# Women, Work, and Family

# Women, Work, and Family

How Companies Thrive with a
21st-Century Multicultural Workforce

**Michele A. Paludi, Editor**

 PRAEGER

AN IMPRINT OF ABC-CLIO, LLC
Santa Barbara, California • Denver, Colorado • Oxford, England

**Library of Congress Cataloging-in-Publication Data**

Women, work, and family : how companies thrive with a 21st-century multicultural workforce / Michele A. Paludi, editor

pages cm
Includes index.

ISBN 978-1-4408-0309-3 (hardback) — ISBN 978-1-4408-0310-9 (ebook)
1. Women—Employment. 2. Work and family. 3. Working mothers. 4. Sex discrimination in employment. I. Paludi, Michele Antoinette.
HD6053.W6455 2014
306.3'6—dc23 2014017555

ISBN: 978-1-4408-0309-3
EISBN: 978-1-4408-0310-9

18 17 16 15 2 3 4 5

This book is also available on the World Wide Web as an eBook.
Visit www.abc-clio.com for details.

Praeger
An Imprint of ABC-CLIO, LLC

ABC-CLIO, LLC
130 Cremona Drive, P.O. Box 1911
Santa Barbara, California 93116-1911

This book is printed on acid-free paper (∞)

Manufactured in the United States of America

For

My Grandmothers:
Rosa Benacquista Peccichio
Lucia DiGiandomenico Paludi

My Mother:
Antoinette Rose Peccichio Paludi

My Sisters:
Rosalie Paludi
Lucille Paludi

My Godmothers:
Anna Paludi
Valerie DiGiandomenico

They may not have all been employed women but they
certainly were/are all WORKING women.

Thank you.

# Contents

# Acknowledgments

Thank you to all contributors to this volume. I admire the work you do to make work-life integration a reality for women and for yourselves. I have enjoyed working with you and have learned a great deal from your work.

I also acknowledge my sisters, Rosalie Paludi and Lucille Paludi.

The following friends and colleagues offered much support during my work on this volume: Steven Earle, Tony LoFrumento, Stephanie Karwan, Jennifer Martin, and Breena Coates.

I thank students in my 2013 graduate course on "Women and Management" for their insights about work-life integration. I am honored to include some of their voices in this volume.

I also thank students in my 2012 undergraduate course, "Women, Work and Families Cross Culturally." You empowered me! You gave me a glimpse as to what our future will be like in terms of feminist changes in workplaces.

I am very appreciative of Hilary Claggett, my editor at Praeger, for her patience, encouragement, and support to me as well as my work. I have been most fortunate to work with her and Debbie Carvalko.

To my clients who have adopted my flexible work policies in their organizations: Thank you on behalf of your employees.

# Introduction

## Michele A. Paludi

Every few years Hollywood produces a movie that begs the question, "Can Women Have It All?" In 1987, the movie was *Baby Boom*, which was introduced as a comedy (is work-life integration really comical?). The plot centered around J. C. Wiatt (notice initials, not a name was used so as to hide the fact J. C. is female), who is known in managing consulting circles as the "Tiger Lady." Her fast paced life in New York City is demanding with no time for a meaningful relationship or children. She inherits a baby girl from a cousin who died and J. C.'s life changes. J. C. exclaims: "I can't have a baby. I have a 12 o'clock lunch meeting."

Eventually J. C. begins her own business making gourmet baby food. Her former employer offers to purchase her company for millions of dollars and return to her the career and Manhattan apartment toward which she has been working. At the end of the movie, J. C. declines this offer, vows to take her company nationwide herself, and returns to her home in Vermont, her new love interest, and her daughter. Thus, the movie ends with J. C. "having it all."

Friedman (2012) described *Baby Boom* as one of the "definitive movies about work-life balance of our time" (p. 1). The movie ends with the theme: there is no incompatibility between family and work roles for women. You can have it all if you are a woman. Friedman notes however that *Baby Boom* is a "feel-good story that's just as much a fairy-tale today as it was 25 years ago" (p. 1).

The reality is that *there is* an incompatibility between work and family roles. For example:

1. Women carry more of the workload at home.
2. Employed women do substantially more caregiving to children and elder parents.

3. While every day more than 350,000 children of employed parents are ill, very few childcare centers have provisions for sick children so parents can go to work.
4. White women have a 7% wage penalty for each child they have (Hewlett, 2002).
5. Women are deliberately treated differently because of their sex, for example, receiving lower starting salaries.
6. Employed women are more likely to lack fringe benefits needed to care for their family (Paludi & Neidermeyer, 2007).
7. Women face the "opportunity gap," factors that bar women from advancing in their careers at the same rate as men (Jandeska & Kraimer, 2005).

In *Baby Boom*, J. C. Wiatt opts for entrepreneurship. The unfortunate theme that is conveyed is that women entrepreneurs can "have it all" since they are their own bosses. While women in corporations face many constrained opportunities as a result of gender and/or race stereotyping and leave to become entrepreneurs, they do not escape the impact of stereotyping when trying to start their own businesses. For example, one obstacle women entrepreneurs face in starting their companies is a relative lack of access to capital to finance their venture (Hedges, 2007; Morris, Miyasaki, Watters, & Coombes, 2006; Neidermeyer, Buenn, & Edelman, 2008). Greene, Brush, Hart, and Saparito (2001) noted that between the years 1997 and 2000, considered the "boom years" for venture investing in the United States, only approximately 5% of venture capital was given to women-owned businesses. In 2003, approximately 4.2% of the $19 billion of venture capital was given to women entrepreneurs.

In the intervening years since the release of *Baby Boom* there has been a substantial amount of research on women integrating work and family/life roles, some of which is addressed earlier. One would assume that Hollywood would recognize these research findings and portray women who are mothers AND who are employed outside the home in a more realistic light. Fast forward to 1996 with the release of *One Fine Day*. The female lead is Melanie Parker, an architect and single mother to her son. Throughout the day, Melanie is juggling maternal and employee roles and demands. Her son has to go to the office with her for part of the day, his toy cars cause Melanie to trip and consequently break her scale model display she must use during a presentation that morning. Asked to accompany potential clients to Connecticut following drinks, Melanie chooses her son and his soccer game rather than her job. This decision is made following an exchange between Melanie and Sammy:

**Melanie Parker:** You're the most important thing in the world.
**Sammy Parker:** No, I'm not. Your job is.
Sammy's classmate's father, who becomes a love interest for Melanie,

comments about Melanie being in control. Their exchange is described as follows (with an acknowledgment to juggling work and life):

**Melanie:** I've got all these little balls up in the air and if someone caught one of them for me I'd probably drop all of them.

**Jack:** But you're not a control freak.

**Melanie:** No. I'm a single working mom.

Fast forward to 2011 and the release of *I Don't Know How She Does It*. The movie is described as being about ". . . a high-powered, multi-tasking working mum Kate Reddy, struggling to balance career and family life" (*The Week*, 2011, p. 1). In the film, Kate Reddy (similar to Melanie Parker) makes it clear that in order to "have it all" it's a matter of juggling.

In this film, Kate Reddy is a manager for an investment firm. She is married to an architect, often unemployed, who becomes the primary caretaker for their children as Kate's career is on the fast track. As Holden (2011) noted:

During much of the movie she behaves like a rat in a maze, hyper-stimulated by constantly buzzing cellphones as she dashes back and forth between Boston and New York to pitch a deal having something to do with retirement funds. . . . The jittery momentum of the movie . . . mirrors Kate's frazzled state all too well. (p. 2)

There is a scene toward the end of the movie where Kate's boss says to her: "Oh we'll give you flexible working, if only you'd asked earlier." The message: women have to ask and that will resolve everything; that it is because women don't ask for things that they don't receive them. The truth is that most employers do not have flexible policies (e.g., telecommuting, desk sharing, job sharing) and those that do must make them known through policies in the employees handbook, onboarding training, and so forth, and not in passing. And, those employers who do not have flexible policies typically don't offer one just because one woman decided to ask. Flexible policies are offered to all.

This movie is adapted from the book of the same name and altered the story line. Critics described the movie as "anti-women, conservative and condescending" (*The Week*, 2011, p. 1). Phillips' (cited in *The Week*, 2011, p. 2) review includes ways the movie "condescends inadvertently to its female characters even as it flatters their juggling abilities." Phillips cites one line in the movie to illustrate his point: "The inside of a working woman's mind is like the control tower at O'Hare Airport." States Phillips: "Doesn't that sort of generic belong to the era of 9 to 5?"

The *New York Times* review of this film (Holden, 2011) included readers' reviews. For example:

This dated post-feminist vignette about how mothers who are good at their demanding job, AND who bring in the bulk of the bacon, should feel guilty about all the homemaking errands they can't complete in a sing day, is a pale, unchallenging, and corny excuse for a movie product. (p. 5)

   I walked out b4 the movie ended. I don't know if this movie is supposed to applaud working mothers but I sure don't think so as it portrayed mainly negative aspects of parenthood as well as installing guilt to all working mothers. (p. 4)

Shipley (2011) in *The f word*, a feminist periodical in the United Kingdom, claimed that "the underlying assumption of most of the film is that everything family-related is automatically a woman's responsibility" (p. 2). Shipley further commented:

That's what annoyed me the most about this film, the fact that the status quo was so rarely challenged by any of the characters. . . . In one scene, Kate's mother-in-law . . . commented that things were easier in the past when men and women had more clearly defined roles. My soul was crying out for Kate to talk about equality or mention the word "feminism", but she just shrugged and winced, saying: "It's more complicated now". . . . I'm disappointed that the film is more post-feminist than feminist in its outlook: it assumes that all struggles are personal. (pp. 2, 4)

This in contrast to the feminist interpretation, that the personal is political; what impacts one woman impacts all women (Hanisch, 1970).

   Furthermore, in all three movies, the films end with the female protagonist (all white) falling into the arms of a man. In only one of these films, *I Don't Know How She Does It* is the female protagonist married. However, during this film Kate is pursued by her boss and she must choose between her husband and her boss. The message: everything will be alright if you have a man's help. The reality that most children are being raised by women in single parent homes has been ignored by Hollywood. Furthermore, the reality that women are in lesbian relationships or are physically challenged and integrating work and life is not addressed by Hollywood. The 2010 movie, *The Kids Are All Right* does address lesbian parenting. However, the theme of the movie is not about work-life integration. I address additional themes from these movies.

## INCOMPATIBILITY BETWEEN WORK AND FAMILY ROLES

   What is also not directly addressed in Hollywood's portrayal of work-life balance is that the incompatibility between the workplace and family demands is exacerbated by a relative lack of provisions that would ease women's integration of these roles (Hewlett & Luce, 2006; Strassel, Colgan, & Goodman, 2006). Traditional occupational policies reflect a separation of family from work life and a societal expectation that mothers remain at home to care for their children (Clark-Stewart, 1993; Paludi et al., 2007; Russo, 1979).

Russo (1979) noted we have a "motherhood mandate" — the belief that the primary career roles of women center around domestic and childcare responsibilities. Equality of the parenting and housekeeping roles has not been achieved (Flouri & Buchanan, 2002). Moss Kanter's (1977) text, "Work and Family in the United States: A Critical Review and Agenda for Research and Policy" brought the issue of work-life balance to the forefront of organizations. Moss Kanter noted the incompatibility between work and family roles, still present 36 years later (Paludi & Neidermeyer, 2007; Paludi et al., 2010; Paludi et al., 2007). Thus, employed women perform "double duty" or what Hochschild (1989) referred to as the "second shift." Maternal employment has increased in the past 25 years dramatically (Paludi et al., 2007). In addition, women with infants have had the fastest growth in labor-force participation of all groups in the United States (Han, Waldfogel & Brooks-Gunn, 2001). Furthermore, women are as likely to be employed when they have infants as they are when they have a preschool-aged child.

Even women who own home-based businesses have a difficult time integrating work and life roles (Beach, 2004; Owen & Winter, 2004). Women owners of home-based businesses must set rules to govern the time they spend in their offices and what they expect from their family during their working time. Family members must be told that even though the entrepreneur is "at home," she is still working. In addition, Shelton (2006) found that women-owned businesses had a high prevalence of team-building and participative management practices. Her research explains this high prevalence as being a response to women entrepreneurs' need to manage work-family conflict.

Furthermore, equality of the housekeeping and parenting roles has not been achieved (Flouri & Buchanan, 2002; Russo, 1979; Strassel et al., 2006). For example, women perform more housework than men, even women in academia and the sciences (Milkie, Raley, & Bianch, 2009). For example:

1. Eighty four percent of women and 63% of men perform housework.
2. Employed women do approximately twice the amount of childcare as employed men (44 minutes versus 23 minutes during a 24-hour period).
3. Dual career families follow traditional husband-wife roles. Women spend approximately 80 minutes more during a day on home and childcare responsibilities while spending 1 hour less at work.

Milkie et al. (2009) also reported examples of the incompatibilities between work and life roles for women. For example, compared to fathers:

1. Mothers have fewer leisure hours per week.
2. Mothers report feeling rushed.
3. Mothers are more strongly impacted by multitasking.
4. Mothers feel less satisfied with how their child is doing.

In addition, as we saw in how J. C., Melanie and Kate were portrayed, personality characteristics are not perceived as gender neutral (Ely & Rhode, 2008). When women engage in behaviors stereotypically linked to men, they are not perceived similarly to men and are often evaluated more negatively than when conforming to stereotypes of employed women. According to Heilman, Wallen, Fuchs, and Tamkins (2004):

> The mere recognition that a woman has achieved success on a traditionally male task produces inferences that she has engaged in counternormative behavior and therefore causes similarly negative consequences. (p. 3)

Furthermore, successful achievement for women is costly. Successful women are described as "cold" vis-à-vis men (Wiley & Eskilson, 1985). Because women are defined culturally as being caretakers of the home and family, women are more likely to experience negative reactions from colleagues for their noncompliance with this role. J. C., Melanie and Kate were all discussed in derogatory terms for violating gender norms, for example, referring to J. C. as the "Tiger Lady."

Furthermore, organizational stereotypes depict men, but not women, as having the requisite skills and characteristics for employment (Denmark et al., 2008; Reuber, Dyke, & Fischer, 2009). For example, business professionals indicate a strong preference for male applicants for a stereotypically masculine job, even when similar information on the resumes of women and men applicants had led to perceptions of similar personality traits. These stereotypes persist even though gender differences are not found in leadership ability, job performance (Duff-McCall & Schweinle, 2008; Eagly & Carli, 2007; Powell, Butterfield, & Parent, 2006), or in the percentage of women and men who aspire to and train to become chief executives (Werhane et al., 2006).

Stereotypes refer to individuals' thoughts/cognitions that typically do not correspond with reality. Stereotypes occur when individuals are classified by others as having something in common because they are members of a particular group or category. Gender stereotyping is a psychological process that describes individuals' structured set of beliefs about the personal attributes of women and men (e.g., nurturing, independent, lacking leadership qualities) (Kite, Deaux, & Haines, 2008).

Psychologists have identified an emotional component to stereotypic cognitions: prejudice, as well as a behavioral component to individuals' cognitions: discrimination and harassment. Individuals' statements and nonverbal gestures toward women and men provide insight into their structured set of beliefs about gender and race (Fiske & Lee, 2008). Stereotypes are not labels, but are assumptions about personality traits and behaviors that people in the labeled categories are thought to possess. Stereotypes have negative effects; the categorization process causes people to emphasize differences between group and similarities within groups. Thus, women are seen as radically different from men; mothers radically different from fathers, for example.

## IMPACT OF INTEGRATING MULTIPLE ROLES

Research has identified noted costs to women who integrate work and family roles. For example, employed women who report work-life conflict are as much as 30 times more likely to experience a significant mental health problem, including depression and anxiety, than women who report no such conflict (Gonzales-Morales, Peiro, & Greenglass, 2006). Psychological symptoms associated with integrating these roles include: isolation, guilt, self-consciousness, frustration, alienation, withdrawal from social situations, and decreased self-esteem (Karsten, 2006). Research has also identified a variety of physical health complaints among women integrating multiple roles, including but not limited to headaches, tiredness, lethargy, gastrointestinal disorders, eating disorders, and inability to concentrate.

In addition, Hewlett and Luce (2006) reported women trying to integrate work and family roles were concerned about the following behaviors of their children: they watched too much television, they engaged in acting out behaviors, ate too much junk food, had too little adult supervision, and underachieved in school.

Research has indicated that maternal employment has been related to positive impacts on children (Han et al., 2001). For example, daughters of employed mothers are more career-oriented (versus home-oriented) than daughters of full-time homemakers. In addition, daughters of employed mothers are more likely to pursue nontraditional careers than daughters of full-time homemakers. Maternal employment influences women's career development through its provision of a role model of women's employment (Gottfried, Gottfried, & Bathurst, 2002). Thus, it is not whether the mother is employed that is the most critical factor, it is their role of satisfaction and assistance with integrating work-life roles that has the most impact on children.

Lundberg and Lindfors (2002) reported research on stress-related effects on women who worked at organizations and those that teleworked. Lundberg and Lindfors (2002) found that blood pressure was significantly higher during work at the office than when teleworking from home or another remote office. In addition, Lundberg and Frankenhaeuser (1999) reported that women were significantly more stressed by their lower salaries and lack of work-life integration vis-à-vis men.

## SHOULD MOTHERS WORK? THEY ALWAYS HAVE!

One question raised in the movies discussed earlier is whether mothers should work outside of the home. The reality is that the majority of women with children are employed. The rate of maternal employment for two-parent families with school-age children is more than 75% (Duncan & Brooks-Gunn, 2000). The reasons for women being employed outside of the home are related primarily to financial needs and self-actualization (Sinacore-Guinn, 1998). Families must have two incomes to support them at a level previously achieved by one wage earner. Single, widowed, and divorced women with children must work to avoid poverty (Duncan & Brooks-Gunn, 2000). Thus, employment for women is not always a choice for women: it is a necessity. The question "Should mothers of young children work?" contains an assumption that mothers do not have to work but simply want to, that they have a choice. Women have always had to work to support themselves and their families (Paludi & Neidermeyer, 2007).

Women with children have also reported wanting to work for the social support, social networks, and adult companionship offered by workplaces (Hakim, 2006). Hyde, Klein, Essex, and Clark (1995) described employment for mothers as a morale boost and a buffer against stress from family roles. The main issue is how satisfied mothers are with the choices they have made regarding integrating work and family (Gilbert, 1994) in addition to support they receive from partners, friends, and employers (Karsten, 2006).

## WHAT'S IN A NAME?

The terminology used to describe women combining work and family roles speaks to how the issue is viewed. The labeling is race-related! The same term for a single woman raising children varies by race of the family. The family situation is referred to as an "alternative life style" if the family is white; a "broken home" if the family is African American. The terminology has implications for how individuals are perceived, treated, and respected. In addition, "juggling" was the first term used in the social sciences to connote women combining work and family lives. This term was changed to "balancing," also connoting that it is women's responsibility to excel in both spheres. The term "integration" is currently in vogue in empirical research. This term, unlike its predecessors, has acknowledged the responsibility of organizations to assist women in meeting work and life demands, including parenting and eldercare. Women have highlighted the necessity for women to have greater flexibility at work as well as assistance with family responsibilities. Miller (2005) noted that the top work-life programs utilized by employees in the United States companies are the following:

Employee Assistance Programs
Leave for School Functions
Wellness Programs
Flu Shot Programs
Fitness Facilities

Work-life programs rated the highest by human resource specialists for reducing unscheduled absences are as follows (Miller, 2005):

Alternative Work Arrangements
Flu Shot Programs
Leave for School Functions
Telecommuting
Compressed Workweek
On-Site Childcare
Emergency Childcare
Employees Assistance Programs
Wellness Programs
On-Site Health Services
Fitness Facilities
Satellite Workplaces
Job Sharing
Eldercare Services

Strategies for employers to assist employees in integrating work life roles include:

Develop and enforce family-friendly policies
Be supportive of job training
Be supportive of parent training
Offer services for quality childcare
Offer services for quality eldercare
Assist employees in aligning work and school calendars
Lessen employee stress
Implement on-site childcare
Recognize the benefits of integrating work and life roles
Offer time-based strategies

Contract with the Employees Assistance Program for employees who wish to receive counseling support
Contract with a local wellness center to provide programs for employees on health issues, proper nutrition, exercise, and so forth.
Facilitate training programs on work-life integration for managers
Offer time off/career breaks
Enforce the Family and Medical Leave Act
Offer relocation assistance for employees

Organizations who implement such policies report positive impacts for employees, including lower absenteeism, less stress, higher morale, improved work satisfaction, lower turnover rate, staffing over a wide range of hours, childcare hours that conform to work hours, and access to quality infant and childcare (Frone & Yardley, 1996; Paludi et al., 2007). These culture climate changes in organizations are necessary if women are ever to achieve parity with men in salary, mentoring, and networking opportunities; unbiased performance evaluations; promotions and tenure awards; and work-life integration. Organizations who implement these policies assist women in realizing we are never going to be perfect in our roles and to love and respect ourselves for what we have accomplished in them.

As Moss Kanter (2012) concluded:

After years of observing individual struggles to achieve work-life balance—and of enlightened companies to provide it—I've concluded that one major hurdle is artificial images of perfection. Certainly institutional structures don't make it easy to balance work and the rest of life. This is especially true in the U.S., where vacations are short, sabbaticals are rare, school schedules don't align with office hours, and working parents cobble together their own costly support systems . . . .

American culture holds up myths of perfection—the perfect body, the perfect job, the perfect child, the perfect lawn—that consume time, money, and attention. This plagues everyone, but especially women who are candidates for high-powered careers. (p. 1)

I wanted to edit this book in order to provide a tapestry of techniques for employees, employers, human resource specialists, consultants, and attorneys to use in valuing ALL women in the workplace. The contributors to this book share my belief that we need to bring together from a variety of disciplines, including the social sciences, law, and management, those concepts, theories, and research that may be useful to people in making decisions about women, work, and family in the 21st-century workforce. Contributors to this volume focus on management strategies that are grounded in case law and empirical research in the social sciences and human resource management. They all recognize that the success of organizations depends on effectively managing work-life integration.

The contributors to this volume offer recommendations to help make women not want to think we have to strive for perfection in both work and life roles but rather remove self-blame and guilt. As Moss Kanter (2012) concludes:

> "Best is the enemy of good," it's often said.
>
> A cultural shift to get out of the perfection trap can also free up time to work on the bigger changes needed to bring work and life into better alignment. (p. 2)

There is a paradox in the film, *I Don't Know How She Does It*: Kate is always rushing around, struggling with integrating work and life demands. However, the movie depicts Kate's friends talking to the camera about Kate and always asking: "I don't know how she does it?" Kate does it the best she knows how, given she is not getting assistance from her employer and her husband, or, for that matter, her friends who wonder what is her secret for perfection. We must feel empowered and stop blaming ourselves. We must get family-friendly policies from our employers. Each of us finds our own way to integrate work and family. There is no universal best way, only the best way for each of us at any given time in our lives.

## REFERENCES

Beach, B. (2004). Family support in home-based family businesses. *Family Business Review, 6*, 371–379.

Clark-Stewart, A. (1993). *Daycare*. Cambridge, MA: Harvard University Press.

Denmark, F., Baron, E., Klara, M., Sigal, J., Gibbs, M., & Wnuk, D. (2008). Women as leaders: From the lab to the real world. In M. Paludi (Ed.), *The psychology of women at work: Challenges and solutions for our female workforce* (pp. 35–56). Westport, CT: Praeger.

Duff-McCall, K., & Schweinle, W. (2008). Leadership and women. In M. Paludi (Ed.), *The psychology of women at work: Challenges and solutions for our female workforce* (pp. 87–99). Westport, CT: Praeger.

Duncan, G., & Brooks-Gunn, J. (2000). Family, poverty, welfare reform, and child development. *Child Development, 71*, 188–196.

Eagly, A., & Carli, L. (2007). *Through the labyrinth: The truth about how women become leaders*. Boston, MA: Harvard Business School Press.

Ely, R., & Rhode, D. (2008). *Women and leadership: Defining the challenges*. Retrieved May 6, 2010, from http://www.hbs.edu/leadership/pdf/ElyRhodepaper.pdf

Fiske, S., & Lee, T. (2008). Stereotypes and prejudice create workplace discrimination. In A. Brief (Ed.), *Diversity at work* (pp. 13–52). New York: Cambridge University Press.

Flouri, E., & Buchanan, A. (2002). What predicts fathers' involvement with their children? A prospective study of intact families. *British Journal of Developmental Psychology, 21*, 81–98.

Friedman, J. (2012). "Baby Boom" 25 years later. Retrieved October 3, 2013, from http:/blogs.wsj.com/juggle/2012/08/06/baby-boom-25-years-later/

Frone, M., & Yardley, J. (1996). Workplace family-supportive programmes: Predictors of employed parents' importance ratings. *Journal of Occupational and Organizational Psychology, 69*, 351–366.

Gilbert, L. (1994). Current perspectives on dual-career families. *Current Directions in Psychological Science, 3*, 101–105.

Gonzales-Morales, M., Peiro, J., & Greenglass, E. (2006). Coping and distress in organizations: The role of gender in work stress. *International Journal of Stress Management, 13*, 228–248.

Gottfried, A., Gottfried, A., & Bathurst, K. (2002). Maternal and dual-earner employment status and parenting. In M. Borstein (Ed.), *Handbook of parenting*. Mahwah, NJ: Erlbaum.

Greene, P. G., Brush, C. G., Hart, M. M., & Saparito, P. (2001). Patterns of venture capital funding: Is gender a factor? *Venture Capital International Journal, 3*(1), 63–83.

Hakim, C. (2006). Women, careers, and work-life preferences. *British Journal of Guidance and Counselling, 34*, 279–294.

Han, W., Waldfogel, J., & Brooks-Gunn, J. (2001). The effects of early maternal employment on later cognitive and behavioral outcomes. *Journal of Marriage and the Family, 63*, 336–354.

Hanisch, C. (1970). The personal is political. In K. Sarachild (Ed.), *Feminist revolution: Redstockings of the women's liberation movement*. New York: Random House.

Hedges, K. (2007). *Women and venture capital*. Women Entrepreneur. Retrieved May 6, 2010, from http://www.womenentrepreneur.com/2007/07women-and-veture-capital

Heilman, M., Wallen, A., Fuchs, D., & Tamkins, M. (2004). Penalties for success: Reactions to women who succeed at male gender-typed tasks. *Journal of Applied Psychology, 89*, 416–427.

Hewlett, S. (2002). *Creating a life: Professional women and the quest for children*. New York: Talk Miramax Books.

Hewlett, S., & Luce, C. (2006, December). Extreme jobs: The dangerous allure of the 70-hour workweek. *Harvard Business Review, 84*(12), 49–59.

Hochschild, A. (1989). *The second shift*. New York: Viking.

Holden, S. (2011). Even a things-to-do list seems to be multitasking. Retrieved October 2, 2013, from http://www.nytimes.com/2011/09/16/movies/i-dont-know-how-she-does-it-review.html?ref=movies&_r=0

Hyde, J., Klein, M., Essex, M., & Clark, R. (1995). Maternity leave and women's mental health. *Psychology of Women Quarterly, 19*, 257–285.

Jandeska, K. E., & Kraimer, M. L. (2005). Women's perceptions of organizational culture, work attitudes, and role-modeling behaviors. *Journal of Managerial Issues, 18*, 461–478.

Kanter, M. R. (1977). *Work and family in the United States: A critical review and agenda or research and policy*. New York: Russell Sage Foundation.

Kanter, M. R. (2012). *The imperfect balance between work and life*. Retrieved October 5, 2013, from http://blogs.hbr.org/2012/08/the-imperfect-balance-between/

Karsten, M. (2006). Managerial women, minorities and stress: Causes and conse-
    quences. In M. Karsten (Ed.), *Gender, race and ethnicity in the workplace: Issues
    and challenges for today's organizations* (pp. 238–272). Westport, CT: Praeger.

Kite, M., Deaux, K., & Haines, E. (2008). Gender stereotypes. In F. Denmark &
    M. Paludi (Eds.), *Psychology of women: A handbook of issues and theories*
    (pp. 205–236). Westport, CT: Praeger.

Lundberg, U., & Frankenhaeuser, M. (1999). Stress and workload of men and women
    in high ranking positions. *Journal of Occupational Health Psychology, 4,* 142–151.

Lundberg, U., & Lindfors, P. (2002). Psychophysiological reactions to telework in fe-
    male and male white-collar workers. *Journal of Occupational Health Psychology,
    7,* 354–364.

Milkie, M., Raley, S., & Bianchi, S. (2009). Taking on the second shift: Time allocations
    and time pressures of U.S. parents of preschoolers. *Social Forces, 88,* 487–517.

Miller, S. (2005, October). Work/life programs tackle unscheduled absenteeism,
    improve the bottom line. Retrieved April 1, 2014, from http://www.shrm
    .org/hrdisciplines/benefits/Articles/Pages/CMS_017137.aspx

Morris, M., Miyasaki, N., Watters, C., & Coombes, S. (2006). The dilemma of growth:
    Understanding venture size choices of women entrepreneurs. *Journal of
    Small Business Management, 44,* 221–244.

Neidermeyer, P., Buenn, E., & Edelman, R. (2008). Women who started up: The
    state of women in entrepreneurship. In M. Paludi (Ed.), *The psychology of
    women at work* (pp. 67–85). Westport, CT: Praeger.

Owen, A., & Winter, M. (2004). Research note: The impact of home-based business
    on family life. *Family Business Review, 4,* 425–432.

Paludi, M., Martin, J. L., Paludi, C., Boggess, S., Hicks, K., & Speach, L. (2010). Pay
    equity as justice: United States and international perspectives. In M. Paludi
    (Ed.), *Feminism and women's rights worldwide* (Vol. 3, pp. 147–176). Westport,
    CT: Praeger.

Paludi, M., & Neidermeyer, P. (Eds.). (2007). *Work, life, and family imbalance: How to
    level the playing field.* Westport, CT: Praeger.

Paludi, M., Vaccariello, R., Graham, T., Smith, M., Allen-Dicker, K., Kasprzak, H., &
    White, C. (2007). Work/life integration: Impact on women's careers, employ-
    ment, and family. In M. Paludi & P. E. Neidermeyer (Eds.), *Work, life, and fam-
    ily imbalance: How to level the playing field* (pp. 21–36). Westport, CT: Praeger.

Powell, G., Butterfield, D., & Parent, J. (2006). Gender and managerial stereotypes:
    Have the times changed? In M. Karsten (Ed.), *Gender, race and ethnicity in the
    workplace: Issues and challenges for today's organizations* (pp. 144–162). West-
    port, CT: Praeger.

Reuber, A., Dyke, L., & Fischer, E. (2009). Gender role stereotypes regarding wom-
    en business owners: Impacts on external resource provision by consultants.
    *Canadian Journal of Administrative Science, 8,* 244–250.

Russo, N. F. (1979). Overview: Sex roles, fertility and the motherhood mandate.
    *Psychology of Women Quarterly, 4,* 7–15.

Shelton, L. (2006). Female entrepreneurs, work-family conflict, and venture per-
    formance: New insights into work-family interface. *Journal of Small Business
    Management, 44,* 285–297.

Shipley, D. (2011). *I don't know how she does it.* Retrieved October 2, 2013, from
    http://www.thefword.org.uk/reviews/2011/10/i_dont_know_how

Sinacore-Guinn, A. (1998). Employed mothers: Job satisfaction and self-esteem. *Canadian Journal of Counseling, 32,* 242–258.

Strassel, K., Colgan, C., & Goodman, J. (2006). *Leaving women behind: Modern families, outdated laws.* New York: Rowman & Littlefield.

The Week. (2011). *Sarah Jessica Parker film betrays modern women.* Retrieved October 2, 2013, from http://www.theweek.co.uk/entertainment/2163/sarah-jessica-parker-film-%E2%80%98betrays-modern-women%E2%80%99

Werhane, P., Posig, M., Gundry, L., Powell, E., Carlson, J., & Ofstein, L. (2006). Women leaders in corporate America: A study of leadership values and methods. In M. Karsten (Ed.), *Gender, race, and ethnicity in the workplace: Emerging issues and enduring challenges* (pp. 1–29). Westport, CT: Praeger.

Wiley, M. G., & Eskilson, A. (1985). Speech style, gender stereotypes, and corporate success: What if women talk more like men? *Sex Roles, 12,* 993–1007.

# Part I

## Why Work-Life Integration?

# Chapter 1

# Women, Work, and How It's Changing

*Michele Kilburn*

"She has a fire in her belly, hire her." That's what a previous employer said to the hiring manager that got me the job.

I suppose that fire is an inherited trait—my great-grandmother and immigrant from Germany was the first woman to earn $100.00 in the early 1900s in a textile mill in Kannapolis, North Carolina. I come from a long line of strong willed, stubborn, and prideful women that have contributed to the evolution of women in the workplace. She worked full-time, without a nanny, or a cleaning lady, or half of the modern technology that we have today and raised eight children. She could be considered an overachiever.

I often feel I've lived my life in reverse in comparison to so many other successful women and my personal peers. Forgoing the college career that my peers took advantage of, I chose to start my career right out of high school as file clerk/receptionist for a local insurance company. I graduated on Saturday and started working on Monday.

While most of my friends were partying, studying, and finding out "who" they were, I was married, working full-time, and I was being formally introduced to my two children through my very early twenties.

I gave birth to my first child two weeks shy of my 22nd birthday in 1992—a lovely baby girl, and upon her first birthday I found out I was pregnant with my son.

Given, my lack of a college education and not earning an income that was anything to rave about, my spouse and I agreed that we did not want our children to be "day care" kids, or to be "latch key" kids, which was a prevalent term at the time. We wanted to be hands-on parents, as much as possible. "Hands on," meant that I would stay home, as my husband earned twice as much as me in the local construction industry. He was the primary breadwinner. Other contributing factors were by the time I would have paid for daycare, commuting, and so forth, I would not have made any money. I would have been working to pay for daycare alone. Looking back now, full-time employment could have assisted in my sanity somewhat though.

I took work, when my family needed it. I had made up my mind that raising responsible adults, with an appreciation for life, love, and family is far more important than any career could offer me monetarily, emotionally, or intellectually.

While raising my children I wanted to be an example of a good work ethic; I am blessed they were able to witness that, not only through me but also through their father, grandparents, aunts, and uncles.

I earned my cosmetology license and later on my real estate license. I volunteered at my children's private school in trade for tuition. I believed my licensures would allow me to generate income while working part-time, build a clientele, be there for the kids, and still have dinner on the table. I quickly realized it is a minimum wage opportunity, with no health benefits, no retirement, and no security. Salon owners treat you as a sub-contractor, and you are easily replaceable. I experienced sexual harassment; a male salon owner spoke inappropriately to me, tried to walk in on me while I was using the tanning beds in the facility after-hours (along with other stylists). I experienced pay negotiations, that is, no pay for products sales and hours worked; it ran the gamut, to where finally I received no pay in the winter months, which is considered the slow season for salons. I have been licensed for 20 years and still practice on family and friends only, for no pay, as a favor to them.

I've accumulated many "aha" moments throughout life, one of them being, if I was the salon owner, then I would have greater job security and so forth. So I opened up shop in my home, again only to be disappointed by cancellations, and trying to create beautiful hair with two kids running around. That lasted about three years. My customers were devastated when I closed up shop, but I had received a corporate job with a great start-up company, with steady pay and health benefits. How could I turn that down?

My children were approximately 8 and 10. I figured, they could handle mom going to work, I was blessed to have my mother and my mother-in-law, alternating days to watch the children . . . for FREE. Two years into this position, the original founder left the organization. A new CEO came in, with little patience, a strong finance background, and a nickname, the "ax-man." He was brought in to lay off 100 people. He analyzed the way we worked, what we did, what our career paths were, interviewed all 175 employees individually, which we all agreed was an unusual approach. During my interview, he questioned my personal life a little more than usual. He asked if I was available to travel at a moment's notice if needed. I said I could more than likely accommodate that, especially if it was going to assist in propelling my career further. He knew I had recently taken time off, as my daughter had an emergency appendectomy. I expressed that my children and family were the most important thing to me. Their well-being came first before anything else. Little did I know that statement sealed my fate. I was the first to be laid off. I was the receptionist and an HR assistant. Not realizing what was happening, the HR director asked me, if I was laid off what I would choose to do, and I unwittingly said, I would open my coffee shop or maybe go back to school. Two weeks later I was called into the conference room at 8:05 A.M., in front of the new CEO, HR director and marketing manager (she escorted me out) I was given my unemployment package, my last paycheck, and I was the **first** of a three-day layoff session.

Shortly after that my spouse took a new position with a new construction company with better pay and benefits. That same organization needed HR/bookkeeping/contract assistance. Having experience, I interviewed and received the job. It was perfect; I could get the kids off to school, work, and be home when they are off the bus. We both truly believed this would be great for our family, and our way of life would improve also.

So here we are, my husband and I are employed at the same company; he was in the field and I was in the office. Mentally I am in place of gratitude, as I believe because it's a small organization my true talents will be utilized and appreciated and I can grow with the company. After two weeks I realize the bitter truth: the books are a mess, there are no HR policies, procedures, and they have front loaded their payment schedules on their contracts. The organization was a sinking ship; it was just a matter of time. If their spending stayed at the pace it was on, they'd be done, in less than a year. Unfortunately my assumptions were right. By Christmas, which was 10 months after we were hired, I was solely laying off approximately 30 workers two weeks before Christmas. See—the owner's and general manager didn't have the heart to do it, so they left it up to me. This time I was on the other side of the table. I was scared and intimidated. I was called names to the extreme of men breaking down in tears scared of how they'd provide for their families. Completely inexperienced as to how to handle this, I just merely functioned and did it. Another item to add to my experience is what I related it to. I stayed with the company and closed the books out into early February of the following year. Then I was displaced and discouraged again.

I moved throughout life from opportunity to opportunity, always believing that I was building on my career and skills. For the most part I truly have. I returned to the same organization twice—a 150-year-old privately owned manufacturing facility in Albany, NY. I worked with a placement agency, where I interviewed four different times. The first two times were with the women of the organization. The very last interview is the most poignant. I was interviewing with the man that would be my direct boss; I walked in with the women. He was the director of operations, and served as the HR point person, as the woman that managed HR was 70 and worked only one day a week. We walked around the corner and we proceeded with normal introductions; he then turned to the director without any hesitation, and said "Yeah she'll do fine." I stayed in the male dominated and chauvinistic office for one year, again taking the position, because my family needed the health benefits and the pay wasn't bad either for a woman without a formal education. My gut was screaming "don't do it, don't take the job" I stayed for two years, because, it paid the bills, and I was gaining experience. I wasn't going to be beaten by a culture that believed "women had a place as mother, and wife," and if they are forced to work, "well as an organization we'll allow them to work, just behind the scenes as support staff." I babysat the owner's children, picked them up from school, worked on multimillion dollar domestic and international bid packages, and contracts, handled trade show events, picked up laundry, arranged for personal vacations, covered up for the service technician's international extramarital affairs, reconciled accounts, created and managed marketing campaigns, created a travel policy, and managed 5S and lean initiatives for the organization. I was the ISO certification manager, and then, I finally couldn't take the rhetoric any longer, and I resigned.

I went back to school, only to be discouraged by the process; with young children, trying to finance it all, it was just too much to bear at the time. I stayed home, and assisted my spouse with his then booming construction business; I did all the same things, just without the discrimination. That worked for a while, although I began to witness that our personal lives and our work lives were so intertwined, that it was hard to tell the difference between them. I decided that I love my husband, but I don't want to work for him. So I called my previous employer for a letter of reference, they said "we're under new management, we have a position open you'd be perfect for come in and interview." I did and I was hired, just like that.

Little did I know, call me naïve, I was going back to the same old chauvinistic culture. I want to believe they had realized the error of their ways. The only thing they realized was they needed to be indiscreet; they changed some titles, gave a modest increase to the female counterparts, although women still had their "place." The female director of operations was demoted for issues unrelated to the fact that she had young children, and her schedule began to reflect that. She's still with the organization in spite of the pay cut, and formal title demotion, because she doesn't feel it will be any better anywhere else.

I have struggled with knowing what my personal talents are and beat myself up for not possessing formal education to warrant the correct pay scale. I now have my BS in Human Resources and Business Administration, I am currently an MBA student, and working in a higher level admin role to keep myself going and assist with paying for my MBA. Our children are grown and pursuing lives of their own to some extent. They are in their twenties, they keep us parents around for the extra cash when they need it. Although our conversations now with our children are a reflection of their "aha" moments of "So many of my friends didn't have dinners like we did growing up, every night," and "we did so many different things, than our friends did." They realize I sacrificed a career in order to be there, they recognize my talents, they have watched me work full-time and go to school, they have watched their father support me through this. That is my greatest accomplishment.

I have found for women, if you do not possess an MBA, or PhD, it is extremely difficult to receive the professional accolades and recognition you deserve. You certainly will not receive the appropriate pay grade either. Organizations are quick to "redefine" admin/secretarial titles, to sound like they are more prominent, although they truly aren't. Neither is the salary attached to them. There is still quite a cultural climate that is not recognizing women in the workplace in certain industries, that is, manufacturing and construction as being valuable in leadership roles. If they are it is in the "softer" roles of marketing and HR. It is unusual to see a woman in contract negotiations, bid negotiations and so forth. If a woman is in leadership roles in male-dominated sectors, they have a stigma attached to them as being overly aggressive and considered to have strong male behaviors.

If a woman exemplifies strength at the wrong time, you are considered too pushy and aggressive, if you are too quiet, you are considered lazy or preoccupied, or "she just doesn't understand or get it." There is a double-edged sword that is still prevalent in business for women. Equal pay for equal talent does not exist fully yet, until you are at the higher ranks, and even then, it's a struggle. Women need to learn how to negotiate. We need to say no to tasks that are not in alignment with the goals of the organization and personal career development.

I still haven't found a company that will recognize my work ethic, and fast track my career as quickly as I would like. At 40 plus years old, I feel the pains of age and sex discrimination. I have a BS and I am an MBA candidate, and I am a serial entrepreneur. My experience is valid. Oftentimes,

I feel underutilized and unfulfilled in my journey to finding the right career. I believe many women do, especially in this volatile employment climate. Unfortunately, people are taking positions that they are overqualified for, to merely make ends meet.

Women offer the ability to multitask, we are planners and doers, we are cheerleaders, and we are leaders. Mothers are the backbone to good families, we will translate that to our work lives, we are able to shift gears fluidly, and we are the highest number of enrollment at universities now. We have the fire in our belly to fuel your organization to the next level. My daughter calls me an overachiever now. I'll take that, I'm just working off of her great-great-grandmother's efforts.

# Chapter 2

# Work-Life Integration: A Personal Reflection

## Tanya Scime

As a wife and mother of three children, I have my hands full. Like many others, I wake up at the crack of dawn; tackle getting my children to the bus on time; work all day; prepare dinner; drive the kids to their extra-curricular activities; and finally sit down for the first time most days by 11 P.M. There are many days when I feel like I didn't give 100% to either my job or my family. Why as parents and career enthusiasts must we feel guilty about trying our best and giving it all that we can? Can't there be a happy medium?

There is no doubt about it. At some point in a woman's life she will be faced with the challenges of integrating the facets of work and family life. There is interdependence between work and life and what happens in each affects the other. Let's face it; more often than not the working role takes precedence over the family role. Why? Well, because in order to feed and clothe our children we need money and in order to have money, we need to keep our jobs. Also, more often than not our family will be more forgiving than our jobs. However, this isn't fair to our families and can also cause a lot of unnecessary stress on them.

Since women have entered the workforce, they have had to overcome challenges of following a male model for career development in order to move up the ranks in their career. In addition to that, most women are burdened with full-time employment and demanding caretaking and household responsibilities, therefore causing women to seek options that reduce the stress of work-family conflict.

So when more and more women entered the workforce, organizations quickly learned they needed to start making changes to their workplace practices to meet the demands of today's diverse family structures. Many have made those changes while others still linger in the old traditional setting.

However, finding an organization that is "family-friendly" can be a challenge. I've worked in many different business sectors; not-for-profit organizations, private business, corporations, and the public sector. Each one approaches the work-life integration model differently. It's a matter of finding what works for you. An organization can offer some fancy on-premise gym membership to ensure better quality of health for its employees; but how is that going to help a working mother who needs flexibility in her schedule to care for her young child?

I think what organizations lack the most is compassion. Too often organizations are more concerned with implementing rules and policies and forget that we are all human and we all have families to care for. Life still goes on outside of the workplace and guess how life will interfere with work at times. While workplace rules and policies are necessary for purposes of conducting business, employees need to have that sense of security that when an emergency arises they can feel confident enough to know they can tend to their family and at the end of the day their job will still be there.

Along with compassion, organizations need to provide flexibility for their employees. Have you ever noticed how your work day spans 9 A.M.–5 P.M. and so do banks, doctor offices, schools, dentist, and so forth? Flextime allows employees to sustain working a full-time schedule but rather working different hours than the traditional 9-to-5 schedule. This works well for employees who may need to be home to care for children or elderly parents. This type of work schedule has shown to increase job satisfaction as well as reduce absenteeism. Employees having the freedom and control over their own schedules will alleviate unnecessary frustration and allow for them to fully integrate work into family life and vice versa. If organizations continue to provide a standard workplace model for work-life integration and don't allow the opportunity for flexibility, they will soon find that their employees will seek positions at other organizations.

Many organizations offer childcare as part of their benefits package as an incentive to employ and retain valuable employees. Some employers even offer childcare for those employees whose children may become ill and cannot attend a regular day care facility. Some of the options that employers may offer are in-house childcare facilities, after-school programs, subsidized childcare, and referral services. It is extremely difficult for parents to obtain safe, dependable, and affordable childcare. Childcare costs these days are so expensive that for some parents, after deducting childcare from what the employee makes, they are barely pulling in minimum wage. This also puts stress on employees. If employers, as part of a benefits package offered either on-site day care facilities or a day care subsidy, they could help alleviate the typical work-family conflicts that arise.

When organizations are able to effectively blend work and life together for their employees, great results such as increased employee morale and reduced employee turnover, can be achieved for both employer and employee.

# Chapter 3

# A Journey to Achieve Work-Life Integration

*Michelle Wildgrube*

When I was initially approached to write this piece, I mentioned the task to my 11-year-old daughter.[1] She responded, "You can't do that, you don't have the time." I think her perception is right, but somehow, over and over, I try to squeeze the most time out of every minute, every hour, every day. I'm a wife, a mother, and an attorney. I have a great husband and two wonderful girls, ages 8 and 11. I am a partner in a small law firm in Niskayuna, New York. I have two law partners, both women, and our law firm is an all-women firm. I enjoy all of my jobs: mom, wife, and attorney; and I am constantly challenged to find balance in my life, to make it work.

It's not easy to be a mother and an attorney in private practice. Some days, I wish I'd chosen a different profession, maybe one that's more family-friendly. It seems that teaching or nursing might offer benefits to my family, summers off or a flexible schedule, that law does not. In college, I remember being encouraged by my mother to carefully consider my career choice and the effect it would have on my family. I also remember thinking, "This is the eighties, it's different now." I remember thinking that times had changed since my mother graduated from college in the 1960s, and I was certain that life for women would be easier by the time

I had children. In college, I minored in women's studies and I knew that the research showed that more women than ever were working outside of the home. It appeared to be a logical conclusion that my community would support my needs as a working woman. I completely underestimated the career that I was preparing to undertake.

I graduated from Rutgers College in the winter of 1988 and started law school at the State University of New York at Buffalo School of Law in the fall of 1989. At my law school, we had nearly equal numbers of men and women; I thought that boded well for my future career. I met my husband in law school and we graduated together in 1992. Following law school, I accepted a position in a small law firm. As a young attorney, my goal was to be a partner in the law firm—that seemed to be a reasonable goal and it was not an unusual goal for a young attorney.

The firm culture dictated long hours for all attorneys, not just for associates, but partners as well. I was expected to be in the office early and leaving before 6:30 P.M. was frowned upon. In addition, I frequently worked on Saturdays, which was also expected. The work never stopped. Private practice is very different from government or municipal practice, where the attorneys work at regular schedule, often 9 A.M. to 5 P.M. There are great benefits with such work, but I have to say that I enjoy the networking of private practice, the ability to see clients and help them, the opportunity to be involved with my community as a part of my work.

In order to represent my clients well, I spent long hours learning the intricacies of the law. I had learned much about the law and legal theories at law school, now I had to learn the process and the application of the law. In addition, I was required by my firm to maintain a heavy case load, to insure that I would be profitable for the firm. There was always pressure to bill the clients and, because I was new, not all of my time could be billed since much of my time was spent learning what experienced attorneys could rattle off from experience. Because of the learning curve, I had to put in long hours in order to bill a reasonable amount. These long hours were at the expense of my personal life. I gave up early mornings, early evenings, and weekends with friends and family so that I could get in my billable hours.

My husband and I were engaged in March 1993. I remember struggling to put together our wedding while working. The week before the wedding, in October 1993, I requested an additional unpaid day off to prepare for the wedding and visit with out-of-town guests. My request was denied. I am certain that the concern was the loss of billable hours and the precedent that such an absence might set for the firm. I have to say that I'm still bitter about that; it's a day I'll never get back. It's one of the things that I think of now as I consider requests from staff for days off.

A couple of years after getting married, my husband and I began to think about starting a family. I thought about the impact that pregnancy and childbirth might have on my work, but I assumed that I'd be able to manage a young family. I had some concerns because I had observed that it was not easy to be a pregnant associate attorney at the firm. I had watched a coworker struggle to work the expected hours while good naturedly managing a high risk pregnancy. This coworker was also the first female associate in the firm to have a baby, somewhat surprising given the fact that the firm had been in existence for over 80 years.

Overall, it seemed to me that the firm was not supportive. I noticed a change in attitude toward my coworker; she was no longer included in discussions about long-term planning and comments were made about her working fewer hours. No concessions were made because of her pregnancy, meetings were scheduled for her before and after work hours, and she was expected to be at those meetings. Despite this, I continued on at the firm, hoping that my experience would be different, hoping that ground had been broken by my coworker and that my path would be easier.

In 1995, I became pregnant with our first daughter, Anna. When I became pregnant, I decided to wait as long as possible before telling the partners at my firm; after all, I didn't want to suffer the same treatment as the last pregnant attorney in the firm. Luckily, my daughter and my body aided me in this endeavor because I wasn't big, at first. I also had the help of a friend who loaned me all of her clothes that were just a little bigger than my clothes, but not maternity clothes. To the outside world, it just looked like I'd gotten a new wardrobe. I waited and waited and waited to share my news while continuing to pretend that it was business as usual. Finally, my parents, who live in the same town and interacted with many of the same people that the partners in the firm did, begged me to tell the partners. At that point, I was nearly six months pregnant.

I continued to work until the day I went into labor, seven days past my due date, because I didn't want to waste any valuable maternity leave time without a baby. The last few weeks of my pregnancy were the only time that any of the partners encouraged me to go home from work at 5 P.M.; I think I made them nervous, hanging out, almost ready to give birth. I took a six-week maternity leave, followed by one week of "vacation" and two weeks of unpaid leave. Because the firm was small, the Americans with Disabilities Act did not apply and I was unable to take any more leave. I also agreed, by taking the maternity leave, that I would continue to work at the firm for a year following the maternity leave or I would refund the firm the six-weeks-paid salary I'd received while I was on leave.

When I returned from maternity leave, I found that it was challenging to be the working mother of an infant. I was nursing my daughter all night and working as hard as I could all day. I hated getting to work early and leaving late. I tried to curb my hours at work during the week and I hardly worked weekends. I was stressed out a lot of the time, either worrying about work or worrying about my family. Before having children, another woman attorney had told me that she had days when she felt as if she was doing nothing well. I could now understand that struggle, that challenge, to spend quality time with my family and to do my job in a competent manner. There were days when it seemed as if everyone was getting short shrift.

After my daughter turned one and my one-year obligation to the firm was complete, I asked the partners if I could work part-time. I wanted to spend more time with my daughter and husband. I proposed working five days a week until 3 P.M. I thought it would be a good compromise, I'd be in the office for most of the day, and I could spend time with my daughter in the late afternoon, hopefully avoiding the evening rush of day care, dinner preparation, and bedtime routine. My request was denied.

I started to consider my options. Unfortunately, at the time, in 1997, I didn't know of any attorneys in private practice law firms who worked part-time. The women who had the flexibility were solo practitioners or they worked for the government. I found it difficult to put together a model of part-time private law practice as there were no local examples to observe. While I struggled with the firm culture, I knew that I wanted a career in private practice. I liked the camaraderie with staff and clients, I liked being able to work with the people in my community. I started to network, seeking support for my ideas. I hoped to work at a firm because I appreciated the support a firm could offer and I liked private practice. I also wanted to work with other attorneys as I saw the value of sharing ideas and legal theories with other attorneys in the office; in addition, I thought that a firm offered clients more options.

I shared my dream of part-time with other attorneys that I worked with in the community. One of the people I talked to was my friend, Deb Slezak, who was an associate at a small firm, Carpenter & Cioffi, that was located close to my home. Deb suggested that I talk to the partners at her office, explaining that there were a lot of part-time employees at Carpenter & Cioffi.

At a luncheon in the spring of 1998, I had the opportunity to speak with Cris Cioffi and I mentioned that I was interested in a part-time job. Cris explained that, at the time, the office of Carpenter & Cioffi didn't have the physical space for another person at the office. I waited. A year later, Deb told me that the firm had expanded its office space and had the space they needed to add another attorney. I called Cris Cioffi again and she invited me to the office to meet with her and her partner, Howard Carpenter. By then, I was eight months pregnant with my second daughter, Zoë. Cris and Howard asked me what I was looking for in a job and I said I was looking to work part-time, three days a week. I suggested Mondays, Tuesdays, and Thursdays, my theory being that Fridays were a quieter day and people could excuse me for being out on Fridays. By the time I got home after the interview there was a message on my machine from Howard and when I called back, I was offered the part-time job, my dream job.

When I gave notice that I would be not be returning to the firm after my maternity leave because I'd been offered employment at Carpenter & Cioffi, the firm asked me to consider staying and also offered me part-time employment. The firm's part-time proposal was for me to work from 9 A.M. to 4 P.M. every day, to be compensated at a reduced rate, and to take an additional pay cut because I wouldn't be maximizing the office space. In effect, they were proposing to rent my office *to me* during the work hours that I wasn't there. I thought that was an outrageous offer and I declined it.

In the summer of 1999, after taking nearly four months for a maternity leave (a glorious and memorable amount of time!), I started work at Carpenter & Cioffi on a part-time basis. This was a launching point for me, embarking on part-time work as an attorney and finally getting to spend time during weekdays with my children.

There were immediate surprises and rewards to working part-time. I found that I was more productive working Mondays, Tuesdays, and Thursdays instead of a full week. I am a conscientious employee, I would never have questioned my productivity while I was working full-time; after all, I work in a business where we keep track of all of our hours and everything we do, billable and nonbillable. I used to joke that I wrote down my hours when I blew my nose or went to the ladies' room before I worked at Carpenter & Cioffi. So, it was a surprise that I found myself working at a firm that was a bit more casual and relaxed, but I was billing even more effectively.

One of the reasons for my increased effectiveness was that working part-time created more deadlines. Because I am committed to returning phone calls and getting tasks done in a timely manner, the days at home created deadlines on a weekly basis. As a result, if I had a client in on a Monday, I'd work to have an answer by Tuesday, because if I didn't, the client wouldn't hear from me until Thursday and, in my mind, that was too long to wait. By completing tasks before my days off on Wednesdays and Fridays, I insured that my clients were happy and that it would be less likely that I would be called by my office for emergencies at home.

I'm sure that it also helped that I was well rested, relaxed, and happier with my life than I'd ever been as a working mother. As a nursing mom, just knowing that I could sleep in on Wednesdays and Fridays was huge help. I was more focused and better able to concentrate at work. It is impossible to sustain a high level of intensity on a constant basis and working full-time dilutes this ability. Working part-time, I was intense much of the time I was at work because I had regular day-long breaks from the practice of law. My clients also had the benefit of the rest because I could use my downtime on days off to mentally work through some of their challenges.

In addition, I was more effective because I was not distracted by home tasks at work. Working full-time, I had no choice but to schedule doctor's appointments, take care of day care issues, and generally plan my life during working hours, distractions that were normal and not extreme, but distractions nonetheless. On the part-time schedule, I took care of these matters on my days off, so I received fewer work day interruptions. I remember a friend who had joked that she needed to go to work to "take care of business," meaning her social life. As a part-time employee, those interruptions occurred infrequently because I knew that within a couple of days I could take care of those matters at home. I also noticed that my attendance at work was nearly perfect working part-time; I also almost never missed a day of work due to a child's illness. My husband and I had always divided the "sick duty" and now that I was home two days a week, my husband always picked up the other days if a child was sick. As the mother of two young children, that was a great benefit to my firm.

And, what about my clients? I did not publicize my part-time schedule. I tried to make my part-time work as seamless as possible so that clients weren't inconvenienced or delayed because I worked part-time. Many of my clients didn't know or realize that I was working part-time because I always returned calls and emails promptly. When I was out on my days off, the receptionist would send the call to my assistant who could take a detailed message, give a status report, and answer basic questions. I had the constant support of a great team at work and I am convinced that part-time would not have worked as well without that team. As technology advanced, I was eventually able to check my email from home and work from home when necessary, as if I was at my desk.

There was also a silver lining to the part-time schedule; I found that I gained clients by working part-time. On my days off, I would have lunch or get together for play dates with other moms, some who worked part-time, some who stayed at home, and I found that these moms were becoming my clients and referring clients to me. A few years later, I attended a seminar on building a law practice and the speakers recommended regular golf outings and entertaining of clients and acquaintances at least two afternoons a week to build a practice. It turned out that my part-time schedule facilitated this kind of networking with the moms of my community and ultimately worked to benefit the firm.

I can't say that the part-time schedule was always perfect. There were some home days when I was on the phone for blocks of time, working out the details of a real estate closing or corporate contract. I'd close myself in my home office and work, letting the kids watch a little too much television or take longer naps. Once, when called by a judge at home while the children were loudly calling for my attention, I walked into the playroom while I was on the phone and silently put down a box of cookies and slowly backed away, as if I were feeding the lions at the zoo. I was able to get in a full, 15-minute conversation with no interruptions! Fortunately, that didn't happen very often and, for the most part, I was able to spend time with my children on my days off.

As my children grew older and entered school, I picked up more hours at work. By the time both children were in elementary school, I was working two full days and three half days. In 2004, when my daughters were eight and five, I was asked to become a partner at the firm. At the time, Cris Cioffi, Howard Carpenter, and Deb Slezak were partners and Howard Carpenter was changing his status to become "of counsel" to the firm. Our new firm, Cioffi Slezak Wildgrube P.C., was 100% woman owned. Remarkably, I was a part-time partner, working at approximately 80% of a full-time attorney's position. Part-time partnership is almost unheard of in the legal community. I was thrilled that I had made my goal of partnership and it was even sweeter to be able to do so while working part-time.

I currently work what the firm considers to be a 90% schedule, working full days on Mondays, Tuesdays, and Thursdays and until 2:00 P.M. on Wednesdays and Fridays. I find that I work additional hours in the evenings and occasionally on weekends, but I always get the kids off the bus on Wednesdays and Fridays and I am grateful to be able to do that. My children look forward to those afternoons; it is a time to catch up with them and work on school projects. That time also allows me to get a head start on household chores and to run errands with the kids.

I am lucky to have a lot of support, both at work and at home. The team work at the office helps me to insure that my clients will have responsive, high quality legal services. At home, I have the help of my husband and parents to care for the children. My husband is truly a partner with me in parenting and he spends lots of time with the children, carpooling, going to their lacrosse practices and games, working with them on their homework, and just spending time with them. I also have the wonderful support of my parents who live about five minutes away from my house and take care of the children after school when I'm working. It helps me to know that my children are spending valuable time with their grandparents when I can't be there. In addition, my parents are always happy to pick up extra time when I have meetings that just can't be moved, or real estate closings that must take place on a Wednesday or Friday.

As a partner in my law firm, it is my goal to give my staff the same opportunities that I have had at the firm. We have 12 employees, 5 of whom work part-time. We have three partners, two of whom work part-time. Our firm has found that part-time staff work well in our framework; we are lucky to have a staff of very talented women who appreciate the concept of team work and who work together to provide excellent legal services to our clients. Because we are amenable to part-time, we have been able to hire great people who want to work outside the home, but who also want to be able to spend time with their families. It's not a compromise to hire part-time employees, it's good business.

## NOTES

Portions of this chapter were published in M. Paludi (Ed.). (2008). *The psychology of women at work: Challenges and solutions for our female workforce. Volume 1: Career liberation, history, and the new millennium.* Westport, CT: Praeger.

1.  My daughter is now 17 years old.

# Chapter 4

# Work-Life Integration: A Woman's Story

*Avigail Moor*

When I was 12 years old, a female prime minister was voted into office in my native land of Israel, and I knew right there and then that this is what I wanted to be when I grew up. Many years have since passed, and I of course abandoned my childhood political aspirations, but I never relinquished the resolve to make a difference in people's lives, on both the collective and individual levels. Deciding to become an activist feminist psychologist was the perfect choice for me, allowing me to affect change in various domains of life and to find tremendous meaning in this pursuit.

When I was 12 years old, I was also one of my neighborhood's leading babysitters, as I truly adored children of all ages and loved caring for them. I was very mature and responsible as well, so parents felt they were leaving their children in safe and loving hands. Electing to become a mother later in life was therefore a most obvious choice for me as well, allowing me to bring all of my nurturing inclinations to bear.

Evolving from these early seeds, the combination of work and life has thus always been entirely natural for me. My work became one of my main sources of meaning and my life outside of work the source of the other half (well maybe somewhat more than half). I cannot imagine my existence without either one of them. Only through their combination is my life whole and complete. Clearly there were times when one received precedence over the other—I intentionally completed my graduate education before having children, and fortunately, was able to slow down my career somewhat when my children where young—but their common meaning always remains.

Has it been challenging? You bet! Were there sacrifices along the way? Of course! But there were never any regrets. At every juncture along the way I was blessed with the freedom to make the exact choices that felt just right for that moment, successfully balancing the two in the most appropriate manner for that time. Consequently, I hardly ever felt that either of my pursuits suffered from its balancing with the other—their harmonizing was usually quite precise.

As time went by I was increasingly able to do even more. About 15 years ago I became a college professor, adding to my activities what I term "academic activism," which involves the creation and dissemination of feminist knowledge through research and teaching. The meaning of my work grew ever stronger, while simultaneously having a fantastic impact on my personal surrounding as well—once again in a harmonious synergetic manner. My daughter was afforded an even stronger role model of achievement in women and my son was given a truly egalitarian upbringing. My spouse enjoyed an equal, reciprocal partnership, and my friends were continuously enlightened by my feminist insights, albeit sometimes irritated by my "preaching" as well (and that was OK too). At the same time, my family continued to enrich me to no end, remaining my number one source of joy and recipient of devotion.

My own life experience hence makes me believe that women can and should combine work and life in whatever manner they desire. It is an idiosyncratic, dynamic process, and no one path is identical to the other. However, the key for a truly fulfilling life is for each woman to look deep into her soul and discover what is right for her, irrespective of social injunctions, and live her life accordingly. Women are entitled to this prerogative, and can handle any and each of its implications. To claim otherwise is a fallacy in my opinion. Clearly, we would be aided tremendously by progressive changes to current social structures and norms, but, nevertheless, not one of us should ever be forced to give up on their dream, as we search for, and find, the perfect balance between all of its pieces.

# Chapter 5

# Inequality in the Division of Household Labor and Childcare

*Miriam Liss*

Women's household labor has declined since 1965 while men's contribution to housework has increased over the same period (Bianchi, Milkie, Sayer, & Robinson, 2000); however, women still do more than men. Over the 40-year period explored in this longitudinal time-diary study, the number of hours women have spent doing housework has been nearly cut in half (from 30 to 17.5 hours a week), while the number of hours men spent on household labor has doubled from 4.9 to 10 hours a week. However, this drop-off has not been consistent over time. The biggest decrease in women's relative contributions to household labor occurred between 1965 and 1975 when women went from doing 6.1 times more household labor than men to doing only 3.3 times as much. The trend continued to decrease, but the gains toward equality have been smaller with each consecutive decade. In 1985, women were doing twice as much housework as were men; however, in 1995 they were doing 1.8 times as much. Thus, one could argue that the gains toward equality in household labor that women made early in the women's movement have stagnated.

Although the ratio of household chore participation varies slightly from study to study, the pattern of women doing more than men is consistent across multiple studies and multiple countries. One study investigating division of labor across 33 countries found that wives ranged from doing 62% of the household labor in Latvia to 90% of the household labor in Japan; in the United States, women reported doing 67% of the household labor (Fuwa & Cohen, 2007). Another study, looking specifically at employed American women with high socioeconomic status (SES) and egalitarian gender attitudes, found that women reported doing 70% of the cooking, 72% of the cleaning, 64% of the childcare, and 58% of the total labor in the household (Claffey & Mickelson, 2009). A recent review article spanning literature from 2000 to 2009 concluded that, overall, North American women perform about two-thirds of the routine household labor (Lachance-Grzela & Bouchard, 2010).

Although some interview studies have suggested that women do from 10 to 15 hours more work than men each week when paid and unpaid labor is combined (Hochschild & Machung, 1989), more recent time-diary studies do not present such a dire picture (Sayer, England, Bittman, & Bianchi, 2009). The work of Sayer et al. (2009) indicated that when paid and unpaid labor was combined, men and women generally worked equal number of hours and that men who worked while their wives stayed home actually worked significantly more hours than women. However, they also found that employed mothers with young children do work more total hours than do men.

However, research that has investigated what full-time working couples do after work has consistently revealed that women suffer from a "leisure gap" where they engage in about 30 minutes per day less of leisure than do men (Mattingly & Sayer, 2006). Although this research is generally conducted utilizing time diaries where people report what they are doing with their time (Mattingly & Sayer, 2006), one study followed couples where both the men and the women worked over 30 hours a week in order to determine how each spent their after-work hours (Saxbe, Repetti, & Graesch, 2011). They found that men spent significantly more time engaged in leisure activities than did women and women spent significantly more time in housework.

## WHY IS THE DIVISION OF LABOR UNEQUAL?

One of the biggest reasons that women do more housework than men is that women have less power than do men (Davis, 2010). One manifestation of greater power is that the individual with more power in the relationship generally makes more of the decisions in the relationship (Fox & Murry, 2000). This means that the more powerful individual in a couple could choose to do less household labor or to do specific tasks that are found more enjoyable or occur less frequently. The influence men have over women's decision making can be subtle. One study found that wives were more likely to agree with earlier stated opinions by their spouse than were husbands (Zipp, Prohaska, & Bemiller, 2004). Regardless of whether the manifestation of power is overt or subtle, it is important to consider the source of the power.

## Gender Ideology

It is typical that men hold more power in relationships, and the traditional view of gender is that men are the head of the household. Thus, individuals who hold traditional views about gender are more likely to endow the male member of the couple with more relational power. Given this, it is important to consider the role of gender ideology on the division of labor. Research has shown that couples who hold egalitarian beliefs about gender were more likely to share household chores relatively equally (Kroska, 2004; Stevens, Minnotte, Mannon, & Kiger, 2006). Men's endorsement of liberal gender attitudes may be more important than women's in determining whether housework is shared equally. Having liberal attitudes predicted husband's participation in domestic tasks considerably more than having liberal attitudes did for wives (Kroska, 2004). Another study found that men who had liberal views as adolescents participated in more household labor than did men who had held more conservative views (Cunningham, 2005). The fact that men's views about equality matter more than women's is consistent with the idea that men have more power in relationships—the men are more likely to determine whether or not there is equality than are the women.

The relationship between gender ideology and amount of household labor completed can be seen on a cultural level as well. In a study of married women across 30 nations, a general trend was found wherein wives in nations with higher levels of gender equality tended to do fewer hours of household labor and less of the total labor in the family (Greenstein, 2009). In this international study, individual women's gender ideology was also a small, but significant, predictor of women's share of the domestic work (Greenstein, 2009).

Nevertheless, simply believing in equality in the abstract is not enough to create an equal division of labor within the family. Attitudes about division of labor tend to be considerably more egalitarian than the actual division of labor (Ferree, 1991). Some research has even found that general attitudes about the importance of equality have absolutely no relationship to the actual division of labor in the family (Wilkie, Ferree, & Ratcliff, 1998). Other sources of unequal power in the relationship also need to be examined.

## Relative Resources

One source of power that has been found to relate to division of household labor is the amount of financial resources each member of the family contributes to the household. Research has consistently found that the individual who contributes more financial resources to the household does less housework (Kroska, 2004). This can be seen from a social exchange perspective where each member of the couple calculates the costs and benefits of being in the relationship (Nakonezny & Denton, 2008). Given that husbands tend to make more money than wives since men's earnings exceed women's (Dey & Hill, 2007), wives may participate in household labor as a way to contribute to the marriage. Research has generally supported the idea that as women's earnings move toward being equal to the earnings of their male partners, the inequity between men and women's division of labor lessens (Ishii-Kuntz & Coltrane, 1992). However, the relative resources perspective is challenged by data reviewed in the following sections, that when women earn more than men, their contribution to housework and childcare actually increases (e.g., Greenstein, 2000).

### Time Availability

A similar perspective to relative resources holds that the individual who has the greater amount of time will engage in the greater amount of household labor. Research has generally supported this perspective showing, for example, that as women's employment hours go up, husbands' contributions to household labor go up as well (Coltrane, 2000; Ishii-Kuntz & Coltrane, 1992; Kroska, 2004). This was found in a study of employed women from 30 nations where women employed either part- or full-time had a total decrease of hours of household labor and did a smaller share of the overall household labor relative to their husbands (Greenstein, 2009). A recent time-diary study found that husbands who had wives who worked more hours did more childcare activities on weekdays (Connelly & Kimmel, 2009). The importance of time availability may differ depending on national context. One study found that, for women who live in more egalitarian countries, full-time employment status (and thus having less available time) was related to a more equal division of labor in the family (Fuwa, 2004). However, this was not true for women in less egalitarian countries. Women in countries characterized by more traditional gender ideologies appeared to benefit less from their individual assets (such as full-time employment) in the negotiation about who did what in the family. This pattern is also seen in Japan where even women who work full-time and earn high incomes tend to do the great majority of household labor and childcare (North, 2009). Furthermore, the research on leisure time reviewed above indicated that women are more likely to use available time to do household chores while men are more likely to pursue leisure activities (Saxbe et al., 2011).

### Other Sources of Power

There are other sources of unequal power in a relationship that have been less frequently investigated as sources of the unequal division of labor in the home. For example, a frequently cited source of relational power is the principle of least interest (Waller, 1938). This is the idea that the individual in the relationship with the least investment in it has the most power in that relationship. Research has found that in couples where there was an inequality in the sense of investment in the relationship, it was usually the man who was less invested (Sprecher & Felmlee, 1997). Furthermore, in heterosexual couples, the member of the couple that was less emotionally invested in the relationship, did, indeed, perceive themselves as having more power in that relationship (Sprecher & Felmlee, 1997; Sprecher, Schmeekle, & Felmlee, 2006). Although perceptions of who is more invested in the relationship has not been studied in terms of the division of labor among actual married couples, research among young adults suggests that there are pervasive stereotypes held by both women and men that men are less interested in marriage and children than women (Erchull, Liss, Axelson, Staebell, & Askari, 2010). Thus, both women and men assumed that the man would be the least invested partner, which would give the man more power in the relationship. However, these stereotypes were found to be false; both men and women were equally interested in marriage and children (Erchull et al., 2010). Furthermore, for young women, but not men, desire for marriage and children was related to willingness to participate in household and childcare chores. Thus, women may feel as though they need to do more chores in order to make up for the fact that they have successfully convinced their supposedly recalcitrant husbands into getting married and having children.

## Doing Gender

Although gender ideology, relative resources, and time availability do explain some of the inequity of the division of household labor, simply being a woman has been found to predict doing more household labor and simply being a man has been found to predict doing less household labor even when all the other variables are taken into account (Kroska, 2004). This has led researchers to hypothesize that men and women are socialized to enact their gender roles in certain ways and that this differential gender socialization influences the division of household labor in a variety of ways.

Women and men are socialized differently, and women may see having a clean house as an important part of their identities and part of their roles as women (e.g., Crawford, 2006; Davis, 2010; Eagley & Steffen, 1984; Mahalik et al., 2005). Research has begun to look at the role of attitudes toward housework as a predictor of how much housework is completed (Poortman & van der Lippe, 2009). Women have been found to enjoy housework more, report higher standards for that housework, and feel a greater sense of responsibility for ensuring the housework is adequately completed (Poortman & van der Lippe, 2009). Furthermore, the more positive women's attitudes and the more negative men's attitudes were toward household labor, the more household tasks the woman did relative to the man even taking into account the contribution of other predictors of division of labor such as time availability and relative resources (Poortman & van der Lippe, 2009). Some research has suggested that men's attitudes toward specific household chores may be better predictors of who completes the chores than women's attitudes (Wilkie et al., 1998). This study found that the personal preferences for household labor predicted the actual division of labor for both husbands and wives, but the preferences of husbands were a better predictor than those of wives. This is consistent with the idea that men have more power in the relationship.

Despite the fact that women are socialized to associate household labor with their sense of themselves as women, research does not actually consistently show women enjoying household tasks. One study showed that women have more positive feelings toward childcare and laundry, but men actually have more positive feelings toward grocery shopping, kitchen cleanup, and housecleaning (Kroska, 2003). This may be because women perform household chores out of obligation while, when men do perform these chores, they are more likely to do it out of choice.

The perspective of doing gender is evident in some research that has pointed to the limitations of the social exchange perspective and resource arguments in explaining the division of household labor. Although it is true that research suggests that as women contribute more to the household their contribution to household labor goes less, this is only true up to a certain level of contribution. In their seminal study demonstrating that women have a "second shift" of household labor after their workday, Hochschild and Machung (1989) found that in every couple they interviewed where the woman earned more than the man, the woman contributed a disproportionate amount to the household labor. Equality in the division of labor was found, however, among some couples that had equal income or where the man earned more. In fact, the couples in which the husband earned the least amount of money were the ones where the wives did the most labor. Another interview study found that when women earned more than men, women participated in more of the labor to decrease the stigmatization for the man of earning less (Atkinson & Boles, 1984).

Several studies have systematically tested this hypothesis (Bittman, England, Sayer, Folbre, & Natheson, 2003). In two of these studies, a relationship was found such that when women's earnings surpassed men's earnings, men's contribution to household labor decreased (Brines, 1994; Greenstein, 2000). Unemployed men, or those who earned the least relative to their wives, contributed the least amount of household labor. A similar finding with an Australian sample indicated that among the 14%

of couples in the sample in which the wives earned 51–100% of the household income, more income was actually related to greater participation in household labor (Bittman et al., 2003). The authors of these studies proposed that couples engage in a process of gender deviance neutralization where the husbands must compensate for the threat to their masculinity of earning less money by contributing less to the household labor. It should be noted, however, that one study looking at data from Austria, Portugal, and the Netherlands did not replicate this finding (Lothaller, Mikula, & Schoebi, 2009).

## An Integrative Theory

Recently, theorists from the study of communication have developed a theory which more specifically helps explain how gender socialization results in an inequitable division of labor (Alberts, Tracy, & Tretheway, 2011). They propose that women generally have a lower threshold of tolerance for when a task needs to be accomplished. So, while a man may see socks on the floor and not be bothered, a woman will be irritated by the socks enough to pick them up. The authors note that this tendency for women to have lower tolerance may have some biological/evolutionary cause (e.g., women having a keener sense of smell) but is also due to the historical social role of women being in the home and thus developing greater attunement to what needs to be done in the home (Wood & Eagly, 2002). Furthermore, women tend to have more skills and competencies in performing household tasks, due to watching their parents perform tasks in a gendered manner and being given chores to do around their childhood home that are gendered in origin. Thus, women have a lower tolerance for performing household labor, become designated as experts in these tasks, and take "ownership" in the relationship for performing them (Clair, 2011). The fact that women tend to perform tasks before men notice that they need to be done creates a self-perpetrating system. The house never gets dirty enough for men to notice that it needs to be cleaned, increasing the gendered division of labor as well as the dynamics of women feeling as though they "own" and are "experts" in the performance of household tasks.

The dynamics of gratitude also contribute to this process. Alberts et al. (2011) proposed that, for women, doing work around the house is expected and they do not expect gratitude for doing such tasks. However, when men perform chores, especially if they are performing a chore before it would naturally reach their level of response threshold, this is seen as a gift and men expect gratitude. On the other hand, many women see their ability to work as a gift given to them by their husband who may prefer that she stay at home (Tracy & Rivera, 2010). Thus, this woman may perform more household labor as a way to compensate for their guilt at being away from the home and family. Thus, the different dynamics of gratitude contributes to our understanding of why women who out-earn men generally do a higher percentage of the division of labor.

Data on this integrative theory suggests that among same-sex roommates, the member of the pair who has a lower threshold for tolerance of dirt and mess is the one who does more than the cleaning (Rigforgiate & Alberts, 2008 cited in Alberts et al., 2011). This theory is also consistent with data that suggests that women have higher standards for household labor (Ferree, 1991). In fact, in this study, 34% of the men reported that they felt it was difficult to meet their wives' standards for housework.

## CONSEQUENCES OF AN UNEQUAL DIVISION OF LABOR

### Marital Satisfaction

Evaluations of fairness in division of labor are important because feeling that the division of labor is unfair in a relationship is an important predictor of relationship dissatisfaction and divorce. Research has suggested that feeling as though the division of labor is unfair is related to dissatisfaction in the relationship for both women and men, but it is only related to the odds of divorce among women (Frisco & Williams, 2003). Research on dual earning Russian families also found that feelings of unfairness were related to marital contention, especially for wives (Cubbins & Vannoy, 2004). Another study utilizing an American group of high SES employed mothers found that an unequal division of household labor was related to feelings of marital distress and personal distress, but this was mediated by perceptions of fairness (Claffey & Mickelson, 2009). In other words, perceived unfairness was the mechanism by which someone with an unequal division of labor became distressed both personally and within the marriage. Just as the relationship between the division of labor and perceptions of inequity differ from country to country, so does the relationship between perceptions of inequity and marital satisfaction (Greenstein, 2009). In countries with high levels of gender equity, perceiving an unfair division of labor was related to lower levels of satisfaction with family life; however, women in low equity nations were generally satisfied with their family life even if they perceived an unfair division of labor. Thus, women make appropriate comparisons within their national context when deciding both whether their unequal division of labor is fair and how perceptions of fairness should influence relationship satisfaction. It should be noted that, although accepting an unequal division of labor as fair may not lead to dissatisfaction or distress among traditional women, research has suggested that believing in equality and actually achieving it (a group called the "congruent liberals") was related to the greatest level of happiness (Crompton & Lyonette, 2005).

The role of division of labor on marital satisfaction becomes even more central when considering the transition to motherhood. Research has suggested that the transition to parenting generally involves a movement to a more traditional division of household labor (Coltrane, 2000; Cowan & Cowan, 1988) as well as the endorsement of more traditional beliefs about gender (Katz-Wise, Priess, & Hyde, 2010). However, research demonstrates that marital satisfaction decreases after the birth of a child (Twenge, Campbell, & Foster, 2003). This is especially the case for individuals in higher socioeconomic classes, is pronounced for mothers of infants, and appears to have a stronger effect on the current cohort of parents than previous cohorts (Twenge et al., 2003). One hypothesis for this trend is that women become disappointed when their expectations for an equitable division of labor after the birth of a child are not met (Twenge et al., 2003). This may be especially true for relatively well-off young women who are brought up to expect equality and have high career aspirations. For these women, the arrival of children and the transition to a more traditional domestic lifestyle may be associated with a feeling of role constriction and dissatisfaction (Twenge et al., 2003). One longitudinal study using data from the National Survey of Families and Households (NSFH) found that the transition to motherhood was related to an increase of housework, which was related to increased perceptions of unfairness about the division of labor, which led to decreased marital satisfaction (Dew & Wilcox, 2011).

### Physical Health

In addition to causing marital strain, research suggests that an unequal division of labor may have negative physical health consequences for women. One study found that the amount of time that women spent on household chores (measured by actual observations within the home) was related to women's inability to physiologically "unwind" after work. Both men and women who spent the most time doing housework maintained higher levels of cortisol throughout the evening (Saxbe et al., 2011). Men who engaged in more leisure activities, which they did more so than women, were better able to unwind, or decrease their cortisol production, after work (Saxbe et al., 2011). In general, the ability to unwind (experience decreases in cortisol levels after work) for women was linked to doing less housework and having husbands doing more housework, while the ability to unwind for men was linked to having more leisure time and having wives who had less leisure time (Saxbe et al., 2011). Given that evening cortisol production has been linked to a number of dire health consequences, including early mortality (e.g., Sephton, Sapolsky, Kraemer, & Spiegel, 2000), it is essential to understand how women's tendency to do more housework than men, even when working full-time, may be negatively impacting their health. Furthermore, other research has suggested that wives who were able to physiologically recover from the stress of work day had higher levels of marital satisfaction (Saxbe, Repetti, & Nishina, 2008).

### Psychological Health

Research has consistently shown that doing a great deal of household labor and childcare is related to increased depression (Coltrane, 2000). These relationships appear to be related by perceptions of fairness such that it is not the inequity per say that is related to depression, but the perception that the division of labor within the family is unfair (Claffey & Mickelson, 2009). Other research has also found that wives who viewed their participation in household labor as unjust were more likely to experience depression (Lennon & Rosenfield, 1994) than those who felt the division, whether equitable or not, was fair.

Recently, research has turned to the effect of inequity in the division of labor on other emotions besides depression. Research has suggested that both individuals who perceived that they under-benefited from inequity in the division of labor (usually the wife) as well as those who perceived that they over-benefited (usually the husband) experienced a variety of negative emotions. Specifically, perceiving that one under-benefited from the division of labor was related to distress, anger, and rage. Men who under-benefited from the division of labor experienced greater negative emotions than women who under-benefited, likely because women were resigned to this situation more than men. The perception that one over-benefited from the division of labor resulted in the negative emotions of fear and self-reproach. Women who over-benefited generally experienced these emotions more strongly than did men. Thus, for both men and women having a division of labor that went against a traditional gendered division of labor resulted in greater negative emotions. Nevertheless, under-benefiting resulted in considerably more negative emotions than over-benefiting for both men and women.

### Professional Consequences

There are profound professional consequences for the inequity in the division of labor and childcare. Although women have made great strides in the workplace and now represent more than 50% of middle management positions, they continue to only represent approximately 2% of top CEO positions ok (Sabattini & Crosby, 2009). Research on the pay gap has found that, among college graduates, women earn 80 cents for every dollar that men earn one year after college (Dey & Hill, 2007). Ten years after college, women earned only 69 cents for every dollar that men earned (Dey & Hill,

2007). The gap in wages and difficulty in advancement are especially salient for mothers, such that some have referred to the existence of a "maternal wall" (Crosby, Biemat, & Williams, 2004). For example, working mothers have been found to earn only 60% of the wages of fathers. One investigation examining whether the motherhood wage penalty has decreased over time found that it did not. Each child significantly decreased a woman's wages, although it had no effect on men's wages (Avellar & Smock, 2003).

Many who interpret this wage gap and lack of advancement of women to the highest tiers of business success do so using the "rhetoric of choice" (Sabattini & Crosby, 2009). The assumption is that many women make an individual personal choice to be less invested in their job and prioritize marriage and family. The assumption is that women choose to cut back on work hours, or even leave the workforce entirely, because it is their personal choice to do so (Sabattini & Crosby, 2009). However, this choice rhetoric is misleading as women's tendency to do more housework and childcare and to take "ownership" over domestic tasks is likely not fully a conscious choice but the result of a complex interweave of socialization pressures and often unspoken interactive patterns with their spouse (Alberts et al., 2011). The tendency to take on the majority of household labor and childcare is a self-replicating process that continues often out of the control of the woman. For example, as discussed previously, the more a woman takes on these tasks the less likely the man will, until habits of who does what becomes entrenched (Alberts et al., 2011).

Furthermore, the choice that women make to scale back their careers or even to opt out of the workforce is often not a choice made freely (Stone & Lovejoy, 2004). Often inflexibility in the workforce forces them to make the decision to opt out of the workforce despite their desire to find a solution that would allow them to continue working and spend time with family (Stone & Lovejoy, 2004). Most companies operate under the assumption that the ideal worker is fully devoted to their careers and should be available to work as many hours as needed by the employer (Blair-Loy, 2003; Crosby et al., 2004). Given that women generally make less than men (Dey & Hill, 2007), the pressure is usually greater for women to opt out of the workforce than men. The gender difference in who takes time off after having children is dramatic. Among college graduates, 27% of mothers were out of the workforce while an additional 17% were working part-time; the corresponding numbers for fathers were 1% out of the workforce and 2% working part-time (Dey & Hill, 2007). Part-time work, even for a short period of time, can be economically devastating. One study estimated that women in the United Kingdom who moved from full-time to part-time work for one year and then moved back to full-time work would earn 10% less after 15 years than women who worked full-time for the entire time period (Francesconi & Gosling, 2005 in Sabattini & Crosby, 2009).

Although the wage gap and the choice for the mother (rather than the father) to cut back on work are mutually reinforcing, there is a social pressure for women to be the one to opt out of the workforce even if she is the primary wage earner (Blair-Loy, 2003). This pressure is both internal and external; women are socialized into believing and embracing the ideology of intensive motherhood (Hays, 1996), which holds that women should be the caretakers of their children and that mothering should be intensive, emotionally consuming, and infinitely rewarding. Although the choice to become a mother, and to dedicate oneself to one's children even to the detriment of one's career success can appear to be a free choice, some have argued that it is the result of our idealization of the motherhood role that is encouraged within a patriarchal culture (Meyers, 2001). In one study of both career- and family-focused women, not a single woman seriously considered that the man quit his job and take care of the children (Blair-Loy, 2003). Women are put in an impossible situation where the notion of the ideal worker, who is completely devoted to work and always available to her job, is necessarily in conflict with that of the ideal mother, who is completely devoted and always available for her children(Crosby et al., 2004). Given the impossible nature of balancing these roles, many women scale back their career aspirations or opt out of the workforce entirely, with grave professional consequences. However, the "choice" to make professional sacrifices is hardly free but constrained by deeply entrenched cultural expectations and stereotypes (Crosby et al., 2004).

## CHANGE

### Interpersonal Communication and Negotiation

There are many individual solutions that may lead to greater gender equality in the home. One possible solution is for women to assert themselves and ask for change in their households. One study found that while the majority of married women (53%) had thought about changing the division of labor in their household, only 26 of 86 reported change and only 11 reported doing so through open discussion with their husbands (Mannino & Deutsch, 2007). Furthermore, the most assertive women were closer to their ideal division of labor as compared to nonassertive women.

Understanding how women and men make sense of and communicate about household labor and childcare can assist men and women in their negotiations. Understanding the dynamics of how threshold tolerance for mess contributes to an unequal division of labor can help couples more clearly and openly discuss the specific dynamics of the division of labor in the home (Alberts et al., 2011). The spouse who does less of the household labor may hold the belief that if they are not bothered by the mess then they should not be responsible for cleaning it up. Furthermore, husbands may argue that if women want to set higher standards for household chore task performance than they feel is necessary, then they should not have to perform up to those standards. However, such an argument would not work in a work environment—one would not imagine an employee telling an employer that their standards for task performance are too high and that they refuse to live up to those standards.

Women may also propagate the inequity of the division of labor by sending mixed messages to their husbands (Alberts et al., 2011). While, on the one hand, they may say they want their husbands to do more, they may continue to want to maintain control and ownership over the household tasks. Furthermore, they may criticize their husbands for not doing the tasks up to their standards, thus causing their husbands to become discouraged and unlikely to continue to try to perform the tasks. Similar dynamics have been found with childcare in which research has suggested that women participate in "gatekeeping" in which they restrict the role of the father because of their beliefs that they are the only ones who can properly care for their children (Fagan & Barnett, 2003). Challenging these gatekeeping behaviors would lead to more equality as would challenging the idea that men are unable to participate in household chores up to the standards of their wives (Ferree, 1991).

On the other hand, it has been argued that instead of assuming that the overperforming (generally the wife) spouse's standards are correct, one should consider that perhaps the tolerance for mess should be raised and women should lower their standards in order to increase equality in household labor (Wood, 2011). Indeed, it is likely that before a home got so messy that it actually became a problem for the health of the residents, the person with the higher threshold for mess (usually the husband) would actually notice the mess and clean it up (Wood, 2011). Thus, negotiations to create a more equitable division of labor in couples should recognize the role that the tolerance for mess plays in the inequity in labor and in who takes ownership over certain tasks. Negotiations could involve both the husband raising their standards and performance levels as well as the wives lowering their standards, being willing to abdicate ownership of certain tasks, and accepting imperfect completion of tasks. For both members of the negotiating pair having a clear language with which to discuss the dynamics of inequity would greatly help communication (Alberts et al., 2011).

## Social System Changes

However, in order to truly effect the division of labor from a societal level, social systems need to change (Lachance-Grzela & Bouchard, 2010). These systems can change both through family-friendly policies of individual companies and through national policy changes. Individual companies have attempted to create programs to allow workers to combine their work and their family life (Sabattini & Crosby, 2009). Such policies include flextime, family or personal leave, and telecommuting. However, these work-family or work-life program, even when available, are often underutilized. This is because the stereotype of the ideal worker as completely committed to the job fosters a corporate culture where work-life policies cannot be taken advantage of without the user appearing to be an uncommitted worker. Another barrier to taking advantage of flexible work schedules is the notion that "face time" in the office is the only way to assess how committed a worker is to the job (Thompson, Beauvais, & Lyness, 1999). When workplace programs appear to benefit certain groups over others (such as parents over nonparents) there tends to be a backlash against their use and a stigmatization and a fear of stigmatization among those who use them (Sabattini & Crosby, 2009). Thus, workplace policy changes need to be framed to benefit all workers, not simply mothers or parents. If these policies are framed as ways to create a happier and more diverse workforce and if organizations actively encourage all workers to use policies that promote flexibility they will be more sustainable. This would benefit the organization as well as the employee as flexible job arrangements and the ability to balance work and personal life is related to productivity and organizational commitment (Sabattini & Crosby, 2009).

National policy can also promote social equality. One way to do so is to promote equal access to the workplace with policies such as affirmative action and antidiscrimination laws. Many liberal countries such as the United States, Canada, and Australia have implemented such policies (Chang, 2000; Fuwa & Cohen, 2007). Another dimension involves providing benefits to families, such as through extended parental leave or state-funded childcare services. These benefits can be seen both in countries that are high in the first dimension of promoting egalitarianism in the workplace, such as Sweden, as well as in countries that have historically valued women's roles in the home, such as the former socialist countries of Hungry and East Germany which provide up to three years of parental leave (Fuwa & Cohen, 2007). Research has found that countries that have antidiscrimination policies have more egalitarian divisions of labor (Fuwa & Cohen, 2007) than countries that solely focus on family policies. Furthermore, in countries with affirmative action policies, women who earn more money have higher levels of egalitarianism in the household. However, in countries with higher levels of parental leave, women's greater income or engagement in full-time employment did not lead to more egalitarian division of labor. Fuwa and Cohen (2007) cautioned that policies that promote women taking off years from the labor force in order to care for children may act to reinforce traditional gender roles and inequality in the family. Instead, they suggested that policies that would reduce the wage difference between men and women would have a greater effect in reducing inequality in the household.

Another social policy that would promote greater equality in the division of labor is offering paternal leave. This policy began in Sweden in 1974 but by 2007 had spread to 66 nations (O'Brien, 2009). Research has indicated that fathers are most likely to take this leave when it provides a high percentage replacement of their income and involves leave that can only be taken by fathers, such as "daddy days" or "father quotas" (O'Brien, 2009). Research has also shown that fathers who take leave are more involved in caretaking activities up to a year later, suggesting that these policy changes do indeed matter (Tanaka & Waldfogel, 2007). Theorists have suggested a positive feedback loop in which fathers who participate more in the home allow mothers to be more active in the workplace, which then further encourages fathers to continue and increase their involvement at home (Coltrane, 2010). Thus, both corporate and social policies, in addition to individual measures, are essential in promoting equality in the household and men's involvement in household labor and childcare.

## NOTE

Portions of this chapter were published in M. Paludi (Ed.), (2013). *Psychology for Business Success, Volume 1: Juggling, Balancing, and Integrating Work and Family Roles and Responsibilities.* Santa Barbara, CA: Praeger.

## REFERENCES

Alberts, J. K., Tracy, S. J., & Trethewey, A. (2011). An integrative theory of the division of domestic labor: Threshold level, social organizing, and sense making. *Journal of Family Communication, 11,* 21–38.

Atkinson, M. P., & Boles, J. (1984).WASP (Wives as senior partners). *Journal of Marriage and Family, 46,* 861–870.

Avellar, S., & Smock, P. J. (2003). Has the price of motherhood declined over time? A cross-cohort comparison of the motherhood wage penalty. *Journal of Marriage and Family, 65,* 597–607.

Bianchi, S. M., Milkie, M. A., Sayer, L. C., & Robinson, J. P. (2000). Is anyone doing the housework? Trends in the gender division of household labor. *Social Forces, 79,* 191–228.

Bittman, M., England, P., Sayer, L., Folbre, N., & Natheson, G. (2003). When does gender trump money? Bargaining and time in household work. *The American Journal of Sociology, 109,* 186–214.

Blair-Loy, M. (2003). *Competing devotions.* Cambridge, MA: Harvard University Press.

Brines, J. (1994). Economic dependency, gender, and the division of labor at home. *The American Journal of Sociology, 100,* 652–688.

Chang, M. L. (2000). The evolution of sex segregation regimes. *The American Journal of Sociology, 105,* 1658–1701.

Claffey, S. T., & Mickelson, K. D. (2009). Division of household labor and distress: The role of perceived fairness for employed mothers. *Sex Roles, 60,* 819–831.

Clair, R. P. (2011). The rhetoric of dust: Toward a rhetorical theory of the division of domestic labor. *Journal of Family Communication, 11*, 50–59.

Coltrane, S. (2000). Research on household labor: Modeling and measuring the social embeddedness of routine family work. *Journal of Marriage and Family, 62*, 1208–1233.

Connelly, R., & Kimmel, J. (2009). Spousal economic factors in ATUS parents' time choices. *Social Indicators Research, 93*, 147–152.

Cowan, C. P., & Cowan, P. A. (1988). Who does what when partners become parents: Implications for men, women, and marriage. *Marriage and Family Review, 12*, 105–131.

Crawford, M. (2006). *Transformations: Women, gender, and psychology.* Boston, MA: McGraw Hill.

Crompton, R., & Lyonette, C. (2005). The new gender essentialism—Domestic and family 'choices' and their relation to attitudes. *The British Journal of Sociology, 56*, 601–620.

Crosby, F. J., Biemat, M., & Williams, J. (2004). The maternal wall: Introduction. *Journal of Social Issues, 60*, 675–682.

Cubbins, L. A., & Vannoy, D. (2004). Division of household labor as a source of contention for married and cohabiting couples in metropolitan Moscow. *Journal of Family Issues, 25*, 182–215.

Cunningham, M. (2005). Gender in cohabitation and marriage: The influence of gender ideology on housework allocation over the life course. *Journal of Family Issues, 26*, 1037–1061.

Davis, S. N. (2010). The answer doesn't seem to change, so maybe we should change the question: A commentary on Lachance-Grzela and Bouchard (2010). *Sex Roles, 63*, 786–790.

Dew, J., & Wilcox, W. B. (2011). If momma ain't happy: Explaining declines in marital satisfaction among new mothers. *Journal of Marriage and Family, 73*, 1–12.

Dey J. G., & Hill, C. (2007). *Behind the pay gap.* Washington, DC: American Association of University Women Educational Foundation.

Eagley, A. H., & Steffen, V. J. (1984). Gender stereotypes stem from the distribution of women and men into social roles. *Journal of Personality and Social Psychology, 46*, 735–754.

Erchull, M. J., Liss, M., Axelson, S. J., Staebell, S. E., & Askari, S. F. (2010). Well . . . She wants it more: Perceptions of social norms about desire for marriage and children and anticipated chore participation. *Psychology of Women Quarterly, 34*, 253–260.

Fagan, J., & Barnett, M. (2003). The relationship between maternal gatekeeping, paternal competence, mothers' attitudes about the father role, and father involvement. *Journal of Family Issues, 24*, 1020–1043.

Ferree, M. M. (1991). The gender division of labor in two-earner marriages: Dimensions of variability and change. *Journal of Family Issues, 12*, 158–180.

Fox, G. L., & Murry, V. M. (2000). Gender and families: Feminist perspectives and family research. *Journal of Marriage and Family, 62*, 1160–1172.

Frisco, M. L., & Williams, K. (2003). Perceived housework equity, marital happiness, and divorce in dual-earner households. *Journal of Family Issues, 24*, 51–73.

Fuwa, M. (2004). Macro-level gender inequality and the division of household labor in 22 countries. *American Sociological Review, 69*, 751–767.

Fuwa, M., & Cohen, P. N. (2007). Housework and social policy. *Social Science Research, 36,* 512–530.

Greenstein, T. N. (2000). Economic dependence, gender, and the division of labor in the home: A replication and extension. *Journal of Marriage and Family, 62,* 322–335.

Greenstein, T. N. (2009). National context, family satisfaction, and fairness in the division of household labor. *Journal of Marriage and Family, 71,* 1039–1051.

Hays, S. (1996). *The cultural contradictions of motherhood.* New Haven, CT: Yale University Press.

Hochschild, A., & Machung, A. (1989). *The second shift: Working parents and the revolution at home.* New York: Penguin Group.

Ishii-Kuntz, M., & Coltrane, S. (1992). Predicting the sharing of household labor: Are parenting and housework distinct? *Sociological Perspectives, 35,* 629–647.

Katz-Wise, S. L., Priess, H. A., & Hyde, J. S. (2010). Gender-role attitudes and behavior across the transition to parenthood. *Developmental Psychology, 46,* 18–28.

Kroska, A. (2003). Investigating gender differences in the meaning of household chores and child care. *Journal of Marriage and Family, 65,* 456–473.

Kroska, A. (2004). Divisions of domestic work. *Journal of Marriage and Family, 65,* 456–473.

Lachance-Grzela, M., & Bouchard, G. (2010). Why do women do the lion's share of housework? A decade of research. *Sex Roles, 63,* 767–780.

Lennon, M. C., & Rosenfield, S. (1994). Relative fairness and the division of housework: The importance of options. *The American Journal of Sociology, 100,* 506–531.

Lothaller, H., Mikula, G., & Schoebi, D. (2009). What contributes to the (im)balanced division of family work between the sexes? *Swiss Journal of Psychology, 68,* 143–152.

Mahalik, J. R., Morray, E. B., Coonerty-Femiano, A., Ludlow, L. H., Slattery, S. M., & Smiler, A. (2005). Development of the Conformity to Feminine Norms Inventory. *Sex Roles, 52,* 417–435.

Mannino, C. A., & Deutsch, F. M. (2007). Changing the division of household labor: A negotiated process between partners. *Sex Roles, 56,* 309–324.

Mattingly, M., & Sayer, L. C. (2006). Under pressure: Trends and gender differences in the relationship between free time and feeling rushed. *Journal of Marriage and Family, 68,* 205–221.

Meyers, D. T. (2001). The rush to motherhood: Pronatalist discourse and women's autonomy. *Signs, 6,* 735–773.

Nakonezny, P. A., & Denton, W. H. (2008). Marital relationships: A social exchange theory perspective. *The American Journal of Family Therapy, 36,* 402–412.

North, S. (2009). Negotiating what's "natural": Persistent domestic gender role inequality in Japan. *Social Science Japan Journal, 12,* 23–44.

O'Brien, M. (2009). Fathers, parental leave policies, and infant quality of life: International perspective and policy impact. *The Annals of the American Academy of Political and Social Science, 624,* 190–213.

Poortman, A.-R., & van der Lippe, T. (2009). Attitudes toward housework and child care and the gendered division of labor. *Journal of Marriage and Family, 71,* 526–541.

Sabattini, L., & Crosby, F. J. (2009). Ceilings and walls: Work-life and "family-friendly" policies. In M. Barreto, M. K. Ryan, & M. T. Schmitt (Eds.), *The glass ceiling in the 21st century: Understanding barriers to gender equality, Psychology of women book series* (pp. 201–223). Washington, DC: American Psychological Association.

Saxbe, D. E., Repetti, R. L., & Graesch, A. P. (2011). Time spent in housework and leisure: Links with parents' physiological recovery from work. *Journal of Family Psychology, 25,* 271–281.

Saxbe, D. E., Repetti, R. L., & Nishina, A. (2008). Marital satisfaction, recovery from work, and diurnal cortisol among men and women. *Health Psychology, 27,* 15–25.

Sayer, L. C., England, P., Bittman, M., & Bianchi, S. M. (2009). How long is the second (plus first) shift? Gender differences in paid, unpaid, and total work time in Australia and the United States. *Journal of Comparative Family Studies, 40,* 523–545.

Sephton, S., Sapolsky, R., Kraemer, H., & Spiegel, D. (2000). Diurnal cortisol rhythm as a predictor of breast cancer survival. *Journal of National Cancer Institute, 92,* 994–100.

Sprecher, S., & Felmlee, D. (1997). The balance of power in romantic heterosexual couples over time from "his" and "her" perspectives. *Sex Roles, 37,* 361–379.

Sprecher, S., Schmeekle, M., & Felmlee, D. (2006). The principle of least interest: Inequality in emotional involvement in romantic relationships. *Journal of Family Issues, 27,* 1255–1280.

Stevens, D. P., Minnotte, K. L., Mannon, S. E., & Kiger, G. (2006). Family work performance and satisfaction: Gender ideology, relative resources and emotion work. *Marriage and Family Review, 40,* 47–74.

Stone, P., & Lovejoy, M. (2004). Fast-track women and the "choice" to stay home. *Annals of the American Academy of Political and Social Science, 596,* 62–83.

Tanaka, S., & Waldfogel, J. (2007). Effects of parental leave and work hours on fathers' involvement with their babies: Evidence from the millennium cohort study. *Community Work and Family, 10,* 409–426.

Thompson, C. A., Beauvais, L. L, & Lyness, K. S. (1999). When work-family benefits are not enough: The influence of work-family culture on benefit utilization, organizational attachment, and work-family conflict. *Journal of Vocational Behavior, 54,* 392–115.

Tracy, S. J, & Rivera, K. D. (2010). Endorsing equity and applauding stay-at-home moms: How male voices on work-life reveal aversive sexism and flickers of transformation. *Management Communication Quarterly, 24,* 3–43.

Twenge, J. M., Campbell, W. K., & Foster, C. A. (2003). Parenthood and marital satisfaction: A meta-analytic review. *Journal of Marriage and Family, 65,* 574–583.

Waller, W. (1938). *The family: A dynamic interpretation.* New York: Gordon.

Wilkie, J. R., Ferree, M. M., & Ratcliff, K. S. (1998). Gender and fairness: Marital satisfaction in two-earner couples. *Journal of Marriage and Family, 60,* 577–594.

Wood, J. T. (2011). Which ruler do we use? Theorizing the division of domestic labor. *Journal of Family Communication, 11,* 39–49.

Wood, W., & Eagly, A. H. (2002). A cross-cultural analysis of the behavior of women and men: Implications for the origins of sex differences. *Psychological Bulletin, 128,* 699–727.

Zipp, J. F., Prohaska, A., & Bemiller, M. (2004). Wives, husbands, and hidden power in marriage. *Journal of Family Issues, 25,* 933–958.

# Chapter 6

# Implicit Bias and Employment Discrimination

*Susan Strauss*

In spite of over 40 years of civil rights law, inequality continues based on gender, race, disability, and other protected classes, as it relates to levels of education, poverty, and success. For example, more and more women are graduating with advanced professional degrees equal to and, in some degrees, surpassing men (U.S. Department of Education, 2011). Women are well represented in middle management, and organizations have implemented diversity and inclusion programs to cultivate women's active participation in leadership roles (Carter & Silva, 2010). Women comprise 40% of the global workforce with anticipated growth by double digits (International Labour Office Bureau of Statistics, 2009).

However, despite the infusion of programs in an to attempt to equalize the playing field between women and men at work, women still comprise only 3% of Fortune 500 CEOs, 15% of corporate board members at those companies (Soares, Carter, & Combopiano, 2009), and less than 14% of executives at the top publicly traded companies worldwide (Carter & Silva, 2010). Women continue to make less money than do men (Carter & Silva, 2010). Why aren't women attaining equal opportunities and pay as are men?

Implicit bias, sometimes called unconscious bias, influences the in-equalities. Attorney Mary Cranston stated "In most organizations there are so many men relative to women. That fact leads to significantly more informal mentoring and coaching being available for men than women. This just opens the door for like-minded bias working itself into the system" (cited in Carter & Silva, 2010, p. 5).

## BIAS AND IMPLICIT BIAS

Bias is defined as the likelihood to prejudice (Prokopeak, 2011). According to Dattner, "We're hardwired to quickly make snap social judgments, distinguishing friend versus foe and simplifying all of the information that's always cascading in, in order to quickly act and react" (cited in Prokopeak, 2011).

Implicit bias is a brain function that assists us in dealing with the deluge of stimuli that we are bombarded with every minute (Reskin, 2005). This brain process helps us instantly categorize people, based on stereotypes. One of the assessments made is whether the person we have met is like us (a member of our "in-group" or "us") or not like us (a member of an "out-group" or "them"). The response is subtle but the consequences have caused disadvantages to women and people of color at work because people automatically favor in-group members. In-group members are trusted more, and are evaluated more positively than are out-group members. They are allowed a broader range of acceptable behavior, not judged as harshly, and are more likely to be rewarded and promoted. There is a cumulative effect in that the stereotyping and out-group rejection may be subtle, but over time the exclusion, being denied credit, and other forms of micro inequality result in in-group members accumulating advantages that are not obtainable to out-group members.

Moule wrote of examples of unconscious bias she sees every day because of her race. In one example, she noticed how a man unconsciously checked his billfold when he saw her walk into the store. A woman moved her purse from the handle of the stroller to her side as she noticed Moule walking toward her. In yet another instance, a husband instructed his wife to move her purse from the back of her chair when he saw Moule approaching.

If a belief is consciously supported, it is said to be *explicit*. A *conscious* or explicit act occurs when an individual is mindful or intentional of the action taken. *Implicit* cognition implies that individuals are not conscious of, or have control over, the perceptions and decision making that spurs them to action. Many mental activities are outside conscious awareness such as implicit memory and implicit stereotypes.

An *attitude* is evaluative and denotes the tendency to either dislike or like, or to act in either a congenial or inhospitable manner (Greenwald

& Banaji, 1995; Greenwald & Krieger, 2006). If we say we like or dislike something or someone, it is an *explicit* expression of attitude. Behavior can also demonstrate explicit attitudes, such as whether we are a democrat or a republican voter. Conversely, some actions may demonstrate an implicit attitude when, for example, we join either government party, and are not aware of why we did so, except *perhaps* because our family has supported that party in the past. Implicit and explicit attitudes toward the same issue or object sometimes differ which is called *dissociations* (Greenwald & Krieger, 2006). Attitudes toward marginalized and minority groups defined by race, age, disability, and sexual nonconformity, for example, may be likely to display dissociations.

A stereotype is an exaggerated belief about a group or an individual (Test yourself for hidden bias, n.d.), and is the basis for discrimination (Fiske, 2002). Stereotypes can portray either positive or negative attitudes, and are learned as children, perhaps as young as three, without them understanding the weight of the message learned. Society is made up of a shared cultural knowledge complete with norms, values, and stereotypes that children absorb unconsciously and through the socialization process. In a study of a child and the skin color of a doll, the child said the black doll looked "bad," and the white doll looked "nice," mirroring society's prejudice (Edney, 2006). In one study, six- to eight-year-old children were read a story and shown pictures of a black, lively, friendly student, and a white, indolent, apathetic student. However, within days, most of the white children remembered the white student as lively and friendly and the black student as apathetic (Bigler & Liben, 1993).

Stereotypes, which operate unconsciously (Devine, 1989), are used to categorize and form judgments (Deaux, 1995). Fiske (1993) asserted that stereotyping is more prevalent with those individuals who hold power, which may result in an increased likelihood of discrimination. According to some, approximately 80% of Western cultures exhibit imperceptible biases and desire positive relations with groups other than their own, while 10% display overt prejudice (Fiske, 2002).

Unfortunately, once stereotypes have been imbedded into our psyche, we resist changing our beliefs even when facts disavow them (Moule, 2009; Reskin, 2005; Ross, 2010). Our beliefs are so ingrained into our unconscious, and so invisible, that it is extremely difficult for us to acknowledge the role they play in our decision making. The human mind will look for those elements to support one's beliefs, sometimes called *confirmation bias* (Ross, 2010). People tend to believe that it is one's consciousness that is in control, but the unconscious is very often what is calling the shots.

People are resistant to accepting behavior that is inconsistent with stereotypes, while accepting behavior that is consistent with stereotypes (Krieger, 1995). Once people have accepted stereotyped behavior of groups, they will remember incidents as consistent with those stereotypes, even when those particular incidents did not occur in the stereotyped manner they remembered.

An *implicit bias* is based on either implicit attitudes or implicit stereotypes (Greenwald & Krieger, 2005). Several studies have shown implicit biases as pliable (Blair, 2002). When study participants imagined *strong* women, their gender stereotypes of *weak* women were diminished (Blair, Ma, & Lenton, 2001). It is not clear how long these changes in stereotypical beliefs hold (Greenwald & Krieger, 2006). When social connections are formed with those from devalued groups, such as race or the physically disabled, remarkable and speedy changes are seen in one's implicit biases (Olsson, 2005).

When obscure situations arise, individuals may revise the situation in their mind so it conforms to their stereotype (Moule, 2009). Stereotyping negatively impacts women who aspire to leadership positions. When women strive for leadership roles, they must demonstrate typical male attributes such as decisiveness, strength, and aggression (Reskin, 2005). This creates a double-bind for her because those attributes are the antithesis of the stereotype of a woman—collaborative, nurturing, and passive. Stereotyping was a pivotal element when Ann Hopkins, a management consultant with a master's degree in mathematics, sued Price Waterhouse for discrimination based on her sex when she was denied a promotion to partner (Hopkins, 2005).

Hopkins was the only female of 88 candidates seeking a promotion to partner (Hopkins, 2005). Ann's minority status in a primarily male workforce created a *solo* situation for her in an otherwise homogeneous group (Frisk, Bersoff, Borgida, Deaux, & Heiman, 1991). Only 6 of the firm's 667 partners were women. She was not selected as a partner by the 47 voting partners. One of the partners who supported her promotion provided her with the following feedback that came from the voting partners: "Needs a course in charm school; matured from a tough-talking somewhat masculine hard-nosed manager to an authoritative, formidable, but much more appealing lady partner candidate; macho; overly aggressive; unduly harsh; difficult to work with; impatient with staff, overcompensated for being a woman; universally disliked" (Frisk et al., 1991, p. 361). When she asked what she could do to be promoted to partner the following year, he told her to "walk more femininely, talk more femininely, dress more femininely, wear makeup and jewelry, have my hair styled" (Frisk et al., 1991, p. 361). She was told after the next nomination that she would never be promoted to partner.

## RESEARCH

Corporations are more likely to have female CEOs when the corporation's home state has more equal employment opportunity laws, and the federal appellate courts in the corporation's district are more progressive (Guthrie & Roth, 1999). When the state, region, or local labor policies take a stand favorable to women, the message sent to employers is that there are consequences when discrimination laws are not adhered to.

If women portray themselves as strong and assertive women in their leadership roles, they are perceived as equally capable as men (Rudman, 1998). However, these same women are also seen as less communal and friendly, which may lead to a "backlash effect" in how they are treated by colleagues and their direct reports, as well as increase the risk of liability (Rudman & Glick, 2001, p. 743). These agentic women are caught in a double-bind—to be respected as agentic women, or to be disliked in the same role. Either way, she may not be seen as a qualified candidate for promotion or hire into leadership positions. This reality reflects female stereotypes as kind, nurturing, and collaborative, rather than strong, assertive, and decisive.

Rudman and Glick (2001) used the IAT to test university students' implicit bias in making hiring decisions for a masculine or feminine management job. The IAT was developed by psychologists at Harvard, the University of Virginia, and the University of Washington in the 1990s to measure individuals' implicit attitudes or stereotypes. Women job applicants' demeanor was either agentic or androgynous. When students used a feminized job description in their hiring, they implicitly discriminated against the agentic female job app stetlicant because she was not viewed as "nice" enough for the job. The androgynous female job applicant was not discriminated against, suggesting that unless a woman is viewed as "nice" enough, she will be punished via discrimination. The women job applicants were seen as less hirable only for those jobs that were feminized, meaning that the job required social skills, thereby suggesting the discrimination was due to gender stereotypes. Those women who were seen as both nice and competent were not discriminated against. The researchers posited that the students who expected female job applicants would be nicer than men were more likely to perceive strong women applicants as unlikeable and socially unskilled.

A Swedish study compared the amount of callbacks for interviews for job applicants with Swedish names and those with Arab/Muslim names (Carlsson & Rooth, 2006). The job recruiters conducting the interviews were measured for both their explicit and implicit attitudes about performance stereotypes of the two categories of applicants' names by use of the means of explicit questions and the IAT. The study found only a weak correlation between implicit and explicit stereotypes but a strong negative correlation between implicit performance stereotypes and the number of applicants with Arab/Muslim names who were called back for second interviews. Testing 193 recruiters who were hiring for 1,552 jobs, Swedish-named applicants were called back for interviews 50% more than the Arab/Muslim-named applicants. The authors asserted that it was possible that both conscious and unconscious negative stereotypes of Arab/Muslims influenced the significantly lowered number called back for a second interview. Recruiters' negative attitudes toward Arab/Muslims did not affect their decision to not call them for a second interview; however, the stereotypes the recruiters believed about the ethnic group's productivity did affect their decision, which was measured implicitly.

A similar study was conducted by submitting fictitious resumes in response to jobs posted in the classified ads in Boston and Chicago newspapers (Bertrand & Mullainathan, 2004). The resumes were assigned either African American or White names. Whites were called back for interviews 50% more often than were African Americans. For every 10 resumes Whites sent, they were invited for one interview, whereas Blacks needed to submit 15 resumes to achieve one interview.

Green and Kaley (2008) evaluated social science research exploring the role of race and gender in implicit bias, employment decisions, and discrimination. Women and minorities were more likely to be judged based on stereotypes when they were underrepresented in their place of employment. The faulty judgment may reduce the expectations employers hold of women and people of color, resulting in unfair treatment which leads to both groups of employees being perceived as less competent.

Height appears to be an implicit bias as it relates to men. Almost 60% of American corporate CEOs are over six feet tall, yet less than 15% of American men are over six feet tall (Judge & Cable, 2004). To delineate even more, 36% of corporate CEOs are over six foot, two inches tall, while only 4% of American men are six foot two inches tall. Height is also associated with Presidents of the United States, Generals, and Admirals. President William McKinley, shorter than most presidents, was mocked in the press as being a "little boy" (Judge & Cable, 2004, p. 428).

## CHANGING BIASES

One of the challenges in changing hidden biases in the workplace is that organizations themselves may display unconscious bias. Perhaps this is one explanation as to why many diversity programs are ineffective in changing the organization's culture (Ross, 2010). The unconscious biases are reflected in the "norms" that have been established over time and incorporated into the very fabric of the organization. These unconscious biases are instrumental in organizational decision making and problem solving, and play a pivotal role in sabotaging change efforts. According to Ross, "Despite our best conscious efforts, the 'organizational unconscious' perpetuates the status quo and keeps old patterns, values, and behavioral norms firmly rooted" (Ross, 2010, p. 4).

Fiske (2002) identified education, increasing economic opportunity, and positive contact with a variety of groups as effective tactics to reduce both unconscious and conscious bias. Automatic biases may be diminished with conscious effort. Fiske pointed out that unconscious bias does not necessarily result in biased behavior, but requires higher level thinking to counteract it. Research demonstrated that if people created purposeful goals that fostered the treatment of the out-group members as individuals, no amygdala activation was present as a reaction to pictures of faces from a race different their own (Wheeler & Fiske, 2001 cited in Fiske, 2002).

A number of strategies have been suggested by Ross (2008) to diminish implicit bias:

1. Become aware of our biases and purposely strive to change them.
2. Conduct an audit of the workplace by critical assessment of resumes; interviewing, hiring, promotion, and termination practices; formal and informal mentoring and coaching; performance management; and new employee orientation.
3. Conduct organization-wide climate surveys specifically designed to assess stereotypes and biases.
4. Conduct exit interviews from departments and from the organization; interviews with former employees to determine why they left the department or the organization.
5. Conduct customized training dealing with hidden bias, stereotypes, and forms of unfairness.
6. Create an ombudsperson role and responsibility who is knowledgeable about nuanced bias.
7. Create projects that demonstrate positive stories and images of people of color, women, and GLBT people to diminish stereotyped perceptions of these groups. Examples include posters, newsletters, and speakers.
8. Establish teams of members from diverse groups.
9. Create an environment in which it is safe to discuss different viewpoint and to disagree.

## NOTE

Portions of this chapter were published in M. Paludi (Ed.), *Women and management: Global issues and promising solutions. Volume 1: Degrees of challenge* (pp. 175–190). Santa Barbara, CA: Praeger.

## REFERENCES

Bertrand, M., & Mullainathan, S. (2004). Are Emily and Greg more employable than Lakisha and Jamal? *American Economic Review, 94*(4), 991–1013. Retrieved September 4, 2011, from EBSCO database.

Bigler, R., & Liben, L. (1993). A cognitive-developmental approach to racial stereotyping reconstructive memory in Euro-American children. *Child Development, 6*, 1507–1518. Retrieved September 4, 2011, from EBSCO database.

Blair, I. V. (2002). The malleability of automatic stereotypes and prejudice. *Personality and Social Psychology Review, 6*, 242–261. Retrieved July 8, 2011, from EBSCO database.

Blair, I. V., Ma, J. E., & Lenton, A. P. (2001). Imagining stereotypes away: The moderation of implicit stereotypes through mental imagery. *Journal of Personality and Social Psychology, 8*, 828–841. Retrieved August 30, 2011, from EBSCO database.

Carlsson, M., & Rooth, D. (2006, September). *Evidence of ethnic discrimination in the Swedish labor market using experimental data*, IZA DP#2281, IZA. Retrieved July 19, 2011, from http://www.docstoc.com/docs/79860244/Evidence-of-Ethnic-Discrimination-in-the-wedish-Labor-Market

Carter, N. M., & Silva, C. (2010). *Pipeline's broken promise.* New York: Catalyst. http://hbr.org/2010/03/women-in-management-delusions-of-progress/ar/1

Deaux, K. (1995). How basic can you be? The evolution of research on gender stereotypes. *Journal of Social Issues, 51*, 11–21. Retrieved August 9, 2011, from EBSCO database.

Devine, P. (1989). Stereotypes and prejudice: Their automatic and controlled components. *Journal of Personality and Social Psychology, 56*, 5–18. Retrieved July 5, 2011, from EBSCO database.

*Donnell Douglas Corp. v. Green*, 411 U.S. 792 (1973).

Edney, H. T. (2006, August 18). 'New doll test' produces ugly results. *Portland Medium, 1*, 7.

Fiske, S. T. (1993). Controlling other people: The impact of power on stereotyping. *American Psychologist, 48*, 621–628. Retrieved July 19, 2011, from EBSCO database.

Fiske, S. T. (2002). What we know now about bias and intergroup conflict, the problem of the century. *Current Directions in Psychological Science, 11*, 123–128. Retrieved June 9, 2011, from EBSCO database.

Gladwell, M. (2005). *Blink: The power of thinking without thinking.* New York: Little, Brown and Company.

Green, T. K., & Kaley, A. (2008). Discrimination-reducing measures at the relational level. *Hastings Law Journal, 59*, 1435–1459. Greenwald, A. G., & Banaji, M. R. (1995). Implicit social cognition: Attitudes, self-esteem, and stereotypes. *Psychological Review, 102*, 4–27. Retrieved August 5, 2011, from EBSCO database.

Guthrie, D., & Roth, L. M. (1999). The state, courts, and equal opportunities for female CEOs in U.S. organizations: Specifying institutional mechanisms. *Social Forces, 78*, 511–542.

Hopkins, A. (2005). Price Waterhouse v. Hopkins: A personal account of a sexual discrimination plaintiff. *Hofstra Labor & Employment Law, 22*, 357–416. Retrieved September 5, 2011, from http://law2.hofstra.edu/pdf/Academics/Journals/LaborAndEmploymentLawJournal/labor_Hopkins_vol22no2.pdf

International Labour Office Bureau of Statistics. (2009). *Economically active population estimates and projections, 1980–2020.* LABORSTA Internet. Retrieved September 5, 2011, from http://laborsta.ilo.org/applv8/data/EAPEP/eapep_E.html

Judge, T. A., & Cable, D. M. (2004). The effect of physical height on workplace success and income. *Journal of Applied Psychology, 89*, 428–441. doi:10.1037/0021-9010.89.3.428.

Krieger, L. H. (1995). The content of our categories: A cognitive bias approach to discrimination and equal employment opportunity. *Stanford Law Review, 47*, 1181–1185.

Olsson, A. (2005). The role of social groups in the persistence of learned fear. *Science, 309*(5735), 785–787. Retrieved September 28, 2009, from EBSCO database.

Prokopeak, M. (2010, July 10). Bias gets a bad rap. *Diversity Executive Magazine.* Retrieved September 15, 2011, from http://diversity-executive.com/articles /view/the-value-of-faithReskin, B. (2005). Unconscious raising. *Regional Review, Q1,* 33–37. Retrieved September 28, 2011, from http://www.bos.frb .org/economic/nerr/rr2005/q1/section3a.pdf

Ross, H. J. (2010). Fighting the bias in your brain. *The Linkage Leader.* Retrieved September 6, 2011, from http://www.linkageinc.com/thinking/linkageleader /Documents/Howard_Ross_Fighting_the_Bias_in_Your_Brain.pdf

Rudman, L. A. (1998). Self-promotion as a risk factor for women: The costs and benefits of counter-stereotypical impression management. *Journal of Personality and Social Psychology, 74,* 629–645. Retrieved September 3, 2011, from http://leadershipexplorationgroup.wikispaces.com/file/view/Rudman_ self_promoing.pdf

Rudman, L. A., & Glick, P. (2001). Prescriptive gender stereotypes and backlash toward agentic women. *Journal of Social Issues, 57,* 743–762. Retrieved September 4, 2011, from EBSCO database.

Soares, R., Carter, N. M., & Combopiano, J. (2009). *Catalyst Census: Fortune 500 women board directors.* New York: Catalyst.

Test yourself for hidden bias. (n.d.). *Teaching Tolerance: A Project of the Southern Poverty Law Center.* Retrieved July 30, 2011, from http://www.tolerance.org /print/activity/test-yourself-hidden-bias

United States Department of Education. (2011, May). *The Condition of Education.* Retrieved September 5, 2011, from http://nces.ed.gov/pubs2011/2011033.pdf

# Chapter 7

# To Return or Not to Return: Women and the Balance between Work and Life

*Katie L. Pustolka*

Now more than ever, employees seek "work-life balance"—the ideal amalgamation between one's professional and personal lives. For women, especially mothers, there is an immense amount of pressure to juggle it all—the desire to be good mothers as well as productive, contributing employees. According to the U.S. Department of Labor, in 2012, the labor force participation rate for mothers with children under the age of 18 was 70.5% (U.S. Bureau of Labor Statistics, 2013). The implication of this number is profound—nearly *three quarters* of mothers in the United States were working or looking for work in 2012. A majority of mothers do work, and as such employers must be aware of the concerns women have when looking to leave or reenter the workforce. In being aware of their concerns, employers will be able to fully maximize women's contributions to the organization, while also allowing them time to be mothers as well.

## THE RETURN-TO-WORK DECISION

After a woman has a child and considers returning to the workplace, a plethora of questions are sure to be running through her mind. Many researchers have analyzed the decisions that mothers make when deciding whether to return to the workforce or not. One of the first points of discussion when women consider workforce reentry is the economic impact of working—comparing potential wages to childcare costs, as well as other work expenditures—cost of gas, transportation, dry cleaning, office lunches, and so forth. A family's financial status has a strong impact on a woman's decision to return to work. Research has shown that women with lower childcare costs, women with higher potential wages, and women with lower family income are all more likely to return to work (Barrow, 1999). Since wages tend to increase over time, older mothers will also have a tendency to return to work quickly because of the opportunity cost of not working (Barrow, 1999). On the other hand, women facing higher childcare costs or having greater other family income are less likely to return to work after becoming a first-time mother (Barrow, 1999). While some women have options available to them, others do not have a choice—a woman may not plan to return to work, but her family's financial situation (unemployment of a spouse, for example) or a forced transition (e.g., divorce) may dictate otherwise. Employment opportunities that are forced can be perceived negatively (Stadelmann-Steffen, 2011). This negative perception certainly will have an impact on the way in which a woman views work and the balance between her many roles.

When a women considers how work fits into her life after the birth of a child—her environment, mental image of herself, skills, abilities, and interests are all forces which come into play (Ericksen, Jurgens, Garrett, & Swedburg et al., 2008). Within these considerations, women's decisions are also affected by the pressure to be "superwoman," to be the perfect wife, mother, homemaker, employee, executive, launderer, chef—the list goes on. Family demands, support (or lack of support) from a spouse/partner, level of education, and amount of work experience all impact a woman's decision to return to the workforce (or not) (Ericksen et al., 2008).

In addition to the economic and environmental factors considered in the return-to-work decision, we must also consider that some women simply *like* to work and enjoy their jobs. Barrow (1999) postulated that some women, even despite having lower wages than some of their counterparts, return to the workforce if they have a "taste for work." A woman is considered to have a strong preference for employment if she chooses to work even though she does not need to for financial reasons, or if employment involves potentially high costs of childcare (Stadelmann-Steffen, 2011). The impact of education on preferences for work also is of interest and open to interpretation. Women with higher levels of education may do so because they are committed to their careers and are more likely to want to return to the workforce. Waldfogel, Higuchi, and Abe (1999), in a cross-cultural sample, found that although children do affect employment, women with college degrees who had infants were more likely to work in the United States, Britain, and Japan, than those who had obtained less education. Also notable—women with less education (less than a high school diploma) are more likely to be employed, presumably due to economic need.

As discussed, support from family and friends, desire to use skills and abilities, and personal opinions on motherhood and career all play a role in a woman's employment decision. In evaluating these influences, women tend to have one of three options: (1) return to work (full-time; part-time; with flexible arrangements such as a reduced work week, job sharing, or telecommuting; or seasonal or temporary employment); (2) develop skills (returning to school for further education, taking training courses, or work-shops); or (3) delay entry into the workforce (Ericksen et al., 2008). Inter-twined with these options is the fact that traditional gender roles do still exist in the 21st century. While strides have been made to level the playing field, when it comes to the family, family women are faced with traditional expectations. Bowman (2009) found that a "gender-based deal" still exists, specifically for women for whom their husbands are the breadwinners ("entrepreneurs" in the study). For the women in the study, the majority admitted that money was an explicit part of "the deal"—it is the respon-sibility of their husbands to earn money and they, as wives and mothers, sacrifice their careers and ambitions for their families. These women de-scribed that when caught between their families and "the market" (the workplace)—the family won; to the women in the study, their aspirations were not valued in the market, their choices and activities were framed around the needs of their husbands and children. Similar to women who are forced to work, some women stay home, but do not actively chose this role. To make sense of the conflict between what they would like versus what they had renounced themselves to, the women justified this choice by describing their selflessness, commitment, and love for their family (Bowman, 2009). With these sorts of social pressures still in existence, there is no doubt why mothers are so conflicted about returning to the workforce. Similarly, Wilby (2005) describes how we have "slipped back in the past 30 years"—that in the early 1970s it was the norm for women to stop working once they had children, but that obstacles to having a career were slowly declining. Women certainly have different personal views on the appropriateness of working when they have children, but it must not be discounted that careers have become more competitive over the years, and child rearing has become more taxing. Employers should take into account the following idea—to "make work more family-friendly, rather than making the family more work-friendly" (Wilby, 2005).

## A GLOBAL ISSUE

The ever-present struggle between balancing employment and family life is an issue felt across the globe. Many countries offer robust leave pe-riods for a mother (and father) to spend time with their newborns. The amount of time that a mother has to spend with her new child may have a significant impact on how she views the transition from employee to mother, and from mother to working mother. In the United States, the standard paid maternity leave is six weeks. If a mother (or father) qualifies, the Family Medical Leave Act (FMLA) provides up to 12 weeks of unpaid leave for the birth of a new child. According to the U.S. Department of Labor, it can "conclude that the FMLA continues to make a positive impact on the lives of workers without imposing an undue burden on employers. The FMLA is working" (U.S. Bureau of Labor Statistics, 2013). While certainly a step in the right direction, some women do not utilize their full FMLA entitlement. Adamo (2013) found that women in the biological sciences in the United States do not take their full leave periods for fear of falling behind on projects, losing grants, and missed tenure opportunities. With the increase of career competition, this sentiment certainly can be extrapolated to other industries as well.

Legally mandated maternity (and paternity) leaves are quite generous in countries outside the United States, and utilization of full leave periods is encouraged and commonplace. For example, leave policies in Norway are some of the most generous in the world—leave for Norwegians "consists of 308 days of paid leave on full wages with a quota of 63 days leave exclusively for mothers, 42 days exclusively for fathers and the rest of the leave available for both parents" (Alstveit, Severinsson, & Karlsen, 2011). Also in Norway, each parent is also entitled to apply for additional unpaid leave of up to 365 days immediately after the "ordinary leave period." In Canada, maternity leave is also legally mandated, with mothers entitled to 17 weeks of maternity leave, as well as 14 weeks of paternity leave at 95% pay. An additional 21 weeks of leave is available with partial pay, for a total of one year (Adamo, 2013). Some Canadian universities even allow a deferral period for women with childcare duties, and leave periods do not negatively impact productivity assessments of faculty.

To compare leave policies with employee retention, Waldfogel et al. (1999) reviewed family leave policies in the United States, Great Britain, and Japan, and found that family leave coverage does increase the probability that women will return to their employer after childbirth, holding true for all three countries. Japan is unique in that there is legislation for national childcare leave, which allows mothers or fathers of children under the age of one to take parental leave. It was found that childcare leave increases retention of women by 35% (Waldfogel et al., 1999). Retention statistics are significant for employers—the costs of recruitment and training are substantial, and organizations cannot afford to lose well-trained employees. Something that policymakers in the United States may want to consider—in the United Kingdom, employees who are for Statutory Maternity Pay (SMP) are also eligible to take up to 10 Keeping In Touch ("KIT") days without affecting their maternity allowance (Vaux,

2007). These days allow mothers to do exactly that—to have an avenue for keeping in touch with their employers while still being on leave. These days may help a mother on leave feel more a part of the organization and may, in turn, help ease their transition back to work when the leave period is up. Employers outside of the United Kingdom are still able to offer employees a way of staying in touch; from sending a quick e-mail "checking in" to a department lunch, small efforts such as these may have a huge impact on a mother's decision to return to work. Employers who are supportive of maternity leave will likely see women return to *their* doors, rather than having productive employees "shop around" for the best employer or leave the workforce entirely.

## AFTER THE DECISION: REENTRY AND REINTEGRATION

We know that when women decide to leave the workforce (and rejoin after a hiatus), there are a number of concerns that dictate if, and when, she will return. Women who are mothers face difficulties not only in the decision to return to work, but might also experience struggles with reintegration and with balancing work and personal responsibilities. Mothers may decide to return to the workforce for many reasons—out of financial necessity, commitment to their careers, or perhaps due to a desire to maintain a sense of self-identity. A survey by MyWorkButterfly.com, a site for mothers returning to the workforce, found that 71% of mothers who went back to work named financial security as the most important benefit. Women are cognizant of why they return to work, but after taking a break, many seek a change. Some mothers know what they are looking for but many women go through a "floundering" period when evaluating different work options (Walecia, 2009). It's important when seeking employment that new moms think about the hours they want (and thus, are willing) to work, the type of schedule that various industries require, and, of course, financial benefits. If income is a concern, it is prudent for mothers to consider associated expenses—fuel and transportation costs, clothing or uniform costs, dry cleaning, office lunches, and childcare benefits, such as medical insurance, life insurance, pension or 401(k) plans, and paid time off should be considered as well.

Once a career direction has been finalized, job seekers, especially those who have been away for a time, should refresh their knowledge. This could mean keeping in touch with former colleagues or supervisors (formally or informally through social networking sites, such as LinkedIn, Facebook, Twitter, etc.), asking other industry professionals for updates on certain processes or tasks, taking a course at a local college, or even planning on how to discuss the time away with potential interviewers.

However, McGinn, Brown, and Adrien (2006) reviewed troubling statistics on high-achieving women who found it difficult to return to work after taking time off. A study conducted by the Harvard Business School found that of women with graduate or college degrees (with honors), 37% took an extended break from work, on average staying home about 2.2 years (as cited in McGinn et al., 2006). Most of these women wanted to return to work, but the statistics are shocking—only about 40% regained full-time employment (McGinn et al., 2006). It is clear there are barriers preventing competent women from returning to the workforce: some hiring professionals assume that women who are serious about their careers would not have left their jobs in the first place (Robinson, 2007). Women may also find employers not as flexible or understanding as they would like.

## IMPLICATIONS FOR EMPLOYERS

The struggles mothers face between work and family responsibilities do not end with the decision to return to work and it is imperative that employers are aware of the conflicts working mothers face. Once she has returned to the workforce, a mother will undoubtedly experience emotional difficulties when leaving her child. She may feel conflicted or guilty in regards to how to be a good mother (or being considered a bad one for going back to work) (Millward, 2006). Many women will also experience guilt for using childcare facilities or at having to stop breastfeeding earlier than is recommended. To this extent, the decision to return to work and the decision to breastfeed are "bound together" (Kimbro, 2006). Some mothers may be less likely to initiate breastfeeding in the first place if they know they will be returning to work and others may quit breastfeeding if they feel their employer would not be supportive. It has been shown that mothers in administrative and manual positions are more likely to quit breastfeeding than those in professional roles (Kimbro, 2006). This is an opportunity for employers to provide support and flexibility to mothers, especially those who wish to breastfeed. An employer may want to consider having a formal "nursing mother's policy" (unpaid or paid time to pump and a discreet area to do so). Human Resources professionals should notify returning mothers of this policy as well as insure managers are aware of it. As it has been shown that women in administrative and manual roles are more likely to quit breastfeeding due to work constraints, employers should seek to provide additional flexibility for these women.

Organizations that are conscious of issues mothers face can help prevent or mediate barriers that typically inhibit returning mothers. Employers should ask themselves—*What do we offer returning employees? Do employees know the benefits available to them? Why should employees want to return to us?* Keeping the lines of communication open—from pregnancy through return—will show an organization is supportive and understanding. Upon learning of an upcoming leave, employers and employees must keep each other in the loop. To avoid feelings of exclusion, managers should keep mothers-to-be informed in regard to coverage preparations: asking for their opinions and requesting feedback on coverage, having her explain nuances of the role, advice, and so forth. Small efforts such as these will keep her feeling a part of the team. It is important for managers to wish mothers-to-be well, and to reassure them that the department/group/company is looking forward to having them back. Little gestures, such as sending a flower arrangement or a card upon the birth of the child, or a quick e-mail to check in, can really go a long way. Of course, it must be noted that each employee is different—some may crave a great deal of contact while on leave, while others will prefer more space.

Once a mother returns, it's important that employers are aware of the insecurities she undoubtedly will face. As Millward (2006) describes, companies must "actively manage the psychological aspects of transition from the woman's point of view" (p. 329). A mother may be concerned about not being able to fulfill performance expectations by needing time off for appointments or a child's sickness, may feel inefficient due to lack of sleep, experience feelings of guilt for working, and may have difficulties integrating. Alstveit et al. (2011) conducted interviews with nine women during the first months of their return, and the following were common themes:

"I no longer feel in complete command."
"I had a guilty conscience for working full-time."
"You do not want to be a burden to your employer because you had a child."
—Alstveit et al., 2011, p. 2155

These concerns could potentially spiral into anxiety or depression, and need to be managed accordingly. An organization may want to explore alternative employment options such as flexible scheduling, telecommuting/working from home, or virtual offices. Benefits administrators should consider comprehensive benefits packages, as well as "fringe" benefits such as on-site fitness centers, free fitness classes, or on-site childcare options. Organizations that provide a supportive environment, as well as a robust benefits package will retain employees they can least afford to lose—and buffer the negative experiences that mothers may have when returning to the workplace.

A majority of women will become mothers at some point in their lives. Coincidentally, the prime time for motherhood often occurs concurrently with a woman's most important professional years. Organizations must be prepared for the ongoing cycle of workplace leaves and reentry. It is prudent for business leaders to be aware of the issues that come into play when a mother decides to return to work. From questions of financial stability to that of a new career, mothers have a great deal of considerations to take into account when returning to the workforce. It is imperative that organizations provide support to their employees (prebirth to return) so that mothers may continue to be productive, contributing employees.

## REFERENCES

Adamo, S. (2013). Attrition of women in the biological sciences: Workload, motherhood, and other explanations revisited. *BioScience, 63,* 43–48.

Alstveit, M., Severinsson, E., & Karlsen, B. (2011). Readjusting one's life in the tension inherent in work and motherhood. *Journal of Advanced Nursing, 67,* 2151–2160.

Barrow, L. (1999). An analysis of women's return-to-work decisions following first birth. *Economic Inquiry, 37,* 432–451.

Bowman, D. (2009). The deal: Wives, entrepreneurial business and family life. *Journal of Family Studies, 15,* 167–176.

Employment characteristics of families summary. (2013, April 26). *U.S. Bureau of Labor Statistics.* Retrieved September 8, 2013, from http://www.bls.gov /news.release/famee.nr0.htm

Ericksen, K., Jurgens, J., Garrett, M., & Swedburg, R. (2008). Should I stay at home or should I go back? Workforce reentry influences on a mother's decision-making process. *Journal of Employment Counseling, 45,* 156–167.

Family and Medical Leave Act—Survey—Wage and Hour Division (WHD)—U.S. Department of Labor. (n.d.). *United States Department of Labor.* Retrieved September 8, 2013, from http://www.dol.gov/whd/fmla/survey

Kimbro, R. (2006). On-the-job moms: Work and breastfeed initiation and duration for a sample of low-omitincome women. *Maternal and Child Health Journal, 10,* 19–26.

Konrad, W. (2009, August). Press restart on your career. *Money, 38,* 63–65.

McGinn, D., Brown, R., & Adrien, C. (2006, September 25). Getting back on track. *Newsweek, 148,* 62–66.

Millward, L. (2006). The transition to motherhood in an organizational context: An interpretative phenomenological analysis. *Journal of Occupational and Organizational Psychology, 79,* 315–333.

Robinson, T. (2007, March 1). Time out. *Black Enterprise,* 87–89.

Stadelmann-Steffen, I. (2011). Dimensions of family policy and female labor market participation: Analyzing group-specific policy effects. *Governance: An International Journal of Policy, Administration, and Institutions, 24,* 331–357.

Vaux, G. (2007). 'Keeping in touch' days offer new mothers flexible return to work. *Community Care, 1682,* 23.

Waldfogel, J., Higuchi, Y., & Abe, M. (1999). Family leave policies and women's retention after childbirth: Evidence from the United States, Britain, and Japan. *Journal of Population Economics, 12,* 523–545.

Wilby, P. (2005, April 4). Maternity leave: An employer writes. *New Statesman,* 30.

# Chapter 8

# Why Work-Life Integration Is Essential for Individuals and Organizations

*Janet Tracey*

Families are busy. School, extracurricular activities, community involvement, and social events fill the schedules of many families. With all of these overlapping and conflicting commitments it is no surprise that working parents often have difficulty finding time to simultaneously meet work and family obligations. More likely than not, both parents have increasingly demanding careers that require more than a 40-hour a week commitment. For these working families, integrating work, family, community involvement, and social commitments may often seem like an impossible task. The goal for many is to organize their time and efforts in meeting the expectations in each area of their lives.

People work out of necessity or desire. For most, it is both. Working professionals need the financial security that a steady income affords and look for opportunities to contribute to meaningful work. While young professionals who have yet to start a family may have more flexibility in the amount of time and energy they can dedicate to their work, dual career families are challenged with coordinating often conflicting work and family obligations. Working professionals with families have less flexibility. In order to support employees in meeting both family and work obligations, employers have initiated family-friendly policies including flexible work schedules, telecommuting, and onsite childcare. Together with the application of technology these policies were intended to help working professionals balance work-time with family commitments. The implementation of these policies, however, may have had the opposite effect, increasing the amount of time parents spend meeting work obligations.

Flexible schedule or telecommuting parents may often answer e-mails at the soccer field, attend conference calls while driving kids to school, or complete work projects at kitchen tables. Work is always there, waiting, calling, making it difficult to dedicate quality time to families. While spending time with family, work is neglected and family time is often neglected while work projects are completed. Work and families are in direct conflict. These situations often foster feelings of guilt and discontent. It is often difficult to feel productive and successful when feeling anxiety over not meeting expectations. To feel successful, working professionals are driven to meet the expectations of those around them, whether in work, family, or community. When these expectations cannot be met, professionals are often left feeling unsuccessful and anxious. Arranging commitments and resources in order to meet various expectations is no easy task and requires a unique set of skills. Replacing standard work-life policies with tools and training is one solution for working professionals to reach the pinnacle of success in all areas of their lives.

While work-life policies are progressive they don't address the root cause of frustrations felt by working professionals. People need freedom and control over their schedules and commitments. Autonomy over schedules, control over commitments, and the freedom to dedicate time as necessary will lead to successfully integrating work into family life. Working professionals need training in identifying expectations, defining, and prioritizing what is most important to them and evaluating their efforts and results. These skills will allow professionals to define boundaries and establish control. This type of training would result in happier, more productive employees. Additionally, companies may want to redefine current work-life policies. These policies are cookie cutter in nature, offering a one-size-fits-all solution to an extremely complex problem. Every professional, every family is different. Open policies that establish a general framework but provide opportunity for flexibility in meeting the needs of individual workers are necessary. If companies continue with standard work-life policies, they may see their most productive employees leave to pursue opportunities that provide more autonomy. Consulting, network marketing, home crafting, freelancing, and starting small businesses allow people more freedom to set their own schedules, prioritize work or family, and work as little or as much as necessary. One need only look at the recent success of network marketing companies and online marketplaces such as Etsy© to recognize a growing trend in professionals opting out of corporate America. The freedom to determine one's commitment level, contributions, and ultimately success is the key to work integration.

# Chapter 9

# The Evolution of Women in the Workforce

*Kathryn Halpin*

From the "Daughters of Liberty," to the revolutionary women of *Newsweek,* to the likes of Sheryl Sandberg, COO, Facebook, and Marissa Mayer, CEO, Yahoo! Inc., the role of women in the workplace has truly evolved. This chapter will explore the history of women's role in the workplace in the United States, including the emergence and importance of work-life balance programs along the way and an evaluation of the perceived "wage gap" between men and women. Finally, Hillary Rodham Clinton's statement about current barriers for women will be assessed, in conjunction with the currently trending question of "are women in a stalled revolution?"

## HISTORY

The Townshend Acts of 1767 were passed by the British Parliament in an effort to exert their authority over the American colonies and ultimately led to the organization of the first society of working women, the "Daughters of Liberty," a subsidiary to the "Sons of Liberty." The

Townshend Acts notably imposed direct revenue duties payable at colonial ports on goods such as lead, glass, paper, paint, and tea, solely for the purpose of collecting revenue for the British treasury. The Daughters of Liberty emerged in New England to make homespun cloth and other goods to assist their fellow colonists with boycotting British products. Eventually, the Daughters of Liberty became key supporters of the American Revolution by making bullets and sewing uniforms for the men on the battlefield—a trend we will see reemerge in future U.S. wars to come. Samuel Adams is often quoted as saying, "With ladies on our side, we can make every Tory tremble" (Townshend Acts, 2013).

The next monumental step in the women's movement came in 1825 with the emergence of the United Tailoresses of New York, the first all-female labor union. Famously led by Lavinia Waight and Louise Mitchell, the group banded together to protest 16-hour work days that failed to guarantee a living wage. The emergence of women in the workforce continued out of the New England area in the late 1820s. Specifically, textile mills in Lowell, Massachusetts, started to hire young women to work in the mills as they were willing to earn less than men. By 1844, working women from the mills joined forces to create the Lowell Female Labor Reform Association (LFLRA) to petition the Massachusetts state legislature for health and safety regulations in the mills. The LFLRA was notoriously led by Sarah Bagley ("Women and the labor movement," 2013).

In 1903, the National Women's Trade Union League (NWTUL) was founded in Boston to advocate for better wages and working conditions. Uniquely, this group included all classes of women, including the working class and wealthy women from prominent families, and recognized that they were united by the "bonds of womanhood." Comparable to what's commonly referred to as a "stiletto network" today, the upper-class women of the NWTUL donated money, served as representatives to the press, and helped to secure legal representation for the group (National Women's Trade Union League of America). The "stiletto networks" of the 21st century, as defined by Pamela Ryckman, author of "Stiletto Network: Inside the women's power circles that are changing the face of business," are networks that can propel women upward in business, while trickling down both guidance and funds to other women and girls (Kenyon, 2013).

Progress continued to evolve through the early 19th century. Massachusetts became the first state to enact a minimum wage law that impacted both women and minors in 1912 (Giang, 2013). In 1913, the Congressional Union for Woman Suffrage, which later became the National Woman's Party, launched the first women's political newspaper in the United States, *The Suffragist*. In addition, Jeannette Rankin of Missoula, Montana, became the female member to be elected to the United States Congress in 1916 and again in 1941 (Rankin, 2013). Finally, the Women's Bureau of the Department of Labor was formed by Congress in 1920.

World War II and President Franklin D. Roosevelt (FDR) served as a major catalyst for women's evolution in the workplace. Soon after taking office, FDR appointed Frances Perkins as his Secretary of Labor from 1933 through 1945, making her the first woman to ever hold a cabinet seat. Perkins held a contributing seat at the table and was a major player in rolling out New Deal legislation, including minimum wage laws and the Social Security Act of 1935 (Perkins, 2013).

When World War II began for the United States, women worked in defense plants, managed the home, and volunteered for war-related activities, including joining men overseas. Per the National World War II museum, nearly 350,000 women served in uniform during the war, including volunteering for the Women's Army Auxiliary Corporation, the Navy Women's Reserve, the Marine Corps Women's Reserve, the Coast Guards Women's Reserve, the Women Airforce Service Pilots, the Army Nurses Corps, and the Navy Nurses Corps. The women in uniform served as clerical workers, mechanics, drivers, pilots, technicians, radio operators, and trainers. General Dwight D. Eisenhower was quoted as saying, "The contribution of the women of America, whether on the farm or in the factory or in uniform, to D-Day was a sine qua non of the invasion effort." Unfortunately, at the war's end, women struggled to hold onto the jobs that they had obtained. They were quickly displaced by men returning home from war and women veterans struggled to receive the same benefits from the G.I. Bill as men (*American women in World War II: On the home front and beyond*, 2013).

Finally, in the 1960s more traction was gained by women in the form of federal legislation for equality. Specifically, the Equal Pay Act was passed in 1963, which prohibits discrimination on the account of sex in the payment of wages by employers engaged in commerce or in the production of goods for commerce. The Civil Rights Act of 1964 (Title VII) prohibits discrimination in employment on the basis of race, color, religion, sex, or national origin. Sexual harassment is also addressed under the Civil Rights Act and is prohibited based on membership in a protected class. Under Title VII, the Equal Employment Opportunity Commission (EEOC) eventually ruled in the late 1960s that it is also unlawful to have separate "help wanted" advertisements for men and women (Equal Employment Opportunity Commission, 2013).

Lynn Povich chronicles her struggles as a young woman working in the 1960s and early 1970s at *Newsweek* in her book *The good girls revolt*. Although legislation was in the place at the time, Povich notes:

*Until around 1970, women comprised fewer than 10 percent of students in medical school, 4 percent of law school students, and only 3 percent of business school students. At Newsweek, our "problem that had no name" in the mid-1960s was sexism, pure and simple. At both Time and Newsweek, only*

*men were hired as writers. Women were almost always hired on the mail*
*desk or as fact checkers and rarely promoted to reporter or writer. Even with*
*similar credentials, women generally ended up in lesser positions than men.*
(Povich, 2012, p. xviii)

On March 16, 1970, 46 female employees of *Newsweek* filed a complaint
with the EEOC, charging that they had been "systematically discriminated against in both hiring and promotion and forced to assume a subsidiary role" simply because they were women (Povich, 2012, p. 1). This
marked the first female class action lawsuit and it quickly inspired others
to spring into action. In the early 1970s, women at *Time, Life, Fortune* and
*Sports Illustrated, Reader's Digest, Newsday,* the *Washington Post,* the *Detroit
News,* the *Baltimore Sun,* the *New Haven Register,* the Associated Press, and
the *New York Times* filed sex discrimination charges on behalf of countless
women (Povich, 2012).

The Civil Rights Act of 1964 was amended in 1978 to include the Pregnancy Discrimination Act, which prohibited sex discrimination on the
basis of pregnancy (Equal Employment Opportunity Commission, 2013).
Soon thereafter, in 1982, 1,700 female flight attendants from United Air-
lines won a $37 million lawsuit against the company for firing them once
they got married (Giang, 2013).

In September 1981, Sandra Day O'Connor was the first woman to be
appointed to the Supreme Court by President Ronald Reagan. O'Connor
was considered to be a "decisive swing vote" and would notably go on
to make several rulings regarding topics like election law and abortion.
She served for 25 years, until 2006 (Sandra Day O'Connor, 2013). Just two
years later, in 1983, Sally Ride became the first American female to go to
space on the *Challenger* shuttle (Sally Ride, 2013).

The early 1990s and the Gulf War marked the first time that women officially served in combat. Estimates reveal that of the 334,000 army soldiers
deployed to the Gulf region, approximately 26,000 were women. In 1992,
*The Washington Post* reported that army officials reviewed the largest female deployment in history as a huge success, despite the fact that investi-
gative reports revealed that at least 24 army servicewomen had been raped
or sexually assaulted in the Gulf, in most cases by high-ranking male service members (24 Army women assaulted, raped during Gulf War, 1992).

Fast forwarding to the 21st century, Lilly Ledbetter is celebrated as a
heroine of female rights. Ledbetter worked for nearly 20 years at Goodyear Tire and Rubber Company in Alabama, before suing Goodyear for
sexual harassment and pay discrimination. Just before her retirement, she
had received an anonymous tip from a male coworker comparing her pay
to that of her male counterparts, which was significantly higher. Ledbetter
found herself testifying before Congress and the Supreme Court in 2007,
which ruled that she was not entitled to compensation that had previously

been awarded by a lesser court due to the fact that she had filed her claim more than 180 days after receiving her first discriminatory paycheck. When President Barack Obama took office in 2009, one of the first pieces of legislation that he signed was the Lilly Ledbetter Fair Pay Act, which changed the Civil Rights Act so that workers can sue up to 180 days after receiving any discriminatory paycheck (Pickert, 2009).

Former First Lady and New York State Senator, Hillary Rodham Clinton, made history in 2008 as the first woman to run for President of the United States. Although she was defeated by President Obama in the democratic primary, speculation looms that she will run again in 2016. From the original supporters of the American Revolution to the presidential campaign trail in the 21st century, the role of women in the United States has undoubtedly evolved.

## WORK-LIFE BALANCE

As the role of women and families in the workplace has expanded and the cultural philosophy on work has changed in the United States, so too have the policies and procedures of many organizations. Nancy R. Lockwood defines work-life balance in her 2003 "Work/life balance: Challenges and solutions" report for the Society for Human Resource Management (SHRM) as "a state of equilibrium in which the demands of both a person's job and personal life are equal." Although the term "work/life balance" was technically coined in 1986, programs supporting this concept existed as early as in the 1930s. Employee Assistance Programs or EAPs were first created in the 1940s and are still offered by many employers today. A typical EAP offers a broad range of services, including drug and alcohol abuse counseling, assistance with financial, legal, family or marital problems, and most other stress-related difficulties.

Although various programs and solutions have been around for years, the need for and importance of work-life balance programs seems to be on the rise. Overall, the sentiment of the American workforce has begun to change from a philosophy of living to work, to that of striking a better balance between personal and work-related obligations. Lockwood highlights the September 11, 2001, terrorist attacks as a major catalyst for this cultural shift in philosophy, as this event led many people to reevaluate their lives and the meaning of work. Lockwood cites a 2001 study conducted by Rutgers University and the University of Connecticut, which revealed that 90% of working adults are concerned that they do not spend enough time with their families. A 2001 Radcliff Public Policy Center survey concluded that 82% of men and 85% of women ages 20 to 39 placed family time at the top of their list of priorities.

Lockwood's report not only highlights the increased desire for more family time, but the increased importance organizations must place on recognizing diversity of family structures and the changing face of the traditional family. Historical research and programs focused on the needs of married couples and couples with children, but there is an increasing need to support single parents, blended families, employees with elder-care responsibilities, and military families, for example. These types of family structures and familial responsibilities warrant serious consideration as organizations review employee engagement and morale, retention, job satisfaction, productivity, and absenteeism. Johnson & Johnson had cited a near 50% decline in absenteeism among employees who utilized the flexible work options and family leave programs offered to employees (Lockwood, 2003). Critical to the success and the effectiveness of any work-life balance program is communication about these programs, including a message of top-down support. If the programs exist, but participation is considered taboo by senior leadership, they will not have the intended impact on the organization.

Topping a 2013 list of the best big companies for work-life balance, as reported by job search engine Indeed.com, is Colgate-Palmolive. *Forbes* magazine reports that Colgate-Palmolive tops the list due to management's focus on setting clear and realistic goals for staff, promoting time management, and clearly communicating expectations to staff. In addition, the company boasts generous benefits, such as flexible work hours, telecommuting options, and nearby back-up childcare centers. As *Forbes* reviews the other finalists, which include Wegman's, Coldwell Banker, and Google to name a few, they highlight that having adequate staffing to ensure that employees don't have to work while on vacation and constantly plug in from home is key to the equation for success (Smith, 2013).

Although companies like Johnson & Johnson are able to boast benefits such as a significant reduction in absenteeism and productivity gains, other companies remain hesitant to jump on the flexible work schedule bandwagon. Specifically, much debate remains over the effectiveness of telecommuting options for employees. The fact remains that employers must be attentive to the priorities of their workforce and note that flexible work-life balance programs are often viewed as attractive perks and retention tools to not only women and families, but to an increasing number of individuals in the workplace.

## TODAY

According to the U.S. Bureau for Labor Statistics (BLS), the average employment status of women in the workplace who are 16 years old and over has increased from 43.3% in 1970 to 58.1% in 2011. Female workforce participation peaked in 1999 at 60%. Statistics for the male portion of the workforce have taken a slightly different trend; the average employment status of men who are 16 years old and over was 79.7% in 1970 and has decreased to 70.5% in 2011. The overall unemployment rate for women in 2011 was 8.5%, as compared to 9.4% for men.

Notably, labor force participation for mothers who have children between the ages of 6 and 17 was at 76.5%, as of March 2011. Mothers who have children under the age of six have a 64.2% participation rate. Finally, 74.9% of unmarried mothers with children under the age of 18 are in the workforce. It is also important to highlight that the educational attainment levels of women between the ages of 25 and 64 has nearly tripled since 1970 and as of 2011, women accounted for 51% of workforce employees in management, professional, and other related occupations.

The weekly earnings of women working in a full-time capacity made up 82% of the median weekly earnings of men in 2011. This ratio has increased from 62% in 1979. In their report "Highlights of women's earnings in 2011," the BLS underscores that among individuals employed in a full-time (35 hours per week or more) capacity, men are more likely to work a longer week. Specifically, 25% of men work 41 hours per week or more, as compared to 14% of women. Among the workforce contributors who had a 40-hour work week, women earned 88% as much as men. There is also a disparity when it comes to the make-up of the part-time employee pool. According to 2011 data, 26% of female workers serve in a part-time capacity (less than 35 hours per week), as compared to only 13% of men (U.S. Bureau of Labor Statistics, 2011).

Wage and salary statistics are one of the main forces fueling the current debate over whether or not women are in a stalled revolution. Groups like Stanford University's Clayman Institute for Gender Research support the theory that there has been a stall. The Clayman Institute titles their "strategic focus" as *Beyond the stalled revolution: Reinvigorating gender equality in the twenty-first century*. They specifically state:

> . . . scholars have identified further evidence of a stall in women's progress. The gender gap in wages, while narrowing over the 1970s and 1980s, has remained relatively constant since the mid 1990s. (*Beyond the stalled revolution: Reinvigorating gender equality in the twenty-first century*, 2013)

At the same time, a report titled "An analysis of the reasons for the disparity in wages between men and women," prepared by CONSAD Research Corporation for the U.S. Department of Labor (D.O.L.) in 2009, seems to take the opposing position as it relates to wage disparities. In the foreword of the report written by the D.O.L., Charles James, Deputy Assistant Secretary for Federal Contract Compliance, highlights the gains made by women in the workforce and notes that data on the "raw wage gap continues to be used in misleading ways to advance public policy agendas without fully explaining the reasons behind the gap." The report underscores several variables that should be factored in to create an "adjusted gender wage gap." These factors include: the variance of women and men who work part-time; the fact that a greater percentage of women leave the workforce for child birth, childcare and eldercare, and the lost tenure or years of experience of women who leave the workforce and then later return; the higher percentage of women who tend to value "family-friendly" policies and the correlating wages and salaries associated with industries and occupations who implement these policies. Taking into account these factors, the " adjusted gender wage gap" is assessed to be between 4.8 and 7.1%.

Wage and salary data aside, the number of women reaching the executive level can seem disheartening to many, especially given that women make up 51% of the workforce in management, professional, and other related occupations. According to a February 2013 *Bloomberg* article just 21 of the CEOs at S&P 500 companies are women, which equates to just 4%, and this number has remained fairly consistent over the last five years. On the other hand, gains have been made when it comes to other positions in the "C-suite." In the last year, the number of women holding the Chief Financial Officer position at an S&P 500 company increased nearly 35%. In summary, women held 14% of senior-executive positions in 2012, but nearly 28% of Fortune 500 companies did not have any women in "C-suite" positions (Frier & Hymowitz, 2013).

Notably, two female executives have recently made waves in the "C-Suite," sparking much conversation and debate. In 2012, Marissa Mayer broke ground by becoming the highest profile pregnant woman to be hired as CEO. Mayer started her new job at Yahoo! Inc. while nearly six months pregnant. Additionally, Mayer was almost 20 years younger than the average-aged CEO at 37. Since her appointment, controversy has been a consistent thread for Mayer. She was slammed when she returned to work after only a two-week maternity leave in October 2012. Shortly thereafter, Mayer banned telecommuting at Yahoo!, sparking yet another debate over working from home. In April 2013, Mayer finally received some praise as she extended the Yahoo! paid parental leave program, allowing new mothers to take up to 16 weeks of time off and providing them with an additional $500 to assist with items like groceries and baby clothes (Pepitone, 2013). In August 2013, Mayer set off a firestorm when she posed for a two-page spread in *Vogue's* September issue. Critics question whether or not the photo which has her lying upside down on a couch is too provocative and sends the wrong message, while others are focused on the accompanying article which highlights the accomplishments Mayer has been able to achieve at Yahoo! thus far (Gross, 2013).

Sheryl Sandberg, Chief Operating Officer at Facebook, published her book *Lean In: Women, work and the will to lead* in 2013. Sandberg evaluates why women's progress has stalled and offers suggestions and solutions for women to reach their full potential, including how to negotiate for more money and how to earn a seat at the decision making table. Critics have contended that Sandberg's expectations are unrealistic for the average female. More recently, in August 2013, Sandberg's LeanIn.org foundation found itself under scrutiny for advertising a job posting for an unpaid intern. The organization made a follow-up statement saying that they will be paying interns moving forward (Yarow, 2013).

The BLS is predicting that between 2008 and 2018 the number of women in the labor force will increase by 9%. This increase will occur in large part due to the projected increase of women between the ages of 65 and older that will remain in the workforce, instead of retiring. During this time frame, the number of women between the ages of 65 and 74 is expected to increase by 89.9% and age 75 and above is expected to have nearly a 62% increase (U.S. Bureau of Labor Statistics, 2011).

## REFERENCES

*American women in World War II: On the home front and beyond.* Retrieved July 20, 2013, from the National WWII Museum website: http://www.nationalww2museum.org/learn/education/for-students/ww2-history/at-a-glance/women-in-ww2.html

*Beyond the stalled revolution: Reinvigorating gender equality in the twenty-first century.* Retrieved July 20, 2013, from Stanford University, The Clayman Institute for Gender Research Strategic Focus website: http://gender.stanford.edu/strategic-focus

CONSAD Research Corporation. (2009, January 12). *An analysis of the reasons for the disparity in wages between men and women.* (Under Contract Number GS-23F-02598, Task Order 2, Subtask 2B). Retrieved from http://www.consad.com/content/reports/Gender%20Wage%20Gap%20Final%20Report.pdf

Equal Employment Opportunity Commission. (2013). *Laws, Regulations, and Guidance.* Retrieved from http://www.eeoc.gov/laws/

Frier, S., & Hymowitz, C. (2013, February 6). Women CFOs reach record level in U.S. as top jobs remain elusive. *Bloomberg.* http://www.bloomberg.com/news/2013-02-06/women-cfos-reach-record-level-in-u-s-as-top-job-remains-elusive.html

Giang, V. (2013, March 27). The incredible rise of women in the workplace. *Business Insider.* http://www.businessinsider.com/women-in-the-workplace-2013-3?op=1

Gross, D. (2013, August 20). Yahoo's Marissa Mayer turns heads with Vogue photo shoot. *CNN.* http://www.cnn.com/2013/08/19/tech/web/marissa-mayer-vogue

Kenyon, J. (2013, May 16). How stiletto networks are blazing the business world. *Forbes.* http://www.forbes.com/sites/learnvest/2013/05/16/how-stiletto-networks-are-blazing-the-business-world/

Lockwood, N. (2003). *Work/Life balance challenges and solutions.* 2003 SHRM Research Quarterly. Retrieved from http://www.shrm.org/research/surveyfindings/articles/documents/0302wl.pdf

National Women's Trade Union League of America. Retrieved July 20, 2013, from Harvard University Library Open Collections Program website: http://ocp.hul.harvard.edu/ww/nwtul.html

Pepitone, J. (2013, April 30). Marissa Mayer extends Yahoo's maternity leave. *CNNMoney.* http://money.cnn.com/2013/04/30/technology/yahoo-materni ty-leave/index.html

Perkins, Frances. Retrieved July 20, 2013, from Social Security Administration website: http://www.ssa.gov/history/fperkins.html

Pickert, K. (2009, January 29). Lilly Ledbetter. *Time.* http://www.time.com/time/nation /article/0,8599,1874954,00.html

Povich, L. (2012). *The good girls revolt.* New York: PublicAffairs.

Rankin, Jeannette. Retrieved July 13, 2013, from Biographical Directory of the United States Congress website: http://bioguide.congress.gov/scripts/bio display.pl?index=r000055

Sally Ride. (2013). In *Encyclopaedia Britannica.* Retrieved July 13, 2013, from http:// www.britannica.com/EBchecked/topic/503056/Sally-Ride

Sandra Day O'Connor. (2013). In *Encyclopaedia Britannica.* Retrieved July 13, 2013, from http://www.britannica.com/EBchecked/topic/424738/Sandra-Day-OConnor

Smith, J. (2013, June 3). The best big companies for work-life balance. *Forbes.* http:// www.forbes.com/sites/jacquelynsmith/2013/06/03/the-best-big-companies-for-work-life-balance/

Townshend Acts. (2013). In *Encyclopaedia Britannica.* Retrieved July 13, 2013, from http://www.britannica.com/EBchecked/topic/601114/Townshend-Acts

24 Army women assaulted, raped during Gulf War. (1992, July 21). *The Washington Post.* Retrieved from http://articles.sun-sentinel.com/1992-07-21/news /9202200757_1_army-records-rapes-or-assaults-army-sergeant

U.S. Bureau of Labor Statistics. (2011). *Highlights of women's earnings in 2011.* (BLS Report 1038). Retrieved from http://www.bls.gov/cps/cpswom2011.pdf

Women and the labor movement. *American Federation of Teachers. (AFT).* Retrieved July 13, 2013, from http://www.aft.org/yourwork/tools4teachers/women /labor.cfm

Yarow, J. (2013, August 16). Sheryl Sandberg caves: After scandal her non-profit lean in will start paying interns. *Business Insider.* http://www.businessinsider .com/sheryl-sandbergs-lean-in-will-pay-interns-2013-8

# Part II

---

# Cultural Considerations of Work-life Integration

# Chapter 10

# Acts of Dignity: Women of Color Balancing Work and Family

*Lillian Comas-Diaz*

Tanya, a 35-year-old biracial woman, was the daughter of an African American woman and a White European American man. Both of her parents worked as teachers, and not surprisingly, they valued education for their children. Although they were Methodist, they sent Tanya and her younger brother to a Catholic private school, to receive a "good" education. A valedictorian in her high school graduating class, Tanya received a college scholarship. She aspired to a PhD education and to become an art history professor.

When Tanya completed her Master's degree, her mother was diagnosed with breast cancer. Tanya took a sabbatical from school to take care of her mother. Sadly, Tanya's mother died a year after being diagnosed. After her mother's death, Tanya entered grief counseling for a brief period. During counseling, Tanya decided to withdraw from the university. She got a job as a fund-raiser for a multicultural art foundation, where she met Ramon, a Puerto Rican painter. Tanya and Ramon got married and soon after had a daughter, Angela. Unfortunately, their marriage ended in divorce when

Angela was three years old. Afterward, Tanya enrolled in a law school. She obtained a student loan and moved in with Gail, her maternal grandmother. Gail enthusiastically agreed to take care of Angela while Tanya attended classes. After completing law school, Tanya found work as an associate in a prestigious law firm. Moreover, she found an influential White woman mentor in the firm.

So far, Tanya's condition as a professional young woman seemed parallel to her White counterparts' experiences. However, let us see what happened when Tanya "comes out" as a woman of color.

After watching the documentary *Good Hair* (Rock, 2009), Tanya decided to "let her hair down" by keeping it in a natural style. In other words, she changed her hairdo from a relaxed style to a kinky one. As a biracial woman, wearing her straight hair made Tanya look "White." She concluded that her practice of relaxing her hair was an example of internalized sexist racism.

A White colleague asked Tanya if she was Black after she saw Tanya's new hair style. Soon after, several colleagues "found out" that Tanya was biracial. Subsequently Tanya noticed a change in her colleagues' attitude toward her. First, she experienced subtle discrimination. Later, Tanya observed a change in her colleagues' behavior. Simply put, her colleagues stopped inviting her to happy hours after work. Tanya confided her frustration to Faith, an African American colleague. Faith advised Tanya to return to her previous hairdo in order to "look" less Black. "Otherwise, you will find out how hard it is for African American women to climb the corporate ladder," Faith said, "Passing as White is not a disgrace," she added.

Tanya rejected the survivalist strategy of "passing" (this concept refers to a person's ability to be regarded as a member of another ethnic/racial or social group other than her own) because she interpreted this strategy as promoting internal oppression. Moreover, Tanya refused to continue to "torture" her scalp with hair chemicals. Unfortunately, Faith's words regarding African American women's obstacles in corporate America seemed prophetic. Tanya's supervisor stopped giving her challenging responsibilities. Instead, she assigned Tanya "diversity" projects, such as becoming the firm's liaison to the inner city African American community. Furthermore, Tanya's colleagues began to question her credentials and to ask if she was a product of Affirmative Action policies. As a result, Tanya felt branded with an Affirmative Action stigma.

Consistent with this notion, Tanya began to experience racial microaggressions. Microaggressions are subtle or preconscious attacks in the form of verbal, behavioral, or environmental insults against members of minority groups (Pierce, 1995). Whether intentional or unintentional, microaggressions are derogatory slights that affect targeted individuals. To illustrate, Tanya's supervisor told her that she looked unprofessional in her appearance during a performance appraisal. Ironically, Tanya's physical appearance and dress fashion remained the same—with the exception of her hairstyle. Therefore, such feedback can be identified as an ethnogender microaggression. Equally important, Tanya's alienation at work became exacerbated when her mentor left the firm for a government position. Regrettably, Tanya became unable to secure another mentor. Furthermore, she gained a new identity—Tanya became a professional "diversity" expert.

Tanya coped with microaggressions at work by refusing to be a showcase for diversity. However, her resistance led her to spend an inordinate amount of emotional capital. Tanya realized that she was the victim of open discrimination when her grandmother Gail called during work and asked her to pick up her daughter Angela from school. Angela was sick and Gail was not feeling well enough to drive to the school. When Tanya informed her supervisor that she was leaving the office to pick up her sick daughter, the supervisor replied: "It's unprofessional to leave during an important meeting." Tanya was shocked at the supervisor's behavior. To illustrate Tanya's surprise more in detail, on the previous week a White woman lawyer left the same meeting to pick up a sick child—without being accused of engaging in unprofessional conduct.

After several months of suffering from discriminatory treatment—what Tanya called undignified affronts—she developed migraines. Tanya stopped expecting fair treatment at her workplace. Instead, she returned to counseling and joined a network of women of color with professional status. Although her colleague Faith recommended Tanya to resign her job and find another employment, Tanya decided to remain at the firm.

"My mother, my mother's mother, and my great grandmother's mother have a legacy of struggle. They engaged in acts of dignity as they endured the double burden," Tanya said. "I continue this legacy, and so will my daughter."

Tanya's behavior seems consistent with what Jones and Shorter-Gooden identified as shifting. According to these authors, African American women spend an inordinate amount of personal resources such as time, mindset, emotional energy watching every step they take, self-regulating an array of emotions, and even changing their outward appearance in order to cope with ongoing stress. Jones and Shorter-Gooden called this coping style shifting because women change their coping strategies according to the specific context. In other words, women of color with professional status need to shift outlook and behavior from the home situation to the work culture and so on.

A growing number of women are entering the workforce (Allen, Herst, Burck, & Sutton, 2000). Two-thirds are mothers who work outside their homes and engage in double duty (Boushey & O'Leary, 2009). As a consequence, many of these women suffer negative consequences such as role conflict, burnout, time pressure, plus impaired physical and mental health problems (Byron, 2005). Indeed, depression—a condition prevalent among a significant number of women—correlates with work-family conflict and is associated with decreased performance in the workplace (American Psychological Association, 2002).

Similar to women in the general population, women of color are rapidly increasing in the workforce (Toossi, 2006). Certainly, women of color have a long history of sustained work inside and outside their home—a legacy of double burden (Booth, 1992). The historical heritage of women of color as slaves, indentured servants, and/or hired maids provides an illustration of such legacy. Later on, the Civil Rights movement opened the doors to other occupations for women of color. Of interest, many female immigrants of color currently engage in domestic work in the United States. Indeed, since 1970, women of color immigrants supply domestic work that supports the United States economy (Domestic Workers United and Data Center, n.d.). Succinctly put, most women of color work to earn a living as well as working at home.

How do women of color balance work and family? For most women of color, this is a rhetoric question. The iconic answer, "I just do it," suggests the challenges that many women of color face. Some of these challenges include sociopolitical realities such as sexism, racism, classism, racist sexism, and heterosexism, among many other challenges, as well as their interaction. Most importantly, women of color cope with psychocultural challenges in the form of internalized oppression, the management of multiple and intersecting identities such as being women, persons of color, mothers, workers, caretakers, and religious/spiritual members; and the resultant conflict within their ethnic, racial, and community loyalties. Moreover, women immigrants of color confront the challenge of mothering in a foreign land (Tummala-Narra, 2004).

Since most women of color juggle family and work responsibilities, they cannot avoid role conflict. However, many women focus on their cultural and gender-specific resilience to cope with such conflicts. As they engage in their double duty, women of color enact acts of dignity—the display of resilience that allows women of color to thrive in the face of adversity.

## WOMEN OF COLOR AT WORK

A multicultural sea is changing the United States workforce. Women are an integral component of this transformation. However, women of color confront a different reality from their White counterparts at the workplace. Indeed, women of color tend to receive the lowest wages. According to the National Partnership for Women and Families (2010), the median average income for African American women who work full-time is $39, 639, and for Latinas or Hispanic women it is $26, 347. These figures are significantly lower than the national average. Moreover, women of color's low earnings are compounded by the fact that most women of color frequently are the primary source of financial support in their families (National Partnership for Women and Families, 2010). According to the United States Census Bureau (2010), a female such as a mother, grandmother, or other female relative is the head of her family and the sole financial support in about 3 million African American families. Furthermore, the same situation occurs in more than 2 million Latino families.

To top it all, women of color tend to have the worst jobs (Baca Zinn & Dill, 1994) as well as to be underemployed. Moreover, three-fourths of low income women do not get paid when they absent themselves from work in order to take care of a sick child. This situation is worse for women of color whose work supervisors frequently label them as irresponsible, unmotivated, and/or lazy.

How do women of color balance their multiple identities, particularly as a worker and caretaker? How do they juggle work with the responsibilities of daily life? More specifically, how do they cope with racism, sexism, and racist sexism? Within this context, how do women of color preserve their dignity?

## Women of Color with Professional Status

For women of color with professional status balancing career and family is more difficult than for White European women (Center for Work-Life Policy, 2002). Anecdotal and clinical data (as you saw in Tanya's vignette) show that women of color report being treated differently from their White sisters at the workplace. Moreover, women of color who request work-life options from their supervisors are often judged unfairly. According to Diversity Best Practice (2011), many supervisors are unfamiliar with women of color's ethnogender context of their personal and family dynamics, and instead of giving women of color the benefit of the doubt, they frequently mislabel them as indolent, aggressive, and/or "ungrateful workers with attitude" (Diversity Best Practice, 2011).

As members of at least two minority groups, women of color's stress due to their double jeopardy increases at the workplace. Like other women in organizations, women of color can be treated as tokens—the condition where superiors, subordinates, and colleagues perceive women's positions as a result of preferential treatment due to their gender and not their merit (Kanter, 1977). However, the token status assigned to women of color is compounded by the interactive effect of ethnicity and gender (Comas-Diaz & Greene, 1994). For example, many women of color are called Affirmative Action Babies (Carter, 1991). Such a designation raises questions around women of color's professional qualifications because they are perceived as products of Affirmative Action policies, regardless of their qualifications, merits, and/or experience.

Following a similar line of thinking, many women of color lose their identity as individuals in the workplace. Indeed, they are stripped from their professional expertise and assigned negative roles. Academia provides a powerful illustration. According to Reyes (1988), many academic institutions attribute to women of color the "one minority in a pot" role. In other words, every academic office needs one minority especially for "Show and Tell" purposes. The "Show and Tell" syndrome means that academic workplaces assign multiple roles to a minority person. More succinctly, this means that a woman of color in academia is appointed to be the representative for the diversity committees, mentor for students of color, diversity expert who teaches diversity coursework and/or provides diversity training, as well as the person who meets the minority requirement on EEO forms (Reyes, 1988). As a result of the "Show and Tell" syndrome, women of color lose their identity as professionals because they are designated as "experts" on diversity, and miss opportunities for career advancement. Similar to Tanya's experience, women of color tend to be perceived as diversity representatives at the expense of their professional development.

Dovetailing this analysis, women of color with professional status can be treated as "showcase pieces" or as examples of how liberal the agencies they work in are. Hiring women of color and showcasing them as diversity experts is an illustration of being a showcase piece for window dressing. Women who refuse the showcase status, like in Tanya's case, frequently confront interpersonal and institutional resistance (Thomas, 2008).

Other harmful roles assigned to women of color with professional status include being treated as "pets" (Thomas, Bailey, Phelps, Tran, & Johnson, in press). Thomas et al. (in press) argued that new professional women can be welcomed at the workplace and given the pet status because just like a pet, they are not considered equal to their superiors (masters), who know what is best for them. Moreover, women of color are treated as pets as long as they are submissive toward their superiors, exhibit a lack of independent thinking, and do not challenge the work culture. Furthermore, women of color can first be treated as pets, later to be perceived as threats (Thomas et al., in press). Let me share a personal experience that illustrates this condition. A mental health clinician "adopted" me as a "pet" when I was a young psychologist working at a Child Guidance Clinic. She introduced me as her "new Puerto Rican psychologist friend" during professional and social events. She seemed to be showing me off as an example of how liberal she was. Needless to say, I felt objectified. Later on, when I became the head of a new unit within the clinic, the clinician stopped inviting me to professional and social events. Apparently, I became a threat when I was appointed director of a clinical unit.

Without a doubt, discrimination threatens women of color's work and family balance. To illustrate, women of color enter the workforce with an integrated ethnic/racial and gender identity. However, once they enter the workforce, they are treated in a compartmentalized manner, separating their gender from their ethnicity or race. In other words, women of color encounter a work culture where they are treated as persons of color for diversity issues, while their work-life struggles are seen as work and family issues (Tucker, Wolfe, Viruell-Fuentes, & Smooth, 1999). Needless to say, such arbitrary compartmentalization creates added stress for women of color in the workforce.

Regardless of their assigned negative labeling, many women of color are rapidly entering most segments of the workforce, including corporate America. A survey of 1,500 Fortune 1000 Companies indicated that about 50% of the women of color reported being in the "sandwich" position, that is, needing to take care of a child under the age of 18 and a dependent adult (Tucker et al., 1999). The survey findings showed major results related to workplace cultures; the connection between workplace cultures and work-life balance; the influence of workplace stress on work-life balance and on women's personal lives; the strategies women use to cope; and, the significance of supportive workplace cultures in helping women maintain work-life balance and in encouraging them to remain with their companies (Tucker et al., 1999). Surprisingly, the survey results appeared paradoxical: Women of color expressed pride at their achievements in working in the corporate world. Nonetheless, they stated that they could not recommend their company to other women of color, due to the company's limited advancement possibilities. Although these women felt free to be themselves at work, conversely, they had to minimize their race and gender in order to fit the corporate culture. Along these lines, most women found their companies' cultural environment to be hostile toward women of color. Many women reported being exposed to racial and gender discrimination. As a result of these occurrences, the women of color in the sample experienced their company as hostile environments.

## Women of Color in Hostile Workplaces

Numerous women of color work in hostile environments. In this fashion, women of color with professional status experience additional pressures. To illustrate, the Diversity Best Practice (2011) identified several barriers to work advancement for women of color with professional status. These barriers included (1) scarcity of mentors; (2) absence of company role models of color; (3) lack of opportunities for informal networking with influential colleagues; (4) omission from high visibility assignments; and, (5) balancing work and family. To provide some points of reference, all five barriers are interrelated, compounding their combined effect on women of color. The absence of mentors in an ethnocentric and androcentric organization is detrimental to women of color because women require mentors at all stages of their education and professional development (Rayburn, Denmark, Reuder, & Austria, 2010). Likewise, absence of company role models of color interferes with women of color's ability to look up and identify with people of color who advanced in the system. Additionally, the lack of opportunities for informal networking with influential colleagues is detrimental to women's professional advancement. Similarly, the lack of opportunities for informal networking with influential colleagues prevents women from forming key connections that facilitate a continued professional advancement. Moreover, the omission from high-level projects limits women of color's visibility and thus erases opportunities for promotion. Unfortunately, a vicious circle emerges where a lack of visibility prevents women of color from demonstrating their competence, and thus, compromising their professional advancement. Finally, juggling work-family responsibilities creates added stress for women of color.

### Effect of Work Stress on Women of Color

Coping with racism, sexism, and racist sexism is common among most women of color in the workplace. The National Women of Color Work/ Life (Tucker et al., 1999) survey found that women of color's work stress affects women's productivity, commitment to their work, and their family life. Certainly, women of color who experience prolonged ethnogender microaggressions frequently develop spirit injuries, a condition that results in psychological distress (Wing, 1997). Lamentably, sustained spirit injuries can become soul wounds. According to Duran (2006), soul wounds result from people of color's legacy of cultural trauma, including ungrieved losses, learned helplessness, and internalized oppression. Definitely, spirit injuries and soul wounds interfere with women of color's work and family balance.

Women of color cope with work stress using diverse mechanisms, including both internal mechanisms and external strategies. According to Shorter-Gooden (2004) the internal coping mechanisms include faith, relying on prayer and spirituality, standing on shoulders or drawing strength and resilience from ancestors, and cultivating a positive self-image. As Shorter-Gooden (2004) posited, the external strategies involve relying on social support, developing role flexibility, altering their outward behavior, diminishing or avoiding contact with certain people or situations, and fighting back to challenge the source of the problem.

Women of color enhance their resilience when they increase their sense of agency. Undeniably, women who experience more control in their life tend to exhibit less psychological distress. As an illustration, women who are self-employed and are entrepreneurial seem to do a better job than women who work in corporations (Center for Work-Life Policy, 2002). This fact highlights the relevance of control in women's psychological health.

Of interest, African American women with professional status are less likely to marry than their lesser-educated sisters (Coontz, 2012). Nonetheless, these unmarried childless women may exercise more control over their lives than their married sisters. However, unmarried women of color display ethnocultural connectedness. In other words, women who are single and/or childless engage in childrearing and family caretaking roles toward biological as well as nonbiological relatives. Regardless of marital status, women of color engage in acts of dignity as a coping mechanism in the workplace.

## Acts of Dignity: How Women of Color Can Cope with Work-Family Stress

The legacy of double burden imparts women of color with ethnogender coping strategies. These approaches reflect indigenous and non-Western values such as dignity, harmony, spirituality, balance, and collective welfare. The heritage of struggle nurtures women of color's cultural resilience. According to Elsass, cultural resilience is a survivalist response to oppression and adversity. Most importantly, cultural resilience draws from values and practices that promote coping mechanisms and adaptive reactions within an ethnic and gender affirmative context. Consequently, cultural resilience empowers women to resist, revise, and subvert the dominant societal discourse (Comas-Diaz, 2012). These strategies promote women of color's acts of dignity. Simply put, acts of dignity are coping mechanisms that allow women of color to thrive in the face of adversity.

Women of color's ethnogender coping strategies include (1) emphasizing collective connectedness; (2) promoting solidarity; (3) fostering positive ethnocultural images; (4) committing to critical resilience; and, (5) engaging in acts of dignity.

When women of color practice collective connectedness, they affirm their relational collective orientation. To illustrate, women of color extend the concept of family to include biological as well nonbiological members. In this way, they develop strong bonds with their Sister Friends, *comadres* (co-mothers), *hermanas del alma* (soul sisters), and other significant women. Indeed, research findings indicated that college-educated African American women identified their women friends and relatives as important sources of support (Brown, Parker-Dominguez, & Sorey, 2000). Likewise, Latinas name their *hermanas del alma* (Castañeda-Sound, in press) and *comadres* (Comas-Diaz, in press) as their source of sustained support. Moreover, women of color promote solidarity as they develop alliances with other women of color and tap into informal networks for mutual support. Due to the negative images promoted by the dominant society, women of color need to foster a positive ethnogender self. To achieve a healthy self-esteem, women of color affirm their ethnogender resilience as a source of empowerment and meaning-making. Indeed, numerous women of color resort to their spirituality for strength. They find solace and comfort in the knowledge that they are the child of God. Furthermore, women of color invoke their ancestors and "stand on their shoulders." As women of color enhance their self-esteem, they attempt to ease their double burden by balancing caretaking with self-care.

In addition to nurturing their cultural and gender-specific resilience, women of color embrace critical resilience. According to Campa (2010) critical resilience is a feminist concept that promotes the cultivation of a larger purpose connected to the social fortification of ethnic families and communities. In other words, as women of color improve their sense of well-being, they commit to enhance the collective well-being of their families and communities at large.

Finally, women of color engage in acts of dignity to cope with work-family stress. This process entails developing a woman of color consciousness that allows her to know when to "pick her battles." More succinctly, this means that women who engage in acts of dignity act in a culturally assertive manner to manage work-family balance. That is, women decide when to resist, adapt, accommodate, fight back, subvert, let go, and/or engage in creative conflict. The goal of behaving with acts of dignity is to thrive in the face of adversity. Acts of dignity represent the culmination of several coping strategies that women of color utilize in private and public spaces.

## CONCLUSION

As the workplace becomes more culturally diverse, it demands institutional changes to accommodate a multicultural workforce. The improvement of women's conditions in the workplace, particularly of women of color, requires organizational and policy transformations (American Psychological Association, 2004). To achieve this goal, the American Psychological Association Briefing Paper on Work and Family Policy (American Psychological Association, 2004) recommended that paid family and medical leave, safe and affordable childcare, extended unemployment benefits, and flexible workplace policies, among other changes be offered to women in the workforce. Similarly, the Report of the National Women of Color Work/Life Survey (Tucker et al., 1999) recommended that employers change the workplace culture to respond to the needs of women of color. The recommendations included linking work-life programs with diversity programs that report to the same unit; the formation of partnerships with stakeholders groups, in order to capitalize on women of color's pride on working in corporate America; and, holding management accountable for the creation of policies that include all employees (Tucker et al., 1999).

## POSTSCRIPT: FROM DIVERSITY EXPERT TO ENTREPRENEURIAL WOMAN

After several years of engaging in acts of dignity, Tanya decided to leave the prestigious law firm where she was employed. As a woman of color, she experienced her head bumping against a glass ceiling (due to her gender), and against a colored glass ceiling (due to her race). "A double coated glass is hard to crack," Tanya told her colleague Faith. However, Tanya valued the experience she gained at the firm. She felt that the firm had provided her with the necessary training to open her own business. Therefore, Tanya invited Faith to join her in a new law office. Both women decided to specialize on women of color's labor issues.

## NOTE

Portions of this chapter were published in M. Paludi (Ed.). (2012). *Psychology for business success. Vol. 1: Juggling, balancing and integrating work and family roles and responsibilities* (pp. 63–75). Santa Barbara, CA: Praeger.

## REFERENCES

Allen, T. D., Herst, D. E., Burck, C. S., & Sutton, M. (2000). Consequences associated with work to family conflict: A review and agenda for future research. *Journal of Occupational Health Psychology, 5,* 278–308.

American Psychological Association. (2002). *APA summit on women and depression.* Retrieved February 1, 2012, from www.apa.org/pi/women/programs/depression/summit-2002.pdf

American Psychological Association. (2004). *APA briefing paper on work and family policy.* Retrieved February 1, 2012, from http://www.apa.org/news/press/releases/2004/04/convention.aspx

Baca Zinn, M. B., & Dill, D. T. (1994). Difference and dominion. In M. B. Zinn & D. T. Dill (Eds.), *Women of color in the U.S.* (pp. 3–12). Philadelphia, PA: Temple University Press.

Booth, M. (1992). *The double burden: Three generations of working mothers.* A film by Marlene Booth Raphael Films.

Boushey, H., & O'Leary, A. (Eds.). (2009, October 16). *The Shiver Report: A woman's nation changes everything.* Shriver Report Publication. Retrieved December 21, 2011, from http://www.americanprogress.org/issues/2009/10/womans_nation.html

Brown, K., Parker-Dominguez, T., & Sorey, M. (2000). Life stress, social support, and well-being among college-educated African American women. *Journal of Ethnic and Cultural Diversity Social Work, 9*(1/2), 55–73.

Byron, K. (2005). A meta-analytic review of work-family conflict and its antecedents. *Journal of Vocational Behavior, 67,* 169–198.

Campa, B. (2010). Critical resilience, schooling processes, and the academic success of Mexican Americans in a community college. *Hispanic Journal of Behavioral Sciences, 32,* 429–455.

Carter, S. L. (1991). *Reflections of an affirmative action baby.* New York: Basic Books.

Castañeda-Sound, C. (in press). Hermanas de corazon y alma. In L. Comas-Diaz & M. B. Weiner (Eds.), *Sisters of the heart. Women therapists' reflections on female friendships* (Special issue) Women & Therapy.

Center for Work-Life Policy. (2002). *Groundbreaking study exposes a crisis among successful women.* Retrieved December 20, 2011, from www.worklifepolicy.org/documents/news-pr03.pdf

Comas-Diaz, L. (in press). Comadres: The healing power of female bonding. In L. Comas-Diaz & M. B. Weiner (Eds.), *Sisters of the heart. Women therapists' reflections on female friendships.* (Special issue) Women & Therapy.

Comas-Diaz, L. (2012). Colored spirituality: The centrality of spirit among ethnic minorities. In L. Miller (Ed.), *The Oxford handbook of psychology and spirituality.* New York: Oxford University Press.

Comas-Díaz, L., & Greene, B. (1994). Women of color with professional status. In L. Comas-Díaz & B. Greene (Eds.), *Women of color: Integrating ethnic and gender identities in psychotherapy* (pp. 347–388). New York: Guilford Press.

Coontz, S. (2012, February 11). The M.R.S. and the Ph.D. *The New York Times Sunday Review.* Retrieved February 14, 2012, from http://www.nytimes.com/2012/02/12/opinion/sunday/marriage-suits-educated-women.html?pagewanted=all

Diversity Best Practice. (2011, November 28). *Five barriers to advancement for women of color at work.* Retrieved January 20, 2012, from http://www.diversitybestpractices.com/news-articles/five-barriers-advancement-women-color-work

Domestic Workers United and Data Center. (n.d.). *Home is where work is: Inside New York domestic work industry. Executive Summary.* Retrieved February 2, 2012, from www.domesticworkersunited.org/index.php/en/pressroom/press-kit

Duran, E. (2006). *Healing the soul wound: Counseling with American Indians and other native people.* New York: Teachers College Press.

Kanter, R. M. (1977). *Men and women of the corporation.* New York: Basic Books.

National Partnership for Women and Families. (2010, December). *Women of color need a paid sick days standard. A fact sheet.* Retrieved December 20, 2011, from http://www.nationalpartnership.org/research-library/work-family/psd/women-of-color-need-a-paid-sick-days-standard.pdf

Pierce, C. M. (1995). Stress analogs of racism and sexism: Terrorism, torture and disaster. In C. V. Willie, P. P. Reiker, & B. S. Brown (Eds.), *Mental health, racism and sexism* (pp. 277–293). Pittsburgh, PA: University of Pittsburgh Press.

Rayburn, C., Denmark, F., Reuder, M. D., & Austria, A. (Eds.). (2010). *Handbook for women mentors: Transcending barriers of stereotype, race and ethnicity.* New York: Praeger.

Reyes, M. L. (1988). Racism in academia: The old wolf revisited. *Harvard Educational Review, 58,* 299–314.

Rock, C. (2009). *Good hair.* Documentary produced by Chris Rock Productions and HBO Films.

Shorter-Gooden, K. (2004). Multiple resistant strategies: How African Americans cope with racism and sexism. *Journal of Black Psychology, 30,* 406–425.

Thomas, K. (2008). *Diversity resistance in organizations.* New York: LEA Taylor-Francis.

Thomas, K. M., Bailey, J. J., Phelps, R. E., Tran, N. M., & Johnson, L. (in press). Women of color at mid career: From pet to threat. In L. Comas-Diaz &

B. Greene (Eds.), *Psychological health of women of color: Intersections, challenges, and opportunities.* New York: Praeger.

Toossi, M. (2006). A new look at a long-term labor force projections to 2050. *Monthly Labor Review, 129,* 19–39.

Tucker, J., Wolfe, L. R., Viruell-Fuentes, E. A., & Smooth, W. (1999). *No more "business as usual": Women of color in corporate America—Report of the national women of color work/life survey.* Washington, DC: Center for Women Policy Studies. Retrieved from www.centerwomenpolicy.org

Tummala-Narra, P. (2004). Mothering in a foreign land. *The American Journal of Psychoanalysis, 64*(2), 167–182.

United States Census Bureau. (2010). *Current population survey, 2010 annual social and economic supplement: Families with related children under 18 by number of working family members and family structure: 2009, Table POVO7.* Retrieved December 20, 2011, from http://www.census.gov/hhes/www/cpstables/032010/pov/new07_100_06.htm

Wing, A. D. (1997). *Critical race feminism.* New York: New York University Press.

# Chapter 11

# The Paradox for Advancing Women in Paid Work and Public Life in Post-EEO Era

*Carolyn Noble*

In 1975 the Whitlam (Labor) government came to power in Australia nationally after 20 years of conservative political rule and embarked on an ambitious social reform agenda that made feminists active at that time believe that the old entrenched patriarchal order was to be, and indeed could be, unsettled (Thornton, 2008). Between 1975 and 1979 this progressive government encouraged by feminist advocacy achieved the biggest social shake-up in last century's political life, where women's success in public life was one of its chief focus of reform. Indeed during this period and for a while after with successive Labor governments, Australia looked like a potential leader in gender equity for women in both paid work and public life. From the late 1970s to the early 1990s a suite of policy initiatives were introduced that were gradually adopted across both State and Federal jurisdictions that focused on changing the culture of male privilege and patronage endemic in the social fabric and reflected most vividly in the paid workforce including Australian corporate culture (Cox, 1995).

Equal Employment Opportunity/Affirmative Action(EEO/AA) policies and practices, sex discrimination legislation, maternity and family

leave, provisions for childcare in the workplace, introduction of griev-
ance procedures, leadership and mentoring programs, and personnel
practices that recognized the value of traditional feminine skills had, by
the middle 1990s, been rolled out across the nation. These legislative initiatives were designed to enhance women's economic and personal free-
doms and provide a more solid footing for women to acquire economic
independence so as to open up more life choices than previously available. Organizations that did not adhere to these legislative imperatives
were to be "named and shamed" in the various state parliaments (Thornton, 2001, 2008).

These EEO/AA strategies and training programs seemed for a while at
least to give women some hope for a changed future—a future that might
include more access to paid employment across the workforce; more access to senior roles in public and private administration and higher education institutions; and more access to the corporate world of male privilege
and patronage as well the heavily masculine dominated manufacturing,
trades, and services industries. Then in the late 1990s, the government
moved its attention from structural policy change to individual organization's behavior by encouraging them to mainstream their EEO/AA initiatives (approved as part of the 1995 UN World Conference on Women,
Beijing) as a strategy for making the concerns for gender equality the responsibility of individual men (Thornton, 2001; Walby, 2005). Now men
were encouraged to be an integral part of the design, implementation,
monitoring, and evaluation of employment and personnel policies and
organizational practices, removing the burden of change from individual
women solely (Noble & Pease, 2011; Probert, 2005). There was a prolifera-
tion of Equal Opportunity Officers positions and EEO/AA committees established across the corporate and public sectors.

One measure of these initiatives, strategies and appointments success
was the feminist push to open the "top jobs" in industry, politics, and corporations to women and, according to Connell (2006), progress on this
front was to become the most visible symbol of gender reform across the
country (p. 837). In challenging the "glass ceiling" in workplaces women
(who were brave enough to leave the domestic realm characteristic of the
1950s and 1960s) have indeed achieved some success, albeit incremental,
idiosyncratic, and uneven. For example by 2010 Australian women had
made great inroads in educational opportunities where women/girls out-
strip high school retention rates for boys and their attendance at university
is higher than men, and women are more likely to hold more postgraduate
qualifications. In professional and allied professional occupations women
have increased their participation to 52% (EOWA, 2011). However, while
more young women are choosing education, career, and "maybe a baby"
the male worker still dominates senior leadership positions in those industries where women dominate (Noble & Pease, 2011).

## SO HOW EFFECTIVE WERE THESE POLICY INITIATIVES?

While it is also impossible to script reform initiatives that will unanimously achieve the desired outcome or predict how they will be deployed and to what effect, sufficient time has elapsed since attempts for gender equity were introduced to look at the phenomena in more detail. The latest research conducted by the Equal Opportunity for Women in the Workplace Agency (EOWA) in 2011 found only 8.0% of key executive management positions in Australian Stock Exchange (ASX) 200 companies were held by women, 9.8% of board directorships were held by women, 2.5% chair positions and 3% of CEOs were women (these roles decreased between 2006 and 2008), and 72 of ASX 200 companies do not have a woman on their board. This report also identified that 17.9% of Australian university vice-chancellors were women; 33.4% of government board members were women, and 30% of seats in the national parliament were held by women compared to 70% by men. Moreover 80% of ministerial positions and senior portfolios were held by men (EOWA, 2011). Overall women made up 45.3% of all employed people and 34% of managers and professional positions. In the wider workforce women accounted for 11% of CEOs or managing directors, while in the lucrative financial industries only 4% were filled by women (EOWA, 2011). Women still only earn 82 cents in the male dollar and the gender gap in pay has widened over the last four years and with bonuses and overtime the gap is wider (The Global Gender Gap Report, 2010). It seems that the disparity between men and women's pay still comes down simply to "being a women" at a cost of the equivalent of 8.5% of Australian GDP and $93 billion a year in productivity (National Centre of Social Economic Modeling (NATSEM)). This ingrained and enduring sexism has seen Australia drop eight places in the Global Gender Gap rankings between 2006 and 2010, from 15th to 23rd, and showed significant deficiency in other areas such as being ranked 40th in ministerial positions and 59th in wage equality for similar work (The Global Gender Gap Report, 2010). The report ranks Sri Lanka and the Philippines ahead of Australia when it comes to gender equity. What is surprising here is that a study by McGregor (2011) found that the majority of women were still unaware whether or not they were receiving equal pay compared to their male counterparts. While no country worldwide has managed to close the gender gap, the Nordic countries, where equality is embedded in the culture, have succeeded best in narrowing it by providing a wider spectrum of educational, political, and work opportunities for women (Bacchi & Eveline, 2009).

So, although gender equality has been a government goal for more than three decades and women's equal rights are now embedded in international law, one can see from the data quoted earlier that women's equal place in paid work and public life is "unfinished business." The promised political, cultural, and social change to free women from employment barriers in the workplace has *not* occurred. Women still face discrimination in recruitment and promotion and will retire with less superannuation and own smaller proportion of the national wealth (Bacchi, 2004). Women are more likely than men to live in poverty, particularly after a relationship breakdown (Leahy, 2011). While equal pay and access to paid employment and senior positions remain an accepted goal for public administration, it remains a distant dream for most women. Many contemporary feminists are arguing that we are entering a postfeminist, hence post–EEO, stage as the challenges facing women in the workforce are now different than previously where governments played a stronger role in workplace relations including supporting workplace equity programs and when the feminist voice was heard loud and clear (Bradley, 1999; Eggins, 1997). Given that government's attempts to promote women's equality in the workplace have been uneven at best and nonexistent at worst, it might be useful (and timely) to ask what are the organizing factors that materially and symbolically still exist that manufacture and maintain this inequality?

## HISTORY OF FEMINIST IDEAS ON EEO-FRAMING THE ISSUE

In Australia, as in many parts of the Western world, feminist scholarship has given serious attention to the "women question," offering numerous explanations as to why women were largely absent from paid work and public life. A significant part of the current literature identifies the sex stereotyping of male and female leaders as still playing a crucial role (Zichy, 2000). Social role theory and role congruity theory's conceptualization of leadership in terms of masculine (agentic) and feminine (communal) qualities still has come currency in explaining women's disadvantage in employment opportunities. For example in seeking why women were absent from senior leadership positions, despite EEO and AA legislation Noble and Mears (2000), Eagly and Karau's (2002) research indicated that in comparison to men, women were seen as lacking the "right" motivation, the "right" skill set, and the "right" leadership aspirations or qualities to aspire for and then secure senior management positions. O'Leary's (2000) work demonstrated that women's career development is still judged through the masculine paradigms of competition, dominance, and the dynamics of winners and losers, and where career steps are regarded as fiercely fought tournaments. Marvin's (2001) research showed the ever-present domination of male business culture where women managers are still "travelers in a male world" and as a result women are treated as mothers while men are treated as workers (p. 185). Rutherford (2001) identifies many cultural barriers to women's success in employment opportunities beyond casual and part-time work such as dual burden of the family-life split, the use of sports, military, and sexual language by men in the workplace and the male defined sexualized culture of organizations. Thornton (2008) names this as "Benchmark men" (p. 3) where women's competencies, motivations, specific skills, or other observable indices are found "wanting" against the male norm. Success in promotion was equated with assertiveness, drive, and competitiveness (all attributes associated with masculinity). By not possessing "the cut and thrust" attributes required for promotion to senior positions, it was inevitable that women were not included in the culture and rewards of work in the same way as men (Martin, 2001; Noble & Moore, 2006). In contrast women's management styles are described as empathetic, supportive, and concerned with relationship building and power and information sharing (Moore & Wen, 2004; Polnick, Reed, Funk, & Edmonson, 2004). While these characteristics are given some prominence in organizational culture most of the research still indicates the preference for the "male" skills with women leaders adopting those stereotypical "male" behaviors in their struggles for an equal place alongside men in public life, and for senior women to break through the proverbial "glass ceiling" and to reach positions of power, leadership, and influence (Moore & Wen, 2004; Noble & Moore, 2006).

Moore and Wen's (2004) study of 40 middle and senior women in public and private organizations in Australia identifies both the positives and negatives of working uncritically in male-dominated corporate businesses. While the women interviewed claimed to be realistic about the personal cost and organizational implications, they chose to work in complex, demanding, and challenging work environments because they enjoyed them; their abilities were tested; and they had more opportunities to extend and apply their skills (Noble & Moore, 2006). Further they wanted to explore and promote a more female-inclusive style of management and leadership than that reported in other management studies as well as to make changes for more women-friendly workplaces and boardrooms. However the downside was that each woman was left to develop a variety of complex arrangements to outsource their private lives and family commitments. Children were put in boarding schools close to the family home; nearly all outsourced all domestic and personal services and struggled to spend "quality" time with partners and children—common stories hinting at the difficulties of being "time poor" most of the time (Noble & Moore, 2006). While some blamed themselves for overwork and lack of work-life balance and others said it was their choice, there were a small number of these top women managers who recognized the contradictions in their behavior. By choosing to work long hours with little work-life balance they were aware they were replicating, rather than challenging the largely masculinist work norms expected from the organization and the organizational politics (Noble & Moore, 2006).

So it seems that acting like men carried a huge burden with limited success. For those women who broke through the "glass ceiling" there were huge expectations from other women that their contribution in public life and senior leadership would not only minimize differences between men and women in the workplace but they were also expected to be champions for women's issues from health reform, increased political and union participation to peace activism and environmental sustainability (Fisher, 1999). Many criticized the actual reforms themselves, especially the push for EEO/AA work-based strategies as signaling women out for preferential treatment implies an acceptance of women's inherent deficits and further assumes that selective policy changes were designed to help them catch up implying an existing inadequacy (Bacchi, 2004, 2009). Not wanting the status of victim in the public space many women preferred to take their chance on merit and distanced themselves from many of the EEO/AA initiatives. Even for those willing to take advantage of EEO/AA legislation they were faced with many unforeseen obstacles.

Noble's longitudinal study (1992–2002) exploring the extent to which EEO/AA legislation has influenced workplace change for women in Australian universities indicates that EEO policies have been markedly limited. This is in spite of programs and skills training specifically developed to address equity and diversity across the sector such as flexible working hours, permanent part-time work, child and family-friendly policies, childcare on campus, special leave and career break schemes, leadership programs, mentoring, networking, and targeting women on special lists for inclusion in senior management positions. Qualitative material indicates bullying, resistances, delays, and reluctance in implementing programs, lack of resources and priorities for women programs, and in some cases active resistance by senior staff (primarily the PVCs) as well as a continued ignorance of the structural issues and their impact on women's employment and "deeply held fears" by those officers charged with the implementation of EEO philosophy and associated practices of women taking "over the workplace" were endemic across the sector.

Even where women have achieved positions in arenas previously the sole domain of men, their achievements are represented as "transformative moments" or as success stories against "overwhelming odds" rather than as a natural occurrence in a woman's working life, thus perpetuating the cycle of disadvantage for women (O'Leary, 2000; Sinclair, 2005). By ignoring how power and the entrenched masculine norms privilege men over women and underestimating how strongly men will resist all such pressures to change their social, political, and cultural dominance in the workplace, it seems in retrospect a venture that was doomed from the start.

Radical feminists realized the futility of liberal reforms from the early days of feminist activism calling for complete transformation of the legal, military, and political structures of patriarchy as well social and cultural institutions such as the family, the church, the academy, and specifically language (Calás & Smircich, 2006). In creating alternative women's spaces in all aspects of societal interaction from social and economic relations, politics, and health issues these feminist advocates' aim was to offer an alternative vision for women from the dominant masculine traits many found alienating. Favoring instead such feminine identified traits as empathy, supportive and engaging relationship building and power and information sharing, nonviolence, and nonaggressive behaviors more generally as well as more cooperative and consultative means of relational interaction these women were keen to see real transformation of social, political, and cultural structures associated with all male forms of power (Polnick et al., 2004).

## RETREAT FROM THE EQUALITY AGENDA

The retreat from the equity agenda is linked to the retreat to individual responsibility in negotiating workplace conditions and is arguably a part of the consequences of the new economic changes that the neoliberalist agenda has inflicted on the workplace culture overall and management culture specifically. Promoting individualism, self-reliance, efficiency, mutual obligation, and competition in the market place and where these attributes are presented as either male-specific or at least gender neutral significantly disadvantages women (Bradley, 1999). By implication these cultural practices assume that women act in the market place as free individuals, as rational, independent players who can achieve success through hard work and talent if only you get "down and dirty" and act to empower themselves and stop whinging like "seventies" feminists (Noble & Moore, 2006). Sinclair (2005) argues that the reemergence of neoclassical economic assumptions and the troublesome concept of merit, as currently organized, work against any improvement in the status of women as equal workers and potential leaders, allowing men to reclaim their "rightful" place as the primary workers, leaders, managers, and great male "heroes" in the corporate, business world, as well as public organizations and institutions (Sinclair, 2005; Thornton, 2008).

Given the competing and complex pressures inherent in responding to global markets and the rate and pace of technological change, being encouraged to be assertive and empower yourself or go out and deal with the battles on your own (now you know what they are!) sounds punitive and naïve in the extreme. Assertiveness, hard work, playing the game, and professionalism in and of themselves can only be piecemeal individual solutions (Noble & Moore, 2006). These individualist approaches work against effective equal opportunity initiatives by virtue of the fact that they challenge the need for an affirmative action strategy and as such become part of the backlash to maintain the status quo. This position ignores the continued social inequality embedded in women's lives as they struggle to balance work with domestic and family responsibilities and the entrenched masculinity of the work culture. While there are some spaces where shifts to more egalitarian politics are evident there are also many more spaces where the shift has been actively blocked. While some extraordinary women do rise to the top and are celebrated in empirical studies, these studies also show that few remain at the top and many more who aspire find it impossible to get there, while others having made it are leaving in disgust at the difficulty of combining work and family life and the unforgiving and relentless battles against the male stronghold of traditional organizational cultures (Hayward, 2005; Noble & Moore, 2006).

These gains and losses have been further exacerbated because of Australia adopting a more neoliberal approach to its labor laws to move toward a more "open market economy" and other neoliberal approaches to workplace agreements. Formal arbitrated agreements have been abandoned for a deregulated workforce that relies on workers to negotiate employment conditions at the workplace. This change has resulted in more flexible, casualized work opportunities, reducing the power of the male worker to negotiate work conditions, yet also providing a supportive environment where gender equity policies remain a priority. This change in workplace practices has resulted in (once again!) inconsistent and unequal outcomes for women employees, despite the existing employment legislation to support their advancement and to minimize discriminatory employment and promotional practices. This, yet another setback and lack of industrial will have been disappointing for women and feminist policy makers alike as women's visibility in public life, industry, business, and the public sectors continues to be underrepresented, despite a large body of feminist scholarship and three decades of EEO/AA legislation at state and federal levels designed to examine this phenomenon and search for solutions (Acker, 1998; Bradley, 1999; Connell, 1995; Probert, 2005; Thornton, 2001, 2008). The lack of progress in the workplace for women's advancement has prompted many writers to resurrect the notions of a "glass ceiling" and a "maternal wall" as still impeding women's progression (Dietz, 2003; Thornton, 2001). These new economic imperatives are evident in the Higher Education (HE) section as well (Probert, 2005). So women find themselves living in the paradox—having to compete on male defined terms despite legislative support for equality and wondering what they have to do to redress this continuing discrimination. Many commentators are arguing that the usefulness of gender equity policy's goal is fundamentally flawed and are arguing for abandoning it in favor of more discursive analysis, in particular the concept of masculinities (coined by Connell, 1987) and male privilege (Pease, 2000, 2002, 2009) as a way of getting beyond the gender divide. This theoretical development might, it could be argued, begin to identify the essence underpinning the issues that proactive gender equity policies are not addressing.

A major criticism of the small 'l' liberal reforms was the underlying assumption that the workplace presented a level-playing field for women and that organizational behaviors are gender neutral. If we see women's access to the workforce as seeking entry into the already well-formed and entrenched male domain, where privileges, power, influence, status and cultural, political, economic, and social rewards are bountiful for all men, then male resistance and fight back now seems obvious. Part of the fight back was men presenting themselves as the silent victims, as workers losing out, or victims being punished for the sins of their elders (Bacchi, 2004) while women are presented as having access to undeserved and yet unproven advantages. By ignoring the ways in which the widespread acceptance of such male norms privileges men keeps the problem of gender discrimination as "women's problem" and men are let "off the hook" from analyzing their role in women's continuing discrimination (Flood & Connell, 2006; Pease, 2000). What they are protecting needs further analysis.

## MASCULINITIES, MALE PRIVILEGE DISCURSIVE POLITICS, AND SUBJECTS WITHOUT BORDERS

Eveline (2004) has drawn attention to "male advantage" in contrast to "women's disadvantage," pointing out that focusing solely on women's disadvantages and ignoring male privilege normalizes and legitimizes masculinist standards. It is the unspoken, the ingrained, the taken-for-granted norms of hegemonic masculinity that reproduces men's power in the workplace (Pease, 2002, 2009) and life generally (Connell, 1995). In this analysis men come into the workforce already scripted with advantages ascribed to their status as men in a patriarchal culture. Acker (1998) calls this factor "doing gender." Martin (2001) names this as men "mobilizing masculinities," McIntosh (2002) named this advantage an "invisible knapsack of privilege," while Flood and Pease (2005) refer to this phenomenon as "doing privilege" which almost unconsciously can be cashed in on a daily basis; from choosing jobs, work conditions, having access to credit, and being free to act in uninhibited ways with confidence because of their position as central actors on the cultural turf (Noble & Pease, 2011). This invisible privilege is so entrenched in the socialization of both men and women that men as the privileged group can easily ignore, or not see how others, in this case women, are denied the same opportunities as them and thus, without analysis blame women for their lack of success (Noble & Pease, 2011). Williams (1992) also named the phenomenon the "glass escalator" as men overtake women in promotional opportunities even in female-dominated industries such as nursing and human service work. This "doing of gender scripts" is not a naïve or innocent activity but one that vigorously constructs, consciously or unconsciously, the gender order of organizations (Calás & Smircich, 2006). That is, men and women act out the scripts of men's privilege and women's subordination as a result of the social construction of men's interests over that of women's, both subjectively and structurally. Men, and by implication women, unconsciously know what the established order is and act in partnership to keep it in place. This may explain why men continue to see gender issues as pertaining to women (not themselves) and seem to have little awareness of the ways in which their behavior and norms operate to exclude women and secure all the benefits from working for themselves at the expense of women colleagues (Noble & Moore, 2006).

From this perspective it is feasible to argue that the culture of patriarchy sustains a workplace with both surface and deep prejudices against women's securing an equal place alongside of men and that this "doing gender" or "doing male privilege" continually acts against and prevents women from making valuable contributions to work or succeeding in securing full-time, career-based employment (Noble & Pease, 2011). One way to challenge these practices is to make visible what is invisible in order to enable the processes that reproduce male dominance to be exposed as harmful and distressing for women in the workplace, whether it is intentional or not, or whether they are aware of it or not (Martin, 2001; Probert, 2005).

Focusing on men and their masculinist assumptions and the way it is played out by both men and women as socially constructed behavior is presented as the new arena for understanding the gender politics of organizational advantage. This focus may give a much-needed new perspective into the gender politics at work that seem so entrenched, not only in Australia but in Western society more generally. Butler's (1993) performative gender theory underlies this notion of male privilege. According to Butler performativity is what makes the doing or scripting of gender intelligible to the actors involved. By examining the possibilities and consequences of gender scripts, it becomes possible to question assumptions about its meaning and thus undermine its seemingly entrenched (now contested) internal logic. It also has the potential to shift the focus from women to men in order to redress the continuing inequality between them in the workplace and public life (Connell, 2006; Flood & Pease, 2005; Hearn & Collinson, 2006; Pringle, 1995). The deconstruction of gender scripts and the unpacking of male privileges could encourage men to explore their position of privilege and take an active role in workforce and organizational change, thus freeing women from bearing the sole responsibility for transforming organizational culture and being blamed for their relative disadvantage (Pease, 2009; Pringle, 1995).

Connell, a forerunner in identifying the theoretical insights attached to the study of masculinities, has more recently argued that these hegemonic practices or gender scripts are not in themselves static or reproduced uncritically and without resistances, especially from more profeminist

conscious men who also want to live in a less restrictive, less oppres-
sive patriarchal culture (Connell, 2006; Pease, 2009). It should also be remembered of course that men are not homogeneous. Not all men benefit
equally from the structures of gender domination. Issues of race, sexuality,
class, disability, and age significantly affect the extent to which men benefit from male privilege (and women are oppressed by them). There are,
according to Connell, subordinate, complicit, and marginalized masculinities as there are for women and that collapsing all masculinities into one
typology undermines any ability for egalitarian masculinities to be constructed. Connell's argument is that instead of placing emphasis on the
dynamics of hegemonic masculinity, analysis on recognizing internal contradictions and fractures within the male script (and the problems these
have for many men) will more likely create new possibilities toward a
male-supported gender democracy (Connell, 2006). That it is men's interest in creating a more human life for themselves may also benefit women.

In some form feminist theorists who espouse democratic plurality and
gender equity and who reject identity-based formulations agree with
Connell. The very effort to totalize, unify, or essentialize a social group, in
this case women, particularly in ways that suppress differences within the
group or do not adequately distinguish between cultural and economic
concerns (such as class, caste, sexuality, age, ethnicity, and ability) (Dietz,
2003) disadvantages women's politics as well. For example by focusing
primarily on white middle class women's lack of employment participation has actually resulted in marginalizing women of color, women with
different abilities, and sexual choices from the gender debate, creating a hierarchy of oppression and ignoring the way oppression also marginalizes
some men (Connell, 1995, 2006). Butler (1993) added to by Young (2000)
argues that the rules of the game (in this case patriarchy) as well as the
players (in this case men and women) are never fully unequivocal, stable,
fixed, or immutable; they are always constituted through acts of power
and shifting alliances. For example if women analyze their positions (sub-
jectivity) as to how it is both produced through political exclusions and
positioned against them, then a more pluralist democracy could possibly
emerge that includes an attack on the complex web of power relations that
enmeshes both genders. The goal here is to replace unifying notions of
gender and feminine gender identity as one relevant strand among others
(Young, 2000). Attending to class, race, ethnicity, sexuality, and ethnicity
as well as gender as constituted constructs than a patchwork of overlapping and potential alliances emerge, which can be harnessed with the
long-term view of disentangling, disempowering these optical entangle-
ments. By demonstrating the inherent unstable, complex, and ambiguous
nature of social reality, women's position in the gendered hierarchy in the
workforce is then seen as both flexible and agential (Butler, 1993). There is,
however, the risk that the rubric of this analysis doesn't promise to resolve

itself into any programmatic consensus or converge into any shared conceptual ground characteristic of the early feminists—liberal, radical, or socialist. Despite the vitality and dynamism in this discursive, contemporary feminist scholarship I come back to the more material world for a reality check. That is to revisit and focus on the real structural barriers and prejudices that prevent women participating equally and in larger numbers from the social, political, and cultural rewards attached to paid work. For this reason, any discussion of workplace reforms must be made within the context of the culture of work, and the culture of work in the new economy of the technological, postmodernist world.

## THE CHANGING CULTURE OF WORK: FLEXIBILITY OR INTENSIFICATION?

In 2006, I and my colleague (Noble & Moore, 2006) posited the argument that the new service industries, new organizations, and new work resulting from the technological revolution and e-based businesses could change current work practices for women in ways yet to be realized. That is what Conti and Warner (1994) refer to as the emergence of the new "greenfield" work environment, with potential to be free of gender stereotypes or discrimination. Women's foray into small businesses, especially those that are home-based and inspired by the development of products to help women with the load of full-time work and household chores, are also growing, offering yet another opportunity for women to enter the workforce with some measure of security, progression, and success (Mattis, 2004). Shifts in the environment and operating contexts of organizations such as more emphasis on collaborative ventures, benchmarking, outsourcing, cross-selling, and networking as well as the impact of the new technologies and increasing economic competition are demanding a new type of workforce, one that might suit women a little more than men. For example in these settings workers need to be able to be effective in decision-making, build "thick" informal networks and coalitions, be flexible and responsive to customer and client needs, to nurture and develop both individuals and a culture through the creation of shared meanings as well as share information, and to operate in an open and transparent manner—attributes still attached to women (Hayward, 2005; O'Leary, 2000). In fact Ritt (2004) argues that as business demands are changing characteristics like multiskilling, good communication skills, more democratic decision-making and attention to employees' needs, understanding the stresses and strains of everyday life, that is, juggling the often conflicting and complex demands of work as actually favoring women. She posits that women can "naturally" deal with internal contradictions, ambiguity, and complexity and are more fluid and adaptable to meet the demands of a rapidly changing workplace. Talking now in stereotypes, these skills, still attributed to women, are more likely to become the norm and hence in demand. However, these developments did not live up to the promise of providing alternative work options for women to succeed. Massive restructuring of the workplace and disruptions to work patterns and the loss of many industries and jobs have heralded yet another "new economy" for workers, which has resulted in new challenges for both men and women, but again more specifically for women.

Even before the GFC crashed markets across the globe, employees were already facing new threats to their employment stability, that is more casualization, less full-time and more part-time or erratic work opportunities, less chance for promotion, increased hours, and stress: in other words less flexibility and worker agency and autonomy. For managers there is increased complexity, work intensification, and reduced job security as they find themselves under increased pressure to produce and reduce costs, while at the same time facing more public scrutiny (e.g., executive salaries and payouts), and targets of hostile comments, and negative press stories. At the same time management roles are being outsourced (e.g., IT, Human Resources) to experts with short-term contracts whose focus is solely on increasing the company's outcomes and short-term profits. This flexibility and cost saving strategies come with a promise and a price. Casual work makes for a compliant workforce where industrial or cultural change is almost impossible to initiate. Further, as changes to consumer-based global capitalism have led to a shift from industrial/manufacturing/service based economies to the more male-dominated, resource-based companies such as mining and engineering, women are ever less in demand for these "hardhat" jobs. In Australia the resources boom uses "fly in and fly out workers" in more remote areas of mining which cater to men rather than women when children are part of the relationship. Even where women are emerging in the new workplaces (professional and associate professional fields) the burden of combining work-life balance can militate against any progress here. The issue of work and the balancing and managing for family and community needs seems to remain the sole providence of women, whether they work in paid employment or in the home.

There is some evidence (Bradley, 1999) that the aspirations of women and men at work regarding career are the same until their early 30s when childcare responsibilities alter women's full-time work and thus promotional expectations, painting a different picture for women and men's career paths (Noble & Moore, 2006). Older women are more ambitious than their male counterparts and are achieving some success in leadership, as women and men's aspirations appear to change as they move between stages in the job and family life cycle. However, demographic changes are gradually impacting once again on older women workers as more and more women are supporting older children's needs often on their own, thus prolonging the childrearing stage and then many are moving on to undertake the granny/nanny role for their working children's children (Probert, 2005). The paradoxes continue.

While young women are moving into work and education at a high rate, their structural position in institutions could also constitute an ideal proletariat and management pool for the new economy—as we can say with confidence that it is easier to introduce flexible contracts, part-time, casual, and temporary work when employing women. Although EEO legislation has broken a small hole in the "glass ceiling," these work changes and different work-life balances are emerging, bringing with them further obstacles for women. At the same time, there seems to be a new push toward female management as women are seen to possess skills in employee and customer care, and to possess required skills to undertake emotion work and relationship management. Again the paradoxes arise when women hit the "glass ceiling" and realize they can't have it all (Noble & Moore, 2006).

## ANALYSIS AND DISCUSSION

Despite a backlash and complexity of analyses of women's position in the workplace and public life, the gender question remains well and truly on the agenda. Even as Australia has the first woman as Prime Minister, ridicule, lack of legitimacy, lack of trust, and sustained criticism of her personal style and appearance suggest that there is more at stake for women who assume positions of power and leadership. Even though the first woman Governor General has escaped much of the embittered criticism of the PM her role seems to have morphed into a "clothes horse" (reference to her sense of style and use of Australian clothes designers) rather than her role as Queens Representative in a democratic monarchy. The ridicule and denigration of successful women is of concern for two reasons. One is that equal rights, equal treatment in private and public life, and equal participation in society are a human rights issue and second, excluding women from leadership roles and by implication full and equal partnership in the workplace impacts on productivity and militates against achieving a diverse workforce characteristic of the community more generally.

Probert, Ewer, & Whiting's (1998) study on gender equity index in Australian workplace performance shows that in private and public institutions of all sizes there is a direct correlation between higher productivity and higher levels of gender equity. Models of women in senior positions and in equal numbers generally benefit the institutions offering different perspectives, experiences, and contributions women can make. It seems a tired argument but one that is worth repeating again. The ongoing wastage of talent and contribution that arises from and is perpetuated by the current underrepresentation of women in the workplace seriously undermines organizations' ability to respond to change and threatens their future viability and vitality in the face of the economic challenges already outlined. The intransigence of barriers preventing the equality between men and women at the highest level of management is also destructive to good management and productive outcomes.

## WHAT NOW?

Liberal feminism, once equated with equal opportunity feminist initiatives, appears to have run out of steam. This is partly a result of the political backlash (Faludi, 1992), differences between women (Segal, 1999), dominance of economic rationalism (Bradley, 1999), the new contractualism (Davis, Sullivan, & Yeatman, 1997), and the rise of managerialism, and the continued existence of the masculinist organizational cultures which continue to sexualize and exclude women (Connell, 2006; Pease, 2009).

Power as exercised though the masculinities discourses still dominates contemporary workplace dialogue, while the work-life balance stifles women's time and focus to achieve in what is still a male-dominated work culture. While there is certainly much less overt discrimination and some culture changes, women still have a limited share of the ongoing secure employment opportunities. The dominant approach still locates the problem in women and does not fundamentally challenge the gendered nature of organizations or men's power within them. Organizational culture may readily accept formal equality and even welcome learning from women and value a more inclusive management style; however, as Burton (1991) and Bacchi (1993) foreshadowed there is a real danger that the new millennium patriarchy may be about subordinating women *within* an equality framework rather than liberating them. This degendering trend (Connell, 2006) is a worry for short- and long-term action, making the task for promoting gender equity that much harder. It is likely that management will continue to see gender equality as a luxury and not core business when workplaces are undergoing such massive and rapid structural change. This attitude will be hard to counter as women's equality in the workplace still needs commitment from both the top managers and the rank-and-file workers and for organizations and businesses to allocate more resources to support women's equal participation like affordable childcare and maternity leave. Even the argument that gender equity is a human rights issue or makes good public policy is hard to maintain as workers lose their jobs in large measure across the manufacturing, retail, and service industries. So after nearly three decades of legislative and various organizational support for more gender equity and inclusive management, the glass ceiling remains an issue for Australian and international policy debate. Changes in the "new" workplace do not give any guarantee that women will be better off in 21st century than they were in the 20th century.

## TOWARD NEW RESEARCH AREAS

Looking ahead it's forgivable if women are asking if any gender equity efforts are available that have not already been tried and, more cynically, why bother trying to change the system when change seems almost impossible! I suppose it is heartening to see that leading EEO researchers are still arguing, despite this pessimism, for the importance of continuing to explore power, sexuality, and differences at work so that women can have free and unfettered access to the benefits of work (Sinclair, 2005; Wajcman, 1999) while some others seem to be willing to give gender strategies another go (Connell, 2006). There is a belief somewhere that women will (eventually!) find a place in society beyond their mothering and caring roles and that it is possible to win the gender democracy debate and achieve a real cultural change for women and men alike.

The answer to moving forward can nearly always be captured by undertaking more research. Future research needs to adopt an agency approach that situates women in the centre of any analysis. That is that their experiences and aspirations, successes and failures, and strengths and weaknesses, become the center of the analysis to help explore the ways in which women as workers make sense of their world and the way women shape and change their own practices, which are socially and organizationally mediated by power axis. Exploring how women construct their working relationships and practices as agents of change and resistance is another area that might shed some light on why women continue to suffer discrimination at work and are denied their rightful place as active contributors to public life. Feminist analysis reminds us that women are not passive victims of masculinist culture and the exercising of male power and privilege at their expense. So, by listening and hearing their voices as a part of a feminist praxis, new gender directions in workplace cultures could be chartered; new strengths identified; and new strategies explored. The process will take into account the competing perspectives reported here and the impact of the "new" economy on the nature of work more generally. Engaging in new research will advance feminist theory as well. Feminist theory as a multifaceted and discursively contested field of inquiry has survived, in part, on its ability to produce its own hybridized critical interpretative positions (Calás & Smircich, 2006).

New research into the way men and women *do* gender at work is also needed and this research might be more fruitful if *both* women and men engage in the process together so that the way men and women do gender is made more visible. Finally I agree with Connell (2006) who argues that gender equity is likely to benefit if it continues to inform the ethos of the public services—not only as part of a good model of a just society but also as a culture shift that encourages male workers to have an ethical and moral duty to support gender equality for the benefit of their female coworkers. It is argued that because men occupy more dominant positions in the workplace that they have a greater responsibility for promoting a nondiscriminatory culture at work. Finally, I would argue there is a need for gender analysis of power and privilege to be included in reworking of equal opportunity theory in order to understand the need for inclusive gender balance workplace to move from the margin of employment to the center of paid work and public life.

## REFERENCES

Acker, J. (1998). The future of "gender and organizations": Connections and boundaries. *Gender, Work and Organization, 5,* 195–206.

Bacchi, C. (1993). The brick wall: Why so few women become senior managers. *The Australian Universities Review, 36,* 36–41.

Bacchi, C. (2004). Policy and discourse: Challenging the construction of affirmative action as preferential treatment. *Journal of European Public Policy, 11,* 128–146.

Bacchi, C. (2009). *Analysing policy: What's the problem represented to be?* Sydney: Pearson Education.

Bacchi, C., & Eveline, J. (2009, March). Gender mainstreaming or diversity mainstreaming? The politics of doing. *Nordic Journal of Feminist and Gender Research, 7,* 2–17.

Bradley, H. (1999). *Gender and power in the workplace: Analysing the impact of economic change.* London: Macmillan.

Burton, C. (1991). *The promise and the price.* Sydney: Allen and Unwin.

Butler, J. (1993). *Bodies that matter: On the discursive limits of "sex."* New York: Routledge.

Calás, M., & Smircich, L. (2006). From the woman's point of view: ten years later: Towards a feminist organisational studies. In S. Clegg, C. Hardy, T. Lawrence, & W. Nord (Eds.), *The Sage handbook of organizational studies* (2nd ed.). London: Sage.

Connell, R. (1995). *Masculinities.* Sydney: Allen and Unwin.

Connell, R. (2006). The experience of gender change in public sector organizations. *Gender, Work and Organization, 13,* 435–452.

Connell, R. W. (1987). *Gender and power.* Cambridge: Polity.

Conti, R. F., & Warner, M. (1994). Taylorism teams and technology in "re-engineering" work organization. *Work, Employment and Society, 9,* 94–102.

Cox, E. (1995). *Leading women.* Australia: Random House.

Davis, G., Sullivan, B., & Yeatman, A. (Eds.). (1997). *The new contractualism? Centre for Australian public sector management.* South Melbourne: Macmillan.

Dietz, M. (2003). Current controversies in feminist theory. *Annual Review of Political Science, 6,* 399–431.

Eggins, H. (1997). *Women as leaders and managers in higher education.* Buckingham, UK: OUP.

EOWA Annual Report 2011. Retrieved July 28, 2011, from www.eowa.gov.au.

Faludi, S. (1992). *Backlash: The undeclared war against feminism.* London: Vintage.

Fisher, H. (1999). *The first sex: The natural talents of women and how they are changing the world.* Australia: Random House.

Flood, M., & Pease, B. (2005). Undoing men's privilege and advancing gender equality in public sector institutions. *Policy and Society, 24,* 19–138.

The Global Gender Gap Report. 2010. Retrieved July 28, 2011, from http://www
.weforum.org/pdf/gendergap/report2010

Hayward, S. (2005). *Women leading*. Hampshire: Palgrave Macmillan.

Hearn, J., & Collinson, D. (2006). Men, masculinities and workplace diversity/
diversion. In A. Konrad, P. Prasad, & J. Pringle (Eds.), *Handbook of workplace
diversity*. London: Sage.

Leahy, M. (2011). Women and work in Australia. *Australian Policy Online*. Retrieved
March 2, 2011, from www.APO.org.au

Martin, P. (2001). Mobilizing masculinities: Women's experiences of men at work.
*Organization, 8,* 586–618.

Marvin, S. (2001). Women's career in theory and practice: Time for change. *Women
in Management Review, 16,* 183–192.

Mattis, M. (2004). Women entrepreneurs: Out from under the glass ceiling. *Women
in Management Review, 19,* 154–163.

McGregor, J. (2011). Confidentiality deals targeted in move for equal employment
opportunities. *The Dominion Post* (4th July), Australia/New Zealand Reference
Centre, EBSCOhost. Viewed July 25, 2011.

McIntosh, P. (2002). White privilege: Unpacking the invisible knapsack. In
P. Rothenberg (Ed.), *White: Essential readings on the other side of racism*. New
York: Worth Publishers.

Moore, S., & Wen, J. (2004). Economic reform and business management in China
today. *International Journal of Applied Management, 5,* 66–84.

Noble, C., & Mears, J. (2000). The impact of affirmative action legislation on women
in higher education in Australia: Progress or procrastination. *Women in Management Review, 15,* 404–411.

Noble, C., & Moore, S. (2006). Advancing women and leadership in the post feminist,
post EEO era: A discussion of the issues. *Women in Management Review, 21,*
598–603.

Noble, C., & Pease, B. (2011). Interrogating male privilege in the human services
and social work education. *WIWE, 10,* 29–38.

O'Leary, E. (2000). *Leadership*. Indianapolis, IN: Macmillan, USA.

Pease, B. (2000). *Recreating men: Postmodern masculinity politics*. London: Sage.

Pease, B. (2002). *Men and gender relations*. Melbourne: Tertiary Press.

Pease, B. (2009). Challenges and directions for profeminist men. In J. Allen, L.
Briskman, & B. Pease (Eds.), *Critical social work: Theories and practices for a
socially just world*. Sydney: Allen and Unwin.

Polnick, B., Reed, D., Funk, C., & Edmonson, S. (2004). Groundbreaking women: In-
spirations and trailblazers. *Advancing Women in Leadership Journal*. Retrieved
from http://www.advancingwomen.com/awl/winter2004/Polnick.html

Pringle, K. (1995). *Men, masculinities and social welfare*. London: UCL Press.

Probert, B. (2005). I just couldn't fit it: Gender and unequal outcomes in academic
careers. *Gender, Work and Organization, 12,* 50–72.

Probert, B., Ewer, P., & Whiting, K. (1998). *Gender pay equity in Australian higher
education*. Melbourne: NTEU.

Ritt, E. (2004). Hearing the opus: The paradox for women leaders in the postmodern university. *Advancing Women in Leadership Journal*. Retrieved from https://
www.humboldt-foundation.de/pls/web/docs/F7981/iab-broschuere-2009.pdf

Rutherford, S. (2001). Organizational cultures, women managers and exclusion. *Women in Management, 16*, 371–382.

Segal, L. (1999). *Why feminism?* Cambridge: Polity.

Sinclair, A. (2005). *Doing leadership differently.* Victoria: Melbourne University Press.

Thornton, M. (2001). EEO in a neo-liberal climate. *JIGS, 6*, 77–104.

Thornton, M. (2008). *Where are the women? The swing from EEO to diversity in the academy.* Working paper No. 22.

Wajcman, J. (1999). *Managing like a man.* St. Leonards: Allen & Unwin.

Walby, S. (2005). Gender mainstreaming: Productive tensions in theory and practice. *Social Politics, 12*, 321–343.

Williams, C. (1992). The glass escalator: Hidden advantages for men in the "female" professions. *Social Problems, 39*, 253–267.

Young, I. (2000). *Inclusion and democracy.* Oxford: Oxford University Press.

Zichy, S. (2000). *Women and the leadership Q.* New York: McGraw-Hill.

# Chapter 12

# Czech Female Professionals and Entrepreneurs between Family and Career

*Martina Rasticova*

When in 1921 Františka Plamínková called Tomáš Garrique Masaryk, the first president of Czechoslovakia, a feminist, this was by no means an offensive attribute. The word feminism, a few years after the end of World War I, which out of necessity conceded the women's ability to carry out, until then, the solely men's professions, carried almost no content. It was, however, clear that Masaryk was a defender of women's rights putting in considerable effort to abolish prostitution and being credited for the first Czechoslovak constitution doing away with every male prerogative. As it happened, one of the first proponents of the Czech women's rights was a man, which only corroborates the old truth that what concerns the woman also concerns the man, that one cannot think about women without at the same time thinking about the relationship between the man and the woman, the relationship between the mother and the son, the father and the daughter, and the brother and the sister (Lenderová, 1999).

The Czech lands had been spared the extreme misogyny; with the Hussite movement even, for a time, lending the active female adherents a feeling of equality and maybe even importance. The time of the Hussite movement and the period before the battle of Bílá Hora (from 15th century till 1620) brought the right appreciation for the mundane woman, the wife, the mother, the housewife, but also for a highbred, beautiful, and educated lady who can stand by her politically active husband. In spite of this, the wife remained "her husband's prisoner"—a husband could kill or imprison his untrue wife; disobedient wives were beaten or repudiated. Until the beginning of the 20th century, matrimony had been the women's only aspiration; it was only in it that they were of any value. The women of high society were only offered two options—either a husband or a convent. Rather than free, the choice was more of a pecuniary nature: an amount that would not have covered the cost of entering a marriage was usually sufficient to enter one of the exclusive convents. Only a fraction of women decided for the life in convent community voluntarily. Brides of Christ were spared the almost incessant pregnancies and repeated mourning over a child's death (child mortality was high) (in the same article).

The Czech feminism trying to achieve women's emancipation was moderate, with women differentiating themselves from men while joining them in a common fight for the rebirth of a nation. The position of a Czech woman in the era of patriotism was no doubt better to some extent than that of her counterpart in the neighboring Germany. Men patriots needed enlightened wives to bear them Czech-minded children bringing them up to love their native tongue, country, and the brotherhood of Slavs. To their daughters, sisters, and wives, men afforded reasonable education, a taste of poetry, and prose writing, letting them even try acting on a stage. However, this idyllic scene was gone once women started to call for qualification that would make them free to choose their own profession. They wanted first secondary and, later, university education. They wanted to enter the labor market. The masculine resistance to such wishes was intuitive, fueled by the foreboding of a cold stove, missing buttons, yellowish cuffs and collars, unwashed children, and economically independent wife getting out of control. For most men, an educated woman destroyed the myth of femininity, unquestionable for centuries. Antonín Gindely (1829–1892), a Czech historian and crown prince Rudolph's tutor, expressed the then prevailing view of feminine education: *let the woman acquire some knowledge, however, only to such an extent as doesn't keep her from her natural job, that is, to bear children and keep the home warm and cosy* (Lenderová, 2002, p. 39). The fight for women's right to be educated, for the content, extent, and places of such education has had a long history; history which is difficult to grasp and a little unclear. One thing is for sure though: until the 19th century, no one had cared much for women's education. Little attention was paid by the rulers, less by the lawmakers, and even by the women themselves. At least, this is true for most of them.

An important milestone in the history of the Czech education was the founding of a girls' gymnasium (a secondary school). A gymnasium, seen as preparation for a university study, was considered a type of education absolutely unnecessary and useless for women. The idea itself of a girls' gymnasium had required years of considerable efforts to take roots. The first attempt in 1868 by Gabriel Blažek, Pavel Jehlička, and František Čupr, a group of Prague professors was doomed to failure. Most of the Czech politicians of that era were bitter opponents of women's education. The efforts were later bravely resumed by Eliška Krásnohorská.[1] It was on her initiative that Minerva, a society for women's higher education, was formed. When she was looking for supporters among the Czech deputies she was met with flat refusal by almost all. In the end it was Deputy Karel Adámek who on March 11, 1890, submitted to the *Reichsrat* an application for the forming of Minerva. It was granted. Minerva became the first girls' gymnasium in Austria Hungary. In the first academic year starting on September 30, 1890, 52 girls applied including 30 from the families of civil servants. Eventually, the gymnasium moved from the old building of a former basic girls' school at St. Adalbert to a villa called Amerika situated in Karlov. However, it was not until 1907 that the girls could take a school-leaving examination at their school; up until that time sporadic girls' exams had taken place at boy's institutes attracting (mostly hostile) attention. Minerva faced financial problems—becoming a public school only in the academic year 1915–1916. Although the first female graduates were no doubt well educated, they left the gymnasium doomed to become spinsters. The fact that they had no dowry to offer because of their family background was not the only reason. There was one more obstacle. Men usually had little interest in an educated woman. And so the *minervistky* often lived their lonely lives as civil servants, governesses, schoolmistresses.

The 19th century came to an end. Women appeared in all the spheres of human activities. They earned their livings in arts, education, public service, business, and offered cheap labor in factories and on farms. Gradually, they even mastered medicine and engineering. Only the legal, clerical, and military professions remained unconquered. Even with their wives entering the world of paid labor, men could still feel that the balance between the masculine and feminine roles was not affected. An overwhelming majority of women still preferred to be mothers readily leaving their professions before getting married to return to hearth and home (Lenderová, 2002).

## WOMEN IN THE SOCIALIST ERA

Vodochodský (2007) points out that one of the key categories of the socialist efforts to equip women with equal rights was "emancipation." Although denoting a positive process of social liberation of women today, this word sometimes has a ring of irony. Šiklová, for one, openly speaks of a "socialist 'pseudo-emancipation' " (Šiklová, 1993, p. 75).

The history of the women's position in the socialist era is usually divided into two periods of approximately the same length (1950s and 1960s, 1970s and 1980s) with the emancipating phase occurring rather in the first one. The principal event that had brought about this change was the crowds of women entering paid employment after 1948 as dictated by the new rulers. Some of the authors (Drakulić, 2006; Einhorn, Sever, 2003; Šiklová, 1997) agree that this was motivated by the narrow economic interests of the postwar regimes. But they also admit that the then Marxist-Leninist ideology, which had a certain intrinsic form of women emancipation, played a certain role, too. Susan Gal and Gail Kligman describe it as follows:

> In most of the communist countries of central and eastern Europe, women were at first primarily seen as working people, which was a dramatic revision of the pre-war concepts. This was part of more general efforts to homogenize and equalize the population with trying to do away with all the social differences including the gender ones with an aim to create a "new socialist citizen." (Gal & Kligman, 2000, p. 47)

The double-edged socialist model of emancipation—economic interests of the state on one side, efforts at gender liberation on the other side—is also described by Ivo Možný:

> Women were presented their labour mobilization as a possibility to become equal to men, as a way to their emancipation: equal job opportunities plus a large-scale, rigorously implemented programme to liberate women from the burden of maternity by building a network of kindergartens and crèches accepting three-month-old babies (the period of the then maternity leave) and even offering an all-week care, which was something that their counterparts defending the egalitarian principles in the western countries could only begin to dream of. (Možný, 1999, p. 154)

Vodochodský further reflects on the main changes for women caused by the egalitarian policy. The rapid increase in the number of economically active women implied that women became independent of men—economically, socially, and psychologically—being virtually self-sufficient in supporting themselves and their families. Also their education and qualification improved. Havelková points out that women in 1950s were taking jobs and, even to a greater extent, becoming teachers while completing and improving their education and skills (Havelková, 1993, p. 91). Women authors emphasize that women in the socialist era became more independent, self-sufficient, and self-assured. Thanks to the new system, they could also very soon get more control over their own bodies by being relieved of their "reproductive duties" with contraception and abortion being easily available. Women could also disengage from marriage easily and attempts were made to free them from the everyday chores by offering the needed services[2] (cleaner's, laundries, and crèches) even if not everywhere, not always, and not of sufficient quality (see the following).

However, most of the authors agree that, under the socialist emancipation, the metamorphosis of the traditional household had not been achieved with women still taking on a majority of tasks and duties.

More independence and self-confidence notwithstanding, women were still under continual physical and psychical strain, fatigue, and stress resulting from the "double load" of a paid job plus domestic chores. Here is how Jiřina Šiklová characterizes this situation:

> In the socialist era, at least two generations of women experienced the impossibility of mastering the dual roles—keeping the household running and being employed—suffering feelings of guilt and permanent frustration from not being able to cope with either of these tasks to their satisfaction. Although crèches and kindergartens were available, other household services as well as the public transport for commuters were of poor quality and women trying to fulfil both roles were not doing so well in their jobs as men. (Šiklová, 1997, p. 267)

Also the pay differences between men and women combined with gender inequalities barring women from advancement to leading positions as well as the overall structure of professions had remained. This also applied to the government, politics, and the "management" of socialist enterprises where women were fewer in number and occupying lower positions. Éva Fodor (2002) says that, in the socialist era, women were assigned professions and offices not only different from but also inferior to those of men (Fodor, 2002, p. 258; cit. by Vodochodský, 2007).

Even though gender-free on the surface, the ideal communist subject was equipped with pronounced masculine qualities and women could never have come up to this standard. In particular, due to their reproductive duties, which the creators of the socialist social policy had not cast any doubt on, women could never be considered equally reliable and committed to the communist cause as men. For this reason, their enforced presence in the world of labor and politics could only be segregated and second-rate (Fodor, 2002, p. 241).

Due to the persisting pay differences between men and women (according to Wagnerová, 1999, p. 80, for example, women's average wage in Czechoslovakia was 67% of men's), women had only become partially economically independent of men. Šiklová points out that in the socialist society, a stereotype had been created of the man as perhaps not the only one but still the main supporter of the family (Šiklová, 1993, p. 75). It is clear that different women authors agree that the process of women's liberation characteristic, mainly of the first half of the communist era, could only be completed in part. Although emphasizing the progress made in liberating women as compared with the Western countries, they are all aware of the ambivalent if not negative impact of this unfinished project.

## WOMEN'S MEMORY

Since 1996, Pavla Frýdlová[3] together with a team of Czech women experts in gender studies and feminism has worked on Women's Memory,[4] a long-term international project. Unique by its scope, this project involves, apart from the Czech teams, also interdisciplinary teams from Germany (the former GDR), Slovakia, Poland, Serbia, Monte Negro, Croatia, and Ukraine. The project focuses on capturing the experiences and views of three generations of women born between 1920 and 1960 using the method of biographic research and oral. This approach lets the narrators themselves select what they think is important in their lives and what they want to speak about and have recorded for the generations to come.[5]

The project aims to record how women lived in recent history, what was their main motives, how they reflected and still reflect themselves, and in what their lives differed from those of their mothers and grandmothers. Although the state controlled model of women's emancipation was more or less the same for all the countries of the Soviet bloc, its particular implementation was fairly different in each country. Note also that different traditions and behavior patterns, together with different historical backgrounds (the Balkans versus the catholic Poland), played a significant role, too. The situation in the immediately postwar Germany might serve as a classic example—after the war women were by 7.3 million less in number than men (3.6 million killed, 11.6 million prisoners of war with most of them returning home within two years, but the last ones from Russia as late as 1955). Entirely unique was the phenomenon of the legendary *Trümmerfrauen*—women who, after the war while the men were absent, had built a new Germany from the ruins only to retreat from the public life and, to a considerable extent, from their jobs, too, to resume their duties in the households as the men returned.

This was not so much the case in the Soviet-occupied East Germany where the trend took the same course as in this country emphasizing the necessity of women being employed. This was not always for ideological reasons—employment as an emancipation factor—but also for the simple reason that the industry needed more and more labor with the women employment rate growing all the time after the war. Born 1919 and graduated from a chemical university after returning from prison in Ravensbrück, Libuše summarizes her experiences of a married woman:

> My husband's friends who married girls educated at a family or convent school so that they had to be supported were envying him that I could earn money and was qualified since the only job their own wives could get was serving coffee in a joint or cleaning. Or rather than taking menial jobs, they scrimped and saved staying at home. I don't see any negatives in women taking jobs and believe that everything can be arranged, depending on the quality of men. My husband, who worked at the directorate of a metal works, seeing women produce up to ten thousand drawing pins per shift, said that this was outright exploitation of women. He saw the maintenance workers in those factories putting on airs on women. Only you can't wait for a man's understanding, they have to be pushed into it by women trying to get the upper hand themselves. It's also a question of bringing up the children well, you're not supposed to say "this is a boys' job, this is a girls' job."

Most of the women, whom the war taught self-sacrifice and self-denial, viewed the huge workload and the inconveniences of the postwar shortages, the rationing, and so forth as part of building a new home accepting the double load (job, household) as a matter of fact. Today, however, almost all the women bringing up their children in the 1950s and 1960s agree that they would have preferred staying longer at home or taking part-time jobs (4 to 5 hours) rather than taking a full-time job after six months' maternity leave with children in crèches and kindergartens.

The Czech women started to realize the unequal distribution of roles only later on, in 1960s when debates were held in women's magazines such as *Vlasta* on the double or triple load, and on the ill-functioning services supposed—through the Liberated Household, which was the name given to a communal agency aggregating various services such as dry-cleaning, laundering, repairing, and cooking—to rid the women of the burden of domestic chores. Men seldom did participate in such debates let alone come up with an idea related to children upbringing or household. On the contrary, they often proclaimed that children were a purely feminine business.

The traditional approach to the distribution of masculine and feminine roles seemed not to have given way in society. The double or triple load that women had to take was so striking that it even gave rise to sayings like "The woman must work in a socialist way for the man to live in a socialist way." The traditional role distribution, however, was not affecting only the private but also the business sphere, particularly, the pay and position at work.

Unequal job opportunities of men and women and the absence of men participating in domestic chores persisted during the whole of the socialist era. A large systematic study of the gender roles of university-educated married couples (as compared with dual-worker couples) was conducted by I. Možný in 1983. Even if some differences were marked in the division of male and female roles between these two respondent groups, the conclusion was that though most egalitarian university-educated couples assumed to agree on an even participation of both spouses in household chores, still most of the work is done by the wife.

## WOMEN IN THE 1990S AND IN THE BEGINNING OF 21ST CENTURY

The turbulent political and social events in Europe of the early 1990s had brought new job opportunities for all, with young Czechs traveling abroad and people having a chance of building a career regardless of their political affiliation. It is, however, clear from the research conducted by Czech authors that the gender role division even in the present-time families remains mostly traditional.

When investigating the division of labor in a household, Ivo Plaňava came to a conclusion that all or most of the domestic chores are done by women. ". . . in 210 out of 260 married couples, it is the wife that does all or most of the household chores," says Plaňava (2000) summarizing the results of research in the division of household roles. His results also imply that even a professionally engaged wife does more to run the household than her husband.

Comparing the attitudes of population toward parent roles using two large-scale ISSP surveys (from 1994 and 2002), Hana Maříková (2003) comes to a conclusion that the present population becomes somewhat more tolerant to the gender role swap. According to the credibility given to the saying "The husband should make a living to support the family while the wife should take care of the household and children," the Czech Republic, with 53% of the respondents agreeing, ranks twelfth among 16 countries, which is almost the last quarter of the scale.[6]

The role of a husband supporting his family is still prevailing today, being often taken for granted by both men and women. As part of a research project, Children, Youth, and the Family in Transformation (Rašticová & Hašková, 2002, p. 100), a survey was conducted to find out whether the respondents would mind money being earned for the family budget solely by one of the spouses.

## GENDER ROLES IN THE FAMILY LIFE CYCLE

The gender roles may change during the family life cycle. Changes taking place in families within the family life cycle are the subject of research by a number of Czech social psychologists ok and sociologists (Čermáková, Maříková, Šanderová, & Tuček, 2000a; Matoušek, 2003; Možný,

1990; Plaňava, 1998) and so here only the gender roles will be dealt with in each phase of the family life cycle that have been investigated as parts of large *Family 1994* and *Family 1996* international projects with the results published by Marie Čermáková et al. in 2000b. The research results imply that Czech men and women living in *nonmarital cohabitation without children* are generally inclined to the opinion that the rights and duties in a household should be equal, both men and women agree that the financial contribution of both partners should be equal (Čermáková et al., 2000a).

It is childless matrimony (i.e., the period after marriage before children are born) that is usually denoted as the first phase of the family cycle. Although both men and women in this phase agree that both partners may contribute to the family budget and that both of them should have equal opportunities to pursue their hobbies, according to the results of the research, the time spent by men for household chores is only half that spent by women. Thus, even in the first phase, a disproportion exists between the attitudes proclaimed toward equal distribution of roles and the actual behavior, which is dominated by gender stereotypes.

Once the first child is born, most families assume the traditional role division. By becoming the mother, the wife is also assigned the role of a household keeper and nurse. In a family with children, the wife does most of the domestic chores: cooking, shopping, and cleaning in three out of four Czech households. Husbands systematically participate in such activities in less than 5% of the households. The results also imply that, according to 61% of women and 51% of men, the mother's role in raising children is more important than the father's. The natural mother-child dyad pattern is also apparent in times of family crises such as during a divorce when, in a majority of cases, children are placed in the mother's custody,[7] which testifies to the predominant stereotype of the mother being irreplaceable as well as to the unequal opportunities men have in child custody lawsuits. Even here, however, things seem to be changing according to some studies published recently dealing with the experiences of the small group of men taking on the role traditionally connected with women—running the household and looking after children (Maříková, 1999, 2003; Šmídová, 2003). Thus, despite the husband's role being still taken to be that of supporting the family (and, in an overwhelming majority of cases, the husband's income *is* larger than the wife's), it is imperative for most of the Czech married couples that both partners be employed to keep the family working. This means that, after the maternity leave[8] expires or even prior to that, the wife has to return to work. Still she carries on the bulk of the domestic chores. At this *preschool-children family stage,* the husband's assistance is not significantly increased. On average, the wife (while going to work) devotes to the household three times as much time as her husband.

At the *school-children family stage,* most Czech wives have a chance of starting their professional careers. It is only during this period that most people think that the wife is entitled to full-time employment without seriously neglecting her family.[9] According to some authors, (Křížková, 2000, 2003), at this family stage, the wife has a double burden to shoulder: in addition to being full-time employed, she still has to cope with the bulk of the household and childcare. The husband, on the other hand, is still the main wage earner at this time as his career has not been disrupted by the birth of a child.

At the last-but-one family life cycle stage sometimes referred to as *flying the nest,* the wife is gradually relieved of the household chores, partly, because some of the work is done by her grown-up children. At this time, the wife devotes significantly more time to work and career. About one half of the Czech wives over 50 say that they devote themselves evenly to family and work with a tenth of them even preferring the family (note that, according to surveys, younger wives overwhelmingly prefer the family — as discussed earlier). The husband at this time does not experience any change in the way he spends his time save that the time he spends at work tends to be a little longer. The time devoted to friends and hobbies in this period is the same in men and women (15 hours weekly).

The last and usually the longest period of the family life cycle described as an *empty nest* begins after the children leave home. This is the time when the wife can devote the most time to her hobbies and profession. Although not raising or taking care of any children, at this stage of the family life cycle, many Czech wives of this generation experience what is called a *sandwich situation,* meaning that they help raise their children's children while supporting and taking care of their aging parents.

Although an attitude shift can be observed toward a more even role division (an overwhelming majority of men and women in Czech society think that, in a family with children, husband and wife are both entitled to the same leisure opportunities and have an equal obligation to contribute to the family budget (Čermáková et al., 2000b), the traditional family model and gender role division persist. The mother is responsible for both running the household and raising the children. The division of labor in a typical Czech family with small children is still markedly asymmetrical with the wife doing most of the chores. The husband is still seen as the principal even if not the only wage earner. That this family model still holds, however, may also be caused by the unwillingness of both partners to give up the dominance in those particular areas assigned to them.

## PERCEPTION OF FEMALE ROLE BY TWO GENERATIONS OF WOMEN AND MEN

In 2004 we conducted an extensive survey of the female and male views of women's roles in family and society (Rašticová, 2004). A sample of 554 respondents was chosen divided into two age groups: students of Prague and Brno universities and their parents. The findings showed that when raising their children, both parents observed the same principles preferring the same educational objectives. To a certain extent, this may have been the result of the choice made (most of the respondents lived in complete families). More interesting, however, was the fact that fathers had different approaches to educating daughters and sons whereas mothers were trying to achieve the educational objectives equally with daughters and sons if not preferring daughters.

Concerning the sharing of educational activities by the parents, the results suggest that it was mothers who participated in education and childcare to a greater extent even if fathers were not altogether absent. The finding that male students expected to have the same if not greater participation in education and childcare as compared with female students' expectations of their partners and fathers of their children offers a number of interpretations. The reason is that the results of our research are equivocal as to whether the lower expectations in female students concerning the participation of their partners in education and childcare is given by their skeptical views of the reality or, on the contrary, results from their desire to keep their exclusive right to raise children. Also, Plaňava (2000) analyzes the differences between the expectations of young men and young women determined by his research.

Comparing the way male and female students saw the sharing of childcare duties in their parents' families with how they expected that this would work in their own future life, both in male and female students, one can perceive a shift toward more equality. *Sick child care* seems ok to be the only exception with more mother involvement expected. In this connection, a study by A. Křížková (2002) describes in detail the different strategies a female manager uses to cope with her double role—as a mother and a woman in a senior position—if she is willing to give up none of these.

In all the respondent groups, the distribution of time of the wife–mother is perceived in conformance with the traditional concept of the wife–mother: mothers devote most of their time to the family (over 50%), one-third of the time to their professions, and the least part (about 10%) to their hobbies. Respondents of all groups think that, in an ideal case, mothers should devote more time to their hobbies and less to the family than they (or their partners) did when raising children. The ideal distribution of the wife's time is only perceived differently by female students and their mothers. The fact that male students (as compared with their mothers) think that the wives should devote twice as much time pursuing their hobbies rather than devoting it to the family again seems to corroborate the existing trend among the young male university students toward removing the differences between gender roles.

Based on the results of the research part investigating the willingness of wives to give up their jobs under certain circumstances, it might be assumed that professional career was more important for female students than for their mothers and for the mothers of male students. Female students were less than their mothers willing to give up their careers provided that their partners *could support them*. If, however, they should find that their job was not bringing them sufficient satisfaction, they would abandon it more readily than their mothers would have. Thus, if J. Joyce found in 1961 that most girls' priority was family with work being not seen as a fulfillment, now, almost 50 years later, the situation seems to be somewhat different. The results of this research imply that, for female university students, professional career is important.

Nevertheless the unequivocal determination of both the female students and their mothers to give up their careers should the *family situation* require this as well as the *child option* (in a model situation of choosing between the child and the professional career) confirm that, even today, child and family are a priority for women of both generations even at the cost of their careers being slowed down or, in over one-third of the cases, even disrupted.

The next section brings some latest statistical data regarding the ratios of male and female in education, labor force, and earnings.

## WOMEN AND MEN IN STATISTICAL DATA

### Education

In the years 2007 and 2008, more than 2.2 million schoolchildren and students from preschools to universities were educated by almost 154,000 teachers and educators. The teachers-per-100-children ratio is the greatest at preschools (7.8) and lowest at universities (6.2). Women form an overwhelming percentage (99.9) of the more than 22,000 teachers at preschools.

The numbers of boys and girls in preschools are basically the same and the situation is not much different at elementary and, on average, at all types of high schools. Differences can be observed between different types of high schools: there are more girls at specialized secondary schools and gymnasiums, particularly specialized colleges attended, however, only by about 1% of all students. Boys, on the other hand, are more numerous at secondary vocational schools and at special schools, particularly those for the attendants of institutional care centers.

## 2007/2008 UNIVERSITY GRADUATE NUMBERS

There were 344,480 students studying at Czech universities in the academic year 2007/2008 with 54% of female students. In 2007 the graduates were 63,473 in number with 55.9% of female students. In absolute numbers, female students studied mostly economics while male students engineering fields. The fields chosen least of all by both female and male students are those of culture and arts.

The highest percentage of female students were among the graduates from medical and pharmaceutical universities (almost 80% of all the graduates being female students), the smallest group of female students were detected in engineering (female students making up about one quarter of graduates here). Save engineering and natural sciences, female students were more numerous in all the fields.

## MALE AND FEMALE LABOR FORCE

Among employees the percentage of women is 45.9. Except for the 25–34 age bracket where there were more female than male employees, men were more numerous. The lowest percentage of female employees was detected in the youngest age group of 15–24.

Male employees could most frequently be found from age 15 to 24. The most self-employed men were between 35 and 49 years old while with self-employed women, the most frequent age, same as with the female employees, was 50 plus.

In 2007 there were over 656,000 men and 200,000 women self-employed in the Czech Republic, thus making up more than one quarter (26.2%). Self-employed men are more numerous in all age brackets.

## MALE AND FEMALE EARNINGS IN 2007

The highest incomes in 2007 were earned by both male and female law makers, managers, and employees in senior positions: the median salary was 40,670 CZK in men and 28,229 CZK in women. Second largest salaries were those of research and white-collar professionals followed by technicians, medical staff, and teachers (gender making no difference). The lowest income group consisted of unskilled workers.

The biggest differences between male and female earnings can be observed in tradespersons and skilled producers, processors, and repairpersons (excluding machine operators) where the 2007 female median earnings only reached 68% of the male ones and in law makers, managers and employees in senior positions (69.4%). Here the Gender Pay Gap[10] (GPG) reaches over 30%, which means that female and male earnings are considerably different. The biggest wage leveling exists in farming, forestry, and related fields. Here, women receive 86.2% of the male median wage. The situation is similar in lower position white-collar workers where female-to-male median wage ratio is 82.5. Thus, the GPG equals 17.5%.

## CONCLUSION

It may be assumed that university female and, more so, male students raised in complete families are less guided by stereotypes in judging the female role than their parents. For female university students, professional fulfillment is important, still the unequivocal willingness of both female students and mothers to give up their careers should the family situation require it as well as the child option (in a model situation of choosing between the child and the professional career) confirm that, even today, family and child-care are a priority for women of both generations. The role of a wife with professional ambitions is not void of the dimension of a nurse and educator.

## NOTES

1. Eliška Krásnohorská (1847–1926) was a famous Czech author, poetess, librettist, translator, and activist in women's movement.

2. Možný (1999) does not interpret such steps as efforts at women's liberation but rather as a blatant attack by the totalitarian regime on the integrity of its arch enemy—the traditional family.

3. Pavla Frýdlová (2006). Life of women in the socialist era in the light of the women's memory project. A paper presented at a conference on *women's emancipation in the socialist era and today*. Held on: November 6, 2006. Venue: Czech Centre, Rytířská 31, Praha 1. Also available at http://www.feminismus.cz/download/Pam.pdf

4. For more information on the project visit www.womensmemory.net. The project is conceived as open, anti-ideological, emancipational, and, above all, feministic. The feministic nature of the project determines its approach to the women questioned: rather than an object, they are the subject of the project as such being both its purpose and aim. The project's uniqueness is not in its scope but rather in its dual character: research with an interdisciplinary concept, but targeted to a wider public.

5. The original objective was to conduct a large interview in each country for each generation. As yet, this objective has been met only by the Czech and German teams, which were the first ones to receive a governmental funding with other teams proceeding slowly mostly due to the lack of funding and some teams—such as the Polish one—even suspending work on the project for the same reason.

6. The following is a list of the 16 countries included in the 1994 ISSP research project (arranged from those agreeing the least with the statement to those agreeing the most): Sweden, Norway, USA, the Netherlands, UK, Australia, Italy, Ireland, Germany (former West Germany), Spain, Slovenia, Czech Republic, Hungary, Bulgaria, Poland, and Russia.

7. Thirty-nine percent of men and fifty-six percent of women agree that, after divorce, the children should be placed in mother's sole custody.

8. The difference between *maternity* and *parental leave* is the following: *maternity leave* (as well as pregnancy and maternity benefits) lasts 28 weeks beginning in the sixth week before the expected date of delivery provided that the woman is no longer earning her wages or receiving a sick pay. Maternity leave and maternity benefit are followed by a *parental leave* and parental benefit, which can be received up to age four of the child (or up to age seven if the child is permanently disabled) (www.mpsv.cz).

9. Only a quarter of the Czech women see their domestic role as a form of fulfillment, three quarters of the women pursue a professional career despite child and family being the top priority for a majority of the Czech women (Čermáková, 2000).

10.  GPG—Gender Pay Gap—is the difference between male and female median pay divided by male median pay and expressed in percentage points. In the previous edition of this publication, a different method was used to calculate GPG (rather than GPG, the percentage of the median hourly female pay to male pay was calculated, which adds up to 100% with GPG).

## REFERENCES

Čermáková, M., Maříková, H., Šanderová, J., & Tuček, M. (2000a). Proměny současné české rodiny (Rodina—gender—stratifikace). Praha: Sociologické nakladatelství.

Čermáková, M., HaM.kov, H., KK., ková, A., Linkova, M., Ma, ova, H., & Musilova, M. (2000b). Souvislosti a změny genderových diferencí v české společnosti v 90. letech. Praha: Sociologický ústav AV ČR.

Drakulić, S. (2006). Jak jsme přežili komunismus. Praha: Nakladatelství Lidové noviny.

Einhorn, B., & Sever, C. (2003). Gender and civil society in Central and Eastern Europe. International Feminist Journal of Politics, 5, 163–190.

Fodor, E. (2002). Gender and the experience of poverty in Eastern Europe and Russia after 1989. Communist and Post-Communist Studies, 35, 369–382.

Gal, S., & Kligman, G. (2000). The politics of gender after socialism: A comparative-historical essay. Princeton, NJ: Princeton University Press.

Havelková, H. (1993). 'Patriarchy' in Czech society. Hypatia, 8, 89–96.

Křížková, A. (2000). Slovník základních pojmů. Gender, rovné příležitosti, výzkum, 1, 2.

Křížková, A. (2002). Životní strategie manažerek: případová studie. Praha: Sociologický ústav AV ČR.

Křížková, A. (2003). Kariérní vzorce žen v. managementu. Strategie žen v rámci genderového režimu organizace. Sociologický časopis, 4, 447–467.

Lenderová, M. (1999). To sin and prayer. The Woman in the last century. Mladá fronta: Prague (in Czech).

Lenderová, M. (2002). Eve not only in paradise. Women in the Czech lands from medieval times to the 19th century. Karolinum: Prague (in Czech).

Maříková, H. (1999). Muž v rodině: demokratizace sféry soukromé. Praha: Sociologický ústav AV ČR.

Maříková, H. (2003). Sociální partnerství muže a ženy v dnešním manželství a rodině—realita nebo fikce? In A. Vodáková & O. Vodáková (Eds.), Rod ženský. Praha: Sociologické nakladatelství.

Matoušek, O. (2003). Rodina jako instituce a vztahová síť. Praha: Slon.

Možný, I. (1983). Rodina vysokoškolsky vzdělaných manželů. Brno: UJEP.

Možný, I. (1990). Moderní rodina. Mýty a skutečnosti. Brno: BLOK.

Možný, I. (1999). Sociologie rodiny. Praha: SLON.

Plaňava, I. (2000). Manželství a rodiny. Struktura—dynamika—komunikace. Brno: Doplněk.

Rašticová, M. (2004). Percipovaná maskulinita a feminita a postoje k roli ženy v rodině. Doctoral dissertation, Fakulta sociálních studií Masarykovy University, Brno.

Rašticová, M., & Hašková, H. (2002). Rodina a/ nebo profese? Role ženy z pohledu mužů a žen více generací. In I. Plaňava & M. Pilát (Eds.), Děti, mládež a rodina v období transformace (pp. 94–107). Brno: Barrister & Principal.

Šiklová, J. (1993). Are women in Central and Eastern Europe conservative? In N. Funk & M. Mueller (Eds.), Gender politics and post-communism: reflections from Eastern Europe and the former Soviet Union (pp. 74–83). New York: Routledge.

Šiklová, J. (1997). Feminism and the roots of apathy in the Czech Republic. *Social Research, 64*, 258–280.

Šmídová, I. (2003). Matkové. In P. Mareš & T. Potočný (Eds.), *Modernizace a česká rodina* (pp. 157–176). Brno: Barrister & Principal.

Vodochodský, I. (2007). Patriarchát na socialistický způsob: k genderovému řádu státního socialismu. *Gender, rovné příležitosti, výzkum, 8*, 34–42.

Wagnerová, A. (1999). České ženy na cestě od reálného socialismu k reálnému kapitalismu. In A. Chřibková, J. Chuchma, & E. Klimentová (Eds.), *Nové čtení světa. 1./Feminismus devadesátých let českýma očima* (pp. 80–90). Praha: One Woman Press.

# Part III

# Work-Life Integration Strategies

# Chapter 13

# Toward a Mother-Friendly Workplace: Workplace Flexibility Intervention Outcomes

*Elise Jones, Joan C. Chrisler, and Ingrid Johnston-Robledo*

Women have become an increasing presence in the U.S. workforce over the past century, in terms of both representation and influence. However, despite the many advances that have opened previously inaccessible careers to female workers, women continue to struggle to attain and succeed in many professional and managerial jobs. Although gender role socialization and gendered expectations can create a challenging climate that impedes women's progress in the workforce, other obstacles may also influence women to scale back on or leave paid employment altogether. Contrary to the personal choice rhetoric in the popular media, women's decisions to scale back or opt out altogether are complex and influenced by primarily work-based factors (Stone & Lovejoy, 2004). Such "choices" may be optimal for some women, but others cannot afford to cut back their work hours or perceive a dearth of viable options that enable them to fulfill their desire to blend caregiving with workforce participation (Watt, 2010). Although flexible work options are important and beneficial to the majority of workers (Golden, 2009), people tend to agree that women need flexibility more than men do (Fursman & Zodgekar, 2009), largely due to their role as primary caregivers. However, because flexibility is often awarded, along with higher wages, to an organization's most valued workers (Winder, 2009), women are less likely than men to have access to flexibility in their jobs (Fursman & Zodgekar, 2009; Zeytinoglu, 2009). In recognition of women's desire for flexibility and their relative lack of access to it, increasing numbers of employers are investing in flexible work interventions as part of an effort to retain and attract female workers.

The effectiveness of these interventions must be considered in context of how women perceive flexibility options. Sometimes the very efforts meant to support mothers can fall short of expectations or even backfire to the extent that they alienate or penalize women in the workplace (Bailyn, 2011). With this in mind, we present background information on women and work and highlight implications for mothers in the workforce, and then share insights related to workplace flexibility that can be used to address the challenges we identified.

## WOMEN AND WORK

In recent decades, organizations have placed importance on building a diverse workforce. Diverse groups have been shown to come up with more and better ideas and to affect more positive outcomes than groups comprising homogenous individuals (Carli, 2010). For example, Catalyst (2007) examined the benefits of women's involvement in the workplace and showed that *Fortune* 500 companies with the highest percentages of women on their boards significantly outperformed those with lower percentages on multiple financial measures. Other studies have confirmed a positive relationship between women's percentage in top management teams of *Fortune* 1,000 companies and their financial performance (Kark & Eagly, 2010). Given that at least 82% of women become mothers at some point (Census Bureau, 2011), and most of them spend a significant portion of their time caring for their children, it is important for organizations to consider the unique needs of mothers in the design and implementation of interventions intended to bolster diverse workforce participation.

## WOMEN'S CURRENT WORKFORCE PARTICIPATION

In 2010, women made up 47% of the workforce, a substantial increase over 29.6% in 1950; 33.9% of women were working outside the home in 1950, and that figure rose to 58.6% in 2010. The gains are particularly noteworthy for mothers; 70% of married mothers were in the workforce in 2010 (Department of Labor, 2011), whereas only 17% were in the workforce in1948 (Cohany & Sok, 2007). Those figures represent dramatically increased access to employment options for women; however, a focus on the amount and type of work currently performed by women sheds light on the remaining gender equity divide.

Despite their increased labor force contributions, women lag behind men in the amount and consistency of their participation in the labor force (Kark & Eagly, 2010). The first distinction between female and male workers concerns the average number of hours worked per week. The Bureau of Labor Statistics counts workers as full-time if they work at least 35 hours per week. In 2010, female workers were more than twice as likely as male workers to work part-time; 27% of all employed women worked part-time, but only 13% of employed men did. Sixty-six percent of female college graduates worked flextime or part-time at some point in their careers (Hewlett, Forster, Sherbin, Shiller, & Sumberg, 2010).

Given the lower status and decreased control experienced by part-time workers in many fields, consideration must be given to full/part-time status in any comparison of workforce participation across gender and across motherhood status. Although those who worked part-time are represented in the employment figures, the rate at which they contribute to and advance within the workforce does not keep pace with that of their full-time counterparts. In addition, U.S. part-time female workers earn 20% less on an hourly basis than those with similar personal characteristics who work full-time (Hudson, 1999). Although the propensity of women to "choose" part-time work need not reflect poorly on employers' efforts to build mother-friendly workplaces, this trend should be considered in any discussion of the composition of the workforce and women's labor force participation rates.

Any discussion of women's rise in the workforce should also reflect the jobs in which male and female workers are employed. Research has shown female workers to be clustered in lower-status, lower-paid jobs relative to male workers (Kelly, Moen, & Tranby, 2011). Although some women take these jobs because they have less education, training, or work experience than is necessary for higher-paid jobs, many women, particularly mothers, work in jobs below their qualifications and educational attainment in exchange for the flexibility they desire or require to invest in caregiving and household labor (Fursman & Zodgekar, 2009). In one study (Connolly & Gregory, 2008), 29% of women with supervisory responsibilities who moved from full-time to part-time work shifted to an occupation or position at a lower level of qualification. Downgrading often occurs earlier in the career lifecycle, as women more often than men enter occupations with lower pay and status due to perceived incompatibilities with home and family (Watt, 2010). As women in the United States now earn 58% of bachelor's degrees and the majority of graduate degrees, the amount and type of women's labor force participation represents a significant gender gap in terms of both underutilized credentials and gender equity in leadership and decision making.

An important point to consider is the lack of representation in the data of women who self-select out of the workforce. Because women who face the greatest conflict between work and family obligations are the most likely to leave the labor force (Kelly et al., 2011), their perspectives and experiences, which are likely to be more extreme than those of their employed peers, are not reflected in the data on how women experience and respond to work-life conflict. If anything, this consideration exacerbates the effects of the forces that impact women in the workforce.

## WORKPLACE OBSTACLES UNIQUE TO WOMEN

Even for women who manage to secure positions of influence and power, the workplace presents obstacles different from those experienced by men. Four characteristics of the work environment in particular create more challenges for women than for men (Kark & Eagly, 2010); each has additional implications for mothers and those who plan to become mothers.

First, many employers equate long hours and the willingness to relocate with success (Kark & Eagly, 2010). The model of the postindustrial full-time worker, with expectations for continuous workforce attachment independent of the need to maintain a home and raise children, is still reflected in most of today's job descriptions, regardless of the changing shape of the workforce (Coltrane & Shih, 2010). This assumption disadvantages women, who experience greater stress from extremely long work hours because they are less likely than men to be able to shift domestic responsibilities to a partner (Kark & Eagly, 2010). Ironically, putting in more hours at work actually yields a lower return for mothers, whose relationship between work hours and managerial advancement has been shown to be weaker than that of nonmothers. Also, as less than one-third of married women earn more than their husbands (Department of Labor, 2010a), few are as willing to relocate as employers may desire.

Second, because well-established organizations (and the broader professional contexts from which newer organizations are derived) were formed and operated by men, women often encounter a male-dominated culture in the workplace (Kark & Eagly, 2010). Characterized by masculine gender-role expectations, the workplace rewards agentic behavior, as manifest through a self-interested, task-focused orientation. Autonomy, dominance, achievement, and control—all stereotypically masculine traits—are likewise associated with professional success. However, feminine gender-role expectations require women to be communal: concerned with the welfare of others and with interpersonal relationships. Women are expected to be kind and helpful, even when they are operating in an environment defined by typical masculine behavior.

Herein is a double bind—although women who behave in an agentic manner are seen as competent, the contrast with the feminine gender role often causes them not to be liked (Chrisler & Clapp, 2008); people tend to find women more likable, albeit less competent, when they perform their traditional roles. For example, participants in social psychology studies have rated homemakers as warmer and more likable than career women (Eckes, 2002) and working mothers as warmer, but less competent, than working fathers and workers of both genders who do not have children (Cuddy, Fiske, & Glick, 2004). Women are therefore required to master both agentic and communal behavior to be seen as competent and likable, a balancing act that is especially difficult for pregnant women, whose physical status makes their gender role salient to coworkers (Glick & Fiske, 2007). To succeed, women must walk the fine line to overcome doubts about their competence, yet not appear to be too assertive or self-serving (Carli, 2010). Mothers also need to be wary of gender-role "spill-over," which has been shown to affect perceptions and expectations of women in the workplace (Glick & Fiske, 2007; Nieva & Gutek, 1981). Spill-over occurs when coworkers are reminded of women's family roles either because they have accepted feminine gendered responsibilities at work (e.g., taking minutes at meetings, making coffee for the group) or because their family responsibilities are obvious to coworkers (e.g., taking "too many" calls from children during meetings, leaving early "too often").

A third challenge women face in the workplace relates to the relationships they build with others. Although in other realms, women's propensity and ability to create close personal relationships is a great asset (Swicker & DeLongis, 2010), those relationships provide far less leverage in the workplace. Because their networks tend to include other women who are likewise in positions of lesser authority and power, women are less likely to form the type of connections that men rely on to advance in their careers (Kark & Eagly, 2010). Women's networks often reflect, rather than challenge, systems of disadvantage in the workplace (Perriton, 2006), and they may not help women to acknowledge and overcome structural barriers to their advancement (O'Neil, Hopkins, & Sullivan, 2011). Furthermore, African American women may be excluded from informal social networks within corporate settings (Combs, 2003).

Differences in social networking behaviors between men and women exacerbate the barriers experienced by mothers. One study (Metz, 2005) indicates that participation in workplace networks actually impedes the advancement of mothers, but not of nonmothers. Perhaps their shared motherhood status leads women with children to network primarily with other mothers and to focus their interactions on non-work-related issues more than other employees do. This could explain the negative relationship between time spent in networking activities and professional advancement for mothers.

A fourth barrier faced by women in the workplace is the challenge of obtaining desirable assignments. In addition to their relative lack of professional connections, women's advancement is threatened by their concentration in staff functions (e.g., human resources, public relations) rather than the line functions (those directly related to the objectives of the organization that directly affect income or customer experience) from which workers are generally promoted to more senior positions. Because of this, few women secure the opportunity to show themselves as high-potential managers (Kark & Eagly, 2010).

## THE SECOND SHIFT

Although each of the foregoing obstacles can be attributed to gender-role stereotypes and gendered expectations, perhaps no barrier is as prominent as the additional responsibilities of caring for children and home. The efforts of diversity advocates to minimize differences between groups of workers, together with "politically correct" attitudes toward fathers' expected involvement in the home, may lead some to disregard the extra weight still carried by mothers. Although women's roles have changed in many respects, a belief in separate gender spheres continues to place a significantly greater portion of household work on women and childcare on mothers (Coltrane & Shih, 2010), many of whom work a "second shift" (Hochschild & Machung, 1989) when they get home from work each day. Even in dual-earner couples, work/family role boundaries have been shown to be asymmetrically permeable for women and men; men more often manage to keep family commitments from intruding on work time, whereas women's family responsibilities regularly impede their work experiences, as well as the amount of time and type of work they do. These commitments include for most women a greater burden of housework—despite significant increases in men's domestic labor, women today still perform two-thirds of all household work (Coltrane & Shih, 2010). In addition, employed mothers of children under age 13 spend an average of 5.4 hours on workdays with their children (Galinsky, Aumann, & Bond, 2011); dual-earner mothers dedicate one-and-a-half times as many hours to childcare as do their husbands (Bureau of Labor Statistics, 2007). Single mothers, who have no partner to share any of the housework and childcare, and low-income mothers, who cannot afford to pay for household help or other services, experience more strain than women with greater resources, but they are often able to rely on extended family and a network of friends and neighbors in order to manage. In sum, the physical and emotional burden born by mothers is significant.

The burden of the "second shift" is often reflected in the work-life conflict reports of mothers. A study (Hill, Jacob, Shannon, Brennan, Blanchard, & Margtinengo, 2008) of multiple companies revealed that being female was associated with greater family-to-work conflict and greater stress and burnout. Similar results were found in another study (Jang, 2009), where female employees reported positive well-being less frequently than male employees did. Employed mothers with young children are more likely to experience work-family conflict than are their male counterparts (Hill, Jacob et al., 2008). For example, in a study of IBM employees in 75 countries, workers in all regions of the world who had a dependent child age five years or younger reported more conflict than workers without a child in that age range. In addition, mothers' well-being has been shown to suffer more than fathers' when they believe they do not have enough time with their children or spouse (Kelly et al., 2011). Men do not typically experience the same familial pressures, as they tend to have wives who are not working or whose work hours are shorter than their own (Kark & Eagly, 2010), and they have not been socialized to feel as responsible as women do for the well-being of their relationships.

## OPTIONS FOR FACILITATING WORK-LIFE INTEGRATION

The pressure felt by women in general, and by mothers in particular, to manage the demands of work and family is significant. Although some mothers manage to tend to home responsibilities and maintain full momentum in their careers, others take alternate routes in response to this combination of barriers.

An increasing number of women opt out of motherhood. In 2002, 5.7% of all ever-married women in their reproductive years indicated a preference not to have children, nearly triple the rate reported in 1976 (Chancey, 2006). The fact that 40% of women in the top percentile of wage earnings in the United States do not have children is evidence of the effectiveness of this strategy (Kark & Eagly, 2010). Other women, as noted previously, take a job for which they are overqualified but that offers the flexibility they need to tend to domestic responsibilities.

Another option, for those who can afford it financially, is to scale back one's work to part-time, which usually entails a step down in responsibility and control as well as pay and benefits. As a result of pressure on employers to offer more part-time options, an increasing number of women in high-status, high-paid professions have secured part-time status (Hill, Grzywacz et al., 2008). That said, the prospects for widespread career-track part-time work reflect numerous financial and cultural complications.

Another choice open to mothers who can afford to consider it is to step out of the paid workforce altogether. As 30% of mothers of children under 18 were not in the workforce in 2010, this appears to be the most viable option for many mothers. Indeed, 43% of mothers with very strong educational credentials, as compared to 37% of similarly qualified women without children and 24% of men, voluntarily drop out of employment at some point (Hewlett, Luce, Shiller, & Southwell, 2005). However, mothers' interrupted workforce participation is associated with a significant loss in lifetime earnings, identified by Crittenden (2001) as the "mommy tax," and slowed career advancement (Chrisler & Johnston-Robledo, 2011; Stone & Lovejoy, 2004). In fact, negative repercussions extend beyond the impact on immediate and future earnings to mothers' psychological well-being and the sensitivity with which they parent their young children (Buehler & O'Brien, 2011).

Although much gender inequity in the workplace hinges on sociocultural expectations of women and men that are changing over time, certain interventions can be instrumental in promoting the retention and advancement of mothers and women who want to become mothers. One of the primary supports is control over when and where work is performed. Mothers of young children have been shown to benefit more than any other group of workers from various workplace flexibility interventions aimed at providing such control, which has led to significant gains in the number of hours they are able to work before work-family conflict surfaces (Hill et al., 2010). Accordingly, workplace flexibility has been identified as a primary mechanism in numerous corporate efforts to retain female workers.

However, whether women feel comfortable taking advantage of these options depends on the perceived climate of support from supervisors and coworkers (Golden, 2009). Unfortunately, a supportive climate does not appear to be the norm. In one study (Fursman & Zodgekar, 2009), 27% of respondents reported that they would be nervous about asking their employers for flexibility, based on the perception that coworkers would have to pick up the slack and that they would progress more slowly in their careers. Many feared being perceived as less committed to their jobs if they were to take advantage of flexible work options. The extent to which this perceived stigma impacts actual utilization and effectiveness of workplace flexibility options is not well known, although negative perceptions of flexibility program participants are noted throughout the literature (e.g., Atkinson & Hall, 2009; Kark & Eagly, 2010; Metz, 2005; Muse, 2011).

Whereas negative perceptions of workplace flexibility can inhibit uptake and thwart effectiveness, a strong organizational culture can support positive perceptions of workplace flexibility, which can help workers to balance work and family responsibilities and to feel happier and less stressed (Jang, 2009). In many ways, flexibility functions as a lens on the effectiveness of an organization, exposing poor management practices that render its implementation problematic. To the extent that organizations can anticipate such difficulties, the establishment of flexible work practices can improve the climate not only for mothers and others who can benefit from greater flexibility, but for all workers.

In the remainder of this chapter we focus on considerations regarding, and steps employers can take to create, a work environment that reduces barriers for and provides direct support to women with children and those who intend to have children. Although much work can be done to address the effects of gender-role expectations that contribute to a difficult climate for women, our analysis focuses on interventions specific to workplace flexibility, with considerations of how cultural factors and negative consequences (e.g., stigma) can impact such efforts. Many examples, both successful and less so, of organizations building mother-friendly policies and programs are mentioned.

It is important to note that fathers, whose rise in work-life conflict over the past 30 years has been documented (Galinsky et al., 2011), and other caregivers can also benefit from the workplace flexibility interventions discussed here. However, the intersectionalities of work and family experienced uniquely by mothers merit treatment of this theme from their perspective. It is encouraging to see increased interest in and efforts to support work-life balance for fathers, as demonstrated by the recent "The New Dad" study conducted by researchers at the Boston College Center for Work and Family (Harrington, Van Deusen, & Humberd, 2011), as well as governmental programs in Scandinavia to help fathers attain greater work-life balance (Kvande, 2009). The growing recognition of the role of fathers, together with their increased use of work-life supports, will not only address their own work-life conflict issues but will also help to confirm the validity of supports currently viewed as "accommodations" for women. Indeed, men's utilization of "family-friendly" flexibility policies may help to counter longstanding workplace norms built around masculine gender-role stereotypes (Kark & Eagly, 2010; Metz, 2005) and thus create greater accessibility for women to positions traditionally held by men, as well as fewer negative perceptions of both men and women in flexible work arrangements.

## ELEMENTS OF THE MOTHER-FRIENDLY FLEXIBLE WORKPLACE

Increasing numbers of employers are initiating flexibility measures to improve the work environment for women, especially mothers. For example, Merck's Global Workplace Flexibility Initiative was created as one of three initiatives to retain women; IBM instituted its "new-concept part-time work" program to retain mothers of preschool children, and has put in practice a host of other flexibility programs as well (Hill, Martinson, Ferris, & Baker, 2004; Hill et al., 2010). Ernst & Young's flexible work arrangements program has contributed to the doubling of the number of female partners in a span of eight years (Powers, 2004). Although examples from the United States are highlighted here, it is important to note the greater availability and more advanced nature of support for mothers outside the United States, particularly in European nations. Examples from other countries are included to illustrate what more can be done in societies with a richer history of supporting mothers in the workplace.

## WORKPLACE FLEXIBILITY

Workplace flexibility can be described as "the ability of workers to make choices that influence when, where, and for how long they engage in work-related tasks" (Hill, Grzywacz et al., 2008, p. 152). In addition to formal dimensions of family-friendly human-resource initiatives, flexible scheduling incorporates informal aspects, such as organizational culture, employee relations, and managerial discretion (Golden, 2009). In its more formal iterations, workplace flexibility can take various shapes, including the ability to vary workday start times, end times, and break times; to work from a remote location; to work fewer hours than those considered full-time; and to vary the workload or typical work schedule across the course of a calendar year.

Although many early workplace flexibility programs were initiated in an effort to retain mothers, these efforts are now generally accepted as an effective business strategy for supporting all kinds of employees across the multiple facets and obligations of their lives (Atkinson & Hall, 2009; Hill et al., 2010). However, flexible work options continue to be of particular interest to mothers given the disproportionate amount of childcare and household labor for which they are responsible. Several specific forms of flexible working are described in the following.

### Flexible Schedules

Flexible schedules can be defined as variable starting and ending times for the workday. They may include the ability to take time off during the workday and make it up at another time without using vacation or sick time. Flexible hours may be used to accommodate individual employee preferences for working early in the morning or late in the evening, or to take care of personal needs (e.g., breastfeeding, breast pumping) and errands most efficiently handled during the workday (e.g., medical appointments). Parents may take advantage of flexible hours to minimize the need for before- or after-school childcare, to volunteer at a school, or to participate in family mealtimes even in times of heavy workloads.

Schedule flexibility has been shown to be the most valued form of flexibility by both corporate men and women in every life stage (Hill et al., 2010), and it is considered by many to be the bedrock of any organizational flexibility initiative due to its broad appeal. In 2008, 31% of U.S. employers allowed flexible hours for at least some workers, up from 24% in 1998 (Galinsky, Bond, & Sakai, 2008).

### Telework

Telework is the ability to work either occasionally or regularly from a location other than the main workplace; it is often referred to as work-at-home. Formal telework may apply to the full workweek or only certain segments of the workweek. Informal telework may be used by workers who are waiting for home deliveries or maintenance calls, and it may be an alternative to taking sick time. Informal telework may enable parents to care for a sick child without taking time off from work. Parents and nonparents alike employ formal telework to avoid lengthy commutes or to secure blocks of uninterrupted work time. Although it is usually not an effective substitute for childcare, formal telework can increase interaction between parent and child during the day, which could be especially helpful to new mothers.

Although home-based workers may report some negative effects of isolation from other workers, these workers have been shown to report levels of work-life balance support and job satisfaction similar to those of office workers (Morganson, 2010). The ability to work from home has been shown to benefit mothers in particular; only 23% of women with children age five years and younger who worked primarily at home reported work-life difficulty, whereas 38% of those who did not work primarily from home reported difficulty (Hill et al., 2010). Based on data from self-report measures of work-life conflict, Hill et al. (2010) concluded that working primarily from home can make a full-time work schedule possible for a woman with small children who would otherwise need to reduce work hours by 25% in order to achieve work-life harmony.

## Reduced or Seasonal Schedules

Reduced hours, or part-time work, refer to the ability to work fewer hours than comprise a standard workweek. Employees on seasonal schedules may work a standard workweek most of the year, then take the summer months off to spend more time with their families. Senior workers often employ part-time work as an alternative to retirement. Others utilize it as a means to continue working while pursuing further education. Parents, most often mothers, tend to choose part-time work to have more time with their children (Hewlett et al., 2005).

Mothers of young children who could afford the option overwhelmingly report that they would prefer to work part-time, regardless of whether they currently have part-time status (Taylor, Funk, & Clark, 2007). This preference for part-time work is not surprising given that number of work hours is positively correlated with work-life conflict across all types of workers (Hill et al., 2010). Mothers with dependent children, in particular, have been shown to perceive fewer conflicts between work and family life when they commit fewer hours to employment (Buehler & O'Brien, 2011). Thus, it is not surprising that the rate of women's part-time employment has been estimated at triple that of men's; women's use of part-time work peaks in the prime childrearing years of 35–44 (Hill, Jacob et al., 2008). However, that only 2% of the professional employees of *Fortune* magazine's "100 Best Companies to Work for 2000" were part-timers re-flects the scarcity of part-time positions for managerial and professional women. In contrast, and in line with their gendered role as breadwinners, men show little interest in and almost no use of flexibility options that would reduce their pay and status (Hill, Jacob et al., 2008).

The use of different forms of flexibility in combination with each other can generate synergistic benefits for workers. At IBM, only 17% of women with children age five or younger who utilized flexible scheduling to-gether with work-at-home options reported work-life conflict difficulties, as compared to 55% of their non-work-at-home, low-flexibility counter-parts (Hill et al., 2010).

It is interesting that, although specific interventions that influence time, place, and hours of work may not apply to all workers in a company, the perception of flexibility positively impacts workers' work-family fit re-gardless of whether these options are used because awareness of the op-tions produces feelings of empowerment and an increased sense of agency (B. L. Jones et al., 2008). In the case of IBM, the perception of schedule flexi-bility was shown to be of greater benefit than the actual practice of working at home in every region of the world (Hill et al., 2010).

Although in general, U.S. employers are not required to extend work-place flexibility to mothers or any other group of workers, certain condi-tions may require flexible options under the provisions of the Family and Medical Leave Act (FMLA). FMLA provides eligible employees 12 weeks of unpaid leave in a 12-month period to care for a spouse, child, or par-ent who has a serious health condition, or to deal with one's own serious health condition. Under some circumstances, this benefit may be taken intermittently, in effect by reducing the employee's usual weekly or daily work schedule (Department of Labor, 2010b).

Many other countries have legislated flexibility supports for parents of young children. For example, since 1978 Swedish parents have had the right to work six hours a day until their children turn eight years old. Fol-lowing the 1997 E.U. Directive on Part-Time Work, Germany, Belgium, and the Netherlands granted similar provisions to parents. A recent U.K. law grants workers the right to request a flexible work arrangement, including part-time, to care for a child under age six (Gornick, Eisenbrey, & Heron, 2007). Likewise, New Zealand's Employment Relations Amendment Act of 2007 enables caregiving workers with at least six months of tenure to request a flexible work arrangement (Fursman & Zodgekar, 2009).

Given the potential to increase positive outcomes for female workers with children, and in hopes of addressing work-life conflict for all work-ers, many U.S. employers have initiated workplace flexibility practices. More than one-half of workers today enjoy some type of flexible schedule; however, female workers (especially those in nonprofessional settings) may be less likely than their male counterparts to have flexible schedules due to the types of jobs that tend to be occupied by women (Fursman & Zodgekar, 2009; Zeytinoglu, 2009). The number of employers in 2008 who said they have allowed staff to work remotely was 42%, up from 30% the previous year (WorldatWork, 2008), and studies show that part-time work options, especially for women, are increasing (Hill et al., 2004). However, although U.S. employers are making strides toward facilitating the flexibility that could help mothers better balance work and life responsibilities, a sizable gap remains. Employers who are considering initiating or bolstering support for workplace flexibility will benefit from a review of the impact that such programs can bring, both to the employees they seek to support and to their own operations and bottom line.

## DEMONSTRATED IMPACT OF WORKPLACE FLEXIBILITY

Although some business leaders initiate mother-supportive programs out of a desire to "do the right thing," most employers do so based on a strong business case. Concerns have been raised that providing specialized supports to women represents "dangerous" tinkering with a market economy, but research has indicated that family-friendly policies do not undermine market efficiency (Wax, 2004). When work-life supports are effectively implemented and utilized, mothers and other workers benefit in significant ways. The benefits are in turn passed on to employers.

## BENEFITS TO WORKERS

Although the original discussion of workplace flexibility was initiated in response to the unique work-life conflict issues facing employed women with children, the benefits of workplace flexibility can be separated into individual factors that contribute to an enhanced state of well-being for mothers and for other workers. Research shows that these benefits are also passed on directly to the families of these workers (Estes, 2004).

Perhaps the most overarching benefit of work-life supports for mothers is their propensity to alleviate the role conflict experienced by women in the workplace, in public life, and at home. Although workplace flexibility options may not directly alter the role of women in the home, they do provide additional options for mothers in balancing home and family roles with their responsibilities in the workplace, and thus increase the likelihood of mothers' continued workforce attachment. That these options impact mothers' workforce participation is evidenced by the 86% employment rate of mothers in Sweden where government-sponsored programs include flexible work arrangements (Bjornberg & Dahlgren, 2003). In contrast, in the United States where fewer supports are offered, just 68% of mothers of preschool children are employed. With flexibility support, women may be more likely to take on positions of greater influence, and thus gain higher earnings and greater negotiating power both in the workplace and at home. From this strengthened position women are more likely to request and obtain support from their partners in managing the needs of the family and the household (Coltrane & Shih, 2010).

The impact of workplace flexibility on work-life balance and work-family conflict has been demonstrated in many settings. At Merck 87% of those who reported having the flexibility they need said that they were able to manage multiple demands, compared with just 29% of those who did not have the needed flexibility (Muse, 2011). Research at IBM indicates that flexibility in both time and place of work is related to less work-life conflict (Hill et al., 2010). Numerous other studies link the perception and utilization of workplace flexibility with an increased sense of work-life balance (Fursman & Zodgekar, 2009; Jang, 2009; Morganson, 2010).

In addition, several studies have identified an association between workplace flexibility and employees' health (Butler, Grzywacz, Ettner, & Liu, 2009; Hill et al., 2008); both stress and burnout are lower among workers in all types of formal flexible arrangements (Grzywacz, Carlson, & Shulkin, 2008). Those who utilize flexibility report getting more hours of sleep and exercise, participating in company-supported stress management activities, and enjoying a better self-appraised lifestyle (Grzywacz, Casey, & Jones, 2007). Thus, the use of workplace flexibility may help prevent chronic illness (Butler et al., 2009).

## BENEFITS TO EMPLOYERS

Although early work-life policies sprang from a desire to respond to the needs of mothers (Hill, Jacob et al., 2008), most organizations now lead with the business case for supporting family-friendly initiatives. Indeed, research on flexible schedules has shown that these supports are often created for business reasons (Zeytinoglu, 2009). Certainly, programs put in place with mothers in mind will reap rewards across all types of employees.

Employee engagement is defined as a heightened emotional and intellectual connection that employees have with their job, organization, manager, or coworkers that, in turn, influences them to apply additional discretionary effort to their work (Richman, Civian, Shannon, Hill, & Brennan, 2008). Engagement has been linked to employer outcomes of customer retention, stock price, and revenue per person (Johnson, Shannon, & Richman, 2008). Research shows that the degree to which employees consider themselves as having the flexibility they desire accurately predicts their engagement; this holds across all types of workers (Pitt-Catsouphes & Matz-Costa, 2008). Other factors that contribute to employee engagement include the existence of supportive work-life policies and the degree to which employees perceive that they have flexibility (Richman et al., 2008). In a study of Merck employees in 77 countries, workers who reported having the flexibility they need were found to have significantly higher engagement than those who did not (9.85 vs. 7.61 on a 10-point scale; Muse, 2011).

With the cost of turnover estimated at 93–150% of departing employees' annual salary and up to 200% of annual salary for highly skilled and senior employees (Johnson, 1995), improved retention is one of the primary factors that motivate employers to enact work-life policies. Indeed, an organization that succeeds in attracting women but is unable to retain them can be likened to a leaky bucket. Much evidence indicates that flexibility programs are effective in promoting the retention of mothers and of all workers. For example, Deloitte's flexibility policies saved more than $45 million a year by reducing turnover (Greenhouse, 2011), and 74% of participants (more than 500 individuals) in IBM's "new concept jobs" program for mothers of preschool children reported that they would have left the company had they not been offered the part-time option (Hill et al., 2004). Forty-nine percent of those surveyed at Merck cited workplace flexibility as the reason they stayed with the company, and turnover intent was twice as high for those who said that they lacked the flexibility they needed. In addition, 65% of employees cited workplace flexibility as part of their reason for joining the company (Muse, 2011). These findings were confirmed in another study (Lee, 2011) that showed that workers' flexibility satisfaction has a greater impact on turnover than overall job satisfaction does.

One of the common concerns on the part of employers new to workplace flexibility is whether work will actually get done outside the realm of the traditional workplace, a concern that is compounded in times of economic downturns and increased workloads. A study of multiple organizations (Johnson et al., 2008) revealed that flexibility is not incompatible with growing work demands. Other research shows that, given the increased ability to control how and when work gets done, workers reward their employers with increased productivity. For example, Best Buy reported that average productivity was 35% greater in groups that implemented the Results Only Work Environment than in groups that did not (Kelly et al., 2011). The Global Work and Life Issues Survey administered to 24,436 IBM employees in 75 countries revealed that employees with schedule flexibility can contribute up to two extra eight-hour days per week before reporting work-life conflict. The benefit was particularly pronounced for women with small children, who reported a difference of 27 hours per week in their work-family conflict breakpoint with and without schedule flexibility (Hill et al., 2010). Finally, Xerox experienced a 30% decrease in absenteeism as a result of their workplace flexibility initiative (Bailyn, 2011).

Work-life support programs have been shown to be successful in attracting female employees by cultivating an image of a mother-friendly workplace (Johnson et al., 2008). Just as important, the existence of these programs has been shown to be instrumental in helping women to advance to become

senior leaders within the organization (Johnson et al., 2008). It is not surprising that the positive results of work-life programs extend beyond the immediate work environment; flexible schedules have been shown to enhance an
organization's reputation with customers as well as employees (Pollitt, 2008).

All of the preceding benefits are assumed to have an indirect impact on
financial performance, but research has identified direct benefits of workplace flexibility as well. For example, one study (Martínez-Sánchez, Pérez-
Pérez, Vela-Jiménez, & de-Luis-Carnicer, 2008) revealed that company
performance is positively associated with the intensity of telework adoption. To summarize, the implementation of work-life policies that benefit
mothers can reap substantial benefits for all employees impacted by such
programs, as well as for employers themselves.

## BARRIERS TO WORKPLACE FLEXIBILITY SUCCESS

Although employer-initiated flexibility can have the positive impacts
discussed earlier, not all workplace flexibility programs are as successful.
Several studies have identified challenges related to the implementation
of family-friendly practices, as well as important factors for the effective
implementation of alternative work arrangements (Fursman & Zodgekar,
2009; Morganson, 2010; Wax, 2004; Wickramasinghe & Jayabandu, 2007).
Among these, perhaps the most damaging, and the most elusive, is the effect of negative perceptions regarding the use of workplace flexibility. In
this section we discuss the roots of such perceptions and their impact on
the utilization and effectiveness of workplace flexibility options.

## NEGATIVE PERCEPTIONS OF USERS OF FLEXIBILITY

Although interest in flexibility is strong across many different types
of workers, and is of particular interest to mothers, negative perceptions about the use of such options is a major obstacle to the implementation, utilization, and effectiveness of workplace flexibility initiatives. The
stigma of workplace flexibility use comes in many forms. Workers may
fear being perceived as less committed to the organization if they place
boundaries on their availability (Atkinson & Hall, 2009). They may fear
being associated with gender stereotypes related to women that are not
in keeping with workplace norms (Kark & Eagly, 2010; Metz, 2005), a reality that may help explain men's relatively low utilization of flexibility
options (Bird, 2002). Furthermore, workers may fear that utilizing flexible
work arrangements may generate resentment, and even hostility, among
coworkers and perhaps prevent them from advancing in their careers
(Metz, 2005). These fears are compounded when an employer's flexibility
programs are not consistent with the organizational culture (Kornberger,
Carter, & Ross-Smith, 2010) and when that culture relies on superficial

means of determining effectiveness (e.g., face time) that are more difficult for those working flexibly to exhibit (Elsbach, Cable, & Sherman, 2010). Given the stigma surrounding such initiatives, some warn that these policies may widen the gender wage gap and contribute to women's continued lower representation in high-status and high-earning management positions (Kark & Eagly, 2010).

Atkinson and Hall (2009) pointed out that, because formal flexibility supports are typically considered a women's issue, much effort is needed to support mothers without negative cultural repercussions. In one poignant example, a flexibility initiative was implemented in a Big Four accounting firm in Australia for the express purpose of retaining women. Given the contrast between the flexibility policies initiated and a workplace culture based on employees' physical presence in the office and total hours worked as opposed to results generated, not only was the program ineffective at retaining women, but it was actually found to reinforce gender barriers among workers. Rather than bolstering women's careers, participation in the program became equated with not being serious about one's career (Kornberger et al., 2010).

The results of a recent study (E. B. Jones, 2011) suggest that forms of flexibility that vary most from accepted ways of working may evoke the greatest negative perceptions. Insights into a possible relationship between stigma and flexibility uptake and effectiveness will be presented in the following. First, however, we consider barriers that may arise in the design and implementation stage, based on the first author's experience working in the human resources department of a large high-tech firm.

## DESIGN AND IMPLEMENTATION ISSUES

It is not uncommon for work-life programs to germinate in the human resources department but never come to full fruition. One of the potential obstacles early in the design phase is the inability to define accurately the problem that needs to be addressed. Before programs move forward they must illustrate a clear link between a problem to be solved and the desired outcome. Because work-life programs address a broad range of issues within an organization, those initiating work-life supports may need to focus in on a few clear objectives rather than trying to solve all organizational problems for all populations at once in order to achieve the clarity needed to take the program beyond conception to actual design and implementation.

A related challenge is the need to gain support from organizational leaders. Although work-life programs are initiated from the top in some organizations, others result from issues identified within individual workgroups or as a result of workers' requests. In addition to clear articulation of the need for such programs, those sponsoring such efforts must be able to define the prospective business impact of implementation. Although sponsors will benefit greatly from quantifying the potential impact based on improved retention rates or other concrete measures, they should not rely wholly on those measures. Incorporating a broad range of benefits (e.g., job satisfaction) to the organization and workers alike will provide the strongest foundation for enlisting the support of business leaders.

A final barrier to design and implementation relates to the structures and systems needed to implement family-friendly policies. Although some policies such as flexible hours are implemented informally within some organizations, and thus require little structural or systemic support, others, such as part-time schedules and telework, can require integration with complex information systems or facilities planning. Overlooking the intricacy of such arrangements or the need to work across groups juggling multiple priorities can stalemate an effort long before it gets off the ground.

## UTILIZATION ISSUES

After investing in the design and implementation of family-friendly initiatives, organizations are eager to reap the rewards of these programs. However, several factors can inhibit the actual adoption of options provided by these programs.

A major barrier to the uptake of flexibility options is a lack of awareness that such options exist (Atkinson & Hall, 2009). Many organizations implement flexibility on a case-by-case basis and fail to communicate the existence of such options to the broad group of workers. This has been cited as a reason for which early career workers, in particular, are less likely to utilize flexible work options (Bird, 2002).

Even when knowledge of flexibility programs is more widespread, workers may feel unsure about initiating a request when the process for doing so is unclear (Atkinson & Hall, 2009). Women with small children, in particular, may not think they have the time or energy to figure out whom to approach or how to propose a flexible arrangement if the request process has not already been made known.

Poor management skills can present a significant barrier to usage of workplace flexibility options (Atkinson & Hall, 2009). Managers who are unaware of, unsure about, or ambivalent toward company flexibility policies and practices can easily dissuade subordinates from pursuing needed flexibility that is, in fact, supported by organizational leaders.

Finally, the stigma of various forms of flexibility has been tied to the rates at which these forms are utilized by mothers. In a recent study (E. B. Jones, 2011) mothers were less likely to use types of flexibility that bear higher levels of stigma; for example, they preferred flexible breaks over part-time work, which was shown to bear the highest level of stigma. Mothers who chose not to use available supports also cited more barriers to utilization of forms of flexible work with higher stigma attached to them.

## POLICY EFFECTIVENESS

Another potential barrier that threatens the success of work-life programs is their actual effectiveness. Programs may be carefully designed and successfully implemented, and employees may sign up to participate, but, unless the benefits for which the program was designed can be achieved through the program, it is unlikely to succeed.

One factor that threatens effective utilization of programs is a disconnect between the programs being implemented and the culture of the locale in which the organization resides. In their study of IBM workers in 77 countries, Hill et al. (2010) demonstrated that telework is less beneficial in countries with collectivist cultures than it is in those with more individualistic cultures. Those whose culture emphasizes the worth of the group may have a harder time accepting subordinates' or coworkers' desire to work in a physical location separate from the rest of the group.

Another obstacle can occur when the benefit offered is not well aligned with individual workers' job functions. A common example is scheduling flexibility for managers. Researchers have identified a number of issues related to the need to be available to subordinates that impedes supervisors' ability to achieve work-life balance through flexibility initiatives (Kelly et al., 2011; Parris, Vickers, & Wilkes, 2008). Likewise, a study of stockbrokers (Blair-Loy, 2009) revealed that schedule flexibility actually increases work-family conflict for these workers because it leads to "workload creep," wherein it broadens the range of hours during which they are expected to respond to customer requests (e.g., during evening hours). Although autonomy and earning power may decrease, scheduling rigidity actually serves the function of buffering these workers from client pressures that intrude on family life.

A final obstacle related to effectiveness is the impact of the perceived stigma of those who use flexibility programs. One study (E. B. Jones, 2011) indicated effectiveness to be high for all forms of flexibility studied; however, effectiveness was also negatively related to perceived stigma across all forms of flexibility. Of particular interest is the significant negative relationship between stigma and effectiveness for formal telework and part-time work, the two forms of flexibility that generally reflect the greatest deviations from accepted forms of working.

## RECOMMENDATIONS TO ORGANIZATIONS

Workplace flexibility can deliver sizable benefits to employers seeking to retain and attract women. However, there are important obstacles to the effective implementation of flexible work initiatives. In this section we highlight a number of suggested approaches gleaned from the experiences of several best-practice organizations mentioned earlier.

Prior to embarking on any organizational change effort (e.g., initiatives to retain women), employers need to understand workers' actual needs. After recognizing an issue with women's retention, Merck formed a task force aimed at identifying the top issues that impact the turnover of female employees. They used a variety of research methods that identified flexibility as one of three issues, and then launched the Global Workforce Flexibility Initiative (GWFI), along with separate initiatives to address low representation of senior women and enhance women's mentoring (Muse, 2011).

Once the desired steps to address workers' needs have been identified, organizations must examine how well such changes mesh with their current culture. Prior to implementing GWFI, leaders at Merck recognized that they would have to change the company's culture to focus on results rather than face time in order to keep participation in flexible work arrangements from becoming a career-limiting move (Muse, 2011). In another example, Best Buy targeted its efforts directly at cultural norms that were holding back flexibility. Each implementation of their Results Only Work Environment approach begins with culture sessions that challenge workers to examine the organizational culture critically and to develop a vision of the desired culture. Role play is used to identify and counter assumptions and expectations not related to actual work results (Kelly et al., 2011).

Employers who recognize the potential detrimental effects of overtly associating work-life programs with women should remove the gender lens before implementing flexibility initiatives. An approach focused on all workers impacts both content and communication. Given the preference shown by men as well as women for flexible scheduling, Hill et al. (2010) recommended including schedule flexibility in addition to reduced schedule and work-from-home options to make flexibility programs universal and relevant for all sorts of caregiving needs. Atkinson and Hall (2009) likewise recommended combining informal flexibility options with more formal implementations to avoid the perception of gender-specific programs. The Best Buy initiative goes by the term "schedule control." Leaders at Xerox opted to name their women's retention effort Collaborative Interactive Action Research, and they focused on redesigning work for effectiveness and creating a humane workplace (Bailyn, 2011). They made flexibility available to all employees for three months without regard to need or performance, as long as the work got done. Although the original intent of flexibility initiatives may be to retain women, making the initiatives applicable and available to everyone helps workers who use them avoid becoming stigmatized and/or marginalized (Kvande, 2009).

Many of employers' as well as workers' concerns about flexible work can be addressed by developing and communicating clear policies, processes, and rationale. Merck utilized input from leaders around the world to develop a consistent global policy supported by well-articulated processes and systems, and then implemented training in 10 languages. A team of 25 employee volunteers conducted an awareness campaign to ensure that the policy was well communicated throughout the organization. A clear communication plan also conveyed that flexibility should not produce negative consequences and helped avoid fostering a culture of entitlement (Muse, 2011).

When obstacles to implementation are identified, effective organizations institute new processes and practices to support program goals. When Boston Consulting Group initiated a regular night off for each team member to address issues of schedule unpredictability, they began assigning a partner to each project to ensure continuous coverage. They also convened weekly team meetings to review the effectiveness of the program and anticipate team members' needs (Bailyn, 2011). In other organizations, flexibility is facilitated by cross-training all employees so that a team member is always available to respond to clients' requests (Lee, 2011).

Finally, employers who wish to reap the full benefits of workplace flexibility initiatives should develop a clear plan to gauge program effectiveness. Those responsible for Merck's Global Workforce Flexibility Initiative identified metrics upfront for measuring continued progress, and they researched employees' attitudes before and after the implementation of the flexibility initiative (Muse, 2011).

Employers who have successfully implemented flexibility policies find themselves engaged in much more than a workplace flexibility plan. As mentioned previously, flexibility can be seen as a lens on the health of the organization and a catalyst for identifying issues of broader impact. Whereas leaders at Xerox started with the intent to address issues of interest to women, they came to see flexibility as a more open and innovative style of managing and an opportunity for rethinking work effectiveness. In addition, they found that flexibility empowered work groups to make decisions more autonomously and enabled divisions to reach their goals (Bailyn, 2011).

Hill, Grzywacz et al. (2008, p. 160) offered a valuable perspective regarding what is at the heart of workplace flexibility and how a flexibility strategy is best implemented:

> Workplace flexibility is more than simply providing a flextime policy or the option to work from home every once in a while—it is a mutual sense of trust and respect between employer and employee, a supportive workplace culture, and an optimal sense of control over one's job and working conditions. . . .

When flexibility is approached in this holistic manner, negative perceptions can be overcome, which then enable women with children, as well as all other workers, to take advantage of options that allow them to balance their work and family responsibilities. Through this approach organizations can both reach their goals of retaining women and create a more effective work environment for all workers.

## CONCLUSION

Our aim was to articulate the unique pressures experienced by employed women with children and to identify measures that can be taken by employers to help mothers balance their work and family responsibilities. Workplace flexibility has been found to be both greatly desired and frequently used by mothers. However, negative perceptions in the workplace about individuals who utilize such options prevent workplace flexibility from reaching and benefiting a large population of those who need them most. Much can be done by employers to prevent and address the stigma attached to flexible work. In line with the assertion that flexibility is a lens on the health of an organization, many of these efforts are as aligned with organizational effectiveness as with workplace flexibility. Understanding employees' needs, setting clear goals and expectations, communicating and making decisions openly, and other effective management practices can go as far or farther in supporting a flexible work environment than any number of awareness campaigns or processes and systems that support formalized flexible work initiatives. However, these formalized steps are essential as well in enabling the flexibility that addresses employed mothers' work-life challenges.

Although the negative perceptions of users of flexibility discussed here are widely acknowledged in the literature (Atkinson & Hall, 2009; Kark & Eagly, 2010; Kornberger et al., 2010; Metz, 2005; Muse, 2011), little attention has been paid to relative levels of stigma among the different forms of flexibility, or to the association between such stigma and the utilization and effectiveness of workplace flexibility options by mothers. Additional research in these areas could help us to pinpoint barriers to implementing successful flexible work environments. Of additional interest are the barriers to part-time work, which continues to be an area of interest for mothers but is not widely available in the professional sector. Further research in these areas, together with application of results of previous research, is needed to create a more equitable professional and social environment that promotes the personal well-being and growth of all employees and enables optimal utilization of the abilities and potential contributions of mothers in the workplace.

## REFERENCES

Atkinson, C., & Hall, L. (2009). The role of gender in varying forms of flexible working. *Gender, Work, and Organization, 16,* 650–666. doi:10.1111/j.1468-0432 .2009.00456.x.

Bailyn, L. (2011). Redesigning work for gender equity and work-personal life integration. *Community, Work, & Family, 14*, 97–112. doi:10.1080/13668803.2010.532660.

Bird, C. E. (2002). Organizational supports for and barriers to part-time work arrangements for professionals: The case of radiology. *Research in the Sociology of Health Care, 20*, 159–182.

Bjornberg, U., & Dahlgren, L. (2003). *Labour supply: The case of Sweden.* Second national report for the Nordic project on Welfare Policies and Employment in the Context of Family Change. Retrieved from http://www.york.ac.uk/inst/spru/research/nordic/swedenlabo.pdf

Blair-Loy, M. (2009). Work without end? Scheduling flexibility and work-to-family conflict among stockbrokers. *Work and Occupations, 36*, 279–317. doi:10.1177/0730888409343912.

Buehler, C., & O'Brien, M. (2011, October 17). Mothers' part-time employment: Associations with mother and family well-being. *Journal of Family Psychology.* Advance online publication. doi:10.1037/a0025993.

Butler, A. B., Grzywacz, J. G., Ettner, S. L., & Liu, B. (2009). Workplace flexibility, self-reported health, and health care utilization. *Work and Stress, 23*, 45–59. doi:10.1080/02678370902833932.

Carli, L. (2010). Gender and group behavior. In J. C. Chrisler & D. R. McCreary (Eds.), *Handbook of gender research in psychology* (Vol. II, pp. 337–358). New York: Springer.

Catalyst. (2007). *Companies with more women board directors experience higher financial performance, according to latest Catalyst bottom line report.* Retrieved from http://www.catalyst.org/press-release/73/companies-with-more-women-board-directors-experience-higher-financial-performance-according-to-latest-catalyst-bottom-line-report/

Census Bureau. (2011, March 17). *Facts for features: Mother's day.* Retrieved from http://www.census.gov/newsroom/releases/pdf/cb11ff-07_mother.pdf

Chancey, L. (2006). *Voluntary childlessness in the United States: Recent trends by cohort and period.* Unpublished master's thesis, Louisiana State University.

Chrisler, J. C., & Clapp, S. K. (2008). When the boss is a woman. In M. A. Paludi (Ed.), *The psychology of women at work: Challenges and solutions for our female workforce* (Vol. 1, pp. 39–65). Westport, CT: Praeger.

Chrisler, J. C., & Johnston-Robledo, I. (2011). Pregnancy discrimination. In M. A. Paludi, C. Paludi, Jr., & E. DeSouza (Eds.), *The Praeger handbook on understanding and preventing workplace discrimination: Legal, management, and social science perspectives* (pp. 105–132). Santa Barbara, CA: Praeger.

Cohany, S. R., & Sok, E. (2007, February). *Trends in labor force participation of married mothers of infants.* Washington, DC: Department of Labor. Retrieved from http://bls.gov/opub/mlr/2007/02/art2full.pdf

Coltrane, S., & Shih, K. Y. (2010). Gender and the division of labor. In J. C. Chrisler & D. R. McCreary (Eds.), *Handbook of gender research in psychology* (Vol. II, pp. 401–422). New York: Springer.

Combs, G. M. (2003). The duality of race and gender for managerial African American women: Implications of informal social networks on career advancement. *Human Resource Development Review, 2*, 385–405.

Connolly, S., & Gregory, M. (2008). Moving down: Women's part-time work and occupational change in Britain 1991–2001. *Economic Journal, 118*, F52–F76. doi:10.1111/j.1468-0297.2007.02116.x.

Crittenden, A. (2001). *The price of motherhood: Why the most important job is still the least valued.* New York: Metropolitan Books.

Cuddy, A.J.C., Fiske, S. T., & Glick, P. (2004). When professionals become mothers, warmth doesn't cut the ice. *Journal of Social Issues, 60,* 701–718.

Department of Labor. (2010a, March). *Women in the labor force: A databook.* Retrieved from http://bls.gov/cps/wlftable25-2010.htm

Department of Labor. (2010b, February). *Fact sheet #28: The Family and Medical Leave Act of 1993.* Retrieved from http://www.dol.gov/whd/regs/compliance /whdfs28.pdf

Department of Labor. (2011, March). *Employment characteristics of families [summary].* Retrieved from http://bls.gov/news.release/famee.nr0.htm

Eckes, T. (2002). Paternalistic and envious gender stereotypes: Testing predictions from the stereotype content model. *Sex Roles, 47,* 99–114.

Elsbach, K. D., Cable, D. M., & Sherman, J. W. (2010). How passive "face time" affects perceptions of employees: Evidence of spontaneous trait inference. *Human Relations, 63,* 735–760. doi: 10.1177/0018726709353139.

Estes, S. B. (2004). How are family-responsive workplace arrangements family friendly? Employer accommodations, parenting, and children's socioemotional well-being. *Sociological Quarterly, 45,* 637–661. doi:10.1111/j.1533-8525.2004 .tb02308.x.

Fursman, L., & Zodgekar, N. (2009). Flexible work arrangements: New Zealand families and their experiences with flexible work. *Family Matters, 81,* 25–36.

Galinsky, E., Aumann, K., & Bond, J. T. (2011). *Times are changing: Gender and generation at work and at home.* New York: Families and Work Institute. Retrieved from https://workfamily.sas.upenn.edu/archive/links/galinsky-e-aumann-k-bond-jt-2009-times-are-changing-gender-and-generation-work-and-hom

Galinsky, E., Bond, J. T., & Sakai, K. (2008). *National study of employers.* New York: Families and Work Institute. Retrieved from http://www.familiesandwork .org/site/research/reports/2008nse.pdf

Glick, P., & Fiske, S. Y. (2007). Sex discrimination: The psychological approach. In F. J. Crosby, M. S. Stockdale, & S. A. Ropp (Eds.), *Sex discrimination in the workplace* (pp. 155–187). Malden, MA: Blackwell.

Golden, L. (2009). Flexible daily work schedules in U.S. jobs: Formal introductions needed? *Industrial Relations, 48,* 27–54. doi:10.1111/j.1468-232X.2008.00544.x.

Gornick, J. C., Heron, A., & Eisenbrey, R. (2007, May 24). *The work-family balance: An analysis of European, Japanese, and U.S. work-time policies.* Washington, DC: Economic Policy Institute. Retrieved from http://www.gpn.org/bp189.html

Greenhouse, S. (2011, January 7). Flex time flourishes in accounting industry. *The New York Times.* Retrieved from http://www.nytimes.com/2011/01/08/busi ness/08perks.html

Grzywacz, J. G., Carlson, D. S., & Shulkin, S. (2008). Schedule flexibility and stress: Linking formal flexible arrangements and perceived flexibility to employee health. *Community, Work, & Family, 11,* 199–214. doi:10.1080/ 13668800802024652.

Grzywacz, J. G., Casey, P. R., & Jones, F. A. (2007). The effects of workplace flexibility on health behaviors: A cross-sectional and longitudinal analysis. *Journal of Occupational and Environmental Medicine, 49,* 1302–1309. doi:10.1097/ JOM.0b013e31815ae9bc.

Harrington, B., Van Deusen, F., & Humberd, B. (2011). *The new dad: Caring, committed, and conflicted.* Chestnut Hill, MA: Boston College Center for Work and Family. Retrieved from http://www.bc.edu/content/dam/files/centers/cwf/pdf/FH-Study-Web-2.pdf

Hewlett, S. A., Forster, D., Sherbin, L., Shiller, P., & Sumberg, K. (2010, June 1). Off-ramps and on-ramps revisited. *Harvard Business Review.* Retrieved from http://www.scribd.com/doc/32365807/Off-Ramps-and-on-Ramps-Revisited

Hewlett, S. A., Luce, C. B., Shiller, P., & Southwell, S. (2005, February 24). The hidden brain drain: Off-ramps and on-ramps in women's careers. *Harvard Business Review.* Retrieved from http://haagsebeek.nl/files/bestanden/hill-erickson-holmes-ferris-2010-8613.pdf

Hill, E. J., Erickson, J. J., Holmes, E. K., & Ferris, M. (2010). Workplace flexibility, work hours, and work-life conflict: Finding an extra day or two. *Journal of Family Psychology, 24,* 349–358. doi:10.1037/a0019282.

Hill, E. J., Grzywacz, J. G., Allen, S., Blanchard, V. L., Matz-Costa, C., Shulkin, S., & Pitt-Catsouphes, M. (2008). Defining and conceptualizing workplace flexibility. *Community, Work, & Family, 11,* 149–163. doi:10.1080/13668800802024678.

Hill, E. J., Jacob, J. I., Shannon, L. L., Brennan, R. T., Blanchard, V. L., & Margtinengo, G. (2008). Exploring the relationship of workplace flexibility, gender, and life stage to family-to-work conflict, and stress and burnout. *Community, Work, & Family, 11,* 165–181. doi:10.1080/13668800802027564.

Hill, E. J., Martinson, V. K., Ferris, M., & Baker, R. Z. (2004). Beyond the mommy track: The influence of new-concept part-time work for professional women on work and family. *Journal of Family and Economic Issues, 25,* 121–136. doi:10.1023/B:JEEI.0000016726.06264.91.

Hochschild, A., & Machung, A. (1989). *The second shift: Working parents and the revolution at home.* New York: Viking.

Hudson, K. (1999, September 1). *No shortage of nonstandard jobs.* Washington, DC: Economic Policy Institute. Retrieved from http://www.epi.org/publications/entry/briefingpapers_hudson_hudson/

Jang, S. J. (2009). The relationships of flexible work schedules, workplace support, supervisory support, work-life balance, and the well-being of working parents. *Journal of Social Service Research, 35,* 93–104. doi:10.1080/01488370802678561.

Johnson, A. A. (1995). The business case for work-family programs. *Journal of Accountancy, 180,* 53–58. Retrieved from http://find.galegroup.com/gtx/infomark.do?&contentSet=IAC-Documents&type=retrieve&tabID=T003&prodId=LT&docId=A17191281&source=gale&srcprod=LT&userGroupName=a03cc&version=1.0

Johnson, A. A., Shannon, L. L., & Richman, A. L. (2008). Challenging common myths about workplace flexibility: Research notes from the multi-organization database. *Community, Work, & Family, 11,* 231–242. doi:10.1080/13668800802048321.

Jones, B. L., Scoville, P., Hill, E. J., Childs, G., Leishman, J. M., & Nally, K. S. (2008). Perceived versus used workplace flexibility in Singapore: Predicting work-family fit. *Journal of Family Psychology, 22,* 774–783. doi:10.1037/a0013181.

Jones, E. B. (2011). *The impact of stigma on workplace flexibility outcomes for mothers.* Unpublished manuscript. Connecticut College.

Kark, R., & Eagly, A. H. (2010). Gender and leadership: Negotiating the labyrinth. In J. C. Chrisler & D. R. McCreary (Eds.), *Handbook of gender research in psychology* (Vol. II, pp. 443–468). New York: Springer.

Kelly, E. L., Moen, P., & Tranby, E. (2011). Changing workplaces to reduce work-family conflict: Schedule control in a white-collar organization. *American Sociological Review, 76,* 265–290. doi:10.1177/0003122411400056.

Kornberger, M., Carter, C., & Ross-Smith, A. (2010). Changing gender domination in a Big Four accounting firm: Flexibility, performance and client service in practice. *Accounting, Organizations and Society, 35,* 775–791. doi:10.1016/j.aos.2010.09.005.

Kvande, E. (2009). Work-life balance for fathers in globalized knowledge work: Some insights from the Norwegian context. *Gender, Work, and Organization, 16,* 58–72. doi:10.1111/j.1468-0432.2008.00430.x.

Lee, G. (2011). Employee satisfaction with schedule flexibility: Psychological antecedents and consequences within the workplace. *International Journal of Hospitality Management, 30,* 22–30. doi:10.1016/j.ijhm.2010.03.013.

Metz, I. (2005). Advancing the careers of women with children. *Career Development International, 10,* 228–261. doi:10.1108/13620430510598346.

Morganson, V. J. (2010). Comparing telework locations and traditional work arrangements: Differences in work-life balance support, job satisfaction, and inclusion. *Journal of Managerial Psychology, 25,* 578–595. doi:10.1108/02683941011056941.

Muse, L. A. (2011). Flexibility implementation to a global workforce: A case study of Merck and Company, Inc. *Community, Work, & Family, 14,* 249–256. doi:10.1080/13668803.2011.571404.

Nieva, V. F., & Gutek, B. A. (1981). *Women and work: A psychological perspective.* New York: Praeger.

O'Neil, D. A., Hopkins, M. M., & Sullivan, S. E. (2011). Do women's networks help advance women's careers? Differences in perceptions of female workers and top leadership. *Career Development International, 16,* 733–754. doi:10.1108/13620431111187317.

Parris, M. A., Vickers, M. H., & Wilkes, L. (2008). Caught in the middle: Organizational impediments to middle managers' work-life balance. *Employee Responsibilities and Rights Journal, 20,* 101–117. doi:10.1007/s10672-008-9069-z.

Perriton, L. (2006). Does woman + a network = career progression? *Leadership, 2,* 101–113. doi:10.1177/1742715006060655.

Pitt-Catsouphes, M., & Matz-Costa, C. (2008). The multi-generational workforce: Workplace flexibility and engagement. *Community, Work, & Family, 11,* 215–229. doi:10.1080/13668800802021906.

Pollitt, D. (2008). Happy employees have a good work-life balance: Staff trusted to balance personal needs with employment responsibilities. *Human Resource Management International Digest, 16,* 27–28. doi:10.1108/09670730810900875.

Powers, V. (2004, July). Keeping work and life in balance. *T + D (American Society for Training & Development), 58,* 32–35.

Richman, A. L., Civian, J. T., Shannon, L. L., Hill, E. J., & Brennan, R. T. (2008). The relationship of perceived flexibility, supportive work-life policies, and use of formal flexible arrangements and occasional flexibility to employee engagement and expected retention. *Community, Work, & Family, 11,* 183–197. doi:10.1080/13668800802050350.

Stone, M., & Lovejoy, M. (2004). Fast-track women and the "choice" to stay home. *Annals of the American Academy of Political and Social Science, 596,* 62–83. doi:10.1177/0002716204268552.

Swicker, A., & DeLongis, A. (2010). Gender, stress, and coping. In J. C. Chrisler & D. R. McCreary (Eds.), *Handbook of gender research in psychology* (Vol. II, pp. 495–515). New York: Springer.

Taylor, P., Funk, C., & Clark, A. (2007, July 12). *Fewer mothers prefer full-time work.* Washington, DC: Pew Research Center. Retrieved from http://pewresearch .org/pubs/536/working-women

Watt, H.M.G. (2010). Gender and occupational choice. In J. C. Chrisler & D. R. McCreary (Eds.), *Handbook of gender research in psychology* (Vol. II, pp. 379–400). New York: Springer.

Wax, A. L. (2004). Family-friendly workplace reform: Prospects for change. *Annals of the American Academy of Political and Social Science, 596,* 36–61. doi:10.1177/0002716204269189.

Wickramasinghe, V., & Jayabandu, S. (2007). Towards workplace flexibility: Flexitime arrangements in Sri Lanka. *Employee Relations, 29,* 554–575. doi:10. 1108/01425450710826087.

Winder, K. L. (2009). Flexible scheduling and the gender wage gap. *The B.E. Journal of Economic Analysis & Policy, 9,* Article 30. doi:10.2202/1935-1682.2197.

WorldatWork. (2008, August 27). *WorldatWork survey finds telework on the rise in the U.S., Canada.* Washington, DC. Retrieved from http://www.awlp.org/about /html/press.jsp

Zeytinoglu, I. U. (2009). Flexibility: Whose choice is it, anyway? *Relations Industrielles, 64,* 555–574.

# Chapter 14

# Making It Work for Women, Children, and the Job

*Tracy C. McCausland, Afra Ahmad, Whitney B. Morgan, Eden B. King, and Kristen P. Jones*

Employed mothers engage in a daily juggling act between caring for their family and meeting their job demands. Marie, for example, entered graduate school immediately after completing her undergraduate studies and has spent the past five years earning her doctorate degree. Now 27, she is on the market for a position as a tenure-track professor. Marie wants to have children and realizes her window of opportunity is limited, but she also knows that if she decides to become a mom while still under the pretenure microscope any mistakes or decreased productivity could be attributed to a lack of job commitment. Does Marie wait to have children until her job security increases or does she risk derailing her career? The choice to become a mother is just the first of many difficult decisions that women with both career and family aspirations will face.

The women's movement has afforded subsequent generations unparalleled opportunities outside the confines of the home. In fact, 71% of mothers with children under the age of 18 are in the workforce (Galinsky, Aumann, & Bond, 2008). These opportunities are also coupled with many new obstacles leaving the most recent generations of women in uncharted territory. Balancing work and family is particularly challenging for women in dual-career families because on top of their job responsibilities women are still expected to perform the majority of household and childcare tasks (Bond, Thompson, Galinsky, & Prottas, 2003). Unfortunately, research finds that occupancy of both the employee and mother role is associated with many negative experiences and outcomes. For example, working mothers are subject to pervasive negative stereotyping and discrimination at work (Budig & England, 2001; Correll, Benard, & Paik, 2007; Heilman & Okimoto, 2008; Ridgeway & Correll, 2004). Working moms are also perceived as less committed, less competent, less involved in work, and less flexible for advancement relative to their childless male and female counterparts (King, 2008; Ridgeway & Correll, 2004). Furthermore, working moms are less likely to be promoted, more likely to be terminated, and make significantly less money as compared to nonparents (Anderson, Binder, & Krause, 2003; Budig & England, 2001; Correll et al., 2007; Fuegen, Biernat, Haines, & Deaux, 2004; Glass, 2004). This phenomenon is so severe that organizational scholars have compared a working women's transition into motherhood to hitting a brick wall (i.e., the "maternal wall"; Williams, 2001) in their career trajectories.

Given these stressful experiences, it is not surprising that working mothers feel a constant push and pull between work and family responsibilities. This tug-of-war is commonly labeled work-family conflict, which is formally defined as "a form of inter-role conflict in which the role pressures from the work and family domains are mutually incompatible in some respect" (Greenhaus & Beutall, 1985, p. 77). This is particularly concerning given the abundance of research linking these experiences to a variety of negative personal and professional outcomes such as increased stress, increased turnover intentions, decreased productivity, and lowered mental and physical health (Bacharach, Bamberger, & Conley, 1991; Bedeian, Burke, & Moffett, 1988; Burden & Googins, 1987; Frone, 2000; Frone, Russell, & Cooper, 1992; Goff, Mount, & Jamison, 1990; Greenhaus & Parasuraman, 1987; Haynes, Eaker, & Feinleib, 1984; Pleck, 1989). Considering that 80–90% of women will undergo the transition into motherhood within the context of work, scholars and employers must continue to evaluate and provide solutions that can empower organizations, managers, and their employees to actively improve the work-family interface (Williams, Manvell, & Bornstein, 2006). Causes for women deciding to exit the workforce and/or pursue careers that are more "family-friendly" may be largely attributed to the difficulties women face in their pursuits to balance work and family. As such, our goal in this chapter is to highlight some of the unique challenges that working mothers encounter in both the work and family domains (as opposed to other nonwork roles) in hopes of providing useful insight that can help working mothers who *want* (or *have*) to stay in the workforce.

In order to achieve this goal, we will start by reviewing the research on common organizational policies and the degree to which working mothers benefit from these supports. Next, we will describe various coping strategies so that individuals can become active agents in the improvement of their own work-family interface. Following this, we will describe the work-family experiences of traditional and nontraditional families and how these experiences overlap as well as differ. Finally, we will summarize current research findings on the work-family interface and conclude with recommendations for future research.

## ORGANIZATIONAL WORK-FAMILY POLICIES AND CLIMATE

Even today, there is evidence that working mothers are commonly being pushed out of the workforce because of uncompromising organizational policies (Williams et al., 2006). Although, there is also evidence that some organizations are responding to women's growing needs for additional support (SHRM, 2009). In this section, we will define and discuss empirical evidence for some of the most common work-family policies. While there are slight variations in classifying work-family initiatives (cf., Butts, Casper, Yan, & Lucas, 2010; Neal, Chapman, Ingersoll-Dayton, & Emlen, 1993), work-family policies include any organizational programs or officially sanctioned practices designed to assist employees' management of both the paid work role and the unpaid family role (Ryan & Kossek, 2008). Ideally, the goal is to maximize workplace productivity through increasing employee well-being and efficiency (Halpern, 2005).

We note that the work-family literature often distinguishes between "work-family" supports and "work-life" supports. This distinction reflects an ongoing discussion that family is only one nonwork role (e.g., participation in religion, community, and leisure are others; Frone, 2002). As implied in the introduction, our population of interest is working mothers, but we will not limit our discussion to policies and programs that are exclusive to the family role. For example, we will discuss policies such as flexible work arrangements even if they can be utilized by those without dependent care responsibilities.

## OVERVIEW AND PREVALENCE

Traditionally, organizations have imposed standardized work schedules on their employees. However, shifts from an industrial to knowledge based economy as well as rapid technological developments have given rise to more flexible work arrangements. Recently, Kossek and Michel (2011) offered a new taxonomy of flexible work schedules allowing employees to exert greater control over four spheres: (1) *when* work occurs (e.g., flextime, compressed work week, rotating shifts), (2) *where* work occurs (e.g., telework, split locations, client visits), (3) the *amount* of work (e.g., job sharing, part-time, phased retirements), and (4) the *continuity* of work (e.g., sabbaticals, vacation).

### Flextime

Flextime schedules permit employees to select their time of arrival and departure as long as they are present during the "core hours" (e.g., 10 A.M.– 3 P.M.). This arrangement permits mothers to respond and react dynamically to life's little unexpectancies that childcare often brings. Employers determine a core band time, which is credited to facilitate meeting coordination (Van Dyne, Kossek, & Lobel, 2007 and other workplace activities that benefit from face-to-face communication (Kossek & Van Dyne, 2008). Flextime schedules can be applied on a daily basis (e.g., have to work 8 hours per day) or a weekly basis (e.g., have to work 40 hours per week, but daily hours may fluctuate). Estimates of organizations that offer flextime vary from approximately 54% (SHRM, 2009) to 79% (Galinsky, Bond, & Sakai, 2008).

Carlson, Grzywacz, and Kacmar (2010) found flextime utilization was associated with enhanced performance and satisfaction at work and in family by minimizing work-family conflict and maximizing work-family enrichment, which is defined "the extent to which experiences in one role improve the quality of life in the other role" (Greenhaus & Powell, 2006, p. 73). Moreover, flextime played a larger role in reducing work-family conflict for women than for men. Ezra and Deckman (1996) also found that mothers benefited more from flextime than fathers. Thus far, empirical investigation supports the use of flextime as a viable solution for effectively managing the work-family interface.

### Compressed Work Weeks

Compressed work weeks allow employees to increase the number of hours worked in a day while simultaneously decreasing the amount of days worked in a week. The most common forms are a 4-day, 10-hour schedule (4/10) and a 9-day, 9-hour schedule (Pierce, Newstom, Dunham, & Barber, 1989). These forms of scheduling permit one day off every week or one day off every other week, respectively. This arrangement affords employed mothers the opportunity to spend longer periods of time with her children and perhaps even catch up with other household obligations (i.e., errands, doctor's appointments, etc.). Estimates of organizations that offer a compressed work week vary from 37% (SHRM, 2009) to 41% (Galinsky, Bond et al., 2008).

Although seemingly attractive, compressed work weeks show a complex relationship with nonwork outcomes depending on their spouses' involvement and employment (Saltzstein, Ting, & Saltzstein, 2001). Compressed work weeks negatively affected work-family balance for unmarried mothers, had no effect on work-family balance for mothers in dual-income households, and positively influenced work-family balance for mothers with an unemployed spouse. Furthermore, compressed work weeks appeared to have no influence on job satisfaction for any family subgroup. However, other research has found that compressed work weeks slightly increased satisfaction with work-family balance (Ezra & Deckman, 1996), but this area merits additional investigation. Explanations for why a compressed work week may not be as beneficial as flextime scheduling are attributed to fatigue (Goodale & Aagaard, 1975) and a lack of flexibility (Saltzstein et al., 2001). Although the latter may seem counterintuitive, mothers have more *scheduling flexibility*, but they don't have *daily flexibility* for issues that may arise unexpectedly.

### Telework

Telework is work that occurs "off-site" (i.e., away from the official organization location). Kurland and Bailey (1999) identified four types of regular telework: home-based telecommuting, satellite offices, neighborhood work centers, and mobile workers. Like the name implies, home-based telecommuting allows employees to work from home. Satellite offices and neighborhood work centers require employees to work both away from the home and main organizational location; however, satellite offices are specific to the operations of a single company while neighborhood work centers are frequented by employees of various companies. Finally, mobile workers are typically on the road (e.g., sales-persons, investment bankers). Approximately 34% of organizations offer part-time telework and 45% offer occasional telework (SHRM, 2009).

Shockley and Allen (2007) found that for mothers with high levels of family responsibilities (e.g., cleaning, planning family life, etc.) telework use resulted in less work-family conflict. However, for mothers with low levels of family responsibility telework actually increased family interference with work, but did not affect work interference with family. Research from Kossek, Lautsch, & Eaton (2005) suggest that working mothers who use telework arrangements experienced less depression. As indicated by Kurland and Bailey (1999), there are four types of telework and the aforementioned studies only investigated home-based telecommuting, which leaves opportunity for empirical exploration.

Although not specific to working mothers, it is worth noting that meta-analyses on flextime, compressed work weeks (Baltes, Briggs, Huff, Wright, & Neuman, 1999) and telework (Golden, Veiga, & Simsek, 2006) typically show a curvilinear relationship with various work outcomes (e.g., productivity, job satisfaction, work-schedule satisfaction). In other words, increased flexibility is good to a point; however, too much of a "good thing" can turn bad. Additionally, this relationship depended on employee type and time since the intervention. Flexibility was more beneficial for general employees, as compared to professionals and managers, and benefits waned over time, suggesting that employees eventually accepted these new flexible schedules as the norm (Baltes et al., 1999). Therefore we recommend imposing some degree of structure in order to avoid schedules being too flexible. For example, only telework part-time, or attempt to arrive at work within a consistent window (e.g., 8–10 A.M.), or travel to a nearby work center to maximize productivity by being in the presence of others when completing simple tasks (see Social Facilitation Theory).

### Part-Time

The definition of part-time fluctuates depending on company policy, but typically these represent work schedules under 30 or 35 hours per week. Research suggests that part-time work is associated with positive family outcomes (e.g., lower work-to-family conflict, improved life satisfaction; Higgins, Duxbury, & Johnson, 2000; Saltzstein et al., 2001), but is also related with negative career outcomes (e.g., reduced compensation, lower status, fewer career opportunities; Barnett & Hall, 2001; Saltzstein et al., 2001). Tilly (1992) proposed a "new-concept" part-time (NPT), which allows professional employees to remain in the same position, but take on reduced workloads when needed. This arrangement ideally permits women to continue making workplace contributions, pursuing professional aspirations, and expanding their family responsibilities. Working mothers classified as NPT did report less work-to-family conflict, more family success, and higher childcare satisfaction, but similar to more traditional part-time jobs, they also reported less career opportunity, work success, and income (Hill, Martinson, & Ferris, 2004). Taken together, these results suggest that part-time work improves family satisfaction, but often at the expense of job satisfaction.

### Childcare

There exist a variety of services or benefits related to childcare, such as on-site care centers, dependent care resources, and/or referral services. Organizations are more likely to offer the last two options, approximately 34% (Bond, Galinsky, Kim, & Brownfield, 2005), in comparison to the first option which is relatively rare. Moreover, 29% of organizations allow employees to bring their child to work in an emergency (SHRM, 2009).

Utilization of employer-supported childcare does not appear to reduce the amount of work-family conflict experienced by mothers (Ezra &

Deckman, 1996). Although, Kossek and Nichol (1992) found that for parents who did not have reliable backup childcare arrangements, employer-supported childcare improved employee attitudes toward work-family balance and decreased absenteeism. Indeed, satisfaction with childcare arrangements (regardless of location) reduced work-family conflict which in turn was related to lower levels of absenteeism (Goff et al., 1990). We strongly recommend taking time to identify childcare that you are confident about and comfortable with since satisfaction with childcare is one of the strongest predictors of managing the work-family interface (King & Knight, 2011).

### Unpaid or Paid Leave

For an organization employing more than 50 individuals, the Family and Medical Leave Act (FMLA) of 1993 permits employees, who have worked at the organization for at least one year, up to 12 weeks of unpaid job-protected leave during any 12-month period. Some employers offer additional family (22%), paternity (15%), adoption (15%), and/or maternity leave (14%) (SHRM, 2009).

Limited research has investigated these policies. Employees with access to maternity leave showed significantly lower turnover intentions, but leave did not influence effective commitment toward the organization (Allen & Russel, 1999). In an experimental study, researchers investigated participants' evaluations following parental level for both men and women. The dependent variables, recommendations to reward and perceived commitment, were most highly influenced by performance; however, males that took parental leave were less likely to be recommended for rewards than females who took leave or males who did not take leave. Furthermore, both males and females that took parental leave were perceived as less committed to work than those that did not take leave. This negative effect was still stronger for males than females. In summary, these results suggest that if you are a high performer, then work evaluations are not likely to suffer after returning from a parental leave. However, in order to keep a high performer status, King and Knight (2011) recommend to: (1) develop and execute a plan to transition projects and tasks to your coworkers and (2) express your gratitude. Your colleagues are going to be carrying the extra work load while you are away and it is important to manage the perceptions of your coworkers, supervisors, and subordinates in order to lessen any negative work-related evaluations.

## A WORK-FAMILY FRIENDLY CLIMATE

In the preceding section we discussed the effect of *utilizing* work-family programs and policies rather than the effect of just having these initiatives *available*. Previous theorizing suggests that these two concepts are different (Sahibzada, Hammer, Neal, & Kuang, 2005) and a recent meta-analysis (Butts et al., 2010) supports this distinction. Program availability was directly and indirectly related to job performance (task performance and organizational citizenship behavior) and attitudinal work outcomes (job satisfaction, affective commitment, and intentions to stay) through improved perceptions of organizational support. In contrast, program use influenced job performance and attitudinal outcomes through reduced levels of work-to-family conflict. Signaling theory explains the benefits of program availability through perceptions of organizational support (Spence, 1973). In offering family-friendly organizational policies and programs, organizations demonstrate their commitment to (or signal that) the well-being of their employees is valued, which in turn, organizations hope, will translate into positive work outcomes. In contrast, self-interest utility model explains the benefits of program use through a transactional exchange. These meta-analytic results suggest that social exchanges may go beyond quantifiable exchanges, highlighting the likely importance of perceived organizational family support (Casper & Harris, 2008).

A second important distinction differentiates policy *adoption* from *implementation*. Although this may appear redundant we believe that this division can offer additional insight into the explanatory mechanisms of why program availability is important. Ryan and Kossek (2008) suggest the answer lies in a "culture of inclusion," which they define as "one that values differences within its workforce and uses the full potential of employees" (p. 296). Regardless if employees currently use available policies, the perceptions of organizational support and/or a culture for inclusion are likely to influence the degree to which employees believe they could use them, if needed. Organizational culture refers to the values, beliefs, and norms in an organization. If the culture is one in which policy use is not typically sanctioned and/or will be met with backlash, then policy availability is likely to be viewed very differently than in culture in which policy use is allowed and/or encouraged. As cited in Ryan and Kossek (2008, p. 299), "Family-friendly policies may originate from the organization, but they are implemented (or not) in the local work context" (Bourne, Barringer, & McComb, 2004, p. 3). This speaks to the importance of organizational climate, such that leadership and organizational structures facilitate work-family policy implementation. Ryan and Kossek (2008) identify four necessary implementation attributes: (1) supervisors must *support* policy use; (2) policies should be *universally* available; (3) employees ought to *negotiate* policies to make them individually tailored; and (4) the *quality of communication* should be high such that it is clear how and when policies can be used.

Research supports that many organizational characteristics positively influence a number of work and family outcomes (Eby, Casper, Lockwood,

Bordeaux, & Brinley, 2005); however, this section also demonstrates that work-family policies demonstrate complex or even unexpected relationships with criteria measures. Therefore, we echo Ryan and Kossek's (2008) caution against a "one-size-fits-all" mentality. While the previous section took an organizational level perspective we will now shift to an individual perspective.

## Personal Coping Strategies

A critical step in women making it work for themselves, families, and their career is for women to first consider their own personal preferences for managing work and family roles and then develop a social support system that will carry them through both celebratory and challenging times.

Boundary theory provides a framework for understanding personal preferences for work and family lives. Specifically, boundary theory states that individuals construct psychological boundaries to manage their work and personal lives (Nippert-Eng, 1996). Clark (2000) extended this notion by developing specific propositions for how people manage different domains, analyzing key factors—permeability, flexibility, and blending—that contribute to its strength (see Border Theory). Ashforth, Kreiner, and Fugate (2000) further explored the boundaries people enact to manage their work and family lives, clarifying that there are both costs and benefits. Together, this body of research suggests that people manage "boundaries" along an integration-segmentation continuum. Integration can be thought of as the overlap or mixing of work and family. Segmentation can be thought of as the separation of work and family. In other words, to what extent do you desire your work and family lives to overlap?

Boundaries between work and family life are blurrier than ever, especially with the growing use of communication and information technology (CIT) (e.g., smart phones, tablets; Major & Germano, 2006). Increases in communication and information technology have been both a blessing and curse for the world of working mothers (and arguably all employees). For example, CIT may allow a mother who must stay home from work to care for her sick child to continue to be productive with her work responsibilities. CIT may also allow for a mother to receive a highly important e-mail after office hours when she is trying to help her child with homework. Such frequent distraction and interference has been shown to lead to lower job satisfaction (Cardenas, Major, & Bernas, 2004). However, Park and Jex (2011) demonstrated that maintaining impermeable (i.e., segmentation) work and family domains related to CIT was better for employees' psychological work-family interface.

Where an individual falls on the integration-segmentation continuum is highly personal and driven by a variety of factors including gender, family status, and organization policies (Kossek, Noe, & DeMarr, 1999).

For example, Rothbard, Phillips, and Dumas, (2005) demonstrated that desire for segmentation moderated the relationship between desire for organizational policies and satisfaction and commitment such that individuals who preferred greater segmentation, but were operating in a more integrated context (e.g., onsite childcare) were less satisfied and committed than those that had a lesser desire for segmentation. Thus, although organizational policies may be specifically directed at integrating families into work, the reactions to such an approach will be in part dependent upon where the employees fall on the integration-segmentation continuum. Although it is impossible to completely control the types of organizational policies in one's place of work, it is important to understand what may or may not complement one's preferred boundary management style.

A second approach to making all spheres "work" is to develop a social support system. We believe that virtually every woman who has successfully navigated the corporate lattice (see Benko & Anderson, 2010) has not done it alone. She has had a support system, both professional and personal, to guide her through the landmines that lie in organizations and family life. It is possible to feel "stuck" in a position with an unsupportive supervisor with no one to whom you can turn. However, one strategy for managing such a situation is to actively pursue other individuals (i.e., mentors) who can provide emotional support, instrumental support, role modeling behaviors, and creative work-family management (see Hammer, Kossek, Yragui, Bodner, & Hanson, 2009). Specifically, we advocate seeking mentoring as a personal strategy women may enact in an effort to make all spheres work.

Mentoring has been shown to have small, but positive effects not only on career outcomes (see Allen, Eby, Poteet, Lentz, & Lima, 2004; Eby, Allen, Evans, Ng, & DuBois, 2008), but also on attitudinal (e.g., satisfaction), health-related (e.g., psychological stress), relational (e.g., helping), and motivational (e.g., involvement) outcomes (Eby et al., 2008). Specifically, individuals who report being more satisfied with are more likely to advance and being committed to their careers. Mentors provide two broad forms of support: career-related and psychosocial (Kram, 1985). Career-related support includes behaviors such as advocating for developmental work assignments, invitations to key networking opportunities, sponsorship for key activities, and protection from adversity. However, there is also psychosocial support that targets a person's sense of self-worth and identity. Behaviors may include role modeling, providing guidance on careers, listening to challenges, and praise over a job well done. Mentoring can be particularly beneficial in organizational settings, as it can lead to both objective (e.g., compensation) and subjective (e.g., career satisfaction) outcomes. Ng, Eby, Sorensen, and Feldman's (2005) meta-analysis demonstrated that indeed both objective and subjective factors were determinants of advancement, an indicator of effectiveness.

Although mentoring in organizations often takes place in a formal fashion (e.g., new employee is assigned to a senior mentor), there is benefit to informal (i.e., unassigned; naturally created) mentoring. Furthermore, mentoring does not (and should not) require the mentor to select the protégé. We advocate that the protégé (i.e., woman) should "select" their mentor(s) in order to maximize benefits for herself. Ibarra (2000) proposed that one should take a "collage" approach when considering mentors. Specifically, the protégé should first identify a range of characteristics one wishes to emulate. Then, the protégé should seek to identify the multiple individuals that best exemplify these characteristics and begin to develop informal mentoring relationships with these individuals. By taking a multiple mentor approach the protégé is able to learn the best strategies for success from a variety of sources. This is particularly relevant when considering dual roles, as it is possible a woman may have one informal mentor she turns to when seeking career advice and another informal mentor she looks to for guidance when developing her boundary management style. Thus, mentoring is not a one-size-fits-all approach, and it is therefore important to sample the best of multiple people to make work and nonwork sync.

It is important to acknowledge that mentoring is not a concept that must be contained to the workplace. The underlying mechanisms that explain why mentoring "works" translate to women's personal lives as well. First, mentors provide helpful information and/or knowledge to the mentee (Mullen, 1994). Second, mentors provide access to social networks (Dreher & Ash, 1990) that may help to strengthen protégé's self-esteem and/or provide unexpected connection to additional support or resources. Finally, mentors provide opportunity for social learning to occur. In other words, role modeling or vicariously learning from individuals behavioral responses to situations are useful in determining what types of behaviors are (and are not ) acceptable (Bandura, 1977). These principles that make mentoring effective in the workplace—information sharing, networking, and role modeling—can be practiced in women's personal lives. We suggest women seek people to serve as mentors for the multiple spheres. For a practical summary of mentoring tips see King and Knight (2011).

One cautionary note when pursuing mentorship is to watch out for the queen bees. Queen bees are individuals, typically senior women who likely had a challenging time rising to the top of their organization and maintain negative attitudes toward confident, attractive, and capable young women (Staines, Travis, & Jayerante, 1973). Queen bees can create psychological distress and barriers to satisfaction. These women would not likely seek out a mentoring role, but it is important to identify these individuals and not let their reactions negatively affect one's well-being. There will always be critics of women's choices and their approach to managing work and family (e.g., "Mommy Wars"), but there are many people (women and men) who are willing to serve as role models and mentors. It is just a matter of finding them.

In summary, we advocate that women should reflect upon what boundary management style works for them and try to surround themselves with supportive people who will provide both career and psychosocial support. In the subsequent section we will highlight research investigating working mothers in less common family types.

## THE WORK-FAMILY INTERFACE OF DIVERSE FAMILIES

The majority of research on the work-family interface has been conducted on middle- and upper-class, heterosexual married couples with children. Indeed, in their review of the literature, Casper, Eby, Bordeaux, Lockwood, & Lambert (2007) lamented the absence of research on diverse families in workplace scholarship. Here, we briefly describe the limited research that has been conducted on the work-family interface in a non-exhaustive set of understudied family structures: women in the sandwich generation, single mothers, and lesbian and bisexual women. In so doing, we review what is known about the work-life interface of women in a range of family types but also highlight the need for additional exploration of these special populations.

## WOMEN IN THE SANDWICH GENERATION

Nearly 2 million women (most between 35 and 45 years of age) in the United States are members of the sandwich generation (Pierret, 2006). This means that nearly 2 million women are responsible for caring for children under the age of 18 at the same time as their aging parents. This requires substantial financial, psychological, physical, and time resources and thus has implications for the work-life interface.

Supporting this view, one study on employees in a major university found that responsibility for taking care of one's parents had worse consequences for employees' well-being than did raising children (Kossek, Colquitt, & Noe, 2001). The increased demands and reduced resources imply that women in the sandwich generation are likely among the most vulnerable to work-life conflict and its most severe consequences. This further implies that organizational efforts to improve employee well-being should attend to dual, simultaneous needs to care for children and elderly parents to reduce the psychological and physical stresses that result for women who are part of the sandwich generation.

## SINGLE MOTHERS

More than ever before, women are having children outside of marriage—nearly a quarter of all children are born to unmarried mothers (Terry-Humen, Manlove, & Moore, 2001). Importantly, the majority of single moms work outside the home (U.S. Census Bureau, 2009). It follows that single mothers typically face heightened levels of responsibility (and lowered levels of support) compared to their married counterparts. An interview study of single moms confirmed that they face challenges that are similar in content to other parents—insufficient time, money, and energy—but that the amount or level of these challenges may be exacerbated among single mothers (McManus, Korabik, Rosin, & Kelloway, 2002). Nearly all of the interviewees in another study of single mothers reported that financial concerns were a major stressor (Quinn & Allen, 1989).

Given these heightened stressors, it is critical to consider ways that organizations and allies might support single mothers. Evidence suggests that organizational structures that allow for flexible or at least controllable scheduling can be particularly helpful for single mothers who are solely responsible for juggling the demands of their children's schedules and needs (Parker, 1994). In addition, support from coworkers and supervisors have been shown to be an important predictor of the job success and satisfaction of single mothers (Robbins & McFadden, 2003).

## LESBIAN AND BISEXUAL WOMEN

The work-life experiences of lesbians and bisexual women are similarly understudied. In their review of the literature, King, Huffman, and Peddie (2012) summarized, "little is known about the ways in which the work-family interface is experienced by [lesbian, gay, bisexual, and transgendered] people." Preliminary research suggests that there may be both similarities and distinctions between heterosexual and nonheterosexual women's experience of work-life conflict. For example, O'Ryan and McFarland (2010) found that LGBT parents and non-LGBT parents report using similar strategies to deal with conflict between work and family. However, additional research shows that the degree to which gay parents are "out" at work is a predictor of work-life conflict above and beyond traditional predictors of conflict (Tuten & August, 2006).

According to King, Huffman, and Peddie (2012), lesbian and bisexual women may experience an additional stressor as a result of their sexual orientation that could contribute to work-life conflict: minority stress (Meyer, 2003). In addition, resources that are available within and outside of organizations to support families may be less available to lesbians and bisexual women. For example, extended family members may not be as supportive of gay parents as heterosexual parents. As another example, lesbians may have to "out" themselves to gain access to family-related resources at work (e.g., family leave, health insurance; Ryan & Kossek, 2008). Together, the limited existing research suggests that lesbians and bisexual women may face additional stressors as a result of others' prejudiced beliefs about sexual orientation that could contribute to their work-life conflict (see also Ragins, 2004).

Overall, limited research on these special populations of women who are balancing work and nonwork demands suggests that they may be particularly susceptible to stressors and conflicts. As a result, this review highlights the need for additional efforts in both research and practice to understand and improve the work-life interface of women in the sandwich generation, single mothers, and lesbian and gay women.

### Synthesis and Future Directions

Employed mothers encounter many obstacles both in their family lives and in the workplace. These challenging experiences are related to increased stress, turnover intentions, decreased productivity, and even lower mental and physical health (i.e., Bacharach et al., 1991; Frone, 2000). Considering these harmful consequences, it is critical that research continues to investigate organizational policies and personal strategies that women with children and careers can utilize. As King and Knight (2011) illustrate, there is no one "right" way to have a balance, it all depends on what is *right* for you and your current circumstances. This recurring theme is demonstrated as we look at both organizational policies and individual coping strategies. Moreover, it is noteworthy to understand the unique experiences of women from both traditional and nontraditional families as well.

## FUTURE DIRECTIONS

We suggest future research should seek to understand strategies that facilitate management of the paid work role and unpaid family role by examining interactions between individual and organizational strategies as well as taking a multilevel approach. The latter could include variables measured within-person, between-persons, and at the team, organizational, and cultural level of analysis. For example, one avenue that can be further explored is how organizational and individual strategies interact to influence important work-related outcomes. Does the success of personal coping strategies depend upon which organizational policies are available (or utilized)? Or is the success of personal coping strategies dependent on the organizational climate? Shinn, Wong, Simko, and Ortiz-Torees (1989) started to investigate pieces of this question by examining whether individual or organizational strategies were more effective for various outcomes. Results supported that individual coping was a better predictor of well-being for parents as compared to flexible job schedules. However, this study was conducted 20 years ago and did not specifically look at working mothers. We encourage researchers to explore under what conditions or situations one may be more effective than the other.

Working in a diverse labor force merits further empirical investigation into the unique challenges that different subgroups encounter. As we've already noted, researchers and organizations cannot take a one-size-fits-all approach to organizational policies and personal coping strategies. In addition to the family structures already discussed, mothers from different ethnic backgrounds should also be studied. Cultural norms are likely to influence women's perceptions of work-family balance and how this balance is achieved. Likewise, mothers from lower income backgrounds and mothers with special needs children should be considered as well.

In addition to rejecting the "one-size-fits-all approach" it is also appropriate to reject the "one-time-fitting approach." Previous researchers have explored within-person variation in life satisfaction arguing that more research needs to take an episodic approach to study dynamic variables (Heller, Watson, & Ilies, 2006). This idea can be extended to mothers as well. Researchers are encouraged to examine how the needs of mothers may change or vary based on the age of the child. For example, the needs of a mother with a baby are different from a mother of a college student. Perhaps the mother of a newborn needs more daily support in terms of allowing for a flexible scheduling and options to work away from the office, as well as more supportive supervisors, whereas a mother going through empty nest syndrome may want to be surrounded by coworkers and be given more opportunities to advance in her career. Thus, organizational policy may need to change and evolve along with the employees' needs in order to maximize employee productivity and satisfaction. Future research in understanding the needs of women in these changing times of their lives can provide insight to organizations as well as women into selecting the appropriate strategy.

## REFERENCES

Allen, T. D., Eby, L. T., Poteet, M. L., Lentz, E., & Lima, L. (2004). Career benefits associated with mentoring for protégés: A meta-analysis. *Journal of Applied Psychology, 89,* 127–136.

Allen, T. D., & Russel, J. E. A. (1999). Parental leave of absence: Some not so family-friendly implications. *Journal of Applied Social Psychology, 29,* 166–191.

Anderson, D. J., Binder, M., & Krause, K. (2003). The motherhood wage penalty revisited: Experience, heterogeneity, work effort, and work-schedule flexibility. *Industrial & Labor Relations Review, 56,* 273–294.

Ashforth, B. E., Kreiner, G. E., & Fugate, M. (2000). All in a day's work: Boundaries and micro role transition. *Academy of Management Review, 25,* 472–491.

Bacharach, S. B., Bamberger, P., & Conley, S. (1991). Work-home conflict among nurses and engineers: Mediating the impact of role stress on burnout and satisfaction at work. *Journal of Organizational Behavior, 12,* 39–53.

Baltes, B. B., Briggs, T. E., Huff, J. W., Wright, J. A., & Neuman, G. A. (1999). Flexible and compressed workweek schedules: A meta-analysis of their effects on work-related criteria. *Journal of Applied Psychology, 84,* 496–513.

Bandura, A. L. (1977). *Social learning theory.* Englewood Cliffs, NJ: Prentice Hall.

Barnett, R. C., & Hall, D. T. (2001). How to use reduced hours to win the war for talent. *Organizational Dynamics, 29,* 192–210.

Bedeian, A. G., Burke, B. G., & Moffett, R. G. (1988). Outcomes of work-family conflict among married male and female professionals. *Journal of Management, 14,* 475–491.

Benko, C., & Anderson, M. (2010). *The corporate lattice: Achieving high performance in the changing world of work.* Boston, MA: Harvard Business Review Press.

Bond, J. T., Galinsky, E., Kim, S. S., & Brownfield, E. (2005). *National study of the employers.* New York: Families and Work Institute.

Bond, J. T., Thompson, C. A., Galinsky, E., & Prottas, D. (2003). *Highlights of the 2002 national study of the changing workforce.* New York: Families and Work Institute.

Budig, M. J., & England, P. (2001). The wage penalty for motherhood. *American Sociological Review, 66,* 204–225.

Burden, D. S., & Googins, B. (1987). *Boston University balancing job and home life study.* Boston, MA: Boston University School of Social Work.

Butts, M. M., Casper, W. J., Yang, T., & Lucas, N. (2010). *How important are work-family support programs? A meta-analysis of their effects on work-related outcomes.* Presented at the annual Academy of Management conference in Montreal, Canada.

Cardenas, R. A., Major, D. A., & Bernas, K. H. (2004). Exploring work and family distraction: Antecedents and outcomes. *International Journal of Stress Management, 11,* 346–365.

Carlson, D. S., Grzywacz, J. G., Kacmar, K. M. (2010). The relationship of schedule flexibility and outcomes via the work-family interface. *Journal of Managerial Psychology, 25,* 330–355.

Casper, W. J., Eby, L. T., Bordeaux, C., Lockwood, A., & Lambert, D. (2007). A review of research methods in IO/OB work-family research. *Journal of Applied Psychology, 92,* 28–43.

Casper, W. J., & Harris, C. H. (2008). Work-life benefits and organizational attachment: Self-interest utility and signaling theory. *Journal of Vocational Behavior, 72,* 95–109.

Clark, S. C. (2000). Work/family border theory: A new theory of work/family balance. *Human Relations, 53,* 747–770.

Correll, S. J., Benard, S., & Paik, I. (2007). Getting a job: Is there a motherhood penalty? *American Journal of Sociology, 112,* 1297–1338.

Dreher, G. F., & Ash, R. A. (1990). A comparative study of mentoring among men and women in managerial, professional, and technical positions. *Journal of Applied Psychology, 75,* 539–546.

Eby, L. T., Allen, T. D., Evans, S. C., Ng, T., & DuBois, D. L. (2008). Does mentoring matter? A multidisciplinary meta-analysis comparing mentored and non-mentored individuals. *Journal of Vocational Behavior, 72,* 254–267.

Eby, L. T., Casper, W. J., Lockwood, A., Bordeaux, C., & Brinley, A. (2005). Work and family research in IO/OB: Content analysis and review of the literature (1980–2002). *Journal of Vocational Behavior, 66,* 124–197.

Ezra, M., & Deckman, M. (1996). Balancing work and family responsibilities: Flextime and child care in the federal government. *Public Administration Review, 56,* 174–179.

Frone, M. R. (2000). Work-family conflict and employee psychiatric disorders: The national comorbidity survey. *Journal of Applied Psychology, 85,* 888–895.

Frone, M. R. (2002). Work-family balance. In J. C. Quick & L. E. Tetrick (Eds.), *Handbook of occupational health psychology.* Washington, DC: American Psychological Association.

Frone, M. R., Russell, M., & Cooper, M. L. (1992). Antecedents and outcomes of work family conflict: Testing a model of the work-family interface. *Journal of Applied Psychology, 77,* 65–78.

Fuegen, K., Biernat, M., Haines, E., & Deaux, K. (2004). Mothers and fathers in the workplace: How gender and parental status influence judgments of job-related competence. *The Journal of Social Issues, 60,* 737–754.

Galinsky, E., Aumann, K., & Bond, J. T. (2008). *The 2008 national study of the changing workforce.* New York: Families and Work Institute.

Galinsky, E., Bond, J. T., & Sakai, K. (2008). *The 2008 national study of employers.* New York: Families and Work Institute.

Glass, J. (2004). Blessing or curse? Work-family policies and mothers' wage growth over time. *Work and Occupations, 31,* 367–394.

Goodale, J. G., & Aagaard, A. K. (1975). Factors relating to varying reactions to the four-day workweek. *Journal of Applied Psychology, 60,* 33–38.

Goff, S. J., Mount, M. K., & Jamison, R. L. (1990). Employer supported child care, work/family conflict, and absenteeism: A field study. *Personnel Psychology, 43,* 793–809.

Golden, T. D., Veiga, J. F., & Simsek, Z. (2006). Telecommuting's differential impact on work-family conflict: Is there really no place like home? *Journal of Applied Psychology, 91,* 1340–1350.

Greenhaus, J. H., & Beutell N. J. (1985). Sources of conflict between work and family roles. *Academy of Management Review, 10,* 76–88.

Greenhaus, J. H., & Parasuraman, S. (1987). A work-nonwork interactive perspective of stress and its consequences. In J. M. Ivancevich & D. C. Ganster (Eds.), *Job stress: From theory to suggestion* (pp. 37–60). New York: Haworth.

Greenhaus, J. H., & Powell, G. N. (2006). When work and family are allies: A theory of work-family enrichment. *Academy of Management Review, 31,* 72–92.

Halpern, D. F. (2005). How time-flexible work policies can reduce stress, improve health, and save money. *Stress and Health, 21,* 157–168.

Hammer, L. B., Kossek, E. E., Yragui, N. L., Bodner, T. E., & Hanson, G. C. (2009). Development and validation of a multidimensional measure of family supportive supervisor behaviors (FSSB). *Journal of Management, 35,* 837–856.

Haynes, S. G., Eaker, E. D., & Feinleib, M. (1984). The effects of employment, family, and job stress on coronary heart disease patterns in women. In E. B. Gold (Ed.), *The changing risk of disease in women: An epidemiological approach* (pp. 37–48). Lexington, MA: Heath.

Heilman, M. E., & Okimoto, T. G. (2008). Motherhood: A potential source of bias in employment decisions. *Journal of Applied Psychology, 93,* 189–198.

Heller, D., Watson, D., & Ilies, R. (2006). The dynamic process of life satisfaction. *Journal of Personality, 74,* 1421–1450.

Higgins, C., Duxbury, L., & Johnson, K. L. (2000). Part-time work for women: Does it really help balance work and family? *Human Resource Management, 38,* 17–32.

Hill, E. J., Martinson, V. K., & Ferris, M. (2004). New-concept part-time employment as a work–family adaptive strategy for women professionals with small children. *Family Relations, 53,* 282–292.

Ibarra, H. (March–April, 2000). Making partner: A mentor's guide to the psychological journey. *Harvard Business Review, 1,* 47–55.

King, E. B. (2008). The effect of bias on the advancement of working mothers: Disentangling legitimate concerns from inaccurate stereotypes as predictors of advancement in academe. *Human Relations, 61,* 1677–1711.

King, E. B., Huffman, A. H., & Peddie, C. (2012). *Work-family interface for LGBT people.* Unpublished manuscript.

King, E. B., & Knight, J. (2011). *How women can make it work: The science of success.* Santa Barbara, CA: Praeger.

Kossek, E. E., Colquitt, J. A., & Noe, R. A. (2001). Caregiving decisions, well-being, and performance: The effects of place and provider as a function of dependent type and work-family climates. *Academy of Management Journal, 44,* 29–44.

Kossek, E. E., Lautsch, B. A., & Eaton, S. C. (2005). Flexibility enactment theory: Implications of flexibility type, control, and boundary management for work–family effectiveness. In E. E. Kossek & S. J. Lambert's (Eds.), *Work and life integration: Organizational, cultural, and individual perspectives* (pp. 243–261). Mahwah, NJ: Lawrence Erlbaum Associates.

Kossek, E., & Michel, J. (2011). Flexible work schedules. In S. Zedeck (Ed.), *APA Handbook of Industrial and Organizational Psychology* (Vol. 1). Washington, DC: American Psychological Association.

Kossek, E. E., & Nichol, V. (1992). The effects of on-site child care on employee attitudes and performance. *Personnel Psychology, 45,* 485–509.

Kossek, E. E., Noe, R. A., & DeMarr, B. J. (1999). Work-family role synthesis: Individual and organizational determinants. *The International Journal of Conflict Management, 10,* 102–129.

Kossek, E. E., & Van Dyne, L. (2008). Face time matters: A cross-level model of how work-life flexibility influences work performance of individuals and groups. In K. Korabik, D. S. Lero, & D. L. Whitehead (Eds.), *Handbook of work-family integration: Research theory and best practices* (pp. 305–330). New York: Elsevier.

Kram, K. E. (1985). *Mentoring at work: Developmental relationships in organizational life.* Glenview, IL: Scott Foresman.

Kurland, N. B., & Bailey, D. E. (1999). Telework: The advantages and challenges of working here, there, anywhere, and anytime. *Organizational Dynamics, 28,* 53–68.

Major, D. A., & Germano, L. M. (2006). The changing nature of work and its impact on the work-home interface. In F. Jones, R. J. Burke, & M. Westman (Eds.), *Work-life balance: A psychological perspective* (pp. 13–38). New York: Psychology Press.

McManus, K., Korabik, K., Rosin, H. M., & Kelloway, E. K. (2002). Employed mothers and the work-family interface: Does family structure matter? *Human Relations, 55,* 1295–1311.

Meyer, I. H. (2003). Prejudice, social stress, and mental health in lesbian, gay, and bisexual populations: Conceptual issues and research evidence. *Psychological Bulletin, 129,* 674–697.

Mullen, E. (1994). Framing the mentoring relationship in an information exchange. *Human Resource Management Review, 4*, 257–281.

Neal, M. B., Chapman, N. J., Ingersoll-Dayton, B., & Emlen, A. C. (1993). *Balancing work and caregiving for children, adults, and elders.* Newbury Park, CA: Sage.

Ng, T.W.H., Eby, L. E., Sorensen, K. L., & Feldman, D. C. (2005). Predictors of objective and subjective career success: A meta-analysis. *Personnel Psychology, 58,* 367–408.

Nippert-Eng, C. E. (1996). *Home and work.* Chicago, IL: The University of Chicago Press.

O'Ryan, L. W., & McFarland, W. P. (2010). A phenomenological exploration of dual-career lesbian and gay couples. *Journal of Counseling & Development, 88,* 71–79.

Park, Y., & Jex, S. M. (2011). Work-home boundary management using communication and information technology. *International Journal of Stress Management, 18,* 133–152.

Parker, L. (1994). The role of workplace support in facilitating self-sufficiency among single mothers on welfare. *Family Relations, 43,* 168–173.

Pierce, J. L., Newstrom, J. W., Dunham, R. B., & Barber, A. E. (1989). *Alternative work schedules.* Needham Heights, MA: Allyn and Bacon.

Pierret, C. R. (2006). The 'sandwich generation': Women caring for parents and children. *Monthly Labor Review, 9,* 3–9.

Pleck, J. H. (1989). *Family-supportive employer policies and men's participation: A perspective.* Unpublished manuscript.

Quinn, P., & Allen, K. R. (1989). Facing challenges and making compromises: How single mothers endure. *Family Relations, 38,* 390–395.

Ragins, B. R. (2004). Sexual orientation in the workplace: The unique work and career experiences of gay, lesbian and bisexual workers. *Research in Personnel and Human Resources Management, 23,* 37–122.

Ridgeway, C., & Correll, S. J. (2004). Motherhood as a status characteristic. *The Journal of Social Issues, 60,* 683–700.

Robbins, L. R., & McFadden, J. R. (2003). Single mothers: The impact of work on home and the impact of home on work. *Journal of Family and Consumer Sciences Education, 21*(1), 1–10.

Rothbard, N. P., Phillips, K. W., & Dumas, T. L. (2005). Managing multiple roles: Work-family policies and individuals' desires for segmentation. *Organization Science, 16,* 243–258.

Ryan, A. M., & Kossek, E. E. (2008). Work-life policy implementation: Breaking down or creating barriers to inclusiveness? *Human Resource Management, 47,* 295–310.

Sahibzada, K., Hammer, L. B., Neal, M. B., & Kuang, D. C. (2005). The moderating effects of work-family role combination and work-family organizational culture on the relationship between family-friendly organizational supports and job satisfaction. *Journal of Family Issues, 26,* 820–839.

Saltzstein, A. L., Ting, L., & Saltzstein, G. H. (2001). Work-family balance and job satisfaction: The impact of family-friendly policies on attitudes of federal government employees. *Public Administration Review, 61,* 452–567.

Shinn, M., Wong, N. W., Simko, P. A., & Ortiz-Torees, B. (1989). Promoting the well-being of working parents: Coping, social support, and flexible job schedules. *American Journal of Community Psychology, 17,* 31–55.

Shockley, K. M., & Allen, T. D. (2007). When flexibility helps: Another look at flexible work arrangements and work family conflict. *Journal of Vocational Behavior, 71*, 479–493.

Spence, M. (1973). Job market signaling. *Quarterly Journal of Economics, 87*, 355–374.

Staines, G., Travis, C., & Jayerante, T. E. (1973). The queen bee syndrome. *Psychology Today, 7*, 55–60.

Society for Human Resource Management. (2009). *Employee benefits.* Retrieved April 2, 2014 from www.shrm.org

Terry-Humen, E., Manlove, M.P.P., & Moore, K. (2001). *Births outside of marriage: Perceptions vs. reality.* Retrieved from http://www.childtrends.org/files /rb_032601.pdf

Tilly, C. (1992). Two faces of part-time work: Good and bad part-time jobs in U.S. service industries. In B. D. Warme, K. Lundy, & L. A. Lundy (Eds.), *Working part-time: Risks and opportunities* (pp. 217–228). New York: Praeger.

Tuten, T. L., & August, R. A. (2006). Work-family conflict: A study of lesbian mothers. *Women in Management Review, 21*, 578–597.

U.S. Census Bureau. (2009). *Custodial mothers and fathers and their child support: 2007.* Retrieved April 2, 2014 from http://www.census.gov/prod/2009pubs /p60-237.pdf

Van Dyne, L., Kossek, E., & Lobel S. (2007). Less need to be there: Cross level effects of work practices that support work-life flexibility and enhance group processes and group-level OCB. *Human Relations, 60*, 1123–1153.

Williams, J. (2001). *Unbending gender: Why work and family conflict and what to do about it.* Oxford, UK: Oxford University Press.

Williams, J. C., Manvell, J., & Bornstein, S. (2006). *"Opt Out" or pushed out?: How the press covers work/family conflict.* University of California, Hastings College of the Law, The Center for Work Life Law.

# Chapter 15

# Valuing Lesbian and Gay Parenting in the Workplace

*Ann H. Huffman, Eden B. King, and Abbie E. Goldberg*

Controversy regarding the rights of sexual minorities continues to exist (Stein, 2005), with one such controversy being whether lesbian, gay, and bisexual (LGB) individuals make suitable parents (The Pew Research Center, 2006). Although there has been much research supporting the notion that sexual orientation is irrelevant to individual's ability to parent (Adams, Jaques, & May, 2004; Goldberg & Smith, 2009; Patterson, 2000, 2004), there are still many who hold the view that only heterosexual individuals should be allowed to parent. Due to such enduring attitudes, individuals who are lesbian, gay, or bisexual *and* are parents can experience unique stressors. These stressors can be experienced in many different domains of the individual's life, including the workplace.

Whereas there is quite a bit of literature that discusses the issues relating to LGB parenting (for a review, see Goldberg, 2010), there is very little research that specifically examines LGB parents and workplace experiences. Lesbian and gay employees who are parents face issues that are common to all working parents. However, in addition, they are also exposed to challenges that are a function of working in a homophobic and heterosexist society. Unfortunately, being an LGB employee *and* being an LGB parent can magnify the potential for social disapproval and discrimination. We propose that LGB parents are exposed to workplace stressors that can have negative effects not only on work-related outcomes such as job performance and job satisfaction but also on overall well-being.

## LGB EMPLOYEES AND WORKPLACE ISSUES

It is very difficult to estimate the exact number of LGB employees in the workforce given that 1) surveys are inconsistent in their measurement and assessment of sexual orientation, and 2) some LGB people do not disclose their sexual orientation on said surveys (Goldberg, 2010). According to different sources, LGB employees constitute somewhere between 4 and 17% of the workforce (4 to 17%, Gonsiorek & Weinrich, 1991; 10 to 14%, Powers, 1996). There is even less information concerning the number of LGB *parents* in the workplace. The U.S. Census Bureau, 2000, reported that 34% of cohabiting lesbians and 22% of cohabiting gay men have children under the age of 18 at home. Based on this statistic, if 4 to 17% of the workforce are LGB employees, then between 1 and 6% of the workforce are made up of LGB parents.

Given the prevalence of LGB employees, it is disheartening that homophobia, or negative attitudes toward an LGB individual, continues to exist in the workplace. Day and Green (2008) describe homophobia as the "last acceptable bias" in the workplace. This description is fitting, given that unlike other minority group statuses such as race, sexual orientation is not a federally protected class by the U.S. government and many other world governments (see King & Cortina, 2010). Additionally, and related to the earlier description, sexual orientation continues to be one of the more controversial minority groups due to value judgments that have been associated with this group. Unlike race or sex, sexual orientation can be seen as "controllable" and is considered a deviance by some religious and political groups. Due to the general negative stereotypes, this group is exposed to unique stressors not evident for majority groups.

## MINORITY STRESSORS

Research suggests that LGB individuals experience unique stressors associated with their sexual identity (e.g., Waldo, 1999). These stressors arise from the negative attitudes held by the heterosexual population regarding homosexuality. "Homophobia" is a commonly used term to describe a general fear of homosexuality. It describes the negative attitudes that society holds toward LGB individuals. While this term is useful, "heterosexism" is a more encompassing term used to describe the bias held by society against homosexuality and in favor of heterosexuality. Herek

(1994) defined heterosexism as "an ideological system that denies, denigrates, and stigmatizes any nonheterosexual form of behavior, identity, relationship, or community" (p. 89). Heterosexism involves the privileging of heterosexuality and the denial of privileges for homosexuals. Further, heterosexism results in prejudice, stigma, and discrimination against LGB individuals (Smith & Ingram, 2004; Waldo, 1999).

Much of the research on heterosexism is based on Meyer's (1995) theory of minority stress. Meyer's theory suggests that LGB individuals experience psychological distress because they typically find themselves in environments in which they are a minority, which leads to their stigmatization. Unlike members of other minority groups (e.g., racial or gender minorities), LGB individuals often spend majority of their lives isolated from fellow minority group members, as they often live in a heterosexual environment (Waldo, 1999). Thus, the discordance between their values, culture, and experiences and those of the dominant culture are highly salient (Meyer, 1995).

Meyer's (1995) framework describes three minority stressors: (1) internalized homophobia, (2) perceived stigma, and (3) discrimination and violent events. *Internalized homophobia* refers to the tendency of LGB individuals to direct negative social attitudes toward themselves, which negatively affects their psychological state. LGB individuals are *stigmatized* because of their sexual orientation. This leads some LGB persons to deny their sexuality in an attempt to avoid stigmatization. However, the stress associated with stigmatization and having to deny their identity leads to feelings of mistrust and fear toward non-LGB individuals. Finally, because homosexuality is not a protected class, LGB individuals are often subjected to legal acts of *discrimination,* and are frequently the victims of antigay violent events. These three stressors, separately or in combination, lead to psychological distress in LGB individuals.

Whereas the broader research on sexual minorities has examined all three types of stressors, much of the workplace research focuses on stigma (Ragins, 2008) and discrimination (e.g., Ragins & Cornwell, 2001). For example, understanding sexual identity management decisions in the workplace has become a more common area of research in recent years (Creed & Cooper, 2008). Research has shown that workers who are open about their sexual orientation at work are more likely to report higher levels of organizational commitment (Day & Schoenrade, 1997) and job satisfaction (Day & Schoenrade, 1997; Griffith & Hebl, 2002). Additionally, studies of LGB employees have found that higher levels of openness about sexual orientation are related to less work-family conflict (Day & Schoenrade, 2000) and lower anxiety (Griffith & Hebl, 2002). Research has also examined how heterosexism (i.e., a system of negative attitudes and behavior directed against LGB individuals) affects LGB employees. This research consistently documents the negative effects (e.g., distress, Smith &

Ingram, 2004; Waldo, 1999) of heterosexism on LGB employees. Finally, a line of research has shown that organizational LGB policies and practices are related to perceived discrimination (Ragins & Cornwell, 2001) and to the degree of openness at work (Rostosky & Riggle, 2002), and that support specifically focused on LBG employees can decrease negative workplace outcomes (Huffman, Watrous-Rodriguez, & King, 2008).

The aforementioned studies, however, focused on LGB employees in general—not LGB employees who are parents. With this in mind, we will also examine how parenting affects LGB individuals in the workplace. Since there is very little research on LGB parent-employees, we will first build on minority stress theory using the conservation of resources framework as an accompanying theory to help provide an understanding of how minority experiences deplete resources that allow successful management of work and family domains. Then, we discuss parenting in general in relation to the work-family interaction. Finally, we provide an overview of some key issues related to LGB employees (i.e., outness and workplace discrimination) with a focus on how these topics affect LGB employee-parents.

## LGB PARENTING IN THE WORKPLACE

The conservation of resources (COR) framework (Hobfoll, 1989) is a useful model that provides a basis from which to examine how minority stress can deplete resources necessary to be successful in the work domain. According to COR theory, individuals seek to acquire and maintain resources, including objects (e.g., homes, clothes, and food), personal characteristics (e.g., self-esteem), conditions (e.g., being married or living with someone provides social support and more financial security), and energies (e.g., time, money, and knowledge). Stress occurs when there is a loss of resources or a threat of loss.

We propose that LGB parent-employees are disadvantaged because resources (e.g., time, energy) "are lost in the process of juggling both work and family roles" (Grandey & Cropanzano, 1999, p. 352), which in turn may lead to efforts to conserve resources such as quitting one's job. Feelings of stress can occur when there is a loss of resources or a threat of loss of resources. Yet, when an employee experiences both minority stress and parenting stress there can be an accumulation of loss of resources. This multiplicative loss can in turn be detrimental to the well-being of the employee.

Utilizing COR theory, several studies have noted the importance of resources in coping with work and family demands (Grandey & Cropanzano, 1999; Lapierre & Allen, 2006; Rosenbaum & Cohen, 1999). One relevant construct in the organizational literature that is related to parenting and workplace experiences is work-family conflict.

## PARENTING SPECIFIC: THE WORK-FAMILY INTERFACE

Work-family conflict (WFC) is a type of interrole conflict (Kopelman, Greenhaus, & Connolly, 1983) that has been defined as the "simultaneous occurrence of two (or more) sets of pressures such that compliance with one would make more difficult compliance with the other" (Kahn, Wolfe, Quinn, Snoek, & Rosenthal, 1964, p. 19). Kahn et al. (1964) posited that interrole conflict will occur when two forces of similar magnitude are competing against each other. Work-family conflict has become a relevant variable in work psychology because of the negative consequences for both the organization and employees (e.g., job burnout: Kossek & Ozeki, 1998; low job satisfaction: Wayne, Musisca, & Fleeson, 2004; poor physical health: Beatty, 1996; and lower life satisfaction: Duxbury & Higgins, 1991).

There has been some empirical evidence to support our contention that parenting can be an additional stressor in the workplace. In the general population, studies have shown that presence of children is a consistent predictor of work-family conflict (e.g., Aryee, 1992; Bouchard & Poirier, 2011; Greenhaus & Beutell, 1985; Kinnuunen & Mauno, 1998). In one of the few studies that explored the work-family interface of LGB parents, Goldberg and Smith (2009) examined perceived parenting skill among 47 lesbian, 31 gay, and 56 heterosexual adoptive parent couples and found that parents who reported higher job autonomy preparenthood viewed themselves as being more skilled at parenting. Indeed, the degree of autonomy that parents have in their jobs (or, the degree to which their jobs allow them freedom to schedule work, make decisions, and select the methods used to perform tasks) facilitates work-related self-efficacy (Paglis & Green, 2002) and general self-efficacy (Gecas & Seff, 1989). Thus, the authors interpreted their findings as providing evidence that all parents, regardless of sexual orientation, who enjoyed more autonomy at work also experienced more self-efficacy at home, such that these persons felt more efficacious as parents.

Research has also found that work-family conflict may increase for LGB workers upon becoming parents. Bergman, Rubio, Green, and Padron (2010) studied 40 gay fathers who had become parents via surrogacy and found that most of the men working fewer hours, getting less sleep, and working late at night while their children were in bed, in an effort to juggle the demands of work and family. Some men revealed that their career goals had shifted upon becoming parents, such that their careers, and career advancement, were less important than they were prior to having children. Some of these men had, in turn, decided to work fewer hours, turn down job opportunities, and travel less in an effort to better manage and shape their work lives around their families. Similarly, in a study of 21 lesbians, Rawsthorne and Costello (2010) found that one-third of their sample described employing similar strategies (e.g., changing jobs, reducing hours, and delaying career aspirations) in an effort to better reconcile work and family responsibilities and reduce work-family conflict.

Finally, some research has begun to examine the factors that predict work-family conflict in LGB parents. For example, Tuten and August (2006) studied 58 employed lesbian mothers and found that working more hours, and being less out at work, predicted higher levels of work-family conflict.

Overall these few studies on LGB employee-parents and their work-family experiences provide some evidence that there are similarities between LGB employees and heterosexual employees in terms of the work-family interface. Individuals, whether they are LGB or heterosexual, who experience work-family conflict are likely to experience "loss spirals" (Demerouti, Bakker, & Bulters, 2004; Hobfoll, 1989). That is, when subjected to work-family conflict, individuals lose resources that help them cope in the environment. The loss of resources can then lead to negative work and personal outcomes. For example, research has shown the benefits of social support in the workplace for both heterosexual (Allen, 2001) and LGB populations (Goldberg & Smith, 2011; Huffman et al., 2008). LGB employees are potentially vulnerable to lower levels of workplace support, especially when they are parents (Mercier, 2007). LGB employees may encounter lack of support or camaraderie from their coworkers on account of their sexual orientation; their parental status may further distance them from some of their workmates, compounding the sense of alienation they may feel. This loss of resources can then lead to more conflict in trying to sustain demands at work and at home.

## LGB SPECIFIC ISSUES: OUTNESS

One concept that is fairly unique to LGB individuals is "outness," or the degree to which an LBG individual is comfortable and willing to share their sexual orientation with others. In the work environment, an environment in which it is not uncommon for coworkers to have some knowledge of their coworkers' personal lives (Day & Schoenrade, 1997), approximately 49% of employees are out (Human Rights Campaign Foundation, 2009). Managing work relationships might not only be quite stressful for an LGB employee, but it can also affect their level of networking and opportunities for mentoring relationships, thus affecting career development and advancement (Badgett, 2008).

There are two helpful frameworks for understanding workplace sexual identity management. First, Woods (1993) provides a framework in which to understand sexual identity management, whereby he discusses a continuum of strategies concerning outness. According to Woods, individuals use one of three strategies to manage their sexual identity in the workplace: counterfeiting, avoidance, or integration. Individuals who use the *counterfeit* strategy consciously behave in a way that suggests that they are heterosexual, even if it means changing truths. The *avoiding* strategy is used when individuals create a rigid boundary between their personal life and their work lives, thus not allowing coworkers and management to get to know them. Finally, individuals who use the *integration* strategy fully reveal their sexual orientation at work.

A second framework is offered by Ragins (2004), who introduced the notion of *disclosure disconnect,* a term that describes the degree to which one is out at different levels depending on whether it is his or her personal work or social network. How to manage one's sexual identity in the workplace is a major decision (Triandis, Kurowski, & Gelfand, 1994) and can become even more complicated when an individual is an LGB employee and parent. Researchers have suggested that LGB employees who deny themselves disclosure of their true identity (Ragins, 2004, 2008) (i.e., individuals who use the counterfeiting and avoiding strategies) will experience stress. Support for this comes from one of the few studies to examine openness in relation to work and family domains (although not specifically parents), in which Day and Schoenrade (2000) found that LGB employees who were more open were more likely to experience less work-family conflict.

It is reasonable to expect that counterfeiting and avoidance strategies would be detrimental for any LGB employee, regardless of parenthood status. Unsettlingly, although integration is ideal, counterfeiting and avoidance can be fairly common strategies (DeJordy, 2008), especially in an unsupportive work environment. Yet these strategies might become harder to accomplish when one becomes a parent. The presence of children, in a sense, provides more opportunity for work and personal life to become intertwined. Parenthood, in general, is one of the most valued experiences of Americans—including LGB persons (Riskind & Patterson, 2010)—and, in turn, it is quite common for parents to want to share stories about their parenting experiences. Indeed, in a survey on LGB employee work experiences, 78% of LGB employees stated that the topic of children comes up at work at least once a week (Human Rights Campaign Foundation). Once an employee allows one aspect of their personal life (parenting) to be disclosed and discussed, it provides opportunities for other areas of their life (sexual orientation) to be exposed (e.g., insomuch as it is difficult to talk about one's children without discussing one's partner and/or relationship status). When this occurs, the LGB employee (who is not out) needs to be more cognitively vigilant and constantly aware of the conversational transactions.

The workplace also provides opportunities for employees and their families to be exposed to colleagues and their families. Parents (whether LGB or non-LGB) have opportunities to bring their children to work-sponsored family events. This act in itself does not necessarily need to out an employee (e.g., it is possible that the parent might engage in conceal-ment strategies, such as by leaving one's partner at home and only attend-ing a work event with one's child). However, once a child becomes verbal, "all bets are off," such that a child may unknowingly out the employee. Therefore, LGB employee-parents, whose management strategy was "de-nial" prior to parenthood, might have more difficulty carrying through with this strategy once children enter the picture.

Yet it should also be noted that LGB employee-parents whose disclo-sure status was *integrated* (i.e., they were out everywhere) or dependent on the situation (*identity disconnect*) might encounter some new challenges as an LGB parent-employee. Whereas, in some cases allowing disclosure at work could provide more meaning to one's life, it might ultimately be det-rimental if others do not approve of one's family situation. Although atti-tudes are changing, and people have become more tolerant of LGB people (Giuffre, Dellinger, & Williams, 2008), contemporary society is still quite divided over the topic of LGB parenting. Thus, although coworkers might have been supportive of an LGB employee, they may not be supportive of an LGB employee-parent. If this is the case, LGB employees who are par-ents will be exposed to new challenges that were not apparent prior to parenthood.

## LGB SPECIFIC ISSUES: EMPLOYMENT DISCRIMINATION

Two interrelated reasons may underlie decisions to conceal a gay or les-bian identity at work. First, majority of the countries around the world do not have legal protection against sexual orientation discrimination. The U.S. government, for example, does not provide protection against em-ployment discrimination, although there is some protection at the state level. As of January 2011, 20 states have included sexual orientation as a protected class. Outside of the United States, as of May 2008, 50 countries have some type of antidiscrimination protection. A second, related reason why individuals may conceal their sexual orientation is concern about dis-crimination: in the United States, an estimated 25 to 66% of LGB employ-ees report experiencing some type of discrimination based on their sexual identity (Croteau, 1996). Even if LGB individuals have not experienced discrimination (due to either not being out or working in a supportive environment), the reason many LGB employees are not open about their sexual orientation at work is because of their fear of discrimination (Day & Schoenrade, 2000).

Discrimination can be overt such as being denied promotion based on sexual orientation, or can be more subtle in nature such as hostile interper-sonal interactions or inappropriate jokes (e.g., Chung, 2001). We propose that beyond the general discrimination that LGB employees might experi-ence, LGB parents are also exposed to and are affected by discriminatory laws. Further, additional discriminatory practices might come into play based on the sex of the LGB parent-employee.

Many of the discriminatory practices that LGB employee-parents are exposed to stem from more general laws related to marriage, civil union, and adoptions. For example, one resource that LGB parent-employees frequently cannot attain is marriage. In our society, not only is marriage symbolically valued, it also has practical, tangible benefits associated with it. Because many organizations do not recognize same-sex partnerships in the absence of marriage (which may not be available at the state level), individuals who are not the legal or biological parents of their children may not be eligible to utilize these benefits for their child(ren). In a qualitative study that examined lesbian employees who were mothers, Mercier (2007) found that lesbian mothers encountered challenges in terms of gaining health care for their children, and other related benefits. In a similar vein, LGB parents may encounter challenges in relation to utilizing family or parental leave when their child is not considered legally theirs (Goldberg, Moyer, Richardson, & Kinkler, in preparation).

In addition to sexual orientation and parenthood status, sex may also contribute to discrimination. Gender is a fundamental element in our own and others' structuring of norms within the work and family domains that can trigger stereotypes. We propose that the gender of the LGB parent can differentially affect the likelihood of occurrence and reason for discrimination. Society has some fairly consistent expectations of the responsibilities each parent should take in the parenting relationship with the key caregiver being the mother (Williams & Best, 1990). Discrimination can be particularly problematic for lesbian parents. Of special note is the concept of a "motherhood penalty," a term used to describe workplace discrimination and lack of accommodation for employees who are mothers (Correll, Benard, & Paik, 2007). These unsupportive practices and overt discriminatory practices have led to slower career advancement trajectories for mothers compared to women without children (e.g., Williams & Segal, 2004). We located only one study that discussed this issue. In a qualitative study on workplace discrimination of LGB employees, Giuffre et al. (2008) commented that although this was not the focus of their research, there was evidence that motherhood penalty existed for lesbian employees. Yet it should be noted that there might also be a "motherhood advantage" for the lesbian mother if outcomes such as income (Baumle, 2009) are taken into consideration.

## VALUING LGB PARENTING: THE ORGANIZATION'S ROLE

Organizational culture describes beliefs, values, and norms that are shared by an organization and influence strategies to achieve organizational goals. Several researchers have examined organizational culture in terms of its role in promoting heterosexism. Waldo (1999), for example, assessed heterosexism in the workplace. He administered surveys to gay and lesbian individuals who either attended a gay event or were part of an LGB community mailing list. He found that LGB individuals, employed in organizations which did not punish those who harassed LGB employees (e.g., made LGB employees feel like they should act straight, used LGB slurs), experienced more heterosexism.

Research has also found evidence for the role of organizational culture—and specifically, organizational support—on lesbian and gay parents' well-being. For example, Goldberg and Smith (2011) studied 52 lesbian and 38 gay male adoptive parents across the first year of parenthood and found that participants who reported their organizations as more supportive preparenthood tended to report lower levels of depressive and anxious symptoms in early parenthood. This finding is notable in that it extends prior work showing a cross-sectional relationship between workplace support and life satisfaction among sexual minorities (Huffman et al., 2008) and suggests that workplaces may play an important role in fostering positive mental health outcomes in LGB workers.

It should also be noted that LGB employees may experience negative, or unsupportive, social interactions following instances of heterosexism (Smith & Ingram, 2004). Instances of heterosexism and discrimination are negatively related to psychological health (Smith & Ingram, 2004; Waldo, 1999), job satisfaction (Button, 2001; Griffith & Hebl, 2002), and commitment (Button, 2001) and positively related to job anxiety (Griffith & Hebl, 2002) among LGB employees.

Although employees may experience minority stress at work, we suggest that a supportive organization will lessen the perceived stigmatization that LGB employees experience. Social exchange theory (Blau, 1964) has been used as a framework to help understand how organizational support affects the relationship between the employee and organization (e.g., Casper, Martin, Buffardi, & Erdwins, 2002). An employee who feels that he or she receives support from his or her organization may feel like the gesture should be reciprocated, and, thus, employees who feel supported and valued by their organizations tend to feel more committed to their organizations (Eisenberger, Huntington, Hutchinson, & Sowa, 1986). Organizational support can be shown in many different ways at many different levels. Support might be demonstrated through tangible benefits (e.g., pay, benefits, and awards) or it could be shown even more through intangible sources (e.g., culture, Thomas & Ganster, 1995; perceptions of a work-family friendly environment, Allen, 2001). To demonstrate a lack of tolerance for heterosexism, many organizations have instituted "gay-supportive" policies that show support for and acceptance of sexual orientation diversity (e.g., LGB employee groups, diversity training). Research has shown that the more widespread these policies are, the less

LGB employees experience discrimination (Button, 2001; Ragins & Cornwell, 2001). Most work that has examined LGB-friendly organizations has been focused on employees in general, and we posit that there is no reason why the LGB friendly culture cannot extend to LGB parents. Most organizations that have an LGB-friendly culture have programs and policies to support their LGB community. We provide several different policies and programs that organizations could initiate to support workplace sexual diversity for LGB parents.

### Diversity Workshops

The goal of an LGB-focused diversity workshop would be to educate all employees concerning issues relevant to gay and lesbian employees. Providing accurate information concerning LGB employees could decrease heterosexual individuals' inaccurate assumptions related to LGB employees. This could be especially important for LGB parents. Workshops could focus on the similarities between LGB and non-LGB parents, in an effort to promote understanding and tolerance of LGB parents.

### LGB Parent Networks

The goal of networks is to provide employees instrumental and social support based on a commonality shared among the group. Many organizations offer networks to provide employees the opportunity to interact and network with other employees. In most cases, these networks are focused on specific factors such as parenting or even more specific such as single parenting. We propose that organizations could offer a network specifically for employees who are LGB parents. Of course, establishing such a group should be dependent on need and desire for such a group.

Finally, we should note that whereas it is important for organizations to have LGB-friendly policies, it is just as important for the organization to show affirmation for the policies (Button, 2001). Open support for these policies can be manifested through simple acts such as written statements confirming the organization's commitment to support for sexual diversity in the workplace. In the case of LGB parents, the organization would need to include a statement that all family types are supported and accepted in the organization.

## LGB PARENTS AT WORK: FUTURE DIRECTIONS IN APPLICATION AND RESEARCH

The issue of LGB parent-employees is very relevant in today's society. It is becoming more common for gay men and lesbian women to want families, and medical advancements and the change in public sentiment are increasingly allowing this to occur. The 2000 U.S. Census showed that more than one-third of lesbians and one-fifth of gay male couples were raising children. Additionally, a study conducted by the national Survey of Family Growth found that 52% of childless gay men (compared to 67% heterosexual men) and 41% of childless lesbian women (compared to 53% heterosexual women) had a desire to have children (Gates, Badgett, Macomber, & Chambers, 2007).

Although gay men and lesbian women have, or would like to have families, there are many gaps in our understanding related to LGB parents and workplace experiences. More needs to be understood about whether theoretical frameworks that have been used to study heterosexual employee-parents (e.g., work-family conflict, social support) apply to nonheterosexual employee-parents. For example, Huffman et al. (2008) found that similar to heterosexual employees, coworker and supervisor support were important to employee outcomes such as satisfaction. Yet they also found that organizational support, specifically for LGB employees, was linked to outcomes for LGB employees. Although social support is just one example, there is a large body of research already conducted on many workplace issues. It would be helpful to understand under what conditions these findings apply to LGB employees who are parents.

Similarly, more research needs to investigate whether current organizational policies focused on helping traditionally defined families are also helpful for LGB families. Research (Human Rights Campaign Foundation) has shown that some programs (e.g., diversity training) are linked to greater outness at work, while other programs (EEO) are not. It is important to understand what types of programs are most effective in developing LGB-family friendly cultures. Similarly organizations would benefit from knowing best practices within each program to ensure that all programs are effective. In other words, how should organizations design their diversity training programs, for example, to ensure that they are effective for all minority groups to include LGB employee-parents?

There is very little known about LGB employee-parents of color. Gay men of color have been described as facing "double jeopardy" due to having two minority characteristics (sexual orientation and race; Ferdman, 1999). One could argue that a lesbian woman of color who has children could face "quadruple jeopardy" since not only are they considered minority status due to sex, sexual orientation, and race, but they also have the additional stigma of being a lesbian parent.

There has been some advancement in the last 10 years concerning LGB employees and their workplace experiences (Wang & Schwarz, 2010). Yet one monumental issue that continues to be problematic for LGB parents is health care benefits for partners and children. Lack of access to health care benefits via a same-sex spouse or via a nonlegal parent creates financial, emotional, and physical stress for LGB-parent families (Mercier,

2007). Indeed, there are still businesses that do not extend domestic part-nership benefits to LGB employees (Human Rights Campaign). It appears that much work is needed at the state and federal levels to expect any pos-itive changes for family benefits of LGB employees.

## NOTE

Portions of this work were published in M. Paludi (Ed.) (2012). *Managing diversity in today's workplace. Volume 2: Work-family integration strategies* (pp. 163–185). Santa Barbara, CA: Praeger.

## REFERENCES

Adams, J. L., Jaques, J. D., & May, K. M. (2004). Counseling gay and lesbian fam-ilies: Theoretical considerations. *The Family Journal: Counseling and Therapy for Couples and Families, 12,* 40–42. doi:10.1177/1066480703258693.

Allen, T. D. (2001). Family-supportive work environments: The role of organiza-tional perceptions. *Journal of Vocational Behavior, 58,* 414–435. doi:10.1006/jvbe.2000.1774.

Aryee, S. (1992). Antecedents and outcomes of work-family conflict among mar-ried professional women: Evidence from Singapore. *Human Relations, 45,* 813–837. doi:10.1177/001872679204500804.

Badgett, M.V.L. (2008). Bringing all families to work today: Equality for gay and lesbian workers and families. In A. Marcus-Newhall, D. F. Halpern, & S. J. Tan (Eds.), *Claremont applied social psychology series. The changing realities of work and family: A multidisciplinary approach* (pp. 140–154). doi:10.1002/9781444305272.ch7.

Baumle, A. K. (2009). The cost of parenthood: Unraveling the effects of sexual orientation and gender on income. *Social Science Quarterly, 90,* 983–1002. doi:10.1111/j.1540-6237.2009.00673.x.

Beatty, C. A. (1996). The stress of managerial and professional women: Is the price too high? *Journal of Organizational Behavior, 17,* 233–251. doi:10.1177/0146167201272004.

Bergman, K., Rubio, R. J., Green, R., & Padron, E. (2010). Gay men who become fathers via surrogacy: The transition to parenthood. *Journal of GLBT Family Studies, 6,* 111–141.

Blau, P. M. (1964). *Exchange and power in social life.* New York: Wiley.

Bouchard, G., & Poirier, L. (2011). Neuroticism and well-being among employed new parents: The role of the work-family conflict. *Personality and Individual Differences, 50,* 657–661. doi:10.1016/j.paid.2010.12.012.

Button, B. (2001). Organizational efforts to affirm sexual diversity: A cross-level examination. *Journal of Applied Psychology, 86,* 17–28. doi:10.1037/0021-9010.86.1.17.

Casper, W. J., Martin, J. A., Buffardi, L. C., & Erdwins, C. J. (2002). Work-family conflict, perceived organizational support, and organizational commitment among employed mothers. *Journal of Occupational Health Psychology, 7,* 99–108. doi:10.1037/1076-8998.7.2.99.

Chung, Y. B. (2001). Work discrimination and coping strategies: Conceptual frameworks for counseling lesbian, gay, and bisexual clients. *The Career Development Quarterly, 50,* 33–55.

Correll, S. J., Benard, S., & Paik, I. (2007). Getting a job: Is there a motherhood penalty? *American Journal of Sociology, 112,* 1297–1338.

Creed, D., & Cooper, E. (2008). Introduction: Offering new insights into GLBT workplace experiences. *Group & Organization Management, 33,* 491–503. doi:10.1177/1059601108321363.

Croteau, J. M. (1996). Research on work experiences of lesbian, gay and bisexual people: An integrative review of methodology and findings. *Journal of Vocational Behavior, 48,* 195–209. doi:10.1177/1059601108321828.

Day, N. E., & Green, P. G. (2008). A case for sexual orientation diversity management in small and large organizations. *Human Resource Management, 47,* 637–654. doi:10.1002/hrm.20235.

Day, N. E., & Schoenrade, P. (1997). Staying in the closet versus coming out: Relationships between communication about sexual orientation and work attitudes. *Personnel Psychology, 50,* 147–163.

Day, N. E., & Schoenrade, P. (2000). The relationship among reported disclosure of sexual orientation, anti-discrimination policies, top management support and work attitudes of gay and lesbian employees. *Personnel Review, 29,* 346–363.

DeJordy, R. (2008). Just passing through: Stigma, passing, and identity decoupling in the work place. *Group Organization Management, 33,* 504–530. doi:10.1177/1059601108324879.

Demerouti, E., Bakker, A. B., & Bulters, A. J. (2004). The loss spiral of work pressure, work-home interference and exhaustion: Reciprocal relations in a three-wave study. *Journal of Vocational Behavior, 64,* 131–149.

Duxbury, L. E., & Higgins, C. A. (1991). Gender differences in work-family conflict. *Journal of Applied Psychology, 76,* 60–74. doi:10.1037/0021-9010.76.1.60.

Eisenberger, R., Huntington, R., Hutchinson, S., & Sowa D. (1986). Perceived organizational support. *Journal of Applied Psychology, 71,* 500–507. doi:10.1037/0021-9010.71.3.500.

Ferdman, B. M. (1999). The color and culture of gender in organizations: Attending to race and ethnicity. In G. Powell (Ed.), *Handbook of gender & work* (pp. 17–34). Thousand Oaks, CA: Sage.

Gates, G. J., Badgett, M.V.L., Macomber, J. E., & Chambers, K. (2007). *Adoption and foster care by gay and lesbian parents in the United States.* Los Angeles, CA: The Williams Institute, University of California at Los Angeles.

Gecas, V., & Seff, M. A. (1989). Social class, occupational conditions, and self-esteem. *Sociological Perspectives, 32,* 353–364.

Giuffre, P., Dellinger, K., & Williams, C. L. (2008). "No retribution for being gay?": Inequality in gay-friendly workplaces. *Sociological Spectrum, 28,* 254–277. doi:10.1080/02732170801898380.

Goldberg, A. E. (2010). *Lesbian and gay parents and their children: Research on the family life cycle.* Washington, DC: APA.

Goldberg, A. E., Moyer, A. M., Richardson, H. B., & Kinkler, A. (in preparation). Challenges encountered by foster-to-adopt parents: Perspectives of lesbian, gay, and heterosexual couples.

Goldberg, A. E., & Smith, J. Z. (2009). Perceived parenting skill across the transition to adoptive parenthood among lesbian, gay, and heterosexual couples. *Journal of Family Psychology, 23,* 861–870. doi:10.1037/a0017009.

Goldberg, A. E., & Smith, J. Z. (2011). Stigma, social context, and mental health: Lesbian and gay couples across the transition to adoptive parenthood. *Journal of Counseling Psychology, 58,* 139–150. doi:10.1037/a0021684.

Gonsiorek, J. C., & Weinrich, J. D. (1991). The definition and scope of sexual orientation. In J. C. Gonsiorek & J. D. Weinich (Eds.), *Homosexuality: Research implications for public policy* (pp. 1–12). Newbury Park, CA: Sage.

Grandey, A. A., & Cropanzano, R. (1999). The conservation of resources model applied to work-family conflict and strain. *Journal of Vocational Behavior, 54,* 350–370.

Greenhaus, J. H., & Beutell, N. J. (1985). Sources of conflict between work and family roles. *Academy of Management Review, 10,* 76–88.

Griffith, K. H., & Hebl, M. R. (2002). The disclosure dilemma for gay men and lesbians: "Coming out" at work. *Journal of Applied Psychology, 87,* 1191–1199. doi:10.1037/0021-9010.87.6.1191.

Herek, G. M. (1994). Assessing heterosexuals' attitudes toward lesbians and gay men: A review of empirical research with the ATLG scale. In B. Greene, & G. M. Herek (Eds.), *Lesbian and gay psychology: Theory, research, and clinical applications* (pp. 206–228). Thousand Oaks, CA: Sage Publications.

Hobfoll, S. E. (1989). Conservation of resources. A new attempt at conceptualizing stress. *American Psychologist, 44,* 513–524. doi:10.1037/0003-066X.44.3.513.

Huffman, A. H., Watrous-Rodriguez, K., & King, E. (2008). Supporting a diverse workforce: What type of support is most meaningful for lesbian and gay employees? *Human Resource Management, 4,* 237–253. doi:10.1002/hrm.20210.

Human Rights Campaign Foundation. (2009). *Degrees of equality: A national study examining workplace climate for LGBT employees.* Washington, DC: Human Rights Campaign Foundation.

Kahn, R. L., Wolfe, D. N., Quinn, R. P., Snoek, J. D., & Rosenthal, D. A. (1964). *Organizational stress: Studies in role conflict and ambiguity.* Oxford, UK: John Wiley.

King, E. B., & Cortina, J. M. (2010). The social and economic imperative of lesbian, gay, bisexual, and transgendered supportive organizational policies. *Industrial and Organizational Psychology: Perspectives on Science and Practice, 3,* 69–78.

Kinnuunen, U., & Mauno, S. (1998). Antecedents and outcomes of work-family conflict among employed women and men in Finland. *Human Relations, 51,* 157–177.

Kopelman, R. E., Greenhaus, J. H., & Connolly, T. F. (1983). A model of work, family, and interrole conflict: A construct validation study. *Organizational behavior and human performance, 32,* 198–215.

Kossek, E. E., & Ozeki, C. (1998). Work-family conflict, policies, and the job-life satisfaction relationship: A review and directions for organizational behavior-human resources research. *Journal of Applied Psychology, 83,* 139–149. doi:10.1037/0003-066X.44.3.513.

Lapierre, L. M., & Allen, T. D. (2006). Work-supportive family, family-supportive supervision, use of organizational benefits, and problem-focused coping: Implications for work-family conflict and employee well-being. *Journal of Occupational Health Psychology, 11,* 169–181. doi:10.1037/1076-8998.11.2.169.

Mercier, L. R. (2007). Lesbian parents and work: Stressors and supports for the work-family interface. In L. R. Mercier & R. D. Harold (Eds.), *Social work with lesbian parent families: Ecological perspectives* (pp. 25–47). New York: The Haworth Press. doi:10.1080/10538720802131675.

Meyer, I. (1995). Minority stress and mental health in gay men. *Journal of Health Sciences and Social Behavior, 36,* 38–56.

Paglis, L. L., & Green, S. G. (2002). Leadership self-efficacy and managers' motivation for leading change. *Journal of Organizational Behavior, 23,* 215–235.

Patterson, C. J. (2000). Family relationships of lesbians and gay men. *Journal of Marriage and Family, 62,* 1052–1069.

Patterson, C. J. (2004). Lesbian and gay parents and their children: Summary of research findings. In *Lesbian and gay parenting: A resource for psychologists.* Washington, DC: American Psychological Association.

Powers, B. (1996). The impact of gay, lesbian, and bisexual workplace issues on productivity. In A. L. Ellis & E.D.B. Riggle (Eds.), *Sexual identity on the job: Issues and services* (pp. 79–90). New York: Haworth Press.

Ragins, B. R. (2004). Sexual orientation in the workplace: The unique work and career experiences of gay, lesbian, and bisexual workers. *Research in Personnel and Human Resources Management, 23,* 35–120.

Ragins, B. R. (2008). Disclosure disconnects: Antecedents and consequences of disclosing invisible stigmas across life domains. *Academy of Management Review, 33,* 194–215.

Ragins, B. R., & Cornwell, J. M. (2001). Pink triangles: Antecedents and consequences of perceived workplace discrimination against gay and lesbian employees. *Journal of Applied Psychology, 86,* 1244–1261. doi:10.1037/0021-9010.86.6.1244.

Rawsthorne, M., & Costello, M. (2010). Cleaning the sink: Exploring the experiences of Australian lesbian parents reconciling work/family responsibilities. *Community, Work & Family, 13,* 189–204. doi:10.1080/13668800903259777.

Riskind, R. G., & Patterson, C. J. (2010). Parenting intentions and desires among childless lesbian, gay and heterosexual individuals. *Journal of Family Psychology, 24,* 78–81. doi:10.1037/a0017941.

Rosenbaum, M., & Cohen, E. (1999). Equalitarian marriages, spousal support, resourcefulness and psychological distress among Israeli working women. *Journal of Vocational Behavior, 54,* 102–113.

Rostosky, S. S., & Riggle, E.D.B. (2002). "Out" at work: The relation of actor and partner workplace policy and internalized homophobia to disclosure status. *Journal of Counseling Psychology, 49,* 411–419. doi:10.1037/0022-0167.49.4.411.

mith, N. G., & Ingram, K. M. (2004). Workplace heterosexism and adjustment among lesbian, gay and bisexual individuals: The role of unsupportive social interactions. *Journal of Counseling Psychology, 51,* 57–67. doi:10.1037/0022-0167.51.1.57.

Stein, A. (2005). Make room for daddy: Anxious masculinity and emergent homophobias in neopatriarchal politics. *Gender & Society, 19,* 601–620.

The Pew Research Center. (2006). *Survey report: Pragmatic Americans liberal and conservative on social issues.* Retrieved October 8, 2010, from http://people-press.org/report/283/pragmatic-americans-liberal-and-conservative-on-social-issues

Thomas, C. A., & Ganster, D. C. (1995). Impact of family-supportive work variables on work-family conflict and strain: A control perspective. *Journal of Applied Psychology, 80,* 6–15. doi:10.1037/0021-9010.80.1.6.

Triandis, H. C., Kurowski, L. L., & Gelfand, M. J. (1994). Workplace diversity. In H. C. Triandis, M. D. Dunnettee, & L. M. Hough (Eds.), *Handbook of industrial and organizational psychology* (2nd ed., Vol. 4, pp. 769–827). Palo Alto, CA: Consulting Psychologist Press.

Tuten, T. L., & August, R. A. (2006). Work-family conflict: A study of lesbian mothers. *Women in Management Review, 21*, 578–597.

U.S. Census Bureau. (2000). *Married-couple and Unmarried-partner Households: 2000.* Census 2000 Special Reports. Retrieved March 25, 2011, from www.census.gov/prod/2003pubs/censr-5.pdf

Waldo, C. R. (1999). Working in a majority context: A structural model of heterosexism as minority stress in the workplace. *Journal of Counseling Psychology, 46*, 218–232. doi:10.1037/0022-0167.46.2.218.

Wang, P., & Schwarz, J. L. (2010). Stock price reactions to GLBT nondiscrimination policies. *Human Resource Management, 49*, 195–216. doi:10.1002/hrm.20341.

Wayne, J. H., Musisca, N., & Fleeson, W. (2004). Considering the role of personality in the work-family experience: Relationships of the big five to work-family conflict and facilitation. *Journal of Vocational Behavior, 64*, 108–130. doi:10.1016/S0001-8791(03)00035-6.

Williams, J. C., & Segal, N. (2004). Beyond the maternal wall: Relief for family caregivers who are discriminated against on the job. *Harvard Women's Law Journal, 26*, 77–162.

Williams, J. E., & Best, D. L. (1990). *Measuring sex stereotypes: A multination study* (Rev. ed.). Newbury Park, CA: Sage.

Woods, J. D. (1993). *The corporate closet: The professional lives of gay men in America.* New York: Free Press.

# Chapter 16

# Promoting Employees' Work-Life Balance: Work, Organizational, and Technological Factors

*YoungAh Park and Tina C. Elacqua*

Most working adults not only engage in work, but also multiple life domains, such as family, community, religion, and leisure. Among others, work is considered as one of the primary domains of life where people invest a great amount of time and effort because they need to make a living through continued employment. As such, work demands easily override the demands in other important life domains (e.g., family, society), and many working adults struggle to manage work and nonwork role responsibilities. The rapidly innovated mobile communication/information technologies, such as smart-phones and portable laptops, contribute to employees' frequent enactment of work-related roles even when they are in the nonwork domain during off-job time (e.g., family, vacation). No wonder that "work-life balance" is or will be a challenging issue for every working individual, at least at some point in his or her life.

Work-life balance is also an important topic of interest for many organizations, managers, and human resource (HR) consultants as our common sense tells us that distress caused by poor balance between work and nonwork life can adversely impact on employees' job attitudes and performance as well as their well-being. In fact, abundant work-life re-search has shown that work-life conflict has negative effects on numerous employee outcomes including job/life satisfaction, commitment to organi-zations, intention to turnover, job performance, and health, to name just a few (e.g., Allen, Herst, Bruck, & Sutton, 2000; Eby, Casper, Lockwood, Bordeaux, & Brinley, 2005; Ford, Heinen, & Langkamer, 2007; Kossek & Ozeki, 1998; van Steenbergen & Ellemers, 2009).

Furthermore, work-life balance plays an important role when orga-nizations attract, hire, and retain talents and high-performing employ-ees (*Work-life balance becoming critical to recruitment and retention*, 2006). Research has further shown that companies promoting their employees' work-life balance tend to achieve better market- and HR-related perfor-mance, such as net profit, new product development, employee morale, and retention (Ngo, Foley, & Loi, 2009). By just glancing at this short list of company and employee outcomes of work-life balance, a strong business case can be built for promoting employee work-life balance in organizations.

## THE CONCEPT OF WORK-LIFE BALANCE

There is a growing popularity of the term *work-life balance* in the popular press and media let alone the field of social science in that many workers ex-perience difficulties in juggling multiple life roles. A quick search in Google Books with a key word, *work-life balance,* gave approximately 1.5 million search results. With this increasing popularity in mind, do we really know what it means? Does work-life balance mean an equal amount of time and efforts allocated into work and nonwork roles? Or does it mean having a little or no difficulty in meeting the demands and responsibilities from the work and personal life domains?

In fact, the concept of work-life balance is not agreed upon and studied as a uniform concept among scholars. It is a rather ambiguous and vague notion to many people; as such it is researched in a variety of different ways (Frone, 2003). Some scholars consider work-life balance as the absence or low levels of perceptions that demands from the work and nonwork life are incompatible due to limited resources (e.g., time, energy)—this is often labeled as work-family or work-life conflict (Greenhaus & Beutell, 1985). Some others argue that we also need to consider positive aspects of the interaction between work and personal life to fully understand work-life balance beyond the concept of work-life conflict (Barnett & Hyde, 2001). For instance, engaging in the work domain can benefit one's effective func-tioning in the family or personal life domains or vice versa—which is la-beled as work-family (life) enrichment or facilitation (e.g., Greenhaus & Powell, 2006; Grzywacz & Marks, 2000). There is another recent perspec-tive that we should view work-life balance as an overall appraisal that parts or elements of life (work and other personal life domains) are arranged harmoniously to the extent that effectiveness and satisfaction in these roles are consistent with one's own life values or priorities (Greenhaus & Allen, 2011).

## WORK-RELATED FACTORS AFFECTING WORK-LIFE BALANCE

### Work Hours and Workload

Many professionals and employees in managerial positions have a feeling of having too much to do in too little time or having not enough time to do it (Milliken & Dunn-Jensen, 2005). We all know that time is a limited resource. As such, the time spent in work-related activities obviously restricts the time needed to fulfill various personal life roles (e.g., spouse, parent, elder care, friends, religion) and enjoy leisure activities that help employees unwind from work stress. Research showed that the more hours employees worked, the less satisfied they were with work-life balance (Valcour, 2007). Research has further shown that imbalance or conflict between the time spent in work and personal life was related to impaired well-being, such as depression among employees in *Fortune* 500 companies (Major, Klein, & Ehrhart, 2002) and life/marital dissatisfaction in various occupations (Allen et al., 2000). We can easily expect these negative life outcomes to have a boomerang effect on important work outcomes over time, such as productivity loss, job dissatisfaction, and turnover.

Then why do employees work longer hours? Work overload (Major et al., 2002) and expectations about time spent at work (Munck, 2001; Thompson, Beauvais, & Lyness, 1999) were shown to be positively related to employees' longer work hours. In other words, when employees have work overload or pressure to get tasks done faster from their superiors and customers/clients, it becomes difficult for them to ignore it because of potentially negative career consequences. If work overload or longer work hours are found to be a major cause of work-life conflict, placing an organizational effort to reduce work load and the pressure can be a direct way to address the time-based work-life imbalance issues in organizations. However, simply removing work overload and time pressure may be something "easier said than done" for many organizations due to fierce competition in the globalized market for survival and increasing customer/client demands.

One potential option for an organization to consider is *reduced-load work arrangement for high-performers*—working less than full-time through a reduction in workload or work hours with commensurate reduction in pay (cf. Hill, Martinson, Ferris, & Baker, 2004; Kossek & Lee, 2008). For example, an employee can opt out for working reduced load/hours of work at

70% with reduced compensation, which can alleviate his or her work-life conflict driven by the lack of time or too much work. On the other hand, the employer can hire a person who can take on some of the responsibilities with the extra money from the salary reduction. According to Kossek and Lee (2008), this type of arrangement can be a useful HR strategy to retain high-talented people who value both work and personal life and the balance between the two. Similarly, another alternative option is creating or allowing part-time track positions in organizations. By opting out for a part-time position (reduced work hours), employees with the birth of a child or preschool child, for example, can still continue one's career and contribute to organizations while being able to devote more time to family when needed (Elacqua, Quinn, & Sax, in press). It should be noted, however, that implementing this type of reduced-load work arrangement requires extra efforts in job redesign, communication, and coordination among the related parties: employer, managers, employees, and employees' work group members (see Elacqua et al., 2012; Kossek & Lee, 2008 for more detailed discussions).

In addition to directly reducing work load or hours, what are other possible ways for organizations and managers to mitigate the negative impacts of longer work hours or work overload on employees' work-life balance? We herein suggest two additional approaches: (1) increasing employees' perceived control over work and (2) supervisors' supportive behaviors for work-life balance.

First, having a greater control over work means to have job autonomy over how one's job is to be performed in general (when, where, how much to work; Elacqua et al., 2012; Thompson & Prottas, 2005). Research evidence supported the beneficial role of employees' job autonomy in managing multiple roles and demands from work and family (Clark, 2001; Grzywacz & Marks, 2000; Thompson & Prottas, 2005; Voydanoff, 2004). In particular, one's control over work time—having a choice in how much and when to work and being able to interrupt work to respond to family demands when needed—was shown to function as a valuable resource especially for those working longer hours leading to employees' satisfaction with work-life balance (Valcour, 2007). Perceived control over time was negatively associated with time-based work-family conflict (Jex & Elacqua, 1999). In addition, as a formal organizational work-life program, flexible work arrangements (e.g., telecommuting, flextime, compressed work week) could be considered to increase the perception of control over work among employees (Casey & Grzywacz, 2008). In short, providing job control in the hands of employees can help mitigate adverse effect of longer work hours or too much work responsibilities, which interferes with their personal life roles. Therefore, organizations are recommended to seek various ways to increase their employees' perceptions of job control. Despite the positive roles of one's job control in work-life balance, it should be noted that increasing control does not solve the fundamental problems of too much workload or longer work hours.

Second, a great amount of research on work-life conflict supports the notion in general that social support from the work domain can help employees deal with work-life conflict (e.g., Michel, Kotrba, Mitchelson, Clark, & Baltes, 2010; Thompson & Prottas, 2005). From a general social support at work, Hammer, Kossek, Yragui, Bodner, and Hanson (2009) have recently differentiated supervisor support that is more specific to work-life balance—*family-supportive supervisor behaviors* (hereinafter, *FSSB*). They offered four categories of FSSB: emotional support, instrumental support, role modeling, and creative work-family management behaviors. According to Hammer et al. (2009), *emotional support* behaviors refer to the behaviors that a supervisor exhibits to make subordinates feel comfortable discussing family-related issues, expressing concerns on how their work roles affect family, and demonstrates sensitivity and respect for employees' nonwork responsibilities. *Instrumental support* behaviors refer to supervisor's providing day-to-day resources or services that help subordinates successfully manage work and family role demands (e.g., backing up subordinates when they have unanticipated nonwork demands). *Role modeling* behaviors include demonstrating examples or strategies that can lead to positive work-life outcomes, so that subordinates can observe and learn them. *Creative work-family management* behaviors refer to behaviors that are individually designed for helping or addressing an employee's work-life management (e.g., creatively reallocating or rescheduling job duties, asking for suggestions to enhance work-life balance). The FSSB were associated with employee's job satisfaction and positive perceptions of their work and family life facilitating each other, and were also related to low levels of turnover intention (Hammer et al., 2009).

Furthermore, Hammer and her colleagues suggested that the FSSB can be highly trainable and applicable based on the results of their rigorous quasi-field experiments on supervisors working in a U.S. local grocery chain (Hammer, Kossek, Anger, Bodner, & Zimmerman, 2011). They found that supervisors—who received a short computer-based tutorial and face-to-face training, and self-monitored their FSSB after the training[1]—greatly improved their supermarket employees' work-life conflict in comparison to the control group who did not receive the training intervention. Beyond the improvement in work-life conflict, Hammer et al. (2011) showed that those employees who worked under the trained supervisors had better physical health, job satisfaction, and a lower level of turnover intentions.

Since the FSSB have been recently introduced, there are not many empirical studies to prove its effectiveness in other job settings, but we agree with the authors that these supervisory behaviors targeting work-family balance can have a great applicability to a wide variety of occupations, industries, and low-paying hourly jobs that lack job autonomy and flexibility (Hammer et al., 2009; Hammer et al., 2011). Considering that supervisors can have a direct impact and changes on employees' work life experience, we believe that training FSSB can be a highly practical approach to promote work-life balance especially for organizations that do not have enough resources to design and implement formal work-life balance programs and policies. Therefore, we suggest that organizations should consider training and rewarding FSSB in order to facilitate work-life balance.

## ORGANIZATIONAL FACTORS AFFECTING WORK-LIFE BALANCE

### Work-Life Culture in Organizations

According to Koppes (2008), the best companies recognized as being good places to work (e.g., *Great Places to Work, Working Mother Best Companies*) seem to have in common a value for work-life balance as a business imperative and actively embrace a supportive culture for work-life balance. More than a decade ago, Thompson et al. (1999) brought great attention to the importance of "work-family culture" in organizations to promote work-life balance. Studies showed that availability of family-supportive benefits/programs is not enough; there must be a work-family supportive culture in order to have effective outcomes of those programs in organizations (Thompson et al., 1999; Thompson & Prottas, 2005). Thompson et al. (1999) recognized that many employees were reluctant to fully utilize family-friendly benefits due to the following components of work-family culture: (1) organizational time demands that interfere with employees' family life, (2) negative career consequences of using work-family programs, and (3) lack of managerial support for employees' work-family balance. In the following section, we address these cultural components in more detail.

#### Organizational Time Demands

We have already noted in the preceding section that employees working longer hours suffer from work-family conflict. It seems that organizational demands for time spent at work are the main driving force for longer hours of working as opposed to employees' preference for working longer (Clarkberg & Moen, 2001). Furthermore, employees perceiving a high level of "visibility norm" (expected amount of time being seen at work) or "face time" culture in their organizations (the more hours put in at work, the better) are more likely to experience poor balance between their work and personal life (Dunn-Jensen, 2006; Munck, 2001). In particular, when job performance has less tangible outcomes (e.g., managerial jobs), spending longer hours at work could be considered an indication of one's dedication to work, which can result in more time demands for work (Milliken & Dunn-Jensen, 2005). Under the pressure and expectations for spending a greater amount of time at work, employees cannot take full advantage of family-supportive programs and policies (Thompson et al., 1999).

### Negative Career Consequences of Using Work-Family Programs

Thompson et al. (1999) also pointed out that when employees perceive negative career consequences associated with using work-family programs or time devoted to family (e.g., extended leave for a new born baby), they would not utilize those programs. In other words, organizations need to examine whether their employees using work-family programs are portrayed as someone who is not serious about one's career and career advancements. For example, if employees who use maternity/paternity leave were not protected from termination or disadvantages in promotions, the leave policies would remain on paper, but not in practice. In that sense, organizations want to make sure that their global organizational culture is in line with work-life programs and policies.

### Managerial Support for Managing Work-Family Responsibilities

There is no doubt that supervisors/managers are the ones who closely interact with employees, and therefore they can have a substantial impact on employees' work-life balance. Supervisors/managers are at the forefront to implement work-life balance programs and policies. As such, regardless of top management decisions, they either can encourage or discourage the use of work-life programs in their work groups and departments (Swanberg, Pitt-Catsouphes, & Drescher-Burke, 2005). Thus, in order to promote work-life balance, organizations must ensure that their supervisors/managers espouse the value of work-life balance. To do it, organizations may hold supervisors/managers accountable for their behaviors in supporting work-life balance culture and educate them of the values of work-life balance and importance of supervisory/managerial roles in employees' lives (Hammer et al., 2011; Koppes, 2008).

## WORK GROUP NORMS

Beyond the work-life specific culture, it is worthy of paying attention to various social norms that exist and differ across work groups, occupations, and job types and levels in an organization. In particular, social norms in a smaller work group or team level are worthy for consideration because the work group employees belong to can impose different demands and expectations, which affect how to manage work and personal life, even when the employees stay within the same organization (Nippert-Eng, 1996). In some work groups, for example, there may be a social norm where members back up each other's work if there is a personal emergency; under this kind of a norm, employees' stress caused by the tension between work and personal life could be reduced (Cioffi, 2007; Hammer, Saksvik, Nytro, Torvatn, & Bayazit, 2004). On the other hand, in some other work groups where high productivity and constant job attendance are the only concerns, employees had a higher level of work-family conflict, which was also related to greater job stress (Hammer et al., 2004). This suggests that constructing a social-relational norm—where mutual respect, caring, and helping are valued—could greatly help employees deal with work-family conflict and job stress (Cioffi, 2007).

## SINGLE-FRIENDLY WORKPLACE CULTURE

When it comes to work-life balance issues, organizations often assume that work-life balance only matters to those married with children. As the diversity in family structures and employees' personal lives increases in our society, we should not exclude childfree single employees (Casper, Weltman, & Kwesiga, 2007). It tends to be easily forgotten that unmarried single working adults without dependent children also have family/personal life responsibilities (their parents, siblings, friends, community). However, the needs of employees with dependent children can be often placed before those of single employees in organizations. For instance, single employees may tend to assume overtime work or business travel responsibilities and have more expectations of deferring their vacation schedule when the business demands are high. If organizations truly want to promote employee work-life balance across the board, they need to actively encompass work-life balance issues of single childfree workers.

Casper et al. (2007) identified several components of single-friendly culture that can address work-life balance issues of single employees. They found that the components of single-friendly culture were related to all components of work-family culture (i.e., managerial support, career consequences, organizational time demands; Casper et al., 2007; Thompson et al., 1999), suggesting that organizations need to be sensitive to work-life issues of single employees when trying to establish an organization-wide work-life balance culture. They also showed that single-friendly culture is associated with higher perceptions of organizational support, which in turn was related to job attitudinal outcomes of single employees, such as turnover intention and commitment (Casper et al., 2007).

Casper et al. (2007) introduced the component of *equal work opportunities* where promotions or work assignments are provided equally to all employees regardless of their family status. For example, an employee with a dependent child would be recognized and given a job opportunity with a greater financial reward as opposed to a single employee who may also need to support an ailing parent financially—but this would not be readily recognized due to the marital status. To ensure equal opportunities, Casper et al. (2007) suggested that work opportunities should be provided based on employees' skills and job performance rather than on employees' family status. Conversely, *equal work expectations* (similar work expectations for single employees and those with immediate families) should be put in place to promote work-life balance for single employees. A working parent, for example, is allowed to miss work for family reasons whereas single employees are often expected to work even on holidays let alone their constant work attendance. This differing level of work expectations with respect to family status can be perceived unfair and aggravate poor work-life balance among single employees.

Casper et al. (2007) also identified that it is important to ensure *equal access to employee benefits* and *equal respect for nonwork roles* of single employees. Most work-life programs and benefits tend to target employees with a spouse/living partner and dependent children (e.g., on-site day care, parental leave) rather than single employees' needs. To make sure equal access to employee benefits is provided organizations may want to implement cafeteria-type of employee benefit programs where employees can select the benefits that best match with their personal life needs (Grandey, 2001). In addition, Casper et al. (2007) pointed out that the nonwork roles among single employees (e.g., family, friends, community member) are not as much respected as those of married employees. Organizations must ensure that their supervisors/managers are trained to be sensitive enough to recognize and respect the nonwork responsibilities of their employees regardless of their marital and family status.

## TECHNOLOGICAL FACTORS AFFECTING WORK-LIFE BALANCE

Many contemporary employees can attend to work-related roles at home and personal/family roles at work through the use of communication/information technologies (hereinafter, *CIT*), such as smart-phones and portable laptops with wireless Internet access. Advancements in CIT increasingly blur boundaries between the work and nonwork domains (Major & Germano, 2006) with employees integrating work roles into the personal life domains and family roles into the work domain (Kossek & Lambert, 2005). There are many beneficial roles of using CIT in integrating employees' work and personal life roles (Elacqua et al., 2012). For instance, a working parent can conveniently grocery shop on the Internet for family meals while at work during break thanks to CIT—this can further save family/personal time at the end of workday. Conversely, an employee can work from home via CIT use when he or she needs to remain at home taking care of his or her children due to unexpected school closings or respond to urgent work-related communication during vacation. These examples illustrate positive episodes of work-life integration through CIT use where employees can fulfill both work and nonwork roles simultaneously regardless of time and place.

The flip side of this work-life integration via CIT includes frequent distractions or interruptions between work and nonwork roles—in particular work easily encroaching upon family/personal time in the nonwork domain (Valcour & Hunter, 2005). Easy access to work or "always on" environment for work through CIT is often pinpointed as one of the culprits that aggravate time demands for work and work-life conflict (Milliken & Dunn-Jensen, 2005; Towers, Duxbury, Higgins, & Thomas, 2006; Valcour & Hunter, 2005). Studies found that CIT use for work after regular business hours was positively related to work-family conflict (e.g., Boswell & Olson-Buchanan, 2007). Chesley (2005) also showed that individuals with persistent use of CIT experienced that negative aspects of their work spilled over to the family domain (i.e., job worries and problems distracted them when they were at home, too tired to do things that needed attention at home)—this negative spillover between work and family was further related to impaired employee well-being.

In line with this research, other occupational health research has consistently supported the notion that employees need to psychologically detach themselves from work during off-job time to recover from work stress (e.g., Sonnentag & Bayer, 2005; Sonnentag & Fritz, 2007). Those who were "switched off" from work during nonwork time reported higher levels of well-being, such as life satisfaction (Fritz, Yankelevich, Zarubin, & Barger, 2010), positive affective experiences (e.g., joviality, serenity; Fritz, Sonnentag, Spector, & McInroe, 2010), and lower levels of depressive symptoms and sleep problems to name just a few (Sonnentag & Fritz, 2007). In addition, this psychological distance from work during nonwork hours buffered the negative impact of work-family conflict and work demands on employee well-being (Moreno-Jiménez, Mayo, Sanz-Vergel, Geurts, Rodríguez-Muñoz, & Garrosa, 2009; Sonnentag, Binnewies, & Mojza, 2010).

## WORK-HOME BOUNDARY MANAGEMENT

Boundary theory posits that individuals construct and maintain more or less permeable psychological, physical, or behavioral boundaries around their multiple life role domains such as work and family/home (Ashforth, Kreiner, & Fugate, 2000; Clark, 2000). Under *permeable boundaries*, individuals are physically in the role's domain, but can psychologically and/or behaviorally engage in another role (Ashforth et al., 2000). Under *permeable work* boundaries, for example, an employee can engage in family-related roles while physically at work (e.g., browse the Internet at work to plan a family vacation). Conversely, under *permeable home* boundaries, an employee can engage in work-related roles at home using a computer and the Internet. Boundary theory posits that highly *permeable* boundaries allow integrating one's work and personal life roles, but this comes with a cost of experiencing frequent work-life conflict and interference. In contrast, *impermeable* boundaries facilitate segmenting work and personal life roles which can reduce work-life interference (Ashforth et al., 2000; Clark, 2000; Kossek & Lambert, 2005; Nippert-Eng, 1996).

Consistent with boundary theory, studies generally support that employees with impermeable work-home boundaries tend to experience a low level of work-family conflict (Hecht & Allen, 2009; Powell & Greenhaus, 2010). A recent qualitative research study also suggests that maintaining impermeable home boundaries could prevent work invasions into the home/family domain (Kreiner, Hollensbe, & Sheep, 2009). When it comes to CIT use for work at home (technological home boundaries), studies showed that keeping impermeable technological boundaries (i.e., more self-restrictions on using CIT for work during nonwork hours) was associated with a lower level of work-life conflict (Kreiner et al., 2009; Olson-Buchanan & Boswell, 2006; Park & Jex, 2011). In summary, creating and maintaining impermeable home boundaries seems favorable to keeping a balance between work and life given the increasingly blurred boundaries where work easily invades in private life domains through the use of CIT.

On the other hand, Clark (2000) and Kreiner et al. (2009) theorized that there are environmental influences on work-home boundary management in that employees live in a social domain (e.g., work) where they tend to conform to the rules, demands, and norms in that domain. Kreiner (2006), in particular, focused on the work environment commensurate with employees' desires for segmenting work from their home domain (e.g., not bringing work home). Kreiner (2006) found that employees' work-family conflict was low when their workplace let them forget about work while they were at home and let them keep work matters at work. Also, Park, Fritz, and Jex (2011) found that employees perceiving that other work domain members actively separated work from their home domain were more likely to "switch themselves off" from work during nonwork hours (psychological detachment from work)—this relationship was even significant when employees' job involvement level was controlled for.

The research on workplace characteristics that supply for work-life segmentation has been fairly nascent. The aforementioned findings and boundary theory bring increasing attention to creating work environments conducive to employees' desired level of work-life segmentation. This is particularly important for an organization to consider when promoting work-life balance because (1) many employees today can run into difficulty in managing the blurred boundaries between work and personal life with the prevalent use of CIT and (2) organizational work-life balance practices have mostly addressed work-life integration rather than segmentation. Some companies even implemented "bring your own computer" program through which employees receive a stipend to purchase a laptop of their own choice for their work and personal use (Madkour, 2008). In some other industries, it may be common that companies provide employees with mobile smart-phones and pay for their fees for work. Despite its benefits, such a program may increase expectations for employees' availability for work by enabling them to transcend temporal and physical boundaries of work.

With the current technological aspects of managing work and nonwork life in mind, we first suggest that organizations need to pay attention to their employees' over-engagement in work-related activities *via CIT during nonwork time*—which should be reserved for family/personal activities to recharge and have energy for the next productive work day. In particular, organizations may want to examine the prevalence of work-related CIT use outside of the office when not required by the job description and when it is related to their employees' poor work-life balance. It is also advisable that organizations educate managers/supervisors so that they can be more attentive to employees' desires for work-home segmentation. For instance, managers/supervisors can refrain themselves from contacting subordinates for work-related matters through CIT outside of office hours, unless it is an emergency.

Second, organizations should be better aware of the positive roles of employees' psychological detachment from work during off-work time to recuperate from work stress for their sustained well-being and work productivity—this was particularly more important for employees who are highly engaged in their work (Sonnentag, Mojza, Binnewies, & Scholl, 2008). Given that intrusive CIT makes many employees harder to detach from their work situations, organizations need to secure and protect nonwork time for their employees' family/personal and recovery activities.

### NOTE

Portions of this chapter were published in M. Paludi (Ed.). (2013). *Psychology for business success. Volume 1: Juggling, balancing, and integrating work and family roles and responsibilities.* Santa Barbara, CA: Praeger.

1. We refer readers who are interested in the FSSB intervention to Hammer et al. (2011) for more detail.

### REFERENCES

Allen, T. D., Herst, D.E.L., Bruck, C. S., & Sutton, M. (2000). Consequences associated with work-to-family conflict: A review and agenda for future research. *Journal of Occupational Health Psychology, 5,* 278–308.

Ashforth, B. E., Kreiner, G. E., & Fugate, M. (2000). All in a day's work: Boundaries and micro role transitions. *Academy of Management Review, 25,* 472–491.

Barnett, R. C., & Hyde, J. S. (2001). Women, men, work, and family: An expansionist theory. *American Psychologist, 56,* 781–796.

Boswell, W. R., & Olson-Buchanan, J. B. (2007). The use of communication technologies after hours: The role of work attitudes and work-life conflict. *Journal of Management, 33,* 592–610.

Casey, P. R., & Grzywacz, J. G. (2008). Employee health and well-being: The role of flexibility and work-family balance. *The Psychologist-Manager Journal, 11,* 31–47.

Casper, W. J., Weltman, D., & Kwesiga, E. (2007). Beyond family-friendly: The construct and measurement of singles-friendly work culture. *Journal of Vocational Behavior, 70,* 478–501.

Chesley, N. (2005). Blurring boundaries? Linking technology use, spillover, individual distress, and family satisfaction. *Journal of Marriage and Family, 67,* 1237–1248.

Cioffi, C. (2007). Finding and keeping the best and brightest—flexible policies in a small workplace. In M. A. Paludi & P. E. Neidermeyer (Eds.), *Work, life, and family imbalance: How to level the playing field* (pp. 79–88). Westport, CT: Praeger.

Clark, S. C. (2000). Work/family border theory: A new theory of work/family balance. *Human Relations, 53,* 747–770.

Clark, S. C. (2001). Work cultures and work/family balance. *Journal of Vocational Behaviors, 58,* 348–365.

Clarkberg, M., & Moen, P. (2001). Understanding the time-squeeze: Married couples' preferred and actual work-hour strategies. *American Behavioral Scientist, 44,* 1115–1135.

Dunn-Jensen, L. M. (2006). *Unmasking face time: The implications of visibility norms in the workplace.* Unpublished doctoral dissertation at New York University.

Eby, L. T., Casper, W. J., Lockwood, A., Bordeaux, C., & Brinley, A. (2005). Work and family research in IO/OB: Content analysis and review of the literature (1980–2002). *Journal of Vocational Behavior, 66,* 124–197.

Elacqua, T. C., Quinn, A., & Sax, E. (2012). From juggling to balancing to integration: Women, work and family lives. In M. Paludi (Series Ed.) & M. Paludi (Vol. Ed.), *Women and careers in management (Series). Managing diversity in today's workplace: Strategies for employees and employers.* Westport, CT: Praeger.

Ford, M. T., Heinen, B. A., & Langkamer, K. L. (2007). Work and family satisfaction and conflict. *Journal of Applied Psychology, 92,* 57–80.

Fritz, C., Sonnentag, S., Spector, P. E., & McInroe, J. (2010). The weekend matters: Relationships between stress recovery and affective experiences. *Journal of Organizational Behavior, 31,* 1137–1162.

Fritz, C., Yankelevich, M., Zarubin, A., & Barger, P. (2010). Happy, healthy and productive? The role of detachment from work during nonwork time. *Journal of Applied Psychology, 95,* 977–983.

Frone, M. R. (2003). Work-family balance. In J. C. Quick & L. E. Tetrick (Eds.), *Handbook of occupational health psychology* (pp. 143–162). Washington, DC: American Psychological Association.

Grandey, A. A. (2001). Family friendly policies: Organizational justice perceptions of need-based allocations. In R. Cropanzano (Ed.), *Justice in the workplace: From theory to practice* (Vol. 2, pp. 145–173). Mahwah, NJ: Lawrence Erlbaum.

Greenhaus, J. H., & Allen, T. (2011). Work-life balance: A review and extension of the literature. In J. C. Quick & L. E. Tetrick (Eds.), *Handbook of occupational health psychology* (pp. 165–184). Washington, DC: American Psychological Association.

Greenhaus, J. H., & Beutell, N. J. (1985). Sources and conflict between work and family roles. *Academy of Management Review, 10,* 76–88.

Greenhaus, J. H., & Powell, G. N. (2006). When work and family are allies: A theory of work-family enrichment. *Academy of Management Review, 31,* 72–92.

Grzywacz, J. G., & Marks, N. F. (2000). Reconceptualizing the work-family interface: An ecological perspective on the correlates of positive and negative spillover between work and family. *Journal of Occupational Health Psychology, 5,* 111–126.

Hammer, L. B., Kossek, E. E., Anger, W. E., Bodner, T., & Zimmerman, K. L. (2011). Clarifying work-family intervention processes: The roles of work-family conflict and family-supportive supervisor behaviors. *Journal of Applied Psychology, 96,* 134–150.

Hammer, L. B., Kossek, E. E., Yragui, N. L., Bodner, T. E., & Hanson, G. C. (2009). Development and validation of a multidimensional measure of family supportive supervisor behaviors (FSSB). *Journal of Management, 35,* 837–856.

Hammer, T. H., Saksvik, P. O., Nytro K., Torvatn, H., & Bayazit, M. (2004). Expanding the psychosocial work environment: Workplace norms and work-family conflict as correlates of stress and health. *Journal of Occupational Health Psychology, 9,* 83–97.

Hecht, T. D., & Allen, N. J. (2009). A longitudinal examination of the work-nonwork boundary strength construct. *Journal of Organizational Behavior, 30,* 839–862.

Hill, E. J., Martinson, A., Ferris, M., & Baker, R. (2004). Beyond the mommy track: The influence of new-concept part time work for professional women on work and family. *Journal of Family & Economic Issues, 25,* 121–136.

Jex, S. M., & Elacqua, T. C. (1999). Time management as a moderator of relations between stressors and employee strain. *Work and Stress, 13,* 182–191.

Koppes, L. L. (2008). Facilitating an organization to embrace a work-life effectiveness culture: A practical approach. *The Psychologist-Manager Journal, 11,* 163–184.

Kossek, E. E., & Lambert, S. J. (Eds.). (2005). *Work and life integration: Organizational, cultural, and individual perspectives.* Mahwah, NJ: Lawrence Erlbaum Associates.

Kossek, E. E., & Lee, M. D. (2008). Implementing a reduced-workload arrangement to retain high talent: A case study. *The Psychologist-Manager Journal, 11,* 49–64.

Kossek, E. E., & Ozeki, C. (1998). Work-family conflict, policies, and the job-life satisfaction relationship: A review and directions for organizational behavior-human resources research. *Journal of Applied Psychology, 83,* 139–149.

Kreiner, G. (2006). Consequences of work-home segmentation or integration: A person-environment fit perspective. *Journal of Organizational Behavior, 27,* 485–507.

Kreiner, G., Hollensbe, E., & Sheep, M. L. (2009). Balancing borders and bridges: Negotiating work-home interface via boundary work tactics. *Academy of Management Journal, 52,* 704–730.

Madkour, R. (2008, September 25). *BYOC: Bring Your Own Computer — to work.* Associated Press. Retrieved May 26, 2011, from http://www.msnbc.msn.com/id/26889537/

Major, D. A., & Germano, L. M. (2006). The changing nature of work and its impact on the work-home interface. In F. Jones, R. J. Burke, & M. Westman (Eds.), *Work-life balance: A psychological perspective* (pp. 13–38). New York: Psychology Press.

Major, V. S., Klein, K. J., & Ehrhart, M. G. (2002). Work time, work interference with family, and psychological distress. *Journal of Applied Psychology, 87,* 427–436.

Michel, J. S., Kotrba, L. M., Mitchelson, J. K., Clark, M. A., & Baltes, B. B. (2010). Antecedents of work–family conflict: A meta-analytic review. *Journal of Organizational Behavior.* Advanced publication. doi:10.1002/job.695.

Milliken, F. J., & Dunn-Jensen, L. M. (2005). The changing time demands of managerial and professional work: Implications for managing the work-life boundary. In E. E. Kossek & S. J. Lambert (Eds.), *Work and life integration: Organizational, cultural and individual perspectives* (pp. 43–60). Mahwah, NJ: Lawrence Erlbaum Associates Press.

Moreno-Jiménez, B., Mayo, M., Sanz-Vergel, A. I., Geurts, S.A.E., Rodríguez-Muñoz, A., & Garrosa, E. (2009). Effects of work–family conflict on employee's well-being: The moderating role of recovery experiences. *Journal of Occupational Health Psychology, 14,* 427–440.

Munck, B. ( 2001). Changing a culture of face time. *Harvard Business Review, 79,* 125–131.

Ngo, H. Y., Foley, S., & Loi, R. (2009). Family friendly work practices, organizational climate, and firm performance: A study of multinational corporations in Hong Kong. *Journal of Organizational Behavior, 30,* 665–680.

Nippert-Eng, C. E. (1996). *Home and work: Negotiating boundaries through everyday life.* Chicago: University of Chicago Press.

Olson-Buchanan, J. B., & Boswell, W. R. (2006). Blurring boundaries: Correlates of integration and segmentation between work and nonwork. *Journal of Vocational Behavior, 68,* 432–445.

Park, Y., Fritz, C., & Jex, S. M. (2011, July). Relationships between work-home segmentation and psychological detachment from work: The pole of communication technology use at home. *Journal of Occupational Health Psychology.* Advance online first publication. doi:10.1037/a0023594.

Park, Y., & Jex, S. M. (2011). Work-home boundary management using communication and information technology. *International Journal of Stress Management, 18,* 133–152.

Powell, G. N., & Greenhaus, J. H. (2010). Sex, gender, and the work-to-family interface: Exploring negative and positive interdependencies. *Academy of Management Journal, 53,* 513–534.

Sonnentag, S., & Bayer, U. (2005). Switching off mentally: Predictors and consequences of psychological detachment from work during off-job time. *Journal of Occupational Health Psychology, 10,* 393–414.

Sonnentag, S., Binnewies, C., & Mojza, E. J. (2010). Staying well and engaged when demands are high: The role of psychological detachment. *Journal of Applied Psychology, 95,* 965–976.

Sonnentag, S., & Fritz, C. (2007). The recovery experience questionnaire: Development and validation of a measure for assessing recuperation and unwinding from work. *Journal of Occupational Health Psychology, 12,* 204–221.

Sonnentag, S., Mojza, E. J., Binnewies, C., & Scholl, A. (2008). Being engaged at work and detached at home: A week-level study on work engagement, psychological detachment, and affect. *Work & Stress, 22,* 259–276.

Swanberg, J. S., Pitt-Catsouphes, M., & Drescher-Burke, K. (2005). A question of justice: Disparities in employees' access to flexible schedule arrangements. *Journal of Family Issues, 26,* 866–895.

Thompson, C. A., Beauvais, L. L., & Lyness, K. S. (1999). When work–family benefits are not enough: The influence of work–family culture on benefit utilization, organizational attachment, and work–family conflict. *Journal of Vocational Behavior, 54,* 392–415.

Thompson, C. A., & Prottas, D. J. (2005). Relationships among organizational family support, job autonomy, perceived control, and employee well-being. *Journal of Occupational Health Psychology, 10,* 100–118.

Towers, I., Duxbury, L., Higgins, C., & Thomas, J. (2006). Time thieves and space invaders: Technology, work and the organization. *Journal of Organizational Change Management, 19,* 593–618.

Valcour, M. (2007). Work-based resources as moderators of the relationship between work hours and satisfaction with work-family balance. *Journal of Applied Psychology, 92,* 1512–1523.

Valcour, P. M., & Hunter, L. W. (2005). Technology, organizations, and work-life integration. In E. E. Kossek & S. J. Lambert (Eds.), *Work and life integration: Organizational, cultural and individual perspectives* (pp. 61–84). Mahwah, NJ: Lawrence Erlbaum Associates Press.

van Steenbergen, E. F., & Ellemers, N. (2009). Is managing the work-family interface worthwhile? Benefits for employee health and performance. *Journal of Organizational Behavior, 30,* 617–642.

Voydanoff, P. (2004). The effects of work demands and resources on work-to-family conflict and facilitation. *Journal of Marriage and Family, 66,* 398–412.

*Work-life balance becoming critical to recruitment and retention.* (2006). Retrieved December 24, 2010, from http://www.management-issues.com/news/2981/work-life-balance-becoming-critical-to-recruitment-and-retention/

# Chapter 17

# Part-Time Employment for Women: Implications for Women and Their Children

*Katherine A. Sliter and Tina C. Elacqua*

For the past several decades, the number of individuals employed in part-time positions in industrialized countries has risen consistently in comparison to full-time employment (Kalleburg, 2000; Sundstrom, 1991; Tilly, 1991), and this is especially true among women with children (Blossfeld & Hakim, 1997; Kalleburg, 2000; Rosenfeld & Birkelund, 1995). Thanks in no small part to the global economic downturn of recent years, the number of mothers seeking employment outside the home has increased, and it seems that mothers are finding this employment most readily in part-time roles.

The motivation for maternal part-time employment can vary greatly, from financial pressure and a need for additional income to an intrinsic desire for fulfillment and self-improvement. As previously noted, the trend is undoubtedly influenced to some extent by the state of the economy. In times of economic hardship, mothers may feel more pressure to seek income outside the home in order to benefit family finances (Blossfeld & Hakim, 1997; Gray, Qu, de Vaus, & Millward, 2002). Full-time positions can be harder to come by during tough economic times, meaning that mothers may find part-time work easier to obtain. Part-time work also offers women with children the opportunity to gain the benefits of employment, financial and otherwise, while still maintaining a distinctly maternal role as caregiver (Brykman, 2006; Elacqua, Quinn, & Sax, in press; Rosenfeld & Birkelund, 1995). Further variation can also be seen in the demographic and social characteristics of part-time maternal employees themselves, the positions that they hold, and the outcomes experienced by both mothers and their children, as will be shown in the coming sections. Clearly, working mothers who take on part-time roles are a unique and diverse subpopulation, and one of particular interest because of their growing numbers. With an increasing number of mothers entering the part-time workforce, there is also an increasing need to understand both the positive and negative impacts of this trend on mothers and their families.

## HISTORY OF MATERNAL EMPLOYMENT: MYTHS OF MOTHERHOOD

The postwar decades of the 1950s and 1960s saw dramatic changes in employment for married women with children (Hofmeister, 2006). Census data from this time period show that in 1957, about 30% of women with children under the age of 18 were working at least part-time, an increase of almost 80% from 1948 (U.S. Census Bureau, n.d.). Yet even during these decades, when maternal employment was creeping ever higher, there still remained a general social expectation that women should remain at home as caregivers, only seeking employment outside the home if they absolutely *must* do so for economic reasons (Stolz, 1960).

This social prejudice against working mothers still persists today (Blair-Loy, 2003; Coltrane & Adams, 2008; Epstein, Seron, Oglensky, & Saute, 1999). Maternal employment, even during the early years of children's lives, is quite common, with 56.3% of mothers of children less than 12 months of age working outside of the home in 2010 (U.S. Department of Labor, Bureau of Labor Statistics, 2011), but societal norms still favor the stay-at-home maternal role. In fact, there is increasing social pressure for women to conform to an emerging norm of "intensive mothering" (Hays, 1996), or investing extremely high levels of time and energy in childrearing in order to produce the healthiest and most successful children possible. As Benard and Correll (2010) point out, this means that present-day mothers who decide to go back to work, and thus devote at least a portion of their time to an activity other than childcare, are almost automatically perceived as falling short of the ideal of motherhood.

The continuation of traditional prejudices against working mothers, and the emergence of new social norms in parallel, is based on several pervasive myths of motherhood. In short, our views of the activities in which women were engaged in the past may not be entirely accurate, thus warping our perceptions of what formal employment actually means for women's time. Furthermore, we may be failing to acknowledge important concomitant social changes when examining the antecedents and consequences of maternal employment. It is important that these myths be identified prior to any discussion of mothers' present-day employment, as doing so will help to put both historical and modern trends and research findings into better perspective.

One common misconception about maternal employment is that when mothers leave the home to work, their children are subjected to reduced maternal involvement (Blankenhorn, 1995; Hughes & Galinsky, 1989). This may have accounted for much of the historical prejudice against women working outside the home when children entered the picture. It was, after all, a woman's duty to raise healthy, happy children and if her absence would result in less direct time with children, that would be undesirable. Contrary to this belief, several studies have shown that this zero-sum view of mothers' time—that time spent engaging in outside employment must automatically result in a reduction of maternal care—may be misleading (Bianchi, 2000; Gauthier, Smeeding, & Furstenberg, 2004; Sandberg & Hofferth, 2001) and that quality time with children may actually *increase* with maternal employment and the modern family structure.

Another myth of motherhood that may unfairly influence perceptions of part-time maternal employees is that maternal employment was almost nonexistent prior to the previously cited postwar boom. The truth is that part-time employment for mothers has been remarkably common throughout history, albeit often in a form that was different from today's corporate setting. In addition to the unpaid farm work that was previously discussed, women with children often held other roles that allowed them to supplement the family's income. One position often held by mothers throughout history was that of assistant for employed husbands, working part-time in a store or office that was run by the patriarch of the family and even running the business if he fell ill or was injured. As early as 1700, there are reports of mothers independently earning money through tasks such as sewing, cleaning, milling, or doing similar domestic tasks for others for a wage (Scott & Tilly, 1975; Tilly, 1987). Mothers could also earn income as midwives or nurses, assisting other women in times of illness or childbirth (Ehrenreich & English, 1978). Modern mothers, even prior to the postwar employment boom, had more choices, including clerical and sales positions, paid childcare, teaching, nursing, and other positions that would take them outside of the home at least part of the time.

All in all, the history of part-time employment for mothers is quite different from the stereotypical conception. Far from being confined to a limited role as caregiver for their children, mothers throughout history have had consistent and varied opportunities for wage earning outside the home. Even among mothers who did not work externally, the role of stay-at-home-mother involved far more than mothering, with only a portion of time being devoted to true childrearing activities. This means that part-time work, or even full-time work, among mothers may not require much separation from the tasks of motherhood.

## MODERN TRENDS IN MATERNAL EMPLOYMENT

In today's rapidly changing, and often uncertain, job market, part-time work has generally become more popular. Although 12.1% of Americans were employed part-time in 1957, that figure grew to 19% in 1993 and to well over 25% in recent years (Tilly, 1991; U.S. Department of Labor, Bureau of Labor Statistics, 2011). It is interesting to note that part-time employment is now markedly higher among females than males. As of 2010, 26.6% of female employees work part-time, compared to only 13.4% of all employed men, and women average 5 fewer hours of employment per week than men when all male and female employees are compared (U.S. Department of Labor, Bureau of Labor Statistics, 2011), a pattern that is seen in industrialized countries worldwide (Kalleburg, 2000; O'Reilly & Fagan, 1998; Rosenfeld & Birkelund, 1995). When parental status is factored into the equation, differences become even more marked. As of 2009, 17.2% of all American mothers worked part-time, a third of all maternal employees (U.S. Congress' Joint Economic Committee Majority Staff, 2010), while the percent of fathers employed part-time continually falls within the single digits.

Interestingly, part-time work may actually be *more* popular among mothers than what is indicated by these already impressive figures: a 2007 Pew Research Center survey found that 60% of mothers who were employed full-time would actually prefer part-time work if given the option. The remaining mothers were split evenly between those who would prefer to be stay-at-home mothers and those who found their full-time work to be ideal. Among fathers, this trend is not seen: fully 72% of fathers in the same survey indicated that they preferred their full-time employment to part-time or stay-at-home arrangements. When these figures were compared to values from 1997, the trend toward part-time work among mothers was even clearer: the number of working mothers preferring full-time work and stay-at-home lifestyles both dropped—a decrease of 11% for the former and 1% for the latter—with only the preference for part-time work increasing by 12% over those years.

It is obvious from the above statistics that mothers not only prefer part-time work to full-time, but that these desires are being reflected in the labor market. However, this trend in employment has not been entirely consistent within the subpopulation of women. Demographic differences exist in the rates of maternal part-time employment, with certain groups being disproportionately represented among part-time employees. These demographic differences, along with the motivation for a woman to seek part-time work (discussed momentarily) play a role in determining how women and their children are impacted by a mother's work status, making them a key factor in understanding the implications of part-time maternal work.

Part-time employees tend to be disproportionately female, as discussed earlier, and other demographic groups disproportionately represented among part-time employees include those who are white (Corcoran & Duncan, 1979), younger in age (Eberhardt & Shani, 1984; Kalleburg, 2000), married (Cull, Mulvey, O'Connor, Sowell, Berkowitz, & Britton, 2002; Walsh, 1999), serving as a secondary income earner (Walsh, 1999), and who have less than a college degree (Nardone, 1995). The latter is perhaps not surprising, given that part-time jobs are often entry-level and lower-ranking positions for which those with fewer academic credentials may be best qualified. It is also more difficult for individuals with weaker academic credentials to compete against more qualified candidates for full-time positions when jobs are scarce and workers are plentiful. This can also be said of younger individuals, who simply have not had the time to build as significant a cache of experience and qualifications as those who have had more years in the job market. It is also not surprising that those who are married and those who have the support of another person with full-time employment status are more likely to work part-time. They are uniquely able to voluntarily select part-time employment because they do not bear the entirety of both the childcare and breadwinner roles within the family.

The finding that white females are more likely to have part-time work than minorities, however, requires some postulation in order to explain. One possible explanation ties back to the topic of marriage and part-time work. White women tend to have higher marriage rates (Manning & Smock, 1995) and lower rates of single motherhood (U.S. Census Bureau, n.d.; U.S. Census Bureau, 2012), meaning that white mothers are more likely to have partners who can offset some of the demands of the household and make part-time work more plausible. Additionally, the average earning of a white female tends to be higher than the average nonwhite female (Alon & Haberfeld, 2007; Pendakur & Pendakur, 2007), meaning that white mothers may be more likely to be able to meet their economic requirements without needing to work full-time. Also possibly contributing to this pattern is the fact that white mothers tend to have fewer children than nonwhite mothers (U.S. Census Bureau, 2012) which both reduces the amount of at-home demands as well as the financial demands on the family. In turn, this could make part-time work more viable for white mothers as there is less pressure either to stay home or to work full-time for financial reasons. Finally, another factor may be that the employment rate for white individuals, in general, is simply higher than that for minority individuals—unemployment rates from 2005 to 2009 averaged 6.1% while this value was over 13% for African American and Native American individuals, for instance (U.S. Census Bureau, n.d.). Once these employment statistics are considered together, the white/nonwhite difference in maternal part-time employment becomes more understandable.

Another important aspect to consider with regards to modern part-time maternal employment trend is the variation in motivation for seeking such employment. Indeed, mothers who secure part-time employment often do so for very different reasons, and the impetus for such a decision on a mother's part can significantly influence the way that she is affected by her employment status. Before discussing the benefits and drawbacks to maternal part-time employment, then, we believe that it is helpful to understand the "why" of maternal employment. Although it is beyond the scope of any one chapter to address the many combinations of factors that are possible, we will now present some of the reasons for maternal part-time employment that are most commonly cited in the contemporary research.

One obvious reason for women to seek part-time employment is finances. In fact, this may be the most common reason, given that a national survey of over 3,700 mothers by the Working Mother Research Institute found that over 70% viewed work merely as a means to obtain a paycheck (2011). Regardless of whether economics are the primary driving force, however, part-time maternal work can have significant economic perks: higher household income is related to numerous familial benefits, including better diet quality (Darmon & Drewnowski, 2008; Galobardes, Morabia, & Bernstein, 2001), better academic achievement for children (Siegel, 2011; Sirin, 2005), and improved healthcare (Nuru-Jeter, Sarsour, Jutte, & Boyce, 2010), to name just a few. It is common for mothers to feel guilty over spending money on themselves (Nyman, 1999), and part-time work may simply offer mothers a chance to earn personal money that can be spent without guilt over taking away from the family finances. Part-time employment, therefore, is viewed by some mothers as a positive opportunity to assist in bettering the lives and social standing of themselves and their partners and children.

Another reason that mothers are increasingly seeking part-time employment is that such a schedule is viewed by many as being ideally conducive to work-life balance (Elacqua et al., in press; Feldman, 1990; Hakim, 1995). Although employment among women, in general, is much higher today than even a few decades ago, women still face notable social pressure to shift their focus to childrearing once they become mothers (Blair-Loy, 2003; Coltrane & Adams, 2008; Epstein et al., 1999). A large percentage of women also find that they simply *want* to spend more time at home once their children are born, regardless of social pressure or stigma

(Declerq, Sakala, Corry, & Applebaum, 2007; Hock, Gnezda, & McBride, 1984), but being a full-time stay-at-home mother may either be financially infeasible or not something they find desirable. In such cases, part-time employment can offer women with children the opportunity to preserve both their maternal and professional identities.

Although finances and a desire for work-life balance are likely two of the most common reasons for mothers to seek part-time employment, innumerable factors besides those noted above can still drive mothers' decisions to work. For instance, women with children may seek part-time employment as a means of self-improvement or accomplishment. In two of the many interviews quoted by author Beth Brykman in her book on maternal employment (2006), one mother recounted how part-time employment was crucial to her sense of emotional and spiritual fulfillment, while another related how she received satisfaction from being able to help others through her part-time job. Part-time work may also be an attempt by mothers in high-powered jobs to preserve their job security, allowing them to keep a hand in at work until they can come back full-time (Epstein et al., 1999). It may also serve as an escape from the stressors of motherhood (Hochschild, 1997) or perhaps a means of trying out a career different from that held prior to having children.

These are, or course, only some of the possible explanations for part-time work among mothers, and every mother is unique. It is beyond the scope of any single chapter to identify all the motivators for maternal employment, and the many combinations thereof, but by identifying some of the more commonly cited motivators, we hope to add yet another piece to the puzzle of understanding part-time maternal employment's effect. In the next section, we will begin to probe the literature on both the benefits and drawbacks of maternal part-time employment for mothers and their children, and many of these motivators will come back due to their effects on various outcomes.

## IMPLICATION OF MATERNAL PART-TIME EMPLOYMENT

### The Benefits

Maternal employment, and more specifically, part-time employment for mothers, has numerous benefits for both mothers and their children. The financial benefits for mothers and their children, previously noted, include extra personal funds for mothers and important factors such as improved academic performance (Siegel, 2011; Sirin, 2005), and access to better healthcare (Nuru-Jeter, Sarsour, Jutte, & Boyce, 2010) for children. However, the positive implications of maternal part-time employment go far beyond simply adding to the household bank account. When mothers work outside the home, at least a portion of the time, both they and their children often experience several notable psychological and social benefits that can result in significant improvement in the quality of life of all members of the family.

One key benefit to part-time work is that by moving from a full-time role to a part-time role, a mother is often able to balance the demands of home and work (Buehler & O'Brien, 2011; Higgins, Duxbury, & Johnson, 2000; Hill, Martinson, Ferris, & Baker, 2004). Perhaps the most parsimonious explanation for this finding is that if a woman feels competing desires to work and to stay home with her children, then part-time work offers a very attractive option: she can do both, and by satisfying this conflict, create a feeling of better balance and harmony. For mothers in professional careers, part-time work may be an alternative to completely abandoning a career path in favor of the "mommy track," as it allows her to maintain a connection to her work and colleagues. Part-time jobs are also perceived by mothers as being more flexible (Hill et al., 2004), and this flexibility likely accounts for at least a portion of the reported reduction in conflict between work and family.

Another benefit for mothers is that employment during the prekindergarten years of a child's life is related to decreased maternal depressive symptoms and lower stress. This relationship has been replicated in multiple studies across various demographic groups. In one such study, over 2,000 low socioeconomic status urban mothers were surveyed multiple times, and the depressive symptoms of those who sought postpartum employment actually decreased over a period of 16 months (Coley, Lohman, Votruba-Drzal, Pittman, & Chase-Lansdale, 2007). Buehler and O'Brien (2011) followed children and their families from infancy to fifth grade and found very similar results, with mothers who were employed at least part-time showing decreasing depressive symptoms over those years. Mothers in this latter study also showed improved self-reported health when employed at least part-time.

Although we were unable to find any studies addressing the possible causal mechanisms of these relationships, we believe that other studies relating to role demands and health may help to explain how part-time employment can be of benefit. A plausible explanation is that work may actually serve as a respite from the stressors of parenting, especially when a mother has a very young child at home. Theoretical support for this hypothesis can be found in Hobfoll's (1989) Conservation of Resources (COR) theory. COR theory posits that individuals have a limited amount of resources for coping with stressors in their environment. When these stressors are depleted, feelings of anxiety, burnout, or other negative emotions may arise. Parenting, especially parenting of an infant, is physically and emotionally draining for a mother, sapping her resources, and leaving her open to negative symptoms. When stressors build up in the workplace, people may withdraw in order to recoup resources (Wright &

Cropanzano, 1998), and it is quite possible that the opposite is also true: withdrawing from the household to work part-time may alleviate the resource drain of parenting, while the part-time status allows a mother to also avoid the drain of full-time work.

It should be noted, however, that one study has previously found that this relationship between part-time work and mothers' health may be moderated by race. Herold and Waldron (1985) found that for African American women, part-time work was actually related to decreased health and well-being and posited that this was likely a result of the lower average socioeconomic status of the jobs that were held by these women. Although, to the best of our knowledge, the relationship has never been retested, the authors' conclusions would seem to be realistic. Other researchers have also found that individuals who are African American and Hispanic/Latino tend to hold positions of lower prestige than Caucasian employees (Bound & Freeman, 1992; Danzinger & Gottschalk, 1991; Xu & Leffler, 1992), and lower income is known to relate to poorer healthcare and higher levels of psychological stress and strain (Cohen, 2011; Nuru-Jeter et al., 2010). This also raises the possibility of moderators in the many benefits and drawbacks being cited in this chapter. Although part-time work is very popular among mothers, it still remains relatively understudied, meaning that there may be other influences on these benefits and drawbacks that simply are not known at this point.

Likely related to this is the finding that part-time employment is linked to increases in certain positive affective outcomes in the workplace than full-time employment. For instance, satisfaction with one's job tends to be highest when a woman is working part-time as compared to full-time employment or a stay-at-home scenario (Booth & van Ours, 2008; Eberhardt & Shani, 1984; Sinclair, Martin, & Michel, 1999). A study conducted by Conway and Briner (2002), however, indicates that this relationship may be mediated by how well a company maintains its promises to employees, as was the positive relationship between part-time employment and intentions to remain with an organization. This relationship between part-time status and intentions to stay was also replicated by Brown and Yoshioka (2003), albeit without the mediation hypothesis. Organizational commitment, another affective outcome, has also been shown to be higher among part-time employees, but only when the part-time employment is the preferred schedule (Lee & Johnson, 1991). This is one area in which the motivation for part-time employment appears to be particularly critical. When mothers are forced to take a part-time job because of financial strain, inability to find a full-time position, family constraints, or other such reasons, this benefit appears to be negated.

The positive affective outcomes of working part-time may actually spill over into nonwork life for women. When women are employed part-time in positions with higher levels of autonomy, responsibility, and prestige, such as professional and managerial roles, they tend to feel a stronger sense of personal fulfillment in their lives (Duxbury & Higgins, 1994; Higgins et al., 2000). According to several studies, positive feelings about one's job also contribute to marital satisfaction (Barling & MacEwen, 1992; Ford, Heinen, & Langkamer, 2007), as well as general positive affectivity after work (Judge & Ilies, 2004). Mothers who work part-time may not only feel happier as a result, but may also feel more energized: Shirom and Shraga (2009) tested the relationship between positive feelings at work and feelings of vigor using a longitudinal framework and found that general positive appraisals of one's work life were related to greater vigor and energy.

Children can experience benefits as a result of their mothers seeking part-time employment outside of the home. One way in which children benefit is through increased quality of parenting. This runs counter to the more traditional belief that when mothers leave the home, children receive less parenting time, and that the time they receive is of inferior quality (Blankenhorn, 1995; Hewlett, 1991). In fact, recent research has shown that neither of these assertions is true. When the number of hours that mothers spend in direct childcare activities is compared across the decades, the surprising finding is that there is an increase (Bianchi, 2000; Gauthier et al., 2004; Sandberg & Hofferth, 2001). Whereas women in the past were required to split their time among numerous demanding household tasks, of which childcare was only one, modern social and technological advances have freed up a significant amount of mothers' time. Instead churning butter, washing clothing by hand, and sewing clothes, today's mothers have the freedom to spend more time with their children while also spending more time in outside employment.

Part-time employment for mothers has also been linked to better quality of parenting in multiple studies. One aspect of parenting in which mothers who are employed part-time have been shown to perform highly is in sensitivity and responsiveness toward their children's needs from infancy through the school-aged years (Belsky & Rovine, 1984; Brooks-Gunn, Han, & Waldfogel, 2010; Buehler & O'Brien, 2011; Horwood & Fergusson, 1999). It is possible that mothers who are employed part-time are better able to fine-tune their communication and reaction skills through more extensive interpersonal reactions outside the home, while also maintaining a closer bond with their children due to reduced working hours. In addition to greater sensitivity and communication, mothers who work part-time have also been shown to provide more learning opportunities to their children and to be more involved with their children's schooling than mothers employed full-time (Buehler & O'Brien, 2011), all indicators of stronger parenting quality.

All of this together may help to explain why researchers have found that traditional beliefs about maternal employment impairing children's future academic achievement are not always true, with part-time employment having either no effect, or even a positive effect, on child achievement (Gregg, Washbrook, Propper, & Burgess, 2005; Vandell & Ramanan, 1992). One such study, conducted by Brooks-Gunn, Han, and Waldfogel (2002), for instance, found that when mothers were employed on a part-time basis, their young children's school readiness scores were statistically comparable to those of stay-at-home moms. Mothers who worked on a full-time basis during these early years, however, had children with average school readiness scores a full 6.25 percentile points lower. Other studies have found some slight reductions in academic ability for children with mothers who work part-time during the first few years of a child's life (see Ruhm, 2004 for a review), but the positive side of this is that these differences are typically quite small and are always less significant than the differences in achievement when mothers work full-time. It is possible that if other considerations were factored in, such as quality of childcare, involvement of fathers, and so forth, these differences may well be even smaller (Parcel & Menaghan, 1994). For mothers who are not socioeconomically disadvantaged, under unusual levels of stress, or otherwise in a uniquely challenging part-time situation, part-time employment may offer the best of both worlds for them *and* their children: an opportunity for mothers to grow and flourish as an individual outside the home while also providing quality parenting and greater economic security and benefits at home.

## The Drawbacks

Mothers who are employed part-time face unique difficulties and concerns within the workplace, as well as in their home lives, that can leave them feeling particularly drained or frustrated. Chief among these concerns are issues of conflict between work and family roles and a mother's need to balance professional desires and demands with those of her maternal position. In addition, there are also issues relating to stigmatization and differential treatment for full-time and part-time mothers, as well as possible negative experiences for the children of part-time mothers.

One issue that mothers may face when employed part-time is lack of a social support network of other mothers. Society tends to categorize mothers as being either working (full-time) mothers or stay-at-home mothers, and being a part-time employee can place mothers in the sometimes awkward and confusing position of being too much of both but not enough of either. Mothers who are employed full-time may not view part-timers as being "real" working mothers and may trivialize their work-related concerns and difficulties, while stay-at-home mothers may look down upon part-time working mothers as not being committed enough to their children. This conflict is not lost on part-time mothers and can become a stressor in itself. When many mothers who were employed part-time were interviewed by

Beth Brykman (2006), an often repeated sentiment was a feeling of never being fully accepted by either maternal camp. Social support is widely known to reduce stress both in and out of the workplace (Cohen & McKay, 1984; Thoits, 1995), and tends to be most effective when the social support comes from those who can be truly empathetic: people who have experienced the same stressors and experiences (Thoits, 1995) and mothers who are employed part-time may not have as easy, or as rich, access to a built-in support network as mothers who are employed or stay at home full-time.

Additionally, women who take on part-time employment schedules often find that they are not accepted as wholly within their organizations as full-time employees. For instance, mothers who work part-time may find their ability to advance within the company, or even to maintain their original rank therein, significantly impaired (Barker, 1993; Burke & McKeen, 1995; Durbin & Tomlinson, 2010; McDonald, Bradley, & Brown, 2009). This is especially true of women who are professionals or managers and executives (Elacqua, Beehr, Hansen, & Webster, 2009; Ragsdale, Beehr, & Elacqua, 2013; Webster, Beehr, & Elacqua, 2011). Mothers in all varieties of positions often face a part-time stigma, with fellow employees and supervisors viewing them as being less committed and professional (Epstein et al., 1999; Whittock, Edwards, McLaren, & Robinson, 2002). Although others in the organization may be legally prevented from openly discriminating against mothers who opt for part-time schedules, mothers who elect to work part-time can be subjected to a host of subtle interpersonal indications of their differential status. They may be excluded from camaraderie outside of work, ostracized within the workplace, given lower quality assignments, and so forth.

Mothers who choose to work part-time face a clear wage penalty. When compared to full-time workers in comparable positions, mothers who choose to work part-time have a much lower per-hour income level (Bardasi & Gornick, 2000, 2008; Rodgers, 2002). In a cross-national study of five industrialized nations, authors Bardasi and Gornick (2000) found that the wage penalty ranged from 8% in Canada to a high of 22% in the United States, indicating that mothers who work part-time in the United State can expect to bring home 22% less money per hour than full-time counterparts performing comparable work. It is not that part-time workers are simply working fewer hours, but that they are actually compensated at a remarkably lower level for the work they do.

Mothers who are employed part-time, then, are likely to find themselves working harder, yet taking home less money. The implications for these findings go beyond simple dollars and cents, because perceptions of inequity in the workplace have been shown to relate to a host of negative experiences, including decreased satisfaction and increased stress, burnout, and intentions to quit (Lawler & O'Gara, 1967; Pritchard, Dunnette, & Gorgenson, 1972; Taris, Kalimo, & Schaufeli, 2002). It is quite possible that some mothers may find this trade-off to be worth the increased time with family and the increased flexibility. However, those mothers who work part-time because they truly are in need of the money, or those who still wish to be viewed as viable and valuable assets to their organizations, may be more prone to inequity-related negative consequences upon realizing that their work efforts are not compensated at a comparable level.

All of these issues can contribute to one of the major problems faced by maternal part-time employees: conflict between work and family roles. Although many mothers who take on part-time roles do report reductions in work and family conflict (Buehler & O'Brien, 2011; Higgins et al., 2000; Hill et al., 2004), as mentioned in the preceding section, it is typically not eliminated entirely. Women who take on both family and work roles, regardless of motivation, will almost inevitably experience some level of conflict between the two. Early research on part-time employment indicated that work-family conflict, in which the demands of work spill over and interfere with family functions, may be more common among part-timers than the opposite, family-work conflict, in which family demands interfere with work roles (Barnett, 1998; Hall & Gordon, 1973). This would seem to make practical sense, as it may be easier for a mother to adjust her home schedule to fit her work schedule—finding childcare that fits her work hours, splitting childcare duties with a partner or family member, postponing nonpriority activities and household duties until the weekend—than to adjust work to fit home. This work-family conflict can be detrimental, as it has been previously shown to relate to greater marital discord (Bolger, DeLongis, Kessler, & Wethington, 1989), withdrawal of the parent from family interactions (Repetti & Wood, 1997), depression (Obidoa, Reeves, Warren, Reisine, & Cherniack, 2011), and even a greater risk of alcohol use (Frone, Russell, & Cooper, 1997).

Finally, although parenting time and quality of parenting time have been shown to be positively related to maternal employment (Belsky & Rovine, 1984; Brooks-Gunn et al., 2010; Buehler & O'Brien, 2011; Horwood & Fergusson, 1999), there are aspects of children's health and well-being that are known to be negatively related. One trend worth noting is that children of employed mothers are more likely to be obese, with the level of obesity increasing with number of hours worked (Cawley & Liu, 2007; Fertig, Glomm, & Tchernis, 2009). The explanation for this is simple: the more time mothers spend outside the home, the less likely they are to have the time and motivation to choose healthy home-cooked meals over restaurant fare, to exercise with their children, and so forth. Yet, these findings may not be entirely negative for mothers employed part-time—because there is a positive relationship between hours worked by mothers and child obesity; this means that the children of mothers who work a moderate amount of hours do not have nearly as strong a chance of becoming obese as the children of full-time employees.

Han, Waldfogel, and Brooks-Gunn (2001) measured six different behavioral problems, including headstrongness, hyperactivity, and dependence, and found that maternal employment during the first year of children's lives was predictive of higher levels of these behaviors. It is worth noting that in this particular study, no significant differences were found between full-time and part-time maternal employment indicating that for this sample, any regular separation from the mother may impact behavioral development. Studies by Blau and Grossberg (1992), Baydar and Brooks-Gunn (1991), and Belsky and Eggebeen (1991) also found negative impacts in these areas that related to maternal employment.

Using the same measure of behavioral problems as Han et al. (2001), and a sample comparable in size and demography, Hill, Waldfogel, Brooks-Gunn, and Han (2005) found that while cognitive ability of children was mildly negatively influenced by maternal employment during the first year, behavioral problems were only related to full-time employment during the first year. Others have found similar patterns to this later work (Han, 2005; Parcel & Menaghan, 1994), making this possible downside to maternal part-time employment a little murkier than those previously noted. With that in mind, we offer this final paragraph as food for thought with the caveat that more research is needed in this area before employed mothers either become too alarmed or breathe too premature a sigh of relief.

## SUGGESTIONS FOR EMPLOYED MOTHERS

### Choosy Moms Choose Supportive Organizations

When searching for part-time work, mothers would be well-advised to investigate the family-friendliness of each organization before deciding whether to accept a part-time position (Cioffi, 2007). Being employed in an organization in which part-time employees are viewed as the equals of full-time employees would very likely help a mother to avoid some of the previously mentioned pitfalls of part-time employment, such as underpayment and reduced probability of advancement.

### Do What You Love and Love What You Do

Employees who are engaged in their work and find meaning in what they do are happier and healthier than those who feel less positive about their jobs (Britt, Adler, & Bartone, 2001; May, Gilson, & Harter, 2004). A mother who really enjoys what she does in her part-time job will typically experience less stress while at work and feel more committed to her job, and in many cases, will even outperform her less engaged counterparts. Not to mention, work-related happiness has been consistently shown to spill over into nonwork life, creating a generally elevated sense of well-being throughout one's life (Ford et al., 2007).

Seeking out more enriching projects or tasks at work (May et al., 2004), taking on projects and activities with greater autonomy and meaning (Bakker, Schaufeli, Leiter, & Taris, 2008), and reframing one's work in order to find greater intrinsic motivation for mastery (Janssen & Van Yperen, 2004) are just a few options related to greater engagement and meaningfulness at work.

### Maintain Beneficial Boundaries

Negative spillover can also occur in the opposite direction, with troubles at home leaching into one's work life and making that time less productive and enjoyable. In short, when the lines between work and home become too blurred, the results can be unpleasant for employed mothers: decreased work performance (St. Onge, Renaud, Guerin, & Caussignac, 2002), marital problems (Bolger et al., 1989), and greater feelings of burnout (Allen, Herst, Bruck, & Sutton, 2000) are just some of the possible undesirable outcomes. Part-time working mothers would be well-advised to consider the importance of boundaries between the realms of work and family life and to take steps to preserve their segmentation.

Mothers can go one step further by actively seeking out ways to recover and detach from work (Park & Elacqua, 2013). Lack of detachment or separation from one's work is linked to an array of negative psychological outcomes (de Jonge, Spoor, Sonnentag, Dormann, & van den Tooren, 2011; Sonnentag, Kuttler, & Fritz, 2010), and making an effort to recover during one's off-time is a great way for mothers to enhance the part-time work experience. Family outings and vacations are one way in which mothers can detach from work while at home, but less costly options can be equally effective. Reading a good (nonwork) book, putting aside time for involvement in a favorite hobby, taking a class to explore a personal interest, or any such activities, large or small, can all help mothers to recover from work and reinforce the work-family boundaries.

### Support, Support, and More Support

Social support, or having a network of friends, family members, coworkers, or other individuals that care about and value you, and on whom you can consistently rely, has been shown to be a powerful tool against numerous negative life outcomes. Among the many benefits of social support are decreases in anxiety (Sarason, Levine, Basham, & Sarason, 1983), depression (Hays, Steffens, Flint, Bosworth, & George, 2001), work-related burnout (Halbesleben, 2006), and even decreased mortality among older adults (Blazer, 1982) and those with chronic illnesses (Uchino, 2006). Social support can also act as a buffer for other stressors. For instance, having a strong social support network can decrease the effects of economic distress in marriages (Conger, Rueter, & Elder, 1999), reduce feelings of overload from conflicting work and family demands (Berkowitz & Perkins, 1984), and even attenuate the negative tendencies related to certain personality traits (Puterman, Delongis, & Pomaki, 2010). This is especially true of women, with social support providing even stronger benefits in many studies (Sarason et al., 1983; Taylor, Klein, Lewis, Grunewald, Gurung, & Updergraff, 2000).

Given the numerous benefits of social support, both in and out of the workplace, mothers who hold part-time employment would be well-served to establish and maintain a solid social support network. This certainly does not mean that working mothers must try to juggle dozens of friends, in addition to their existing work and family demands, as early research on social support indicated that the quality of relationships was far more important in predicting positive outcomes than the quantity of supporters (Porritt, 1979). Having a handful of trusted friends and reliable family members or coworkers can be enough to provide significant psychological benefits and stave off many of the stressors that come with being a working mother. This may be particularly beneficial for mothers employed in lower-level part-time jobs, who have been shown to have the lowest levels of social satisfaction (Warren, 2004).

Perhaps even more essential than having the social support network, though, is *using* that network. One important way that mothers can do this is by working out a system for household work distribution with other adults and older children in the household. Research consistently shows that women still tend to take on a disproportionately large share of household tasks—cooking, cleaning, childcare, and the like—than men (Bianchi, Milkie, Sayer, & Robinson, 2000; Blair & Lichter, 1991), leaving them with less time for personal tasks and stress reduction. Mothers who work part-time and who also have a partner, spouse, or parent living in the home should establish an equitable distribution of family tasks so that all members of the household have time for rest and recovery. Mothers in part-time situations owe it to themselves to resist the feeling that they must do it all alone, and should take advantage of those who are eager to provide support: their spouses or partners, family members, friends and coworkers. Accepting support is not a mark of failure; it is a mark of a *smart* mother and employee!

### Value and Promote Your Own General Wellness

A sizeable body of research exists which highlights the psychological, physical, and even interpersonal benefits of mothers devoting time and care to their own health and wellness, and we would believe that it is worth noting some of the more commonly identified factors. One such factor is consumption of a balanced diet, which has significant physical health and disease-prevention benefits and also promotes energy, alertness, and memory (Centers for Disease Control and Prevention, n.d.). This healthy diet can be shared with a mother's children and spouse or partner, meaning that it can truly benefit the entire family. Other health and wellness factors to consider include adhering to a consistent sleep schedule, known to promote both physical and psychological health (Ellenbogen, 2005), eliminating or at least significantly reducing the consumption of cigarettes, and simply adjusting one's workspaces at home and in the office to ensure that they are ergonomically beneficial.

Physical fitness is another important aspect to consider and is, in many ways, nature's perfect remedy for what frequently ails mothers who are employed part-time. Exercise can, for example, reduce stress (Fleshner, 2005; Penedo & Dahn, 2005), depressive symptoms (Penedo & Dahn, 2005), and the probability for becoming ill (Warburton, Nicol, & Bredin, 2006), while also increasing feelings of vigor (Hoffman & Hoffman, 2008) and cognitive ability and attention (Weuve et al., 2004) and promoting better sleep quality (Singh, Clements, & Fiatarone, 1997). Add to this the well-publicized medical benefits of maintaining fitness and a healthy weight, and the benefits of exercise for mothers becomes clear. The Centers for Disease Control and Prevention (n.d.) guidelines on physical fitness recommend 150 minutes of moderate intensity aerobic activity each week, but busy working mothers need not feel overwhelmed by this number: the same guidelines state that this can be accomplished in segments as brief as 10 minutes.

## NOTE

Portions of this chapter appear in M. Paludi (Ed.). (2013). *Psychology for business success. Volume 1: Juggling, balancing and integrating work and family roles and responsibilities* (pp. 77–104). Santa Barbara, CA: Praeger.

## REFERENCES

Allen, T. D., Herst, D. E., Bruck, C. S., & Sutton, M. (2000). Consequences associated with work-to-family conflict: A review and agenda for future research. *Journal of Occupational Health Psychology, 5,* 278–308.

Alon, S., & Haberfeld, Y. (2007). Labor force attachment and the evolving wage gap between white, black, and Hispanic young women. *Work and Occupations, 34,* 369–398.

Bakker, A. B., Schaufeli, W. B., Leiter, M. P., & Taris, T. W. (2008). Work engagement: An emerging concept in occupational health psychology. *Work & Stress, 22,* 187–200.

. Bardasi, E., & Gornick, J. C. (2000). *Women and part-time employment: Worker's "choices" and wage penalties in five industrialized countries.* Luxembourg Income Study Working Paper, Luxembourg, Belgium: Cross-National Data Center, 223.

Bardasi, E., & Gornick, J. C. (2008). Working for Less? Women's part-time wage penalties across countries. *Feminist Economics, 14*(1), 37–72.

Barker, K. (1993). Changing assumptions and contingent solutions: The costs and benefits of women working full- and part-time. *Sex Roles, 28*, 47–71.

Barling, J., & MacEwen, K. E. (1992). Linking work experiences to facets of marital functioning. *Journal of Organizational Behavior, 13*, 573–583.

Barnett, R. C. (1998). Toward a review and reconceptualization of the work/family literature. *Genetic, Social, and General Psychology Monographs, 124*, 125–182.

Baydar, N., & Brooks-Gunn, J. (1991). Effects of maternal employment and child-care arrangements on preschoolers' cognitive and behavioral outcomes: Evidence from the children of the National Longitudinal Survey of Youth. *Developmental Psychology, 27*, 932–945.

Belsky, J., & Eggebeen, D. (1991). Early and extensive maternal employment and young children's socioemotional development: Children of the National Longitudinal Survey of Youth. *Journal of Marriage and Family, 53*, 1083–1110.

Belsky, J., & Rovine, M. J. (1984). Social-network contact, family support, and the transition to parenthood. *Journal of Marriage and the Family, 46*, 455–462.

Benard, S., & Correll, S. J. (2010). Normative discrimination and the motherhood penalty. *Gender & Society, 24*(5), 616–646.

Berkowitz, A., & Perkins, H. (1984). Stress among farm women: Work and family as interacting systems. *Journal of Marriage and Family, 46*, 52–67.

Bianchi, S. M. (2000). Maternal employment and time with children: Dramatic change or surprising continuity? *Demography, 37*(4), 401–414.

Bianchi, S. M., Milkie, M. A., Sayer, L. C., & Robinson, J. P. (2000). Is anyone doing the housework? Trends in the gender division of household labor. *Social Forces, 79*, 191–228.

Blair, S. L., & Lichter, D. T. (1991). Measuring the division of household labor: Gender segregation of housework among American couples. *Journal of Family Issues, 12*, 91–113.

Blair-Loy, M. (2003). *Competing devotions: Career and family among women executives.* Cambridge, MA: Harvard University Press.

Blankenhorn, D. (1995). The state of the family and the family policy debate. *Santa Clara Law Review, 36*, 431–437.

Blau, F. D., & Grossberg, A. J. (1992). Maternal labor supply and children's cognitive development. *Review of Economics and Statistics, 74*, 474–481.

Blazer, D. G. (1982). Social support and mortality in an elderly community population. *American Journal of Epidemiology, 115*, 684–694.

Blossfeld, H. P., & Hakim, C. (1997). *Between equalization and marginalization: Women working part-time in Europe and the United States of America.* New York: Oxford University Press.

Bolger, N., DeLongis, A., Kessler, R. C., & Wethington, E. (1989). The contagion of stress across multiple roles. *Journal of Marriage and the Family, 51*, 175–183.

Booth, A., & van Ours, J. (2008). Job satisfaction and family happiness: The part-time work puzzle. *Economic Journal, 118*, 77–99.

Bound, J., & Freeman, R. (1992). What went wrong? The 1980s erosion of the economic well-being of black men. *Quarterly Journal of Economics, 107*, 201–232.

Britt, T., Adler, A. B., & Bartone, P. T. (2001). Deriving benefits from stressful events: The role of engagement in meaningful work and hardiness. *Journal of Occupational Health Psychology, 6*, 53–63.

Brooks-Gunn, J., Han, W., & Waldfogel, J. (2002). Maternal employment and child cognitive outcomes in the first three years of life: The NICHD study of early child care. *Child Development, 73,* 1052–1072.

Brooks-Gunn, J., Han, W., & Waldfogel, J. (2010). First-year maternal employment and child development in the first 7 years: What distinguishes women who work full-time, part-time, or not at all during the 1st year? *Monographs of the Society for Research in Child Development, 75,* 35–49.

Brown, W. A., & Yoshioka, C. F. (2003). Mission attachment and satisfaction as factors in employee retention. *Nonprofit Management and Leadership, 14*(1), 5–18.

Brykman, B. (2006). *The wall between women: The conflict between stay-at-home and employed mothers.* Amherst, NY: Prometheus Books.

Buehler, C., & O'Brien, M. (2011). Mothers' part-time employment: Associations with mother and family well-being. *Journal of Family Psychology, 25,* 895–906.

Burke, R. J., & McKeen, C. A. (1995). Work experience, career development, and career success of managerial and professional women. In *Gender in the Workplace* (pp. 81–98). Corte Madera, CA: Select Press.

Cawley, J., & Liu, F. (2007). Maternal employment and childhood obesity: A search for mechanisms in time use data. NBER Working Paper 13600, Cambridge, MA: National Bureau of Economic Research.

Centers for Disease Control and Prevention. (n.d.). *Nutrition facts.* Retrieved from www.cdc.gov/healthyyouth/nutrition/facts.htm

Cioffi, C. (2007). Finding and keeping the best and brightest—flexible policies in a small workplace. In M. A. Paludi & P. E. Neidermeyer (Eds.), *Work, life, and family imbalance: How to level the playing field* (pp. 79–88). Westport, CT: Praeger.

Cohen, P. N. (2011). *Poverty, hardship, and families: How many people are poor, and what does being poor in American really mean?* Briefing paper prepared for the Council on Contemporary Families.

Cohen, S., & McKay, G. (1984). Social support, stress, and the buffering hypothesis: A theoretical analysis. In A. Baume, S. E. Taylor, & J. E. Singer (Eds.), *Handbook of psychology and health* (pp. 253–267). Hillsdale, NJ: Erlbaum.

Coley, R. L., Lohman, B. J., Votruba-Drzal, E., Pittman, L. D., & Chase-Lansdale, L. (2007). Maternal functioning, time, and money: The world of work and welfare. *Children and Youth Services Review, 29,* 721–741.

Coltrane, S., & Adams, M. (2008). *Gender and families* (2nd ed.). Thousand Oaks, CA: Pine Forge Press.

Conger, R. D., Rueter, M. A., & Elder, G. H. (1999). Couple resilience to economic pressure. *Journal of Personality and Social Psychology, 76,* 54–71.

Conway, N., & Briner, R. B. (2002). Full-time versus part-time employees: Understanding the links between work status, the psychological contract, and attitudes. *Journal of Vocational Behavior, 61,* 279–301.

Corcoran, M., & Duncan, G. J. (1979). Work history, labor force attachment, and earnings differences between the races and sexes. *The Journal of Human Resources, 14*(1), 3–20.

Cull, W. L., Mulvey, H. J., O'Connor, K. G., Sowell, D. R., Berkowitz, C. D., & Britton, C. V. (2002). Pediatrician working part-time: Past, present, and future. *Pediatrics, 109,* 1015–1020.

Danzinger, S., & Gottschalk, D. (1991). *Uneven Tides.* New York: Russell Sage.

Darmon, N., & Drewnowski, A. (2008). Does social class predict diet quality? *American Journal of Clinical Nutrition, 87,* 1107–1117.

Declerq, E. R., Sakala, C., Corry, M. P., & Applebaum, S. (2007). Listening to mothers II: Report of the second national U.S. survey of women's childbearing experiences. *Journal of Perinatal Education, 16*(4), 9–14.

de Jonge, J., Spoor, E., Sonnentag, S., Dormann, C., & van den Tooren, M. (2011). "Take a break?!": Off-job recovery, job demands, and job resources as predictors of health, active learning, and creativity. *European Journal of Work and Organizational Psychology, in press.*

Durbin, S., & Tomlinson, J. (2010). Female part-time managers: Networks and career mobility. *Work, Employment, and Society, 24,* 621–640.

Duxbury, L., & Higgins, C. (1994). Interference between work and family: A status report on dual-career and dual-earner mothers and fathers. *Employee Assistance Quarterly, 9,* 55–82.

Eberhardt, B. J., & Shani, A. B. (1984). The effects of full-time versus part-time employment status on attitudes toward specific organizational characteristics and overall job satisfaction. *The Academy of Management Journal, 27,* 893–900.

Ehrenreich, B., & English, D. (1978). *For her own good: 150 years of experts' advice to women.* London: Pluto Press.

Elacqua, T. C., Beehr, T. A., Hansen, C. P., & Webster, J. (2009). Managers' beliefs about the glass ceiling: Interpersonal and organizational factors. *Psychology of Women Quarterly, 33,* 285–294.

Elacqua, T. C., Quinn, A., & Sax, E. (in press). From juggling to balancing to integration: Women, work and family lives. In M. Paludi (Series Ed.) & M. Paludi (Vol. Ed.), *Women and careers in management (Series). Managing diversity in today's workplace.* Westport, CT: Praeger.

Ellenbogen, J. M. (2005). Cognitive benefits of sleep and their loss due to sleep deprivation. *Neurology, 64,* 25–27.

Epstein, C. F., Seron, C., Oglensky, B., & Saute, R. (1999). *The part-time paradox: Time norms, professional lives, family, and gender.* New York: Routledge.

Feldman, D. C. (1990). Reconceptualizing the nature and consequences of part-time work. *Academy of Management Review, 15,* 100–112.

Fertig, A., Glomm, G., & Tchernis, R. (2009). The connection between maternal employment and childhood obesity: Inspecting the mechanisms. *Review of Economics of the Household, 7,* 227–255.

Fleshner, F. (2005). Physical activity and stress resistance: Sympathetic nervous system adaptations prevent stress-induced immunosuppression. *Exercise and Sport Sciences Review, 33,* 120–126.

Ford, M. T., Heinen, B. A., & Langkamer, K. L. (2007). Work and family satisfaction and conflict: A meta-analysis of cross-domain relations. *Journal of Applied Psychology, 92,* 57–80.

Frone, M. R., Russell, M., & Cooper, M. L. (1997). Relation of work-family conflict to health outcomes: A four-year longitudinal study of employed parents. *Journal of Occupational and Organizational Psychology, 70,* 325–335.

Galobardes, B., Morabia, A., & Bernstein, M. S. (2001). Diet and socioeconomic position: Does the use of different indicators matter? *International Journal of Epidemiology, 30,* 334–340.

Gauthier, A. H., Smeeding, T. M., & Furstenberg, F. F. (2004). Are parents investing less time in children? Trends in selected industrialized countries. *Population and Development Review, 30,* 647–672.

Gray, M., Qu, L., de Vaus, D., & Millward, C. (2002). *Determinants of Australian mothers' employment.* Research paper No. 26, Australian Institute of Family Studies, Melbourne.

Gregg, P., Washbrook, E., Propper, C., & Burgess, S. (2005). The effects of a mother's return to work decision on child development in the UK. *The Economic Journal, 115,* 48–80.

Hakim, C. (1995). Five feminist myths about women's employment. *British Journal of Sociology, 46,* 429–455.

Halbesleben, J. R. (2006). Sources of social support and burnout: A meta-analytic test of the conservation of resources model. *Journal of Applied Psychology, 91,* 1134–1145.

Hall, D. T., & Gordon, F. E. (1973). Career choices of married women: Effects on conflict, role behavior, and satisfaction. *Journal of Applied Psychology, 58,* 42–48.

Han, W. (2005). Maternal nonstandard work schedules and child cognitive outcomes. *Child Development, 76,* 137–154.

Han, W. J., Waldfogel, J., & Brooks-Gunn, J. (2001). The effects of early maternal employment on later cognitive and behavioral outcomes. *Journal of Marriage and Family, 63,* 336–354.

Hays, J. C., Steffens, D. C., Flint, E. P., Bosworth, H. B., & George, L. K. (2001). Does social support buffer functional decline in elderly patients with unipolar depression? *American Journal of Psychiatry, 158,* 1850–1855.

Hays, S. (1996). *The cultural contradictions of motherhood.* New Haven, CT: Yale University Press.

Herold, J., & Waldron, I. (1985). Part-time employment and women's health. *Journal of Occupational Medicine, 27,* 405–412.

Hewlett, B. S. (1991). Demography and childcare in preindustrial societies. *Journal of Anthropological Research, 47,* 1–37.

Higgins, C., Duxbury, L., & Johnson, K. L. (2000). Part-time work for women: Does it really help balance work and family? *Human Resource Management, 39,* 17–32.

Hill, E. J., Martinson, V. K., Ferris, M., & Baker, R. Z. (2004). Beyond the mommy track: The influence of new-concept part-time work for professional women on work and family. *Journal of Family and Economic Issues, 25,* 121–136.

Hill, J. L., Waldfogel, J., Brooks-Gunn, J., & Han, W. J. (2005). Maternal employment and child development: A fresh look using newer methods. *Developmental Psychology, 41,* 833–850.

Hobfoll, S. E. (1989). Conservation of resources: A new attempt at conceptualizing stress. *American Psychologist, 44,* 513–524.

Hochschild, A. (1997). *The time bind: When work becomes home and home becomes work.* New York: Metropolitan Books.

Hock, E., Gnezda, M. T., McBride, S. L. (1984). Mothers of infants: Attitudes toward employment and motherhood following birth of the first child. *Journal of Marriage and Family, 46,* 425–431.

Hoffman, M. D., & Hoffman, D. R. (2008). Exercises achieve greater acute exercise-induced mood enhancement than nonexercisers. *Archives of Physical Medicine and Rehabilitation, 89,* 358–363.

Hofmeister, H. (2006). Women's employment transitions and mobility in the United States: 1968–1991. In H. P. Blossfeld & H. Hofmeister (Eds.), *Globalization, uncertainty, and women's careers: An international comparison* (pp. 302–326). Cheltenham, UK and Northampton, MA: Edward Elgar.

Horwood, L. J., & Fergusson, D. M. (1999). A longitudinal study of maternal labour force participation and child academic achievement. *Journal of Child Psychology and Psychiatry, 40,* 1013–1024.

Hughes, D., & Galinsky, E. (1989). Balancing work and family lives: Research and corporate applications. In A. E. Gottfried & A. W. Gottfried (Eds.), *Maternal employment and children's development: Longitudinal research* (pp. 233–268). New York: Plenum Press.

Janssen, O., & Van Yperen, N. W. (2004). Employees' goal orientations, the quality of leader-member exchange, and the outcomes of job performance and job satisfaction. *Academy of Management Journal, 47,* 368–384.

Judge, T. A., & Ilies, R. (2004). Affect and job satisfaction: A study of their relationship at work and at home. *Journal of Applied Psychology, 89,* 661–673.

Kalleburg, A. L. (2000). Nonstandard employment relations: Part-time, temporary, and contract work. *Annual Review of Sociology, 26,* 341–365.

Lawler, E. E., & O'Gara, P. W. (1967). Effects of inequity produced by underpayment on work output, work quality, and attitudes toward the work. *Journal of Applied Psychology, 51,* 403–410.

Lee, T. W., & Johnson, D. R. (1991). The effects of work schedule and employment status on the organizational commitment and job satisfaction of full versus part time employees. *Journal of Vocational Behavior, 38,* 208–224.

Manning, W. D., & Smock, P. J. (1995). Why marry? Race and the transition to marriage among cohabitors. *Demography, 32,* 509–520.

May, D. R., Gilson, R. L., & Harter, L. M. (2004). The psychological conditions of meaningfulness, safety and availability and the engagement of the human spirit at work. *Journal of Occupational and Organizational Psychology, 77,* 11–37.

McDonald, P., Bradley, L., & Brown, K. (2009). "Full time is a given here": Part-time versus full-time job quality. *British Journal of Management, 20,* 143–157.

Nardone, T. (1995). Part-time employment: Reasons, demographics, and trends. *Journal of Labor Research, 16*(3), 275–292.

Nuru-Jeter, A. M., Sarsour, K., Jutte, D. P., & Boyce, W. T. (2010). Socioeconomic predictors of health in middle childhood: Variations by socioeconomic status measure and race. *Issues in Comprehensive Pediatric Nursing, 33,* 59–81.

Nyman, C. (1999). Gender equality in the most equal country in the world: Money and marriage in Sweden. *The Sociological Review, 47*(4), 766–793.

Obidoa, C., Reeves, D., Warren, N., Reisine, S., & Cherniack, M. (2011). Depression and work family conflict among corrections officers. *Journal of Occupational and Environmental Medicine, 53,* 1294–1301.

O'Reilly, J., & Fagan, C. (1998). *Part-time prospects: An international comparison of part-time work in Europe, North America, and the Pacific Rim.* London, NY: Routledge.

Parcel, T. L., & Menaghan, E. G. (1994). Early parental work, family social capital, and early childhood outcomes. *American Journal of Sociology, 99,* 912–1009.

Park, Y., & Elacqua, T. C. (in press). Promoting employees' work-life balance: Work, organizational, and technological factors. In M. A. Paludi (Series Ed.) & M. A. Paludi (Vol. Ed.), *The psychology for business.* Westport, CT: Praeger.

Pendakur, K., & Pendakur, R. (2007). Minority earnings disparity across the distribution. *Canadian Public Policy, 33,* 41–61.

Penedo, F. J., & Dahn, J. R. (2005). Exercise and well-being: A review of mental and physical health benefits associated with physical activity. *Current Opinion in Psychiatry, 18,* 189–193.

Pew Research Center. (2007). *Fewer mothers prefer full-time work.* Retrieved from http://pewresearch.org/assets/social/pdf/WomenWorking.pdf

Porritt, D. (1979). Social support in crisis: Quantity or quality? *Social Science & Medicine, 13,* 715–721.

Pritchard, R. D., Dunnette, M. D., & Gorgenson, D. O. (1972). Effects of perceptions of equity and inequity on worker performance and satisfaction. *Journal of Applied Psychology, 56,* 75–94.

Puterman, E., Delongis, A., & Pomaki, G. (2010). Protecting us from ourselves: Social support as a buffer of trait and state rumination. *Journal of Social and Clinical Psychology, 29,* 797–820.

Ragsdale, J. M., Beehr, T. A., & Elacqua, T. C. (2013). Glass ceilings and sticky floors: Barriers to the advancement of women at work. In M. Paludi (Series Ed.) & M. Paludi (Vol. Ed.), *Women and management: Global issues and promising situations.* Westport, CT: Praeger.

Repetti, R. L., & Wood, J. (1997). Effects of daily stress at work on mothers' interactions with preschoolers. *Journal of Family Psychology, 11,* 90–108.

Rodgers, J. R. (2002). Hourly wages of full-time and part-time employees in Australia. *Australian Journal of Labour Economics, 7,* 231–254.

Rosenfeld, R. A., & Birkelund, G. E. (1995). Women's part-time work: A cross-national comparison. *European Sociological Review, 11*(2), 111–133.

Ruhm, C. J. (2004). Parental employment and child cognitive development. *Journal of Human Resources, 39,* 155–192.

Sandberg, J. F., & Hofferth, S. L. (2001). Changes in children's time with parents: United States, 1981–1997. *Demography, 38*(3), 423–436.

Sarason, I. G., Levine, H. M., Basham, R. B., & Sarason, B. R. (1983). Assessing social support: The social support questionnaire. *Journal of Personality and Social Psychology, 44,* 127–139.

Scott, J. W., & Tilly, L. A. (1975). Women's work and the family in nineteenth-century Europe. *Comparative Studies in Society and History, 17,* 36–64.

Shirom, A., & Shraga, O. (2009). *Emotions in groups, organizations, and cultures* (pp. 73–101). Bingley, UK: Emerald Group Publishing, Ltd.

Siegel, S. M. (2011). *An analysis of the impact of parent education level and family income on the academic achievement of students of Hispanic and white ethnicities.* Doctoral dissertation. Retrieved from ProQuest Dissertation and Theses. (Publication number 3451752).

Sinclair, R. R., Martin, J. E., & Michel, R. P. (1999). Full-time and part-time subgroup differences in job attitudes and demographic characteristics. *Journal of Vocational Behavior, 55,* 337–357.

Singh, N. A., Clements, K. M., & Fiatarone, M. A. (1997). A randomized controlled trial of the effect of exercise on sleep. *Sleep, 20,* 95–101.

Sirin, S. R. (2005). Socioeconomic status and academic achievement: A meta-analytic review of research. *Review of Educational Research, 75*, 417–453.

Sonnentag, S., Kuttler, I., & Fritz, C. (2010). Job stressors, emotional exhaustion, and need for recovery: A multi-source study on the benefits of psychological detachment. *Journal of Vocational Behavior, 76*, 355–365.

St. Onge, S. S., Renaud, S., Guerin, G., & Caussignac, E. (2002). An assessment of the work-family conflict through a structural model. *Industrial Relations, 57*, 491–516.

Stolz, L. M. (1960). Effects of maternal employment on children: Evidence from research. *Child Development, 31*(4), 749–782.

Sundstrom, M. (1991). Part-time work in Sweden: Trends and equality effects. *Journal of Economic Issues, 25*, 167–178.

Taris, T. W., Kalimo, R., & Schaufeli, W. B. (2002). Inequity at work: Its measurement and association with worker health. *Work and Stress, 16*, 287–301.

Taylor, S., Klein, L., Lewis, B., Grunewald, T., Gurung, R., & Updergraff, J. (2000). Biobehavioural responses to stress in females: Tend and befriend, not fight or flight. *Psychological Review, 107*, 411–429.

Thoits, P. A. (1995). Stress, coping, and social support processes: Where are we? What next? *Journal of Health and Social Behavior,* Extra issue, 53–79.

Tilly, C. (1987). *Women, work, and family.* New York: Routledge.

Tilly, C. (1991, March). Reasons for the continuing growth of part-time employment. *Monthly Labor Review, 114*(3), 10–18.

Uchino, B. N. (2006). Social support and health: A review of physiological processes potentially underlying links to disease outcomes. *Journal of Behavioral Medicine, 29*, 377–387.

U.S. Census Bureau. (n.d.). *2005–2009 American community survey 5-year estimates.* Retrieved January 2, 2012, from www.factfinder.census.gov/

U.S. Census Bureau. (2012). *The 2012 Statistical Abstract, section 86.* Retrieved January 9, 2012, from www.census.gov/compendia/statab/cats/births_deaths_marriages_divorces/births.html

U.S. Congress' Joint Economic Committee Majority Staff. (2010). *Women and the economy 2010: 25 years of progress but challenges remain.* Retrieved from http://jec.senate.gov/public/?a=Files.Serve&File_id=8be22cb0-8ed0-4a1a-841b-aa91dc55fa81

U.S. Department of Labor, Bureau of Labor Statistics. (2011, March 24). *Employment Characteristics of Families Summary.* Retrieved from www.bls.gov/news.release/famee.nr0.htm

Vandell, D. L., & Ramanan, J. (1992). Effects of early and recent maternal employment on children from low-income families. *Child Development, 63*, 938–949.

Walsh, J. (1999). Myths and counter-myths: An analysis of part-time female employees and their orientations to work and working hours. *Work, Employment, & Society, 13*(2), 179–203.

Warburton, D. E., Nicol, C. W., & Bredin, S. S. (2006). Health benefits of physical activity: The evidence. *Canadian Medical Association Journal, 174*, 801–809.

Warren, T. (2004). Working part-time: Achieving a successful work-life balance? *The British Journal of Sociology, 55*, 99–122.

Webster, J., Beehr, T. A., & Elacqua, T. C. (2011). The advancement of women at work: The continued struggle to break the glass ceiling. In M. A. Paludi (Series Ed.), M. A. Paludi & B. Coates (Vol. Eds.), *Women and careers in man-*

*agement (Series). Women as transformational leaders: From grassroots to global interests.* Westport, CT: Praeger.

Weuve, J., Kang, J. H., Manson, J. E., Breteler, M. M., Ware, J. H., & Grodstein, F. (2004). Physical activity, including walking, and cognitive functioning in older women. *Journal of the American Medical Association, 292,* 1444–1461.

Whittock, M., Edwards, C., McLaren, S., & Robinson, O. (2002). "The tender trap": Gender, part-time nursing and the effects of "family-friendly" policies on career advancement. *Sociology of Health and Illness, 24,* 305–326.

Working Mother Research Institute. (2011). *The working mother report: What moms choose.* Cincinnati, OH: Ernst & Young.

Wright, T., & Cropanzano, R. (1998). Emotional exhaustion as a predictor of job performance and voluntary turnover. *Journal of Applied Psychology, 83,* 486–493.

Xu, W., & Leffler, A. (1992). Gender and race effects on occupational prestige, segregation, and earnings. *Gender & Society, 6,* 376–392.

# Chapter 18

# Moving Beyond Offering Flexible Work Arrangements

*Sue A. Epstein and Janet H. Marler*

Flexible work arrangements (FWAs) offer employees some control over where and when their work is conducted (Lambert, Marler, & Gueutal, 2008). The number of organizations interested in offering flexible work arrangements, such as flextime or compressed workweeks, has been growing (Baltes, Briggs, Huff, Wright, & Neuman, 1999; Bond, Galinsky, Kim, & Brownfield, 2005). In fact, interest in offering FWAs has moved beyond the walls of the corporate America and now includes unions that incorporate flexible work arrangements in the negotiation processes between employers and union members (Mesmer-Magnus & Viswesvaran, 2006). President Obama, First Lady Michelle Obama, and the White House Council on Women and Girls recently hosted a Forum on Workplace Flexibility in which President Obama and First Lady Michelle Obama's opening comments and remarks both focused on the growing need for employers to offer flexible workplaces that meet the needs of employees (Remarks by President at Workplace Flexibility Forum, 2010).

However, despite the increasing availability of and interest in FWAs, research suggests that the *offering* of FWAs does not necessarily result in their actual use (Sutton & Noe, 2005). What stands in the way of employees using FWAs even though research shows that FWA use is associated with many positive organizational and individual benefits (Hayman, 2009; Olmstead, 1995)? We explore this question with a brief overview of FWAs. In the remainder of the chapter we discuss factors that appear to facilitate or inhibit employee use of this organizational benefit.

## OVERVIEW OF FWAS

The term "flexible work arrangements" is typically used to describe work arrangements that offer employees the ability to work outside traditional workday and workplace boundaries (Lambert et al., 2008; Rau, 2004). Flexibility is built into when an employee is present in the workplace, where the employee performs work, and the length of time in which employees perform their work. For example, in one version of FWAs (sometimes referred to as flextime) the employee has flexibility over when to begin and end the workday as long as they are present during designated core hours (Olmstead, 1995; Rau, 2004). Organizations may also use a flextime arrangement that does not involve a set of established core hours in which employees must be present but instead simply allows employees to set their work hours according to individual scheduling needs and interests (SHRM, 2010; Stuart, 2010). According to the government labor force statistics about 30% of the workforce use flextime. Use of flextime, however, varies across industry and occupation (Torpey, 2007). For instance only 12% of production shift workers use flextime compared to over 50% of those working in computer occupations (Torpey, 2007).

In a compressed workweek arrangement, the employee has flexibility over the design of the workweek in that the employee works fewer than five days a week, but works a greater number of hours each day as compared to a traditional workday (Olmstead, 1987; Rau, 2004). In both flextime and compressed workweek arrangements, the employee is still working full-time but the hours of his or her schedule differs from the traditional 9–5 workday, five days a week schedule (Olmstead, 1995; Rau, 2004).

With telecommuting, the employee works at least part of his or her work schedule at a different location than the official workplace, thus allowing for flexibility in the place where work is conducted. Telecommuting is a relatively new flexible work arrangement and as such the government has not yet collected reliable estimates of the proportion of the workforce using this type of FWA. At the low-end, the estimated proportion is 3% of the workforce but this does not include many informal telecommuting arrangements negotiated by employees.

Finally, regular part-time and job sharing give the employee flexibility to work less than full-time (Olmstead, 1995; Rau, 2004). About 17% of the labor force is in part-time jobs, working less than 35 hours per week. This proportion has not changed appreciably over the last few years (Schaefer, 2009).

Additionally, while FWAs typically refer to an arrangement that is in place for some designated period of time, a broader conceptualization is to think of some FWAs as on an as-needed basis. For example, an employee working a traditional schedule at the office may need to, on occasion, change his or her work hours or work from home.

## GROWTH IN THE OFFERING OF FWAS

Initially, FWAs were targeted toward women in the workplace and more specifically toward working mothers (Stuart, 2010). However, changing workforce demographics, war for talent, and technological advances have all contributed to the increasing demand for these workplace benefits.

First, in addition to the increased participation of women in the workforce, there are now increasing numbers of dual-career households, employees close to retirement, and new entrants into the workforce who demand more balance with their personal life. Consequently, women are no longer the only employee group for whom FWAs are of interest (Rapoport, Bailyn, Fletcher, & Pruitt, 2002).

Older employees close to retirement are also a growing segment of the workforce interested in using FWAs. Given current economic circumstances, older workers are choosing to remain in the workforce longer than they had originally anticipated (Glaeser, 2011). FWAs therefore provide this growing demographic group with the ability to combine work with nonwork interests they had anticipated being part of their retirement years. From the organization's perspective older workers are desirable employees because they bring experience and knowledge and tend to have higher levels of job satisfaction than younger employees (Kooij, Jansen, Dikkers, & Lange, 2010). Thus, organizations may want to minimize the number of older workers who choose full retirement (Herrbach, Mignonac, Vandenberghe, & Negrini, 2009). One way to potentially entice older workers to remain in the workforce is offering FWAs that will enable older employees to actively pursue nonwork interests.

Interestingly, there has also been a change in how the younger generations view the workplace and the development of their careers. Members of Generation X (i.e., workers born from 1965 to 1976), also known as GenMe, express stronger interests than previous generations in pursuing employment opportunitites that allow for their concurrent pursuit of nonwork interests (Twenge, Campbell, Hoffman, & Lance, 2010). Millennials (i.e., workers born from 1977 to 1998) are entering the workplace seeking greater work-life balance and even prioritizing the ability to pursue nonwork interests in their criteria for selecting job and careers to pursue (Smith, 2010).

Deloitte's Mass Career Customization program is an example of how the relevance of FWAs appeals to a growing demographic of employees beyond those who are mothers. Deloitte's program acknowledges that employee's personal responsibilities and interest evolve and change over time and impact the employee's interest and availability for a variety of work assignments (McClelland, Koestner, & Weinberger, 1989). For example, following the birth of a child an employee may want to temporarily switch to a part-time position. Perhaps once the child is in school full-time, that same employee may want to return to a full-time schedule with a flex-time arrangement. Some years later, the employee may desire a full-time, traditional schedule working five days at the worksite. And still later in time, that employee may desire phased retirement and a switch to a part-time position. A critical element of the Deloitte program is the career view of the employee and employer relationship. FWAs are therefore a major component of career development practices at Deloitte and not simply associated with an isolated event that occurs at one point in time.

Deloitte's Mass Career Customization program's original intention was to increase retention and advancement by letting women design their preferred work schedules and assignments (McClelland et al., 1989). Upon introduction, however, demand for the program reached beyond female employees with caregiving responsibilities, resulting in Deloitte's decision to offer the program to all employees (Fitzpatrick, 2009). The changes in the target audience for Deloitte's Mass Career Customization program may be indicative of a broader social and demographic trend. Once conceived as the solution for helping working mothers manage work-life balance at Deloitte, a broader target of employees (e.g., males, employees without caregiving responsibilities) was interested in using Deloitte's program. Deloitte's Mass Career Customization program even now includes an added type of FWA, the "Personal Pursuits" program, which allows employees to temporarily leave Deloitte for up to five years (Development, 2010).

The growth in organizations offering FWAs can also be seen as a strategic response by organizations who want to remain competitive in attracting talented employees (Robinson, 2005; Sutton & Noe, 2005). Organizations offering FWAs send a positive message to potential employees about the employee's potential experience of work-life balance. As more organizations offer FWAs, peer pressure may result in additional organizations offering FWAs (Sutton & Noe, 2005).

Lastly, advances in technology represent another reason for the growth in organizations offering FWAs and the ability of employees to use FWAs (Stuart, 2010; Valcour & Hunter, 2005). Internet-based technologies can facilitate an employee's ability to perform work-related activities while physically remote. For example, access to the Internet and thus servers with needed documents permit the employee to be productive without being physically present. Technology such as mobile videoconferencing (i.e.,

Movi) enables users to connect via video to their office from any remote location (e.g., home, airport). Desktop cameras and Skype can also be used for communication between remote and local users. Using these types of technology, employees at alternative locations can see and talk with colleagues at the main location thus enabling a "face-to-face" interaction with a video-enabled physical presence. Web-based document sharing allows remote and local users to view the documents simultaneously. Additionally, since technology now fosters work interactions during nonwork hours (e.g., cell phone calls and e-mails during nonwork hours) employees may seek FWAs such as flextime days as compensation for their 24 x 7 availability. For instance, an employee who frequently takes work calls in the evening at home may offset these additional hours of work with having the ability to come in later to compensate for working during nonwork hours.

## BENEFITS ASSOCIATED WITH FWAS

Many research studies show that FWAs are associated with a broad variety of organizational benefits. These include increased organizational citizenship behaviors (Richman, Civian, Shannon, Jeffrey Hill, & Brennan, 2008; Scandura & Lankau, 1997), employee retention (Allen, 2001; McNall, Masuda, & Nicklin, 2010; Richman et al., 2008), job satisfaction (Allen, 2001; Butler, Grzywacz, Ettner, & Liu, 2009; Carlson, Grzywacz, & Kacmar, 2010; McNall et al., 2010; Scandura & Lankau, 1997), productivity (Baltes et al., 1999), as well as reduced absenteeism (Baltes et al., 1999).

Research also establishes that FWAs have positive consequences for individual employees. FWAs reduce employees' experience of work-life conflict (Beauregard & Henry, 2009; McNall et al., 2010), stress and burnout (Grzywacz, Carlson, & Shulkin, 2008), as well as positively contribute to work-life enrichment (Carlson et al., 2010) and employees' perceptions of their physical health (Butler et al., 2009).

Some empirical evidence supporting the hypothesized relationships between FWAs and beneficial organizational outcomes have shown mixed results (Baltes et al., 1999; Hayman, 2009). One potential explanation for the differing results is that a distinction needs to be made between organizations offering FWAs, employees perceiving that the FWAs are available (Hayman, 2009), and employees' actual usage of FWAs. If employees do not feel they can actually use the FWAs that are offered by the organization, the benefits associated with FWAs are unlikely to be realized (Hayman, 2009).

## CONCEPTUALIZATIONS OF FWAS

Researchers use different conceptualizations of FWAs in empirical studies which has important consequences. Some researchers operationalize FWAs according to organizational offerings of FWAs (Beauregard &

Henry, 2009; Scandura & Lankau, 1997), others operationalize FWAs as perceived availability of FWAs (Butler et al., 2009; Hayman, 2009; Richman et al., 2008) and explore usage of FWAs (Baltes et al., 1999; Carlson et al., 2010; Rogier & Padgett, 2004; Thompson, Beauvais, & Lyness, 1999). In some cases, researchers measure more than one conceptualization in a particular empirical study. For example, Allen (2001) measured organizational offerings of FWAs as well as employee usage of FWAs. McNall et al. (2010) describe their research as exploring the availability of FWAs but the items in their measure were a combination of organizational offering of FWAs (i.e., "Does your company offer flexibility in when you start or end your workday (also known as flextime)?") and perceived availability (i.e., "Does your company allow you to work four longer days per week instead of five regular days (also known as a compressed workweek)?") (McNall et al., 2010, p. 68). The subtle distinction is that perceived availability is a more personal question (e.g., Do I, the employee, feel I have access to the FWA?); whereas offering is a more general question for all employees (e.g., Does my organization offer this FWA to employees?). A respondent might know the company offers flextime but, for reasons to be discussed shortly, may feel that flextime is not truly available for their personal use.

Do differences in how researchers define and measure FWAs matter? The answer to this question depends on whether the ability to synthesize and integrate research results is considered important. As mentioned earlier, seemingly contradictory research results may be a matter of differing definitions and measurements. And, as discussed in the next section, it is important to make certain that "apples are compared with apples and not with oranges" in order to create relevant evidence-based research implications for practitioners.

## CONNECTIONS BETWEEN CONCEPTUALIZATIONS OF FWAS

The Human Resource (HR) department of an organization develops FWA programs and lists these as the "official" FWAs programs offered by the organization. These programs are promoted internally (e.g., to managers and employees) and externally (e.g., to job applicants, for analyses of FWA offerings). An employee's belief that a particular FWA is available and accessible (e.g., the employee's manager will support the employee's interest in participating in the FWA) is part of the conceptualization. Not all employees are aware of organizational FWAs or, if aware, believe they can be used. Organizations must offer the FWA, employees must perceive the FWA as being available to them, and the employee must feel that their actual use of the FWA is feasible (e.g., he or she can afford part-time work).

So how can understanding the connections between these different conceptualizations help us understand seemingly contradictory research results? Let's say one researcher measures organizations offering FWAs and finds a positive relationship with an outcome variable such as job satisfaction. Another researcher using the same variables may find no relationship between these variables. In the first case, the organization offering FWAs may also have employees who perceive these FWAs as available for use and employees who then subsequently use the FWAs. As the organization's offering of FWAs increases, more employees will perceive FWAs as being available and, thus, more employees also use the FWAs and more job satisfaction results. Thus, the positive relationship is found in the research analysis.

For the second researcher, some employees do not believe the FWAs that their organization offers are available for their use. The nature of the employee's job or the belief that the supervisor would not approve the employee's request for using the FWAs are two factors that might impact perceived availability. Since the employee does not perceive the FWAs as available for his or her usage, even as the organization increases the offering of FWAs there is no change in the employee's job satisfaction or, potentially, there is a decrease in the employee's job satisfaction as the employee becomes frustrated because they are prevented from using this benefit. In both these cases, the researcher has measured organizational offerings of FWAs but because the studies don't account for differences in employee perceptions of availability, comparison of results are misleading. The way in which FWAs are measured (offered versus perceived as available) can make a big difference in the studies' conclusions.

In addition to helping interpret seemingly contradictory research results, it is also important to understand the relationships between these different ways of measuring FWAs. For example how are perceptions of availability and employee use related? Is there a causal relationship and if so what is the direction of causality? Do employees have to first perceive availability in order to use FWAs or does use of FWAs precede perception of availability? A better understanding of these relationships can help researchers and practitioners better understand how to change employee behavior.

Grzywacz et al. (2008) indicate that employees who are using FWAs are more likely to have perceptions of FWAs availability compared to employees who are not using FWAs. Is a perception of availability needed before employees use FWAs? If so, what factors explain whether there will be a relationship between an organization offering FWAs and employees perceiving those FWAs as being available to them (e.g., supervisory attitudes, job structure)? Next, what are the barriers between employees' perceiving FWAs as available and employee usage of FWAs (e.g., perceived negative career consequences, financial issues associated with reduced work schedule)? For practitioners, while there may be short-term gains from offering FWAs (e.g., attraction of applicants), if perceived availability and, ultimately, FWA usage do not follow then longer-term gains (e.g., reten-tion) may be hindered.

Interestingly, Grzywacz et al. (2008) conclude that it is not the perceived availability of FWAs that lead to usage but, instead, the use of FWAs leads to perceptions of FWA availability which then leads to reduced stress and burnout. Since Grzywacz et al.'s (2008) research is cross-sectional the di-rection of causality cannot be established and, thus, we cannot determine the direction of the relationship or if there exists a reciprocal relationship. Regardless of the direction of the relationship between usage of FWAs and perceived availability of FWAs, Grzywacz et al.'s (2008) research re-sults do support our notion that *both* FWA use and perceived availability are related and that each has a relationship with outcomes associated with FWAs.

## INTERVENING FACTORS IN EXPLAINING THE RELATIONSHIPS BETWEEN FWAS AND OUTCOMES

Some researchers have suggested that the relationship between FWAs and outcomes of interest is not a simple direct relationship. The relation-ship is instead more complicated (Beauregard & Henry, 2009; Carlson et al., 2010; McNall et al., 2010; Mesmer-Magnus & Viswesvaran, 2006). Beauregard and Henry (2009) propose a model in which several personal outcomes and organizational outcomes intervene and therefore mediate the relationship between organizational offerings of work-life balance practices and organizational performance. While Beauregard and Henry's (2009) framework focuses on work-life balance practices, flexible work ar-rangements are an integral part of work-life balance practices and, thus, it seems reasonable to apply their work-life practices mediation framework to the FWAs. In Beauregard and Henry's (2009) framework the organiza-tional offering of work-life balance practices influences mediator variables such as work-life conflict, retention, attraction of applicants, and job satis-faction. These intervening explanatory variables then have a positive rela-tionship with organizational performance.

In one mediation path, the *use* of work-life practices is positioned as a mediator between the *offering* of work-life practices and the employees' ex-perience of reduced work-life conflict (Beauregard & Henry, 2009). Build-ing on Beauregard and Henry's (2009) framework, we suggest a linkage that incorporates all three constructs of FWAs (i.e., organizational offer-ing of FWAs, employees' perceptions of FWA availability, and employees' usage of FWAs). McNall et al. (2010) explore work-to-family enrichment as a mediator of the relationship between the availability of FWAs, spe-cifically flextime and compressed workweeks, with employees' job sat-isfaction and turnover intentions. McNall et al.'s (2010) research results support our notion that Beauregard and Henry's (2009) model of the more general work-life practices can be applied to FWAs. McNall et al. (2010) found support for work-to-family enrichment acting as a mediator of the relationship between FWAs and job satisfaction and turnover.

We also suggest a second model in which the relationships reflect partial mediation. In both models, we have provided a simplified overall approach to communicate the concept to mediation and multiple variables rather than a detailed, descriptive model.

Research conducted by Carlson, Grzywacz, and Kacmar (2010) further illustrates how our mediation modelcan be applied. Carlson, Grzywacz, and Kacmar (2010) found work-to-family conflict and work-to-family enrichment acted as full mediators of the relationship between usage of FWAs and job satisfaction and performance in family-related responsibilities and, additionally, work-to-family enrichment was a partial mediator of the relationship between usage of FWAs and family satisfaction. These findings highlight the importance of increasing work-to-family enrichment and reducing work-to-family conflict in achievement of outcomes that have been associated with FWAs. This research also highlights the importance of distinguishing between different measures of FWAs. If organizations offer FWAs but do not actively allow or facilitate perceived availability and usage of FWAs, then can employees experience improvements in work-to-life enrichments and reductions in work-to-life conflict? It is likely that in order to better understand the relationships between FWAs and positive individual and organizational outcomes, researchers and practitioners need to consider relationships with intervening factors (Beauregard & Henry, 2009) and pay attention to the way in which FWAs are measured (i.e., offered, perceived availability, and use).

## MODERATING FACTORS IN THE RELATIONSHIP BETWEEN FWAS AND OUTCOMES

In addition to mediators, the presence of moderating variables in the relationships between FWAs and organizational and individual outcomes is also likely (Baltes et al., 1999; Beauregard & Henry, 2009). There has been increased interest in the manager's role in FWAs (Allen, 2001; Goff, Mount, & Jamison, 1990; Hammer, Kossek, Yragui, Bodner, & Hanson, 2009; Hammer, Kossek, Zimmerman, & Daniels, 2007; Lapierre & Allen, 2006). Two potential moderating factors are the role of an employee's manager in FWAs and the influence of organizational culture.

## THE MANAGER'S ROLE

Managers may moderate the relationship between each of the FWA conceptualizations. At the initial level of the organization offering FWAs, the manager can be the conduit through which organizational information on

FWAs flows to employees (Mesmer-Magnus & Viswesvaran, 2006; Swody & Powell, 2007). In this way the manager serves as the filter through which the employee develops a perception of which of the FWAs offered by the organization are available to the employee.

A manager also signals whether usage of available FWAs will affect career progression, project assignments, and managers' perceptions of the employee's commitment to the workgroup and to the organization. In this way the manager's support of FWAs can affect the direction of the relationship between employee's perceptions of FWA availability and employee usage of FWAs. Employees who fear negative career consequences are less likely to use FWAs. Anecdotal evidence suggests that employees' fear is linked to their belief that their managers' responses to employee FWA usage will be negative (e.g., lack of promotions, perceptions of employee not being as committed to the workplace) (Stone, 2007). Stone (2007) claims the presence of unsupportive managers is part of the real reason for why talented women leave the workplace rather than the stereotypical rationale that women leave so that they can become full-time caregivers (Stone, 2007).

Managers also play a role in the development of a workgroup culture. Lambert et al. (2008) found that employees who had coworkers using FWAs were more likely to use FWAs than those employees who did not have coworkers who used FWAs. In fact, among the variables measured (i.e., tenure, hours worked per week, supervisory responsibilities, and personal lifestyle), coworker usage of FWAs was the strongest predictor of an employee's intention to use FWAs. A manager's behavior of either encouraging or discouraging employees' usage of FWAs plays a critical role in shaping the departmental/workgroup atmosphere and the continued usage of FWAs by member of the workgroup (Kossek, Barber, & Winters, 1999; Lambert et al., 2008).

## ORGANIZATIONAL CULTURE

An interesting dichotomy exists in today's workplace between FWAs and organizational culture. Organizational culture can be defined as the shared beliefs, norms, and values of the members of an organization (Pinder, 2008). On the one hand, we see an increase in the number of organizations offering FWAs. On the other hand, the predominant culture of the workplace is still influenced strongly by social norms that associate men as the primary breadwinners and women as primarily full-time homemakers. When these social norms are incorporated into strongly held beliefs within an organization, then the "ideal" worker is seen as an employee able to dedicate *himself* to the workplace whereas all nonwork responsibilities are handled by the at-home female spouse (Bailyn, 2006; Rapoport et al., 2002; Williams, 2000). Within an organization built upon this ideal worker framework, there is no need for FWAs. The employee has no need for flexibility since he is fully committed to his work and career advancement the primary focus of his efforts and has no conflict with other non-work responsibilities since those are fully handled by his female spouse.

When male breadwinner social norms strongly influence organizational culture, it should not be surprising to find differences between organizational offerings of FWAs (e.g., listed in HR manuals and documents) and employee perceived availability of FWAs. In this way, organizational culture can affect the strength of the relationship between what organizations offer in the way of FWAs and whether employees perceived such FWAs as being available for use. Thus although some organizations offer FWAs for the reasons cited earlier (e.g., to appear competitive, to attract employees), employees may not feel that FWAs should be used because the organizational normative culture tacitly stigmatizes any need for workplace flexibility (Bailyn, 2006; Rapoport et al., 2002; Williams, 2000). As noted by Kathleen Christensen, Program Director at the Alfred P. Sloan Foundation, "There is a structural mismatch: the rigid schedules of most American workplaces, with little flexibility in how, when or where work is done, are mismatched to the needs of an increasingly diverse workforce, composed of working parents, older workers and others with distinct work-life needs" (SHRM, 2010, p. 5).

## FUTURE DIRECTIONS

Technological advances have contributed to the blurring of the lines between employees' personal and work lives and employees' interest in FWAs. For example, employees might wonder, "if I use my computer at home to check and answer work-related e-mails during the evening, can I come in later during the workday if I have personal obligations to attend to in the morning (e.g., child's school function, medical appointment)?" Given the expectation that the use of technology in our work and personal lives will continue to increase, it follows that employees will experience increasing work-life boundary issues and thus we can expect continued interest in FWAs as a way to help address these challenges. To that end, the link between organizations' FWAs benefits, employees' perceptions of FWA availability, and subsequent employee use of FWAs will need to be strengthened.

Right now FWAs are largely positioned as an employer's reaction to workforce demographic changes and demands. However, if the organization has the potential to benefit in multiple ways from the employee's usage of FWAs (e.g., greater retention, greater productivity), then why wouldn't organizations seek to proactively encourage usage of FWAs? One reason may be employer concern over reduced employee productivity when employees use FWAs (Eaton, 2003). Galinsky et al. (2005) note that employers should be careful to not associate employees who have nonwork interests with reduced productivity since these employees may in fact be more productive than work-centric employees. Indeed, an analysis by Families and Work Institute of approximately 1,000 adults age 18 and older working full-time found the feeling of being overworked was *less prevalent* among employees who had either a greater emphasis on family or an equal emphasis on work and family as compared to those employees who had work as their primary focal point (Galinksy et al., 2005). Could we then argue that organizations in an effort to improve morale and productivity (e.g., fewer mistakes) might proactively encourage usage of FWAs? Could encouraging workers to pursue nonwork interests and use of FWAs result in greater productivity? This type of thinking certainly represents a paradigm shift in how we conceptualize FWAs and how it would likely impact future use of FWAs.

Technology has certainly blurred the boundaries between employees' personal and work lives—calls on cell phones for home and work, access to e-mails from work and home. While one result of these blurred boundaries can be an increase in work-to-life conflict, there may be a positive side in terms of the implications for employees' usage of FWAs. If some of the resistance to employees' usage of FWAs has stemmed from a fear of not being able to monitor employee productivity, the Internet and advancements in information technology eliminate this concern. Technology now allows employees to access documents located on workplace-based servers from home, and also enables employees to share and edit those documents in real-time with other employees in different physical nonoffice based location(s).

Interestingly, Robinson (2005) raises the question of the ethical obligations that employers have when employees use FWAs. She suggests that if an organization is going to allow employees to use FWAs, the organization must also provide the appropriate resources (e.g., technology) and support (e.g., access to career advancement). Additionally, is it ethical for employers to list multiple FWAs in their Human Resource handbooks but then not ensure all employees have equal access?

## NOTE

Portions of this chapter were published in M. Paludi (Ed.). (2013). *Psychology for business success: Volume 1: Juggling, balancing, and integrating work and family roles and responsibilities.* Santa Barbara, CA: Praeger.

## REFERENCES

Allen, T. D. (2001). Family-supportive work environments: The role of organizational perceptions. *Journal of Vocational Behavior, 58,* 414–435.
Bailyn, L. (2006). *Breaking the mold: Redesigning work for productive and satisfying lives* (2nd ed.). Ithaca, NY: Cornell University Press.

Baltes, B. B., Briggs, T. E., Huff, J. W., Wright, J. A., & Neuman, G. A. (1999). Flexible and compressed workweek schedules: A meta-analysis of their effects on work-related criteria. *Journal of Applied Psychology, 84,* 496–513.

Beauregard, T. A., & Henry, L. C. (2009). Making the link between work-life balance practices and organizational performance. *Human Resources Management Review, 19,* 9–22.

Bond, J. T., Galinsky, E., Kim, S. S., & Brownfield, E. (2005). *2005 National Study of Employers.* New York: Families and Work Institute.

Butler, A. B., Grzywacz, J. G., Ettner, S. L., & Liu, B. (2009). Workplace flexibility, self-reported health, and health care utilization. [Article]. *Work & Stress, 23,* 45–59.

Carlson, D. S., Grzywacz, J. G., & Kacmar, K. M. (2010). The relationship of schedule flexibility and outcomes via the work-family interface. *Journal of Managerial Psychology, 25,* 330–355.

Development, D. (2010). *Redesigning the workplace: Fitting life into work and work into life.* Retrieved April 2, 2014 from www.dspace.mit.edu

Eaton, S. C. (2003). If you can use them: Flexibility policies, organizational ommitment and perceived performance. *Industrial Relations, 42,* 145–167.

Fitzpatrick, L. (2009, May 25). We're getting off the ladder. *Time,* May 14, 2009, 45.

Galinksy, E. M., Bond, J. T., Kim, S. S., Backon, L., Brownfield, E., & Sakai, K. (2005). *Overwork in America. When the way we work becomes too much.* New York: Families and Work Institute.

Glaeser, E. (2011, November 20). Goodbye, Golden Years. *New York Times Sunday Review,* pp. 1–2.

Goff, S. J., Mount, M. K., & Jamison, R. L. (1990). Employer supported child care, work/family conflict, and absenteeism: A field study. *Personnel Psychology, 43,* 793–809.

Grzywacz, J. G., Carlson, D. S., & Shulkin, S. (2008). Schedule flexibility and stress: Linking formal flexible arrangements and perceived flexibility to employee health. [Article]. *Community, Work & Family, 11,* 199–214.

Hammer, L. B., Kossek, E. E., Yragui, N. L., Bodner, T. E., & Hanson, G. C. (2009). Development and validation of a multidimensional measure of family supportive supervisor behaviors (FSSB). *Journal of Management, 35,* 837–856.

Hammer, L. B., Kossek, E. E., Zimmerman, K., & Daniels, R. (Eds.). (2007). *Clarifying the construct of family-supportive supervisory behaviors (FSSB): A multilevel perspective* (Vol. 6). Oxford: Elsevier Ltd.

Hayman, J. R. (2009). Flexible work arrangements: Exploring the linkages between perceived usability of flexible work schedules and work/life balance. *Community, Work & Family, 12,* 327–338.

Herrbach, O., Mignonac, K., Vandenberghe, C., & Negrini, A. (2009). Perceived HRM practices, organizational commitment, and voluntary early retirement among late-career managers. [Article]. *Human Resource Management, 48,* 895–915.

Kooij, T.A.M., Jansen, P.G.W., Dikkers, J.S.E., & de Lange, A. H. (2010). The influence of age on associations between HR practices and both affective commitment and job satisfaction: A meta-analysis. *Journal of Organizational Behavior, 31,* 1111–1136.

Kossek, E. E., Barber, A. E., & Winters, D. (1999). Using flexible schedules in the management world: The power of peers. *Human Resource Management, 38,* 33–49.

Lambert, A. D., Marler, J. H., & Gueutal, H. G. (2008). Individual differences: Factors affecting employee utilization of flexible work arrangements. *Journal of Vocational Behavior, 73*, 107–117.

Lapierre, L. M., & Allen, T. D. (2006). Work-supportive family, family-supportive supervision, use of organizational benefits, and problem-focused coping: Implications for work-family conflict and employee well being. *Journal of Occupational Health Psychology, 11*, 169–181.

McClelland, D. C., Koestner, R., & Weinberger, J. (1989). How do self-attributed and implicit motives differ? *Psychological Review, 96*, 690–702.

McNall, L. A., Masuda, A. D., & Nicklin, J. M. (2010). Flexible work arrangements, job satisfaction, and turnover intention: The mediating role of work-to-famiy enrichment. *The Journal of Psychology, 144*, 61–81.

Mesmer-Magnus, J. R., & Viswesvaran, C. (2006). How family-friendly work environments affect work/family conflict: A meta-analytic examination. *Journal of Labor Research, 17*, 555–574.

Olmstead, B. (1987). Flextime is money. *Management Review, 76*(11), 47–51.

Olmstead, B. (1995, Summer). Flexible work arrangements: From accommodation to strategy. *Employment Relations Today, 22*(2), 11–19.

Pinder, C. C. (2008). *Work motivation in organizational behavior.* New York: Psychology Press.

Rapoport, R., Bailyn, L., Fletcher, J. K., & Pruitt, B. H. (2002). *Beyond work-family balance: Advancing gender equity and workplace performance.* San Francisco, CA: Jossey-Bass.

Rau, B. (2004). Flexible work arrangements. In *A Sloan Work and Family Encyclopedia Entry.* Sloan Work and Family Research Networks.

Remarks by President at Workplace Flexibility Forum. (2010). Retrieved from www.whitehouse.gov/the-press-office/remarks-president-workplace-flexibility-forum

Richman, A. L., Civian, J. T., Shannon, L. L., Jeffrey Hill, E., & Brennan, R. T. (2008). The relationship of perceived flexibility, supportive work-life policies, and use of formal flexible arrangements and occasional flexibility to employee engagement and expected retention. [Article]. *Community, Work & Family, 11*, 183–197.

Robinson, W. (2005). Ethical Considerations in Flexible Work Arrangements. [Article]. *Business & Society Review, 110*(2), 213–224.

Rogier, S. A., & Padgett, M. Y. (2004). The impact of utilizing a flexible work schedule on the perceived career advancement potential of women. *Human Resource Development Quarterly, 15*, 89–106.

Scandura, T. A., & Lankau, M. J. (1997). Relationships of gender, family responsibility and flexible work hours to organizational commitment and job satisfaction. *Journal of Organizational Behavior, 18*, 377–391.

Schaefer, H. I. (2009, October). Part-time workers: Some key differences between primary and secondary earners. *Monthly Labor Review, 132*(10), 3–15.

SHRM. (2010). *SHRM executive roundtable on workplace flexibility: Executive summary.* Alexandria, VA: Society for Human Resource Management.

Smith, K. T. (2010). Work-life balance perspectives of marketing professionals in generation Y. *Services Marketing Quarterly, 31*, 434–447.

Stone, P. (2007). *Opting Out? Why women really quit careers and head home.* Berkeley, CA: University of California Press.

Stuart, A. (2010). The perils of flextime. *CFO, 26,* 38–44.

Sutton, K. L., & Noe, R. A. (2005). Family-friendly programs and work-life integration: More myth than magic? In E. E. Kossek & S. J. Lambert (Eds.), *Work and Life Integration*. Mahwah, NJ: Lawrence Erlbaum Associates.

Swody, C. A., & Powell, G. N. (2007). Determinants of employee participation in organizations' family-friendly programs: A multi-level approach. *Journal of Business and Psychology, 22,* 111–122.

Thompson, C. A., Beauvais, L. L., & Lyness, K. S. (1999). When work-family benefits are not enough: The influence of work-family culture on benefit utilization, organizational attachment, and work-family conflict. *Journal of Vocational Behavior, 54,* 392–415.

Torpey, E. (2007, Summer). Flexible work: Adjusting the when and where of your job. *Occupational Outlook Quarterly, 51*(2), 14–26.

Twenge, J. M., Campbell, S. M., Hoffman, B. J., & Lance, C. E. (2010). Generational differences in work values: Leisure and extrinsic values increasing, social and intrinsic values decreasing. *Journal of Management, 36,* 1117–1142.

Valcour, P. M., & Hunter, L. W. (2005). Technology, organizations, and work-life integration. In E. E. Kossek & S. J. Lambert (Eds.), *Work and Life Integration* (pp. 61–84). Mahwah, NJ: Lawrence Erlbaum Associates.

Williams, J. (2000). *Unbending Gender. Why family and work conflict and what to do about it.* New York: Oxford University Press.

# Chapter 19

# Sandwiched In: Women as Child and Elder Caregivers and Employers' Responses

*Michele A. Paludi*

## THE IN-BETWEEN OR SANDWICH GENERATION

*As a member of the sandwich generation, I can relate. I often feel like the peanut butter between two slices of bread: I'm trying to hold it together for my two teenage daughters, and also meet the needs of my 89-year-old mom, Elinor*

—*(Katie Couric, 2013, p. 1)*

In the United States, many women are postponing childbearing until their late 30s and early 40s (Lockwood, 2003). By the time these women begin their families, their parents are aged 60 years or older. In addition to caring for young children, employed women are simultaneously caring for one or more of their elderly parents. Lockwood (2003) noted that between 40 and 60% of women caring for elders also have childcare responsibilities in addition to their careers. Lockwood (2003) and Hammer, Neal, Newsome, Brockwood, and Collton (2005) further noted that women spend approximately 17 years of their lives caring for children and 18 years caring for one or both parents. The term "sandwich generation" (coined by

Miller, 1981) or "in-between generation" has been used to describe the
middle-aged generation who is simultaneously caring for children (under
18 years of age) and elders (65 years and older). More women than men
are "sandwiched in."

Research has (Ingersoll-Dayton, Neal, & Hammer, 2004) noted that the
time involved in caring for children and elders is comparable to a second
occupation. On average, women's caregiving responsibilities include:

- 4.7 hours per week on making arrangements
- 2.6 hours per week traveling to the elder's home assisted living
  community
- 4.1 hours per week on caregiving tasks
- 4.5 hours per week on driving children to and from school
- 9.6 hours per week taking children to and from extracurricular activities
- 10.4 hours per week on childcare responsibilities

Women caregivers indicate they sleep approximately six hours per
night. Furthermore, they report experiencing sadness and grief over parents' declining health; fear and worry about ability to give adequate care,
financial issues; anger over having to deal with the added responsibilities,
guilt for not doing enough for anybody; fatigue and isolation (Clark &
Weber, 1997). Research also identified that employees providing eldercare
were in fair or poor health themselves. Among women employees aged 50
and older, 17% of those elder caregivers reported fair or poor health versus
9% of women who were not caregivers. Illnesses likely to be reported by
women caregivers include depression, hypertension, and pulmonary disease. There is a direct impact on women's health as well: women caregivers
were less likely to report annual mammograms than noncaregivers and
deferred other preventive health screenings (Cole & Van Houtven, 2009).

Women caregivers report more stress at home than noncaregiving employees in every age group. Furthermore, stress is additive. Each new
stressor adds to a woman's stress level. Time pressures are not the primary
cause of stress when dealing with work-life conflicts. Rather, it is the psychological inclusion of family life into the work domain and, conversely,
work into the family domain (Ezzedeen & Swiercz, 2002). Ezzedeen and
Swiercz (2002) found that this cognitive intrusion of work results in lower
job satisfaction, a greater incidence of work-life conflict, job burnout, and
less overall happiness. Furthermore, the experience of intrusion is rooted
in the organizational culture of the employer, including whether or not the
employer has family-friendly policies.

Caregiving to children and elders is thus a workplace issue. Women
report they must take off 18.9 vacation days and sick days per year to
deal with caregiving responsibilities of children and elders. Women have
indicated they have had to make work-related adjustments as a consequence of eldercare and childcare responsibilities (MetLife Mature Market

Institute and National Alliance for Caregiving, 2006). These adjustments involved early retirement, telework, taking a reduced salary, and quitting their jobs. Hunt (2004) found that employed caregivers have lost job benefits, turned down a promotion, changed work shifts, took a less demanding job, and refused overtime work. In addition, MetLife (2006) reported that additional health care cost to employers is 8% more for employees with eldercare responsibilities. This percentage translates into approximately 13.4 billion dollars annually.

The National Alliance for Caregiving and Center for Productive Aging reported that women employees who were dealing with eldercare responsibilities had to miss work:

81% took time off during their workday to make arrangements and/or provide care for elders

70% reported needing days off in order to fulfill caregiving obligations
64% admitted to coming to work late and/or leaving work early
41% spent part of their workday discussing eldercare issues with coworkers

We must also acknowledge that the majority of women in the sandwich generation are single. Their salaries are typically not sufficient to bear costs of both childcare and eldercare and take care of household expenses and themselves (Lin, Fee, & Wu, 2012). The Pew Research Center (2013) reported that providing financial support for aging parents is related to financial strain; not being able to live comfortably. Women re-entering the workplace following taking leave for caregiving lose approximately 11% of their earning power; when they spend three or more years away from the workplace, women lose approximately 37% of their earning power (Hewlett & Luce, 2005). Furthermore caregivers' social security and pension benefits over the course of their work career suffer as well.

MetLife (2006) concluded:

Employers can serve the best interests of their employees as well as those of their corporation by anticipating and responding to the challenges of eldercare for their employees. (p. 5)

Middle-aged women, many of whom are employed, provide the majority of care to older, frail, disabled, and chronically ill relatives. The increasing labor force participation of women, along with older relatives living longer but with chronic illness, raises important questions about how effectively and at what cost the roles of family caregiver and worker can be combined. (p. 6)

However, employer support for women simultaneously caring for adults has not yet reached the level offered for childcare services, for example, on-site child care, day care referral services. Only 29% of organizations provide employees with information about eldercare services (Bond, Galinsky, Kim, & Brownfield, 2005). In fact, research conducted by *USA Today* (cited in Rose, 2006) found that employers typically do not know which employees are impacted by eldercare issues and "sandwich" issues. Eighty percent of the respondents in this research didn't know or "guessed" at the percentage of caregivers in their organization. In addition, data suggest that employees are reluctant to use any services related to eldercare (Families and Work Institute, 2002) as a consequence of the following:

1. Discomfort when discussing eldercare issues, especially about terminal illnesses and not being able to juggle responsibilities.
2. Employers who discourage discussion about ways family demands impact work.
3. Beliefs that family issues should not be made public.

The purpose of this chapter is to provide recommendations for employers to assist employees, especially women employees who provide the majority of caregiving to children and elders in coping with these multiple caregiving roles.

## DETERMINING CHANGES TO BE INSTITUTED IN THE ORGANIZATION

### Human Resource Audits

In keeping with the recommendations from the EEOC and human resource management literature (e.g., Dessler, 2009; Smith & Mazin, 2004), I suggest companies utilize an audit checklist to review their multiple caregiving management program. The following audit is adapted from Paludi and Barickman's (1998) recommendations for managing sexual harassment in the workplace. Audits provide information for administrators on ways caregiving respect is operating in their organization. As Greenberg-Pophal stated, a human resource audit is "an analysis by which an organization measures where it currently stands and determines what it has to accomplish to improve its human resource function" (in Dessler, 2009, p. 412). Audit questions cover all aspects of the four major functions of human resource management, that is, recruitment and selection, training and development, motivation (performance appraisals, compensation) and maintenance (health and safety, communications, labor relations, discipline) (DeCenzo & Robbins, 2007). Sample audit questions for caregiving management include:

1. Are there flexible work policies for employees who are providing care and need assistance? For example:

   Part-time Work
   Job Sharing

Flextime
Telecommuting
Compressed Work Week
Desk Sharing

2. Are the policies well publicized? Are they circulated periodically among all members of the company? Are they available on the company's website?
3. How do employees learn to whom they should request leave for caregiving responsibilities?
4. Does the company have procedures to inform new employees about eldercare and childcare leaves during onboarding training?
5. Does the company work with an Employees Assistance Program to offer services, for example:

Stress-reduction techniques
Eldercare referrals
Support groups/workshops dealing with wills, trusts, estate planning
Housing options, long-term care choices

6. Do we train our managers and supervisors so they understand their role as "agents" of our company with respect to employees informing them of their caregiving responsibilities?
7. Are our policies, procedures, and training program resources available in other common languages in addition to English?
8. Does our Employees Assistance Program have counselors who speak languages common to our workforce?
9. What metrics do we have in place to measure the success of our caregiving management program?

The employer must learn from the audit the reason(s) for the disconnect between the company's policies and its practices with respect to childcare and eldercare. Subsequently, the employer must correct the problems uncovered in the audit.

## Cultural Climate Surveys

I also recommend conducting organizational cultural climate surveys with employees in order to determine their perceptions about the effectiveness of the company's management of childcare and eldercare responsibilities (Cooper, Cartwright, & Earley, 2001; Driskill & Brenton, 2005). These climate surveys typically measure organizational values and practices, organizational effectiveness, organizational leadership, communication, and performance management. Climate surveys profile the alignment between the organization's stated mission with respect to caregiving and behaviors of management and employees, effectiveness of training programs, policies, investigations, and corrective action.

## SWOT Analysis

In order to evaluate the **S**trengths, **W**eaknesses, **O**pportunities, and **T**hreats involved in developing or improving caregiving management program, I recommend conducting a SWOT analysis (Williamson, Cooke, Jenkins, & Moreton, 2003). This analysis provides information that is useful in matching the organization's resources and capabilities to the competitive environment in which it operates. The SWOT analysis serves as a filter to reduce the information to a management quantity of major issues. It classifies internal aspects of the organization as strengths or weaknesses and the external situational factors as opportunities or threats.

Using this analysis, the organization can leverage its strengths associated with its caregiving program, correct its weaknesses in its program (e.g., lack of resources), capitalize on opportunities (e.g., assistance from consulting firm), and deter devastating threats to the program's success (e.g., failure to have confidential procedures).

A completed SWOT analysis may be used for goal setting, strategy formulation, and implementation. This analysis is best conducted with many stakeholders, including the organization's president, human resource director, employees, strategic partners, vendors, clients, and consultants (Williamson et al., 2003).

## Barrier Analysis

A barrier analysis may be used when there is an employment issue, for example, policy, procedure, training program, hiring practice, performance evaluation, that limits opportunities for women who are multiple caregivers (Dineen & Bartlett, 2002). Through this analysis, an investigation of the triggers found in the employment issue are identified and resolved. Triggers include a disparity or trend that suggests a need for an inquiry into an employment issue, for example, lack of promotion for women in the "sandwich" generation, high separation rate of women who are multiple caregivers. Barriers may be found in all functions of human resource management, that is, recruitment, hiring, promotions, training, incentive programs, disciplinary actions, and separation from the company. All of these strategies have been linked to positive ramifications for the organization as well as for women caregivers, for example, lower absenteeism; less stress; higher morale; improved work satisfaction; lower turnover rate; staffing over a wide range of hours; childcare hours that conform to work hours; and access to quality infant, child, and eldercare.

Barriers may be institutional, attitudinal, for example, managers believe that women employees who are caring for children and elders are not as committed to their job as are other employees, or physical, for example, training materials and employee handbooks are not available in languages in addition to English, Braille, and so on.

There are six components to a barrier analysis:

1. Review practices, policies, procedures. Documents include handbooks, directives, staffing charts, hiring records, promotion records.
2. Analyze the source material.
3. Identify triggers from workplace statistics, complaints data, culture climate surveys, reports by outside organizations.
4. Determine the root cause of the triggers.
5. If the root cause is a barrier, develop an action plan to remove the barrier.
6. Monitor the action plan periodically.

## ADDITIONAL ORGANIZATIONAL RESPONSES

Research findings summarized in this chapter highlight the necessity for women to have greater flexibility at work as well as assistance with family responsibilities. Organizations that recognize the need and adapt work to employees' lives (to be obtained by the human resource metrics discussed earlier in this chapter) will garner employees' loyalty and thus have a competitive advantage. The challenge for employers is to help restore the balance of work and caregiving responsibilities. This has been accomplished through four major strategies: time-based, information-based, direct services, and culture change policies (Strassel, Colgan, & Goodman, 2006). Time-based strategies include family-friendly policies, including job sharing, desk sharing, flextime, part-time work, career break/sabbatical, and telecommuting (Golden, 2001).

Information-based strategies include programs such as Intranet work, relocation assistance, and eldercare resources. Direct services include on-site child and/or eldercare, emergency back-up care, subsidy of eldercare costs, eldercare referral services, paid eldercare, concierge services, and on-site health services. Culture change strategies include programs that provide training for management to help deal with work-life conflicts. These culture change programs include:

1. Policy revisions to ensure they are not discriminatory toward caregivers of children and/or elders.
2. Using a variety of recruitment and selection techniques that are not biased toward applicants who are simultaneously caring for children and elders.
3. Ensuring legal recruitment and selection techniques, for example:

   Employers must not ask applicants about their elder caregiving (or childcare) or whether they will be providing eldercare services in the future. The focus of questions of applicants must be on their qualifications. This applies to both the application and interview.

4. Not interpreting periods of absence from work as negative; this could be an indication of elder caregiving.
5. Using a variety of recruitment resources that are targeted at diverse applicant pools.
6. Establishing effective, objective criteria for evaluating job candidates.
7. Establishing criteria for evaluating employees' performance that are reliable, valid, and free from bias.
8. Using several interviewers to minimize the impact of discrimination and bias by any single interviewer.
9. Training managers to be aware of stereotyping and hidden biases that may operate in all human resource functions with respect to women employees who are caregivers.
10. Measuring the organization's return on investment, that is, the net benefit of the caregiver management program divided by the initiative costs (Gates, 2004; Hubbard, 2004; Jayne & Dipboye, 2004).
11. Ensuring there is no retaliation against caregivers who request leaves or voice complaints about unfair treatment.
12. Posting work schedules as soon as possible, so employees have ample time to arrange for alternate care for their elders or children.
13. Ensuring managers are knowledgeable about legal obligations that impact caregivers, for example, Family and Medical Leave Act, Employee Retirement Income Security Act, Americans with Disabilities Act.
14. Making reentry as easy as possible for women who have been out of the workforce due to caregiving responsibilities.
15. Cross-training employees.
16. Offering Employee Assistance Programs that focus on:

Substance abuse treatment
Stress management
Crisis intervention
Individual and family counseling
Bereavement counseling

Several organizations have time-based, information-based, direct services, and culture change policies. For example, Booz Allen uses a "ramp up, ramp down" flexible work program that contracts with current and recently exited workforce to assist them in remaining connected through projects and training programs. Lehman Brothers instituted the "Encore Program" that provides women traders and bankers who have been out on leave with opportunities to update their work skills, including resume building and interview skills. Goldman Sachs provides employees with access to 1,500 childcare centers and in-home agencies for child and/or eldercare.

At AstraZeneca, employees receive six hours per year with an expert on geriatric care. Services provided include reviewing private nursing homes, interviewing home-health aides and physicians, and tasting food served at nursing homes. AstraZeneca also offers elder referral services workshops/seminars during the lunch period on geriatric topics, for example, Alzheimer's disease. At IBM, employees are provided discounted long-term care insurance and a phone button connected to an ambulance.

In 1999, at the beginning of the "sandwich" generation concerns, Fannie Mae hired a full-time eldercare consultant whose responsibilities include grief counseling, wills and estate planning, and helping to select nursing homes. Fannie Mae's evaluation of these offerings indicated that 28% of their employees in need of eldercare resources would have had to quit their jobs without this assistance.

Arnold and Porter's programs include on-site childcare, national day care network that provides full-time and back-up childcare, and a new Parent Mentor Program.

The Equal Employment Opportunity Commission (EEOC, 2007) has identified employer's best practices for the sandwich generation. According to the EEOC, employer support for multiple caregiving responsibilities benefits the workplace as well as individuals, for example, employee productivity is enhanced, absenteeism is reduced, and profits are increased:

> Employers adopting flexible workplace policies that help employees achieve a satisfactory work-life balance may not only experience decreased complaints of unlawful discrimination, but may also benefit their workers, their customer base, and their bottom line. (p. 1)

By the year 2030, one of five citizens in the United States will be 65 years or older (Dreifus, 2006). The requirement for caregiving progressively ascends after 65; at age 85 and older, more than half of elderly individuals cannot function without caregiving. Since women live, on average, five to seven years longer than men, they will continue to form the majority among caregivers (Remennick, 1999). The Radcliff Public Policy Center (2001, cited by Lockwood, 2003) found that 85% of women aged 20 to 39 put family time and commitments first, not work. In 2001, Rutgers (cited in Lockwood, 2003) reported that 90% of employees indicated they are not pleased with the amount of time spent with families; that they want more time with them.

Employers must offer options to permit women to integrate work and family roles. The management philosophy that demands all employees to put work above family is no longer welcome by women and men employees.

## REFERENCES

Bond, J., Galinsky, E., Kim, S., & Browfield, E. (2005). *National study of employers.* New York: Families and Work Institute.

Clark, J., & Weber, K. (1997). *Challenges and choices: Elderly caregiving.* Retrieved October 16, 2013, from http://extnsion.missouri.edu/p/GH6657

Cole, N., & Van Houtven, C. (2009). Caring for mom and neglecting yourself? The health effects of caring for an elderly parent. *Health Economics, 18,* 991–1010.

Cooper, C., Cartwright, S., & Earley, C. (2001). *The international handbook of organizational culture and climate.* New York: Wiley.

Couric, K. (2013). *Katie Couric on caring for elderly parents.* Retrieved October 17, 2013, from www.womansday.com/life/personal-stories/katie-couric-on-caring-for-elderly-parents

DeCenzo, D., & Robbins, S. (2007). *Fundamentals of human resource management.* New York: Wiley.

Dessler, G. (2009). *Fundamentals of human resource management.* Upper Saddle River, NJ: Prentice Hall.

Dineen, M., & Bartlett, R. (2002). *Six steps to root cause analysis.* Oxford: Consequence.

Dreifus, C. (2006). Focusing on the issue of aging, and growing into the job. *The New York Times,* November 14.

Driskill, G., & Benton, A. (2005). *Organizational culture in action: A cultural analysis workbook.* New York: Sage.

Equal Employment Opportunity Commission. (2007). *Employer best practices for workers with caregiving responsibilities.* Retrieved October 16, 2013, from www.eeoc.gov/policy/docs/caregiver-best-practices.html

Ezzedeen, S., & Swiercz, P. (2002). *Rethinking worklife balance: Development and validation of the cognitive intrusion of work scale-A dissertation research proposal.* Proceedings of the 2002 Easter Academy of Management Meeting.

Families and Work Institute. (2002). *Highlights of the national study of the changing workforce.* New York: Families and Work Institute.

Gates, S. (2004). *Measuring more than efficiency: The new role of human capital metrics.* Retrieved September 20, 2009, from www.conference-board.org

Golden, L. (2001). Flexible work schedules: Which workers get them? *American Behavioral Scientist, 44,* 1157–1158.

Hammer, L. B., Neal, M. B., Newsom, J., Brockwood, K. J., & Colton, C. (2005). A longitudinal study of the effects of dual-earner couples' utilization of family-friendly workplace supports on work and family outcomes. *Journal of Applied Psychology, 90,* 799–810.

Hewlett, S., & Luce, C. (2005). Off ramps and on ramps: Keeping talented women on the road to success. *Harvard Business Review, 83,* 43–46, 48, 50–54.

Hubbard, E. (2004). *The diversity scorecard: Evaluating the impact of diversity on organizational performance.* Burlington, MA: Elsevier Butterworth.

Hunt, G. (2004). Caregiving and the workplace. In C. Levine (Ed.), *Always on call: When illness turns families into caregivers* (p. 126). Nashville, TN: Vanderbilt University Press.

Ingersoll-Dayton, B., Neal, M., & Hammer, L. (2004). Aging parents helping adult children: The experience of the sandwiched generation. *Family Relations, 50,* 262–271.

Jayne, M., & Dipboye, R. (2004). Leveraging diversity to improve business performance: Research findings and recommendations for organizations. *Human Resource Management, 43*(4), 409–424.

Lin, I., Fee, H., & We, H. (2012). Negative and positive caregiving experiences: A closer look at the intersection of gender and relationship. *Family Relations, 61,* 343–358.

Lockwood, N. (2003, June). *Work/life balance: Challenges and solutions.* Alexandria, VA: Society for Human Resource Management Research Quarterly.

MetLife Mature Market Institute and National Alliance for Caregiving. (2006). *The MetLife caregiving cost study: Productivity losses to U.S. business.* Westport, CT: MetLife Mature Market Institute.

Miller, D. (1981). The sandwich generation: Adult children of the aging. *Social Work, 26,* 419–423.

Paludi, M., & Barickman, R. (1998). *Sexual harassment, work, and education: A resource manual for prevention.* Albany: State University of New York Press.

Pew Research Social and Demographic Trends. (2013). *The sandwich generation: Rising financial burdens for middle-aged Americans.* Retrieved October 17, 2013, from www.pewsocialtrends.org/2013/01/30/the-sandwich-generation/

Remennick, L. (1999). Women of the "sandwich" generation and multiple roles: The case of Russian immigrants of the 1900s in Israel. *Sex Roles, 32,* 247–378.

Rose, K. (2006). *Elder care: A responsibility that requires a collaborative effort.* Retrieved October 16, 2013, from www.worldatwork.org/advancesearch

Smith, S., & Mazin, R. (2004). *The HR answer book.* New York: AMACOM.

Strassel, K., Colgan, C., & Goodman, J. (2006). *Leaving women behind: Modern families, outdated laws.* New York: Rowman & Littlefield Publishers.

Williamson, D., Cooke, P., Jenkins, W., & Moreton, K. (2003). *Strategic management and business analysis.* Burlington, MA: Butterworth-Heinemann.

# Index

# About the Editor and Contributors

## EDITOR

**MICHELE A. PALUDI,** PhD, is the series editor for *Women's Psychology* and for *Women and Careers in Management* for Praeger. She is the author/editor of 50 college textbooks, and more than 200 scholarly articles and conference presentations on sexual harassment, campus violence, psychology of women, gender, and discrimination. Her book *Ivory Power: Sexual Harassment on Campus* (1990, SUNY Press) received the 1992 Myers Center Award for Outstanding Book on Human Rights in the United States. Dr. Paludi served as Chair of the U.S. Department of Education's Subpanel on the Prevention of Violence, Sexual Harassment, and Alcohol and Other Drug Problems in Higher Education. She was one of six scholars in the United States to be selected for this subpanel. She also was a consultant to and a member of former New York State Governor Mario Cuomo's Task Force on Sexual Harassment. Dr. Paludi serves as an expert witness for court proceedings and administrative hearings on sexual harassment. She has had extensive experience in conducting training programs and investigations of sexual harassment and other Equal Employment Opportunity (EEO) issues for businesses and educational institutions. In addition, Dr. Paludi has held faculty positions at Franklin & Marshall College, Kent State University, Hunter College, Union College, Hamilton College, and Union Graduate College, where she directs the human resource management certificate program. She is the Equal Opportunity and Employee Relations Specialist/Title IX Coordinator and ADA/504 Coordinator at Siena College.

## CONTRIBUTORS

**AFRA AHMAD** is from George Mason University with a BA in psychology and a minor in Islamic studies. Her primary research interests include diversity and cross-cultural issues in the workplace. After earning her bachelor's degree, Afra was selected for a Fulbright Fellowship to conduct research in the United Arab Emirates. Currently, she is involved in research projects with her advisor, Dr. Eden King, related to age diversity, religious minorities, women, and ethnic leaders. In addition, she is working with Dr. Seth Kaplan and several other students in developing a well-being program to help employees improve their workplace emotions. Afra's undergraduate honors thesis, which examined discrimination toward Muslim women in job applications, was recently published in *Personnel Psychology*. In addition to research, Afra enjoys mentoring undergraduates and teaching undergraduate courses.

**JOAN C. CHRISLER**, PhD, is the Class of 1943 Professor of psychology at Connecticut College, where she teaches courses on the psychology of women and health psychology. She has published extensively on the psychology of women and gender, and is especially known for her work on women's reproductive health and body image. Her most recent books are *Reproductive Justice: A Global Concern* (2012, Praeger), *Handbook of Gender Research in Psychology* (2010, Springer), and *Women over 50: Psychological Perspectives* (2007, Springer). She is the editor of *Women's Reproductive Health*, an interdisciplinary, feminist journal, and she is currently working on a book about women's embodiment.

**LILLIAN COMAS-DIAZ** is a private practitioner in Washington, D.C., executive director of the Transcultural Mental Health Institute, and a clinical professor at the George Washington University Medical School. She has written extensively on the interaction among culture, gender, ethnicity, race, social class, and mental health. She serves on several editorial boards. She is a past president of the American Psychological Association Division of Psychologists in independent practice.

**TINA C. ELACQUA** has 20 years of teaching and research experience in the field of higher education, including the roles of research scientist, professor, industrial/organizational consultant, and author. Dr. Elacqua earned her BA degree in psychology with a concentration in human services and presocial work and minored in sociology and women's studies from Russell Sage College in Troy, NY, and her MA and PhD degrees in industrial and organizational psychology from Central Michigan University in Mt. Pleasant, MI. Dr. Elacqua teaches graduate-level business courses and undergraduate business and psychology courses for LeTourneau

University. She enjoys teaching, writing, and publishing. Her scholarly productivity includes publications in journal articles, books, conference papers and presentations, technical reports, and technical presentations. Her main research interests and publications are in the areas of career development (e.g., glass ceiling, work-life interface) and faith-based bereavement postviolent death. Her most recent projects led to two books (entitled *Hope Beyond Loss* and *Hope Beyond Homicide*) and an intervention for counseling the bereaved through a Biblical worldview.

**SUE A. EPSTEIN** is assistant professor in management, business, and economics at SUNY Empire State College. Her research interests include work-life issues and leadership. Her doctoral research combined these two areas and explored the theoretical antecedents of work-life supportive leadership. She completed her PhD in organizational studies at The University at Albany, SUNY.

**ABBIE E. GOLDBERG** received her PhD in clinical psychology from the University of Massachusetts Amherst and completed her predoctoral internship at Yale Medical School. She is currently an associate professor of psychology at Clark University, where she has been since 2005. Her research and teaching interests involve diverse families, sexuality, and gender. She is the author of over 30 peer-reviewed journal articles as well as the book, *Lesbian and Gay Parents and Their Children: Research on the Family Life Cycle,* which in 2010 received the Distinguished Book Award from Division 44 of the American Psychological Association. She has received grant funds from a variety of sources, including the National Institutes of Health, the American Psychological Foundation, the Alfred P. Sloan Foundation, the Williams Institute, and the Gay and Lesbian Medical Association. Dr. Goldberg currently serves on the editorial boards of several journals, including the *Journal of Marriage and Family, Family Relations,* and *Adoption Quarterly.*

**KATHRYN HALPIN** graduated summa cum laude from Bentley University in 2008 with a BS in marketing and from Union Graduate College in 2012 with her MBA. Katie also obtained her professional in human resources (PHR) certificate in 2012. She currently works as a manager in the human capital management department at Capital District Physicians' Health Plan (CDPHP) in Albany, NY. She was previously employed by Time Warner Cable and Harvard University serving in various human resource roles.

**ANN H. HUFFMAN** is an associate professor of psychology and management at Northern Arizona University. She received her PhD in industrial and organizational psychology from Texas A&M University in 2004. Prior to Texas A&M University, Dr. Huffman worked as a principal investigator with the Walter Reed Army Research Institute, Europe. Her primary research interests include the work-life interface, high stress occupations (e.g., police, military), diversity in the workplace, and environmental sustainability issues. Dr. Huffman has published in journals such as the *Academy of Management Journal, Journal of Occupational Health Psychology, Psychological and Educational Measurement, Sex Roles,* and *Human Resource Management* and has received grants from the Society for Human Resource Management Foundation and the Society of Industrial-Organizational Psychologist Small Grant to support her research. She was selected in 2007 as a Sloan Early Career Work-Family Scholar and in 2009 was honored as Northern Arizona University Most Promising New Scholar Award.

**INGRID JOHNSTON-ROBLEDO**, PhD, is director of women's studies and associate professor of psychology at SUNY, Fredonia. She teaches courses on the psychology of women, women's health, and human sexuality. Her areas of expertise are women's health, reproductive health education, and women's experiences with pregnancy, childbirth, breastfeeding, postpartum adjustment, and motherhood.

**ELISE JONES** is a master's candidate in psychology at Connecticut College, where she studies how individuals' investments in the roles they most value impacts their overall well-being and performance. Prior to returning to school, Elise led the diversity effort for the mobile communications business at Microsoft Corporation where she founded the company's flexwork-focused employee affinity group and served as workplace flexibility advisor to several executives. Elise is president of E Jones Consulting and holds a bachelor's degree in business administration from Brigham Young University.

**KRISTEN P. JONES** is an assistant professor at George Mason University (GMU), and her main research interests include building an understanding of the work experiences of socially disadvantaged individuals. Kristen is currently teaching a course on the psychology of gender at GMU, and her past teaching experience includes advanced statistics and research methods at the graduate and undergraduate level. In addition to research and teaching, she serves as the editorial assistant at *Organizational Research Methods* and is about to begin collecting data for her dissertation exploring the work-pregnancy interface.

**MICHELE KILBURN** graduated with her bachelor of science in human resources and business administration in 2011. She is pursuing her MBA at Union College, with a certificate in human resources and healthcare administration, 2015. She is the president of the Graduate Student Assembly at Union Graduate. Michele is 22-year professional in human resources, marketing, contract negotiations, and project management. She recently completed a project in assessing green jobs and education with the NYS Department of Labor and the College of Nanoscale Science and Engineering in 2011. Michele works full-time in the construction industry as support staff to business development and marketing. She also consults for her spouse in managing the family construction business and other entrepreneurial efforts. Michele resides in Upstate New York with her spouse, their two college-age children, and pets. She and her spouse are avid motorcyclists, and they ride, own, and have built custom choppers. Michele is a licensed cosmetologist since 1992, a previously licensed New York real estate sales associate, and a carry concealed weapons licensure. When Michele has downtime, besides spending time with her family or riding motorcycles, she also likes to spend time riding her horse.

**EDEN B. KING** joined the faculty of the industrial and organizational psychology program at George Mason University after earning her PhD from Rice University in 2006. Dr. King is pursuing a program of research that seeks to guide the equitable and effective management of diverse organizations. Her research integrates organizational and social psychological theories in conceptualizing social stigma and the work-life interface. This research addresses three primary themes: (1) current manifestations of discrimination and barriers to work-life balance in organizations, (2) consequences of such challenges for its targets and their workplaces, and (3) individual and organizational strategies for reducing discrimination and increasing support for families. In addition to her academic positions, Dr. King has consulted on applied projects related to climate initiatives, selection systems, and diversity training programs, and she has worked as a trial consultant.

**MIRIAM LISS** is an associate professor of psychology at the University of Mary Washington. She received her PhD in clinical psychology from the University of Connecticut in 2001. Her research on gender issues includes feminist identity, sexualization and objectification, expectations regarding the division of household labor, and ideologies about motherhood. She has also published on psychoanalysis, self-injury, sensory processing sensitivity, and autism. She lives in Fredericksburg with her husband and two children.

**JANET H. MARLER** is an associate professor and chair of the management department at the School of Business at University at Albany, State University of New York. Prior to earning a PhD from Cornell University's School of Industrial and Labor Relations, she held several senior executive positions in the financial services industry. She was also a doctoral fellow at Cornell's Employment and Family Careers Institute, a Sloan Center on Working Families funded by the Alfred P. Sloan Foundation. Her research centers on the strategic use of e-HRM, compensation strategy, alternative and flexible work arrangements, and work and family careers and has been published in leading scholarly journals and books including *Corporate Governance: An International Review, Human Resources Management Review, International Journal of Human Resources, Journal of Management, Journal of Organizational Behavior, Journal of Vocational Behavior, Journal of Managerial Psychology, Personnel Psychology,* and *Strategic Management Journal.*

**TRACY C. MCCAUSLAND** is a fifth year doctoral candidate in the industrial and organizational psychology program at George Mason University. She completed her bachelor of science from Davidson College in North Carolina. Her primary research interests include age diversity, multiteam systems, and leadership. Specifically, she is interested in how technology impacts age diverse interactions and team processes of multicultural distributed teams. In addition to her main research pursuits, Tracy has conducted research investigating the development of situational judgment items, electronic mentoring programs at the United States Office of Personnel Management, and global leadership at Booz Allen Hamilton.

**AVIGAIL MOOR**, PhD, is a clinical psychologist who specializes in the study and treatment of survivors of sexual violence. She heads the gender studies program at Tel Hai College in Israel, and is also on the faculty of the social work department. In addition, she serves as a psychological consultant to several rape crisis centers in Northern Israel. Her past and present research focuses primarily on the social context of sexual violence against women and its psychological sequelae. She has also written many articles on the treatment of survivors. Other research interests concern the psychology of women, including the effects of the gender-based power imbalance on women's mental health in general, and on body image and eating disorders in particular. She lives in Israel with her family and is the proud mother of a daughter and a son.

**WHITNEY B. MORGAN** (PhD, George Mason University) is an assistant professor at the University of Houston—Downtown in the department of management, marketing, and business administration. The overarching goal of her program of research is to provide theoretical and empirical evidence guiding the advancement of women and mothers in the workplace. Her line of research touches a variety of content areas including performance appraisal, developmental opportunities, extra-role behavior, and retention. She has published in *Human Resource Management Review, Journal of Occupational Health Psychology, Equal Opportunities International,* and *Sex Roles.*

**CAROLYN NOBLE,** PhD, is professor emerita at Victoria University, Melbourne, and inaugural professor of social work at the Australian College of Applied Psychology (ACAP) in Sydney, Australia. Her research interests include social work theory and practice, social movement and progressive practice, and gender democracy and equality in higher education.

**YOUNGAH PARK** received her PhD in industrial and organizational psychology from Bowling Green State University (BGSU) in Bowling Green, Ohio. Before she pursued her academic career, she worked for multinational companies in the field of employee training and development and trade marketing. Park is an assistant professor of psychology at Kansas State University. Her scholarly productivity includes extramural research grants receipt and publications in journal articles, books, conference papers and presentations. Her main research interests include work-life interface, recovery from work stress, and interpersonal mistreatment at work.

**KATIE L. PUSTOLKA,** PHR, is the human resources generalist at Ballston Spa National Bank, a community bank located in Saratoga County, New York. She is primarily responsible for the overall staffing and recruitment initiatives for the bank, benefits administration, and employee health and wellness initiatives. Pustolka is a certified professional in human resources and holds a bachelor of science degree in psychology with a minor in classics from Union College; as well as a certificate in human resources management from Union Graduate College. She is a member of the Society of Human Resource Management's national and local chapter. Pustolka has published several chapters and writing pieces and recently acted as a panel moderator at the 2013 conference of the International Coalition against Sexual Harassment.

**MARTINA RASTICOVA,** PhD, is a social and organizational psychologist. She graduated from Masaryk University, Brno, Czech Republic in 2004 (PhD studies). Then she worked as a researcher in the Centre for Research of Personality Development and Ethnicity at Faculty of Social Studies of Masaryk University of Brno (gender studies specialization). She has been involved in several international cooperation and projects. In 2006 she received associate research scholarship at George Washington University, Washington, D.C. She is currently leading the Institute of Management at Faculty of Business and Management of Brno University of Technology. Her professional research interest includes diversity management, cross-cultural psychology, and gender problematic in leadership. She is a member of *International Association for Cross-Cultural Psychology* and *Society for the Psychology of Women* (APA, Div 35) and regularly publishes in European journals.

**TANYA SCIME** is currently the executive assistant to the president at Union Graduate College in Schenectady, New York. She received her BS in public policy from SUNY Empire State College and will pursue her masters in social policy. In addition to her full-time work, she is also a member of the board of directors for the YWCA in Schenectady and serves as chair to their advocacy committee. She currently resides in Rotterdam, New York, with her husband, three children, and their three dogs.

**KATHERINE A. SLITER** received her bachelor's degree from Central Michigan University, where she studied psychology, political science, and business management. She later received her master's and PhD degrees in industrial-organizational psychology from Bowling Green State University, with a specialty in psychometrics and measurement. She is currently completing a postdoctoral fellowship at IUPUI where she conducts research and teaches graduate and undergraduate courses relating to statistics, measurement, and psychology. Following her postdoctoral fellowship, Katherine plans to pursue a professorship in the field of industrial and organization psychology. Her research interests are varied, with a primary focus on applied psychometrics and secondary focuses on personality assessment and the effects of obesity in the workplace. Katherine and her husband Michael, also an industrial and organization psychologist, live in Indiana with their three birds, adopted one-eyed Chihuahua, and a steady stream of foster dogs.

**SUSAN STRAUSS** has worked as a registered nurse (RN) in the operating room, pediatrics, medical-surgical, psychiatry, and public health. She is a seasoned health educator working with a variety of community, education, and professional groups. She has also been the director of health care quality improvement, director of education and development, and held other health care leadership roles. She researched physician abuse to RNs in the OR to determine if the abuse varied based on the gender of the nurse. Dr. Strauss has authored over 30 books, book chapters, and articles, as well as written curriculum and training manuals. Susan has been featured on *20/20, CBS Evening News,* and other television and radio programs as well as interviewed for newspaper and journal articles such as the *Times of London, Lawyers Weekly,* and *Harvard Education Newsletter.* Susan has presented at international conferences in Botswana, Egypt, Thailand, Israel, and the United States, and conducted sex discrimination research in Poland. She has consulted with professionals from other countries such as Israel, England, Australia, Canada, and St. Martin. In addition to her RN, Susan has a master's degree in community health science, and holds a doctorate in organizational leadership.

**JANET TRACEY** is earning her MBA at Union Graduate College. She is also earning a graduate certificate in human resource management, also at Union Graduate College. She is the mother of a son and a daughter and lives in Schenectady, New York.

**MICHELLE WILDGRUBE** has been a principal attorney at Cioffi, Slezak, and Wildgrube, P.C. since 2004, and has been with the firm since 1999. Before joining the firm, Ms. Wildgrube worked for a general practice firm that provided a broad foundation for her law practice, which now concentrates on estate planning and administration, corporate and business law, and real estate. Ms. Wildgrube holds a BA in English from Rutgers College and a JD from the State University of New York at Buffalo School of Law.